Unde

in the
Light of Christianity

A Comparison
of the
Messenger, Message and Mission
of the
Qur'an and the Bible

Abridged Version

James F. Gauss, Ph.D.

Unless noted otherwise, all Bible scripture quotations are from the Serendipity Bible for Groups, New International Version, ©1988. Published by Serendipity House, Littleton, Colorado with scriptures taken from The Holy Bible, New International Version, ©1984, Zondervan Bible Publishers.

Scripture quotations designated NKJV are from The Holy Bible, New King James Version, ©1982, Thomas Nelson, Inc.

Scripture quotations designated NLT are from Holy Bible, New Living Translation, ©1996, 2004 by Tyndale Charitable Trust. Used by permission of Tyndale House Publishers.

Quotations from the Qur'an are from The Qur'an translated by M.H. Shakir, ©2004. Published by Tahrike Tarsile Qur'an, Inc., Elmhurst, New York.

ISBN: 9781468000061

Published by UI Publications. U.S.A.

Endorsements

Your book is the finest and most thorough analysis I have ever seen of the teachings of the Quran in comparison to the Bible. It is a treasure trove of biblical truth, theological insight, and practical application.

My granddaughter is using it in her Global Studies class on Islam this very semester. I think a college-level text book version would be very helpful.

Dr. Ed Hindson, *Founding Dean | Distinguished Professor of Religion*
John W. Rawlings School of Divinity, *Liberty University*

In today's ever charged torrent of religious and political unrest, it is becoming increasingly vital for the people of the world to understand the truth of both the religious and the geo- political nature of Islam. The heart, purpose and vision of the Islamic system governed by a complete way of life known as Shari'ah is dangerously misunderstood and highly under-estimated by the West. It has been that way for 1400 years, numbing the minds of people like a shot of Novocain before treating an abscessed tooth. This compendium, 'Understanding Islam in the Light of Christianity' by Dr. James Gauss, is a vital and valuable resource that will be called upon again and again. If you are a pastor, spiritual leader, governmental leader, business leader or simply a curious person with a sincere desire to understand the heart of both Islam and Christianity, get this book.

Rev. Dale Witherington, Chief Steward, Restore Minnesota State Director, Minnesota Prayer Caucus Network

James Gauss' Understanding Islam in the Light of Christianity is a thought provoking and needed resource which brings deep truths into a discussion which continues to be mired by lies and deception. Challenging the doctrine of Islam from a factual yet loving basis, Gauss exposes how normative and universally taught Islam is directly contrary to the basic teachings of Jesus and his Church. This book promotes great discussions and offers a significant amount of information which is valuable to students of history and of the truth. I recommend it for all open-minded and open-hearted people wanting to expand their understanding of these matters.

John D. Guandolo, Former U.S. Marine Officer, Operations Desert Shield/Storm. Former FBI agent & counter-terrorism expert.
President & Founder of Understanding the Threat

Contents

Acknowledgements

First and foremost, I would like to thank my dear wife Kathleen for her tireless effort of praying and interceding for this project and for her countless hours of proofreading, editing and helpful suggestions. I also am deeply appreciative of her understanding for the many times she sacrificed her time with me in exchange for increased research and writing time.

I also deeply appreciate and extend my gratitude to the numerous brothers and sisters in Christ for their prayerful support and encouragement.

Preface

Unlike all other religions of the world, Christianity should stand as an extroverted belief system. That is to say that the Christian faith must proclaim and protect the truth of God unto all men. As the Apostle Paul puts it, the church, the representative of the Christian faith, is the pillar and foundation of the truth—internally as well as externally (1 Timothy 3:15).

Jesus said, "For this purpose I was born and for this purpose I have come into the world—to bear witness to the truth" (John 18:37).

Truth of what, Jesus?

Truth of God.

Actually better phrased would be, the truth that originates from God.

God is the God of truth. Everyone agrees on that, I mean everyone who believes in one true God. That is all the monotheistic religions, including Islam, Judaism, and Christianity. Although these religions believe that God is truthful, do they know His truth?

Truth is the very ingredient of life. Any perverted form of the truth is perverted life. Unfortunately we live in an age where lies are believed to be the truth.

Upholding the truth and protecting it in these days of politically correct and morally confused world is not an easy task. There will be strong resistance to the truth, similar to that of Jannes and Jambres who opposed the Word of God through Moses, so there will be those who oppose the truth, men of depraved mind (2 Tim 3:8).

In regards to ideologies, one of the strongest opposing forces to God and His truth is the religion of Islam, a belief system that is in utter contradiction to the truth of God's Word.

If the Apostle Paul lived in our days, he would include Islam in Romans chapter one: "They exchanged the truth of God for the lie" Romans 1:25

As believers and true followers of Christ, we must live by the truth as well as protect it no matter what the cost may be. If we fail, we have lost our savor, and as Jesus puts it, we are good for nothing but to be thrown out and trampled underfoot (Matthew 5:13).

If Christianity is tasteless, mocked, and ridiculed is solely on the ground of being indifferent to the truth.

So the question is what must the church do when Islam, a world religion, claims unashamedly Mohammad as a prophet of God, Jesus as only a prophet ranked even inferior to Mohammad; and when Islam holds in its religious fangs 1.7 billion people denying them the truth of the Gospel?

If the church remains silent in the name of political correctness or fear of persecution or whatever the reason may be—then the church is not the pillar and the ground of the truth!

The church of Christ upholds the truth because she is a Steward of God, a representative for God for this dying humanity.

It is calculated that in the year 2050, the continent of Europe will become an Islamic continent, just by the means of birth rate of the Muslim families immigrated to Europe in the past few decades. Why is Islam, an antichrist religion growing so rapidly in a continent that used to proclaim the Gospel of Jesus Christ from every corner? It is simply because the light of the Gospel has dimed and the church is no longer a Pillar of the truth.

Dr. Gauss, in this profound study, is upholding the truth of the Gospel, revealing the fallacies of a false religion. His pen is sharp but the imprint of his spirit is marked with compassion and love for a lost people who believe they are worshipping the one true God.

I commend Dr. Gauss on writing such an informative book bringing out the darkness that covers every page of the Quran and delusions of the Islamic faith.

May there be more voices such as Dr. Gauss proclaiming the truth of God with boldness and in the spirit of Christ. And may we witness freedom for millions of Muslims who are bound by a dark and evil force!

Blow the trumpet in Zion; sound the alarm on my holy hill. Let all who live in the land tremble....

Pastor Reza Safa
(Former Iranian Shi'a Muslim)
President, TBN Nejat TV
Director, TBN Middle East
Author of *Inside Islam: Exposing and reaching the world of Islam*

Introduction

It is hard to escape the harsh realities of Islamic terrorism since it is reported in one form of media or another on a daily basis. For older generations of Americans it is especially difficult to forget since the fateful day of September 11, 2001, when 19 Muslim fanatics succeeded in crashing four commercial American passenger jets on American soil, killing almost 3,000 people. Some Americans, myself included, from time to time, like to point the finger at America's new evil of choice—Islam, and too often, all of its adherents. The truth, however, is that Americans, including the Christian Church in America, have embraced evil for many decades—evil that Islam proclaims to abhor. Perhaps, that is why America finds itself under another attack that is not easily defended against and which is attracting younger Americans to its fold.

In truth, Americans and the Church in America cannot point the finger at the evils of Islam without first pointing the finger at ourselves and the failing Christian faith in America. Many of the evils that Islam claims to be against, America has come to embrace. This will be presented throughout the book, but briefly, here are some of the challenges in the Church's and the Christian's witness to Muslims.

- For the devout Muslim, Allah is welcome in every aspect of his or her life. In America, the Church and Christians have permitted the government to take control of education and remove prayer and the Bible from schools.
- Muslims are dedicated to prayer—five times per day. Most Christians (according to polls) rarely pray to God, unless they need something from Him.
- Muslims detest homosexuality while some Christians not only practice it, but the Church has largely turned a blind eye to it.
- Abortion in most Muslim societies is rare and forbidden, but in America it has been entitled as the law of the land and exported in philosophy around the world. The Church in America and its followers have mostly remained silent.

Such divergences in thought and practice, and much more, for Islam and Christianity, will be presented throughout the book. The challenge for America: Most Muslims are serious about practicing their faith and their adherents are growing in numbers in America at a time when Christianity is weakening and declining. The other challenge is, how does one present the Gospel of Christ to the Muslim who is witness to so much perversion in a self-proclaimed Christian nation? To do so, the Christian must not only present the true Gospel, but at the same time disavow the sin in America and that of the Church.

Where will it all end? It is up to the people of God—Jehovah God. If the Church in America does not repent for its past failings and its distortion of the Gospel of Christ, it is quite possible, as some believe, that God may use Islam to "purify" the Church, much like He did with Israel and her enemies.

The Author's Quest. My initial search for the truth about Islam was spurred on by two events early in the new millennium—the September 11, 2001 Islamic terrorist attack on the world trade towers in New York City, the Pentagon in Washington, DC and the plane crash in Somerset County, Pennsylvania. That day changed America's way of life forever. I remember that day well. As soon as the radio broadcast at my place of employment announced the first plane crash into the World Trade Center, I told my co-workers that it was a terrorist attack. How did I know that? Having grown up in New Jersey I was a several time visitor in downtown Manhattan where the towers were built. The towers were clearly visible and any commercial pilot who found himself in trouble could easily avoid them and, if necessary, crash land in the Hudson River, the East River or Upper New York Bay nearby. Any plane, especially commercial, crashing into the towers had to be deliberate.

Not long after this momentous event and aftermath I surprisingly found myself managing a large apartment complex where nearly 90% of the residents were Somali refugees. I knew nothing about the Somali, the country they called home or their struggle. Although I had started to research Islam due to 9/11, I was still very new to my understanding of the religion.

I entered into my new responsibilities with absolutely no foregone conclusions about the Somali or Islam, but, rather dedicated myself to get to know individual Somali, befriend them and learn about their history and personal stories. At the same time I continued my research and studies into Somalia and Islam and visited with Somali imams (Islamic religious leaders), Somali leaders, and teachers of the Qur'an and Somali community leaders. Countless hours were spent visiting with the Somali residents in their homes and getting to know them.

After many months of such intense experience and study and after inquiring of their leaders on multiple subjects I came to the inescapable conclusion that the Somali, and perhaps followers of Islam as a whole, operated and carried out their lives in a manner that I was completely unfamiliar with and had little understanding.

Understanding the Qur'an vs. the Bible. It is hard, perhaps, for the majority of patriotic Americans and Christians alike to comprehend the approach to life that most Muslims exhibit. However, if one objectively looks at the perversion and lifestyles of many Americans, including Christians, a Muslim would likely be equally perplexed.

Christianity, though a religion of "free choice," is often lived out too freely by its followers. Christian freedom is too often interpreted as, "I can do what I want and I'm forgiven."

One does not become a Christian because one's parents or family are, because of where you live or went to school or church. To be a true Christian, one must make a personal decision to accept Jesus Christ as Lord and Savior and submit to His teachings and Lordship. In Islam, personal choice is not a factor for the majority of Muslims. If you are born to a Muslim father (the mother's religion does not matter), you are a Muslim for life – you have no say in the matter, EVER! In addition, millions of people over the centuries, as well as today, become Muslims due to threats, bodily harm to themselves or family members, destruction of their livelihood or because of marrying a Muslim man. To become a new Muslim it is quite easy, just recite the Shahada (the Muslim statement of faith): *there is no god but Allah, and Muhammad is the messenger of Allah.* That is all that is needed. No understanding of the faith or nature of the commitment is needed.

The Qur'an claims that Allah is the God of Muslims, as well as Jews and Christians. It is important to note and remember that no other faiths are considered legitimate in the Qur'an or by today's Muslims. "And do not dispute the followers of the Book [Bible] except by what is best, except those of them who act unjustly, and say: We believe in that which has been revealed to us and revealed to you, and our God and your God is One, and to Him do we submit" (**Qur'an 29:46**). The author will deal with this concept thoroughly in Chapter 2 (and elsewhere).

Despite this assertion, that the God of the Jews, Christians and Muslims is one and the same, much of the Qur'an condones hatred toward Jews and Christians ("People of the Book"), referring to them continually as "infidels" and "unbelievers," ones that are only worthy of the sword of Allah's wrath.

There is some difficulty for the non-Muslim, and perhaps for Muslims as well, in piecing together the message of the Qur'an. Some of the challenges follow:

- Unlike much of the Bible, the sequence of chapters in the Qur'an are not chronological. The Qur'an is not written with any sequential theme nor is it written in a chronological manner. The chapters (often called *surah*) are arranged by the longest (that appear first) to the shortest (which appear last). The Bible, by comparison, is somewhat easier to follow due to many chronological and historical sequences that bring together a clear story of God's faithfulness and purpose for His people.
- Much, but not all of the events mentioned in the Bible and many of its characters have been verified through historical records,

period writing, artifacts or archeological evidence. The same cannot be said of the Qur'an where little historical context is provided and, therefore, little to be verified.

- The Qur'an was originally composed on any organic material handy, including bones, leaves, bark, reed mats, stones or just "recorded" in the minds of men. The "original" Qur'an was not written by Muhammad, the one who received Allah's revelation, because he was illiterate, but by others decades later who tried to recall his teachings. The Bible, on the other hand, was written largely by those who experienced what they were writing about at the time of the events, or shortly thereafter.

- Since Muslims claim that the only true Qur'an is in Arabic (the language of Muhammad and Saudi Arabia, where he lived), any other translations are suspect even if translated by Muslim scholars. However, this has not stopped the Muslim proselytizers for using the Qur'an in multiple languages to spread their message, but it also makes it convenient for Muslims to dispute whatever non-believers find objectionable in non-Arabic translations. Muslims can claim that the verse does not hold true in the original Arabic language.

- The Qur'an's reliability as Allah's word rests solely on the character and trustworthiness of one person, Muhammad, the prophet of Islam. In the Qur'an, Muhammad is the only participant with Allah and the only reporter. There are no collaborating witnesses or recorders of the events to which Muhammad speaks. The Bible, on the other hand, was composed by 40 different prophets, sages and Apostles who were eyewitnesses to God's intervention in human history and provided clear testimony to the same.

- In the Qur'an there are only about three dozen characters mentioned, but only two unique to the Qur'an other than Muhammad. The other people mentioned in the Qur'an are just references to persons mentioned in the Bible. By contrast, the Bible mentions 3,237 participating individuals.

- The Qur'an is based on the testimony of one man, one prophet. The Bible, however, contains the testimony and writings of 16 prophets (4 major and 12 minor by Judeo-Christian tradition). However, according to a study by Steve Shirley of the Jesus Alive website (http://jesusalive.cc/ques233.htm), he has enumerated 73 prophets mentioned in the Bible, but not all contributed to biblical writings.

- Much of the Qur'an appears to be verses of revelation that Muhammad received to fit his self-serving ambitions, warring nature or sexual proclivities, rather than holy guidance for lost

12

souls. By comparison, the Bible presents a clear and consistent message of God's purpose and plan for mankind that was fulfilled through Jesus Christ.

- Despite Muslim claims to the contrary, no original copy of the Qur'an exists anywhere in the world. However, there are original copies of biblical texts that exist in their original form.
- The Bible was written and composed over a period of more than 1500 years (1450 BC to 95 AD) and yet provides a harmonious story of God's grace, love and salvation for all mankind. The Qur'an was supposedly written over 22 years (610-632 AD) and is a disjointed narrative of mostly self-serving and violent "revelations."
- Some of the teachings of the Qur'an violate the Ten Commandments which the Jews and Christians consider sacred. The Qur'an also completely reverses God's plan of salvation as revealed in and through Jesus Christ.
- While the Qur'an claims that Jews and Muslims (and Christians through Christ) are descendants of Abraham and therefore "brothers," much of the Qur'an denigrates and demeans Jews and Christians and repeatedly calls for violence against them or, at the bare minimum, to be subjugated by the followers of Allah.

Purpose of this Abridged *Compendium*. The purpose of this *Compendium* is not to denigrate or condemn the Muslim faithful. The majority of Muslims desire the same things as most people: love, freedom, security, good health, family, friendship, etc. However, they have been indoctrinated to look at those things somewhat differently.

The primary purpose of this abridged version of the full *Compendium* is to educate the non-Muslim world of the true teachings of Islam; the threat it poses to the Free World and Judeo-Christian values, beliefs and way of life, and to provide a path for Muslims to emerge from the darkness of Islam into the light of Christ. After reading this version, perhaps you will desire the *Compendium* as your go-to educational resource on all matters concerning Islam, whether you are interested for yourself or as a homeschooling parent, Christian and public school educator, university professor, seminary student or teacher, or a Christian Church leader. The *Compendium* has considerably more detailed information, charts, images, addendums and other resources not available in this version.

Throughout the text, Bible, Qur'an and hadith (Muhammad's sayings) citations are in **bold** for easier reference for the student. Certain verses may be repeated throughout, due to their significance or because of their pertinence in more than one chapter or topic.

Islamic Law citations are from *Reliance of the Traveller*, translated by Nuh Ha Mim Keller, ©1991 and 1994, Amana Publications.

The reader should be aware, that in order to produce this abridged version, many addendums, images, graphs and charts had to be eliminated and some chapters greatly edited to the degree of cutting lengthy chapters in half. Therefore, for the serious student and for a thorough study, it is highly recommended that you consider getting the full version of *Understanding Islam in the Light of Christianity.*

Chapter 1

Understanding the Origin of Islam

And you shall know the truth, and the truth shall make you free.
John 8:32 (NKJV)

Every Muslim is taught that the Qur'an and other Islamic sacred texts are the unchangeable, perfect word of Allah and must be adhered to. Why should the non-Muslim world be concerned? The Islamic faith is growing and Muslim populations have some of the highest birthrates in the world.

Perhaps the naiveté of the Western world can be summed up in the assessment of Islam's future dominance by Pavel Kohout of the Center for Economics and Politics in Prague. In an article titled, *Why al-Qaeda Will Dominate the European Union*, published October 7, 2004. Kohout wrote:

> The *first reason* extreme Islam will prevail is the intellectual advantage that al-Qaeda leaders have over western European politicians. The latter want to believe that there is no clash of civilizations; that terrorism is just a product of misery and lack of education; that the solution lies in a multicultural, tolerant society; and that the stubbornness of the Americans and Israelis is to blame for all the problems.
>
> . . . The *second reason* is the unification of foreign policy in the EU [European Union]. In the UN [United Nations], all member states of the European Union dutifully voted against Israel as a flock of sheep under the leadership of France. France is home to millions of Muslims, who are a decisive factor in its politics.
>
> . . . The *third reason* is an advantage of the Islamic society in terms of evolution: a high birthrate.

The World Islamic Population

In 2010, Pew Research Center estimated that the world's Muslim population was around 1.6 billion or 23% of the world population. While the Muslim population has the greatest density (by percent of population) in the Middle East and North Africa, it is the Asia-Pacific region that has the most Muslims (986.4 million) or 62% of the world Muslim population. This region includes the highly Muslim populated countries of Bangladesh, India, Indonesia and Pakistan. By 2050, Pew Research estimates that the world Muslim population will grow to 2.76 billion or 29.7% of the total world population.

An Islamic web site, www.muslimpopulation.com, stated that the 2017 world Muslim population was 2.18 billion, thus outnumbering the 2.01 billion Christians in the world. The majority of Muslims (up to 90%) are Sunni Muslims with the next largest group, Shi'a Muslims.

In 2015 the Pew Research Center (http://www.pewresearch.org/ fact-tank/2016/01/06/a-new-estimate-of-the-u-s-muslim-population/) estimated that the Muslim population in the United States was 3.3 million or about 1% of the total U.S. population. One of the largest influx of Muslim refugees or immigrants has been the Somali. However, estimates of the U.S. population vary widely and appear to be largely unknown. Various sources put the Somali population at 35,760 to 150,000.

The lower estimate seems unlikely since a 2015 estimate put the Minnesota Somali population at 57,000. Although a year later another estimate put the Minnesota population at 40,000. But that also seems improbable since Allied Media reported that Minneapolis alone had an estimated 60,000 Somali. In the same report it was stated only 25,000 lived in Minnesota (http://www.allied-media.com/Somali_American/ Somali_American_demo-graphics.html). Only two things are clear: Minnesota is home to the largest Somali population in the United States and that no one knows how many Somali live in the U.S.

Countries Dominated by Muslims. The Muslim population is growing rapidly in many parts of the world, namely the Middle East, Africa, all of Europe and Russia. Following is a list of 50 countries with Muslim populations of 51% or more in 2010 with projected populations in 2030 in parenthesizes ( ). Nigeria is also included even though the Muslim population is less than 50% (47.9) because, although a minority, the Muslim population is very oppressive and violent there. However, there are many other countries with less than 50% Muslim population—representing 10% of the population or more—but where Islam has a major influence on the political and social fabric of those countries through oppression, intimidation, coercion and violence.

Afghanistan, 99.8% (98)	Albania, 82.1% (83.2)	Algeria, 98.2% (98.2)
Azerbaijan, 98.4% (98.4)	Bahrain, 81.2% (81.2)	Bangladesh,90.4% (92.3)
Brunei, 51.9% (51.9)	Burkina Faso, 58.9% (59)	Chad, 55.7% (53)
Comoros, 98.3% (98.3)	Djibouti, 97% (97)	Egypt, 94.7% (94.7)
Gambia, 95.3% (95.3)	Guinea, 84.2% (84.2)	Indonesia, 88.1% (88)
Iran, 99.7% (99.7)	Iraq, 98.9% (98.9)	Jordan, 98.8% (98.8)
Kazakhstan, 56.4% (56.4)	Kosovo, 91.7% (93.5)	Kuwait, 86.4% (86.4)
Kyrgyzstan, 88.8% (93.8)	Lebanon, 59.7% (59.7)	Libya, 96.6% (96.6)
Malaysia, 61.4% (64.5)	Maldives, 98.4% (98.4)	Mali, 92.4% (92.1)
Mauritania, 99.2% (99.2)	Mayotte, 98.8% (98.8)	Morocco, 99.9% (99.9)
Niger, 98.3% (98.3)	Nigeria, 47.9% (51.5)	Oman, 87.7% (87.7)
Pakistan, 96.4% (96.4)	Palestinian Terr., 97.5% (97.5)	Qatar, 77.5% (77.5)
Saudi Arabia, 97.1% (97.1)	Senegal, 95.9% (95.9)	Sierra Leone,71.5% (73)
Somalia, 98.6% (98.6)	Sudan, 71.4% (71.4)	Syria, 92.8% (92.8)

Tajikistan, 99% (99)   Tunisia, 99.8% (99.8)   Turkey, 98.6% (98.6)
Turkmenistan, 93.3% (93.3) United Arab Emirates, 76% (76)
Uzbekistan, 96.5% (96.5)   Western Sahara, 99.6% (99.6)   Yemen, 99% (99)

Other countries with 10% or more Muslim populations by 2030 include: Benin (24.5%), Bosnia-Herzegovina (42.7%), Bulgaria* (15.7), Cameroon (19.2%), Cyprus* (22.7%), Eritrea (36.5%), Ethiopia (33.8%), Gabon (11.9%), Georgia (11.5%), Ghana (18.2%), Guinea Bissau (42.8%), India (15.9%), Israel (23.2%), Ivory Coast (39.9%), Liberia (12.8%), Malawi (12.8%), Mauritius (16.6%), Montenegro (21.5%), Mozambique (22.8%), Republic of Macedonia (40.3%), Russia (14.4%), Singapore (14.9%), Suriname (15.9%), Tanzania (25.8%), Togo (12.2%) and Uganda (10.9%).

In addition, numerous European countries are on the verge of collapse as their Muslim populations approach 10% or more by 2030. They include: Austria* (9.3%), Belgium* (10.2%), France* (10.3%), Germany* (7.1%), Greece* (6.9%), Netherlands* (7.8%), Norway (6.5%), Sweden* (9.9%), Switzerland (8.1%) and the United Kingdom* (8.2%).

Source: *Muslim Population by Country.* Pew Research Center, January 27, 2017.

Of the 28 European Union countries (marked with an asterisk), ten have or will have significant Muslim populations by 2030. It should be noted that there are countries like Australia, Canada, Denmark, Finland, Ireland, Italy, Spain and others, while having far less than a 10% Muslim population, are plagued with continuous riots, sexual assaults and violence at the hands of their Muslim residents.

The Origin of Islam

Some non-Muslims in the West and even some in the Christian church believe that Ishmael, Abraham's illegitimate son in the Bible, was the "founder" of Islam. Undoubtedly, this belief stems from the Qur'an's attempt and that of Muslims for over 1400 years to link Islam, ironically, with the Jewish faith and patriarchs (more on this later in this chapter and Chapter 3).

Muhammad, The Prophet of Islam or The Apostle, as he is called, was born in 571 A.D. (some sources use 570). His father, Abdullah, died before Muhammad's birth and his mother, Amina, died in 577 when he was only six. Muhammad then stayed with his grandfather until he died two years later. Muhammad was then raised by his uncle, Abu Talib (2).

"The evidence that a prophet was active among the Arabs in the early decades of the 7th century," wrote Patricia Crone, professor of

Islamic history at Princeton University, "must be said to be exceptionally good" (3).

Everything else about Mohammed," Crone continued, "is more uncertain. . . we can be reasonably sure that the Qur'an is a collection of utterances that he made in the belief that they had been revealed to him by God."

When he was in his early twenties, Muhammad had the good fortune of being introduced to the wealthy Hadrat Khadija. Muhammad took on the responsibility of managing her prosperous trade caravan. A year later, in 595, although Khadija was fifteen years his senior, Muhammad took her as his first wife. He would live with her monogamously for 25 years until her death in 619 (4). In his early years of searching for divine guidance, Muhammad seemed uncertain of his status. "Say: I am not the first of the apostles, and I do not know what will be done with me or with you: I do not follow anything but that which is revealed to me, and I am nothing but a plain warner" (**Qur'an 46:9**).

Muhammad's First Revelation. In 610, around age forty, Muhammad had his first "revelation" in a cave on Mt. Hira from a manifestation he referred to as the angel Gabriel. His experience is recounted in the writings of the 8th century Muslim, Ibn Ishaq, in his *Sirat Rasul Allah*:

> *When it was the night on which God honored him with his mission, and showed mercy on His servants thereby, Gabriel brought him the command of God. "He came to me," said the Apostle, "while I was asleep, with a piece of brocade whereon was writing, and said 'Recite!' and I said 'What shall I recite?' He pressed me with it so tightly that I thought it was death; then he let me go and said 'Recite!' I said 'But what shall I read?'*
>
> *And this I said only to deliver myself from him lest he should do the same to me again, but he said:*
>
> *'Recite: In the Name of thy Lord who created, Created man from blood clotted,*
>
> *Recite! Thy Lord is the most beneficent, who taught by the Pen, Taught that which they knew not unto men.'*
>
> *So I recited it, and he departed from me. And I awoke from my sleep, and it was as though these words were written on my heart.*
>
> *Now none of God's creatures was more hateful to me than an (ecstatic) poet or a man possessed; I could not even bear to look at them. I thought, 'Woe is me – poet or possessed. Never shall Quraysh [Muhammad's pagan Arabian tribe in Mecca] say that of me! I will go to the top of the mountain and throw myself down that I may kill myself and gain rest.'*

18

I raised my head towards heaven to see, and lo! Gabriel in the form of a man, with feet astride the horizon, saying, 'O Muhammad! Thou art the Apostle of God, and I am Gabriel.' I stood gazing at him, moving neither forward nor backward; then I began to turn my face away from him, but towards whatever region of the sky I looked, I saw him as before.

"I continued standing there, neither advancing nor turning back, until Khadija sent her messengers in search of me . . ." (5, 6).

Problems with Muhammad's Revelation. If it is to be accepted that the preceding account of Muhammad's first revelation is true, then there are several problems with it.

Ibn Ishaq's recounting of Muhammad's experience was written more than a century and a half after the visitation. According to the Muslim Sacred Texts web site, "[Ibn Ishaq's] original work survived only in quotations from it by other authors . . . However, it has been possible for modern scholars to re-establish much of the original text" (7).

"Muhammad's doubts are troubling," wrote Mark Gabriel, "for what major prophet doubts the source of his prophetic revelation? . . . Certainly no major prophet in the Bible attributes God's revelation to demons, as Muhammad believed . . ." (8).

The prophets of the Old Testament always referred to God as the author of their spoken words. Muhammad was the first (of the class of prophets that he put himself in—Moses, David, Isaiah, et al) that proclaimed his prophetic words came from an angel—and one that he first thought was demonic.

After this visitation, Muhammad thought that he had been visited by Satan and that he was possessed by a demon (9). So much so, that he wanted to commit suicide. He thought he was crazy and wanted to die. Not an encouraging beginning for a prophet who later became convinced that he was chosen as Allah's last and most important prophet.

It was only after he returned from Mt. Hira to the waiting arms of his wife Khadija that his demeanor changed. When he saw her, he said, "Woe is me—a poet, or a man possessed!" Khadija reassured him with these words: "Rejoice, O son of my uncle, and be of good heart! Verily by Him in whose hand is Khadija's soul, I have hope that thou wilt be the prophet of these people" (10). Muhammad did not receive words of reassurance from Allah but from a woman. He considered Khadija's words to be reliable confirmation of the visitation and his calling, even though later revelations from Allah disclosed that women were only half as intelligent as men and could not be relied upon because they were often deceivers.

In hadith 3:826, Muhammad is quoted as saying, "'Isn't the witness of a woman equal to half of that of a man?' The woman said, 'Yes.' He said, 'This is because of the deficiency of a woman's mind.'"

The Source of God's Word. Gabriel also told Muhammad that God taught man by *the pen* or written word. This is ironic since it is believed in Muslim circles and elsewhere that Muhammad could neither read nor write. While the *written* word of God of the Bible has been essential in spreading God's truth over the centuries, it was first the spoken word that the Old Testament prophets received from God to warn and teach the faithful and the unbelievers. While Muhammad declared he proclaimed God's word, Jesus *was* God's Word. "In the beginning was the Word," John's Gospel offers, "and the Word was with God, and the Word was God. He was with God in the beginning. Through him all things were made; without him nothing was made that has been made. In him was life, and that life was the light of men" **(John 1:1-4)**.

The words of God, according to Jesus, are not presented to man by the angels, by mere mortal men (such as Muhammad) or even by sacred writ, but by the Holy Spirit of God Himself. "But the Counselor, the Holy Spirit," Jesus told His disciples, "whom the Father will send in my name, will teach you all things and will remind you of everything I have said to you" (John 14:26).

> *But when he, the Spirit of truth, comes, he will guide you into all truth. He will not speak on his own; he will speak only what he hears, and he will tell you what is yet to come. He will bring glory to me by taking from what is mine and making it known to you. All that belongs to the Father is mine. That is why I said the Spirit will take from what is mine and make it known to you* **(John 16:13-15)**.

Throughout human history, and in current times, God has sent angels to bring a message to His people or to provide protection. However, God's primary method of communication is through the revelation knowledge of the Holy Spirit.

This dubious beginning for Muhammad's prophethood was further complicated by what followed or did not follow. Unlike the prophets of old, where God revealed his word to them on a regular basis, Allah did not reveal himself again to Muhammad through Gabriel for three years. Once again Muhammad became depressed and suicidal. As he received revelations in the years following, his wives believed the visions were authentic because Muhammad would frequently go into trances or convulsions (11)—a state of being that the New Testament of the Bible attributes to demon possession **(Matthew 12:22; 17:14-18; Mark 9:20)**.

Unlike Moses and other prophets before him, Muhammad never had a personal encounter with the god of his affections. "Narrated Aisha: 'Whoever claimed that (the Prophet) Muhammad saw his Lord, is committing a great fault, for he only saw Gabriel in his genuine shape in which he was created covering the whole horizon'" (hadith 4:457).

At one point Muhammad even claimed to have communicated with the dead (12) and on numerous occasions changed Allah's revelations to suit himself (13). Jesus also spoke to the dead, but He did so because He had power over death as demonstrated in the resurrection of Lazarus (**John 11**).

In the year, 613 A.D., Muhammad began to preach the tenets of Islam in Mecca. The word, Islam, means *submission* to Allah. To be a Muslim, is to be one who is completely submitted to Islam and Allah; to be a slave of Allah. Almost from the very beginning of this new faith, "The goal of Islam [wa]s to produce a theocracy with Allah as the ruler of society, a society with no separation between religion and the state. This society would have no democracy, no free will and no freedom of expression" (14).

Satanic Verses—The Islamic Challenge

Six years after Muhammad started preaching his Islamic philosophy, in 619, he received a revelation that became known in Islamic tradition as "the Satanic Verses."

"According to Islamic tradition," stated Robert Spencer, a noted researcher and author on Islam, "Satan, not Allah, once actually spoke through Muhammad's mouth."

As the story has been handed down, Muhammad yearned for the conversion of his own tribe, the Quraysh, to his new found religion of Islam. But the Quraysh leaders wanted to continue to worship their gods, al-Lat and al-'Uzza. They offered Muhammad a deal: Muhammad would worship their gods for a year and then they would worship Muhammad's god for a year. In exchange, they would give Muhammad money, wives and make him their king. Muhammad was tempted, but then this revelation came to him:

> *Say: What! Do you then bid me serve others than Allah, O ignorant men?*
> *And certainly, it has been revealed to you and to those before you: Surely if you associate (with Allah), your work would certainly come to naught and you would certainly be of the losers.*

> *Nay! But serve Allah alone and be of the thankful*
> (**Qur'an 39:64-66**).

The Quraysh persisted, however, and Muhammad sought for a solution to the stalemate. "And finally he hit on a solution. He received a revelation saying that it was legitimate for Muslims to pray to al-Lat, al-'Uzza, and Manat, the three goddesses favored by the pagan Quraysh, as intercessors before Allah." The Quraysh, of course, accepted this new revelation with great enthusiasm and word rapidly spread that the Quraysh had indeed acknowledged Allah as one of their gods.

But then Muhammad received another revelation strongly rebuking him for placing Allah in this grouping of pagan gods.

> *And surely they had purposed to turn you away from that which We have revealed to you, that you should forge against Us other than that, and then they would certainly have taken you for a friend.*
>
> *And had it not been that We had already established you, you would certainly have been near to incline to them a little;*
>
> *In that case We would certainly have made you to taste a double (punishment) in this life and a double (punishment) after death, then you would not have found any helper against Us* (**surah 17:73-75**).

"The Satanic verses incident," commented Spencer, "has naturally caused Muslims acute embarrassment for centuries. Indeed, it casts a shadow over the veracity of Muhammad's entire claim to be a prophet....

". . . While events may be explained in other ways, those who would wish away the Satanic verses cannot get around the fact that these elements of Muhammad's life were not the inventions of his enemies, but were passed along by men who believed he was indeed the Prophet of Allah" (15).

During the same year of the Satanic Verses incident, Muhammad's first wife, Khadija and uncle, Abu Talib died. A year later, Muhammad began his polygamous lifestyle with his marriage to the widow, Sauda bint Zam'ah (or Sawda) (16, 17). At the same time he was also betrothed to six-year old Ayishah (or Aishah), the one who would become known as his favorite wife at age nine. After his marriage to Ayishah, from 626 to 629, Muhammad would marry ten more women; sometimes for no other reason than to cement tribal alliances (see Chapter 7 for more on Muhammad's wives).

Ayishah, would later narrate that, "Once the Prophet was bewitched so that he began to imagine that he had done a thing which in fact he had not done" (**hadith 4:400**).

Exactly what *things* he supposedly did or did not do is not as troubling as the observation by his wife that Muhammad was under the influence of witchcraft. In the following **hadith (4:490)**, Ayishah again proclaims that, "Magic was worked on the Prophet . . ." In a dream, Allah revealed to Muhammad the source of the spell: "A comb, the hair gathered on it, and the outer skin of the pollen of the male date-palm." Muhammad went to the site of the date-palms and discovered, "Its date-palms . . . are like the heads of the devils." Ayishah asked him, "Did you take out those things with which the magic was worked?" Muhammad answered, "No, for I have been cured by Allah and I am afraid that this action may spread evil amongst the people."

Muhammad's Night Journey to the Seven Heavens

In 620, perhaps in an effort to solidify his status as the Prophet of Allah, Muhammad revealed his celebrated "Night Journey" or ascension to Paradise and the seven heavens. The event is recounted in the following hadith (or words of Muhammad). Note, how self-serving the words of the heavenly biblical figures were for Muhammad.

Narrated by Abu Huraira:

> *The Prophet said, "I met Moses on the night of my Ascension to heaven." The prophet then described him saying, as I think, "He was a tall person with lank [lifeless] hair as if he belonged to the people of the tribe of Shanu's." The prophet further said, "I met Jesus." The Prophet described him saying, "He was one of moderate height and was red-faced as if he had just come out of the bathroom. I saw Abraham whom I resembled more than any of his children did." The Prophet further said, "(That night) I was given two cups; one full of milk and the other full of wine. I was asked to take either of them which I liked, and I took the milk and drank it. On that it was said to me, 'You have taken the right path (religion). If you had taken the wine, your (Muslim) nation would have gone astray'"* (**hadith 4:647**).

The visionary trip or *miraj* (ascension) took Muhammad to Jerusalem and the Temple Mount. From there he ascended to the first heaven where he was met by Adam, who told Muhammad, "You are welcome, O pious son and pious Prophet." Then the angel Gabriel took him to the second heaven where both John the Baptist and Jesus

23

greeted Muhammad with, "You are welcome, O pious brother and pious Prophet."

This "vision" was still during Muhammad's conciliatory phase, when he was trying to win over the Jews in the Middle East. To state that he ascended from the Jewish Temple Mount gave him more credibility, at least in his eyes.

Muhammad continued his journey with Gabriel through the 3rd, 4th, 5th, 6th and 7th heavens where he met many of the prophets before him, including Moses and Abraham. When Moses met Muhammad in the 6th heaven, he wept. When Muhammad asked him why he wept, Moses said "I weep because after me there has been sent (Muhammad as a Prophet) a young man, whose followers will enter Paradise in greater numbers than my followers."

Again, this is clearly an attempt of Muhammad to elevate his status among the people, especially the Jews and Christians. That Moses would weep over Muhammad, a false prophet, and ignore the prophetic ministries of the great Jewish prophets like Elijah, Isaiah, Jeremiah, Ezekiel and many others, as well as God's prophetic fulfillment through Jesus Christ, is not biblical.

When Muhammad reached the 7th heaven he met Abraham, who told Muhammad that Muslims must pray *fifty* times a day. But the Prophet of Islam balked at such a burdensome number and appealed to Moses on his journey backwards through the heavens. "The prophet of Islam kept going between Allah and Moses until the number of daily prayers for the Muslims was only five" (18). It is interesting, that it was Abraham, not Allah that instructed Muhammad about prayer.

This negotiation with God over prayer is strangely similar to Abraham's negotiation with God over God's planned destruction of Sodom and Gomorrah in **Genesis 18**. In that chapter of the Old Testament, Abraham asks God if He would destroy the two cities if God found 50 righteous people in Sodom. God told Abraham He would not. Emboldened, Abraham kept negotiating with God until God agreed that He would not destroy the cities if 10 righteous people could be found in Sodom. Once again, God said He would not.

Although Muhammad was illiterate, he supposedly had been to Jerusalem before and would likely have heard many of the stories from the Pentateuch, the first five books of the Bible. As you will see in the next chapter, Muhammad's understanding or remembrance of these biblical tales became very convoluted and erroneous.

In an attempt to *seal the deal* with the Christians in the region, Muhammad had another eye-opening revelation—that he and Jesus and all the prophets of the Bible were really tight knit buddies.

This *journey*, at least in the eyes of Muhammad, elevated his status with Allah. In **hadith 4:651**, narrated by Abu Huraira, Muhammad equates himself with Jesus. "I heard Allah's Apostle saying, 'I am the nearest of all the people to the son of Mary, and all the prophets are paternal brothers, and there has been no prophet between me and him (i.e. Jesus).'"

"Allah's Apostle said, 'Both in this world and in the Hereafter, I am nearest of all the people to Jesus, the son of Mary. The prophets are paternal brothers; their mothers are different, but their religion is one'" (hadith 4:652).

It was during his *flight into the seven heavens* that Muhammad would later relate to his wives, Khadija and Aisha, that Allah wedded him to Mary, the mother of Jesus, the sister of Moses and to the wife of Pharaoh.

"It was Allah's special divine blessing that Muhammad was husband to three of the Bible's most noted women," wrote the Caner brothers. "Clearly he was not bound to the very Qur'an he said he had received" (19).

Muhammad's claims about the *Night Journey* were more than some of the followers of this new religion could tolerate. Members of his own tribe, the Quraysh, whom Muhammad had been trying to sway toward Islam, mocked and ridiculed him. Two years later, amid the growing tensions and threats in Mecca, Muhammad and his band of followers fled to Medina.

The *Hijra* or Flight to Medina

After *The Hijra*, or flight from Mecca to Medina in 622, the tenets of the new faith went through a radical transformation. Muhammad, stung, rejected and ridiculed by Jews and Christians and his own tribe, found a way to retaliate. Allah's revelations to Muhammad became more vengeful and oppressive. From a human standpoint, this would make sense, if one were under the threats and oppression of others. But it also illustrates very concretely that Allah is a changeable and vengeful god that apparently has no clear plan for mankind or mankind's salvation (see chapter 11).

Former radical Shiite Muslim and now a pastor, author and Christian evangelist, Reza Safa, has claimed that, "Many rituals practiced within Islam are similar to those of Baal worship. In my opinion, the spirit that raised Baal worship in Phoenicia and Canaan, and later in Babylon, is the same spirit that raised Islam in Arabia" (20).

Baal worship—worship of multiple gods—was first mentioned in the Bible during the time of Moses (**Numbers 22:41**). Baal, the supreme male deity, was worshipped throughout the Canaanite and Phoenician Middle East and such pagan worship preceded the arrival of the Jewish people in the "promised land" of Canaan. During the time of Moses and the prophets of the Bible, many of the region's kings submitted to the worship of Baal.

Muhammad, after settling in Medina, began to receive revelations from Allah laying down the "Law" to be followed by Muslim adherents. Despite his distaste for the Jews, much of what he *received* was heavily influenced by Judaism in Medina and beyond. "From nearly the beginning of his prophetic career," author Robert Spencer stated, "Muhammad was strongly influenced by Judaism—situating himself within the roster of Jewish prophets, forbidding pork for his followers, and adapting for the Muslims the practice of several daily prayers and other aspects of Jewish ritual" (21).

"We must realize," concluded Safa, "that many of the teachings of Islam are a reflection of Arabian culture and society of the seventh century. Many rituals and practices enforced by Islam can be traced back to pre-Islamic Arabia. . . . Muhammad constructed his religion and the Koran from pre-existing material in Arabian culture" (22).

With Muhammad's death in 632 A.D. at the age of sixty-three, the faith of Islam was left with no clear successor. Muhammad had no male children and no "second lieutenant" in command. According to the traditions of Islam, Muhammad singled out his rich neighbor and one of his first converts, Abu Bakr, as his successor. A small group of Muslims insisted that it was Hadrat Ali (or Ali), Muhammad's son-in-law and cousin that the Prophet had chosen (23). With his hatred for the Jews, his death came with a twist of irony. Bukhari's hadith 4:165 says, "Allah's Apostle died while his (iron) armor was mortgaged to a Jew for thirty Sas of barley."

Muslims that chose to follow Abu Bakr became known as Sunni or ones that follow the Sunnah (i.e., the traditions of Muhammad). The smaller group that followed Ali became known as the Shi'a or Shiites (i.e., the Party of Ali). Today, Sunni Muslims comprise about 83% of the world's Muslims (24). Other sources put the Sunni population at 87-90%. They are the predominant form of Islam in such countries as Afghanistan, Algeria, Egypt, Gaza Strip, Jordan, Kuwait, Libya, Maldives, Pakistan, Somalia, Sudan, Syria, Tajikistan, Turkey, United Arab Emirates, Uzbekistan and the West Bank. The majority of Muslims in Iran and Iraq are Shi'a Muslims or Shiites (25).

Chapter Conclusion

The origin of Islam arises from the troubling "vision" and testimony of one man, Muhammad, a man who believed he had been visited by a demon. Unlike the prophets of the Bible, he had to be persuaded by his wife that his vision was from Allah, his chosen god. The majority of the people in Saudi Arabia and the adjoining regions, including, Christians, Jews, pagans and his own tribe rejected him and believed Muhammad was a false, self-serving "prophet". Indeed, the vast majority of Muhammad's revelations, particularly those he "received" after his flight to Medina, were clearly self-serving and his way of inflicting revenge on his non-believing enemies.

Despite this dubious beginning for Islam, the adherents to this new 7th century "faith" exploded throughout the Middle East and beyond over the centuries. Not so much because of the superior heavenly vision of a new way of life, but because the majority of new adherents were either born into the new belief or were strongly impressed, oppressed or subjugated into the faith as new areas were conquered by the Muslim hoards. More on these topics will be presented in succeeding chapters.

References

1.   *This was no insult to Islam.* The First Post, September 15, 2006.   Source: http://www.Thefirstpost.co.uk/index.php?menuID=1&subID=751&WT.srch=1. Accessed January 4, 2007.
2.   Caner, Ergun Mehmet and Emir Fethi Caner. *Unveiling Islam,* 2002. Kregel Publications, div. of Kregel. Inc., p. 40.
3.   Crone, Patricia. *What Do We Actually Know About Mohammed?* Open Democracy, August 31, 2006. Source: http://www.openDemocracy.net. Accessed June 2, 2007.
4.   Caner & Caner, p. 40-41.
5.   *Muhammad the Messenger.* Source: http://www.sacred-texts.com/isl/isl/isl11.htm. Accessed February 19, 2007.
6.   Wood, David. *A Bewitched Prophet? Examining Muhammad's Psychological and Spiritual Stability.* Source: http://answering-islam.de/Main//Authors/Wood/bewitched_prophet.htm. Accessed February 19, 2007.
7.   *Muhammad the Messenger.*
8.   Gabriel, Mark A. *Islam and Terrorism,* 2002. Published by FrontLine, a Strang Company, Lake Mary, Florida, p. 42.
9.   Ibid.
10. *Muhammad the Messenger.*
11. Caner & Caner, p. 44.
12. Ibid, p. 44.
13. Ibid, p.45.
14. Safa, Reza F. *Inside Islam: Exposing and Reaching the World of Islam,* 1996. Charisma House, Lake Mary, FL., p. 19.
15. Spencer, Robert. *The Truth About Muhammad, Founder of the World's Most Intolerant Religion,* 2006. Regnery Publishing, Inc., Washington, DC., pp. 78-83.
16. Caner & Caner, p. 56.
17. Gilchrist, John. *Muhammad and the Religion of Islam. 2C. The Circumstances of His Marriages,* 1984. Online edition at: http://www.answering-islam.org/Gilchrist/Vol1/2c.html.
18. Spencer, p. 83-85.
19. Caner & Caner, p. 136.
20. Safa, p. 22.
21. Spencer, p. 90.
22. Safa, p. 18-19.

23. Spencer, p. 167-168.
24. Wehner, Peter. *Why They Fight, and what it means for us.* OpinionJournal, from The Wall Street Journal, January 9, 2007.
25. *The World Fact Book*, Updated December 12, 2006. Source: http://www.cia.gov/cia/publications/factbook/fields/2122.html. Accessed December 19, 2006.

Chapter 2

The Bible vs. the Qur'an

I am the way the truth, and the life.
No one comes to the Father except through me.
John 14:6

Allah supposedly revealed to Muhammad, "Surely the [only] (true) religion with Allah is Islam, and those of whom the Book had been given did not show opposition but after knowledge had come to them, out of envy among themselves; and whoever disbelieves in the communications of Allah then surely Allah is quick in reckoning" (**Qur'an 3:19**). As for those who refused to accept Islam as the only true religion, then the true believers were to proclaim to them a severe chastisement (spiritual and moral punishment; **verse 21**).

A hadith narrated by Aisha, Muhammad's child bride, proclaims, "Allah's Apostle said, 'If somebody innovates something which is not in harmony with the principles of our religion, that thing is rejected'" (**hadith 3:861**).

Biblical Contrasts and Islamic Abrogation

At first glance, with even a cursory reading of the Qur'an and comparing it to the New Testament message of Jesus and the Apostles, one will not be able to escape the great contrast between the two texts. The Bible presents a clear message of God's love, forgiveness, reconciliation, peace and assurance of eternal life in heaven. The message of the Qur'an and Allah's messenger, Muhammad, presents Allah as unforgiving, vengeful, changeable, deceptive, one to be feared, and a god that takes pleasure in the oppression and slaughter of those who do not believe in him. In spite of that image of Allah, "The worst thing the enemies of Allah [or infidels] can do is to persuade Muslims to 'reject the Truth'" of the Qur'an or teachings of Muhammad, claim the Caner brothers, former Muslims that are now serving Christ (1).

"If they [the infidels] find you, they will be your enemies, and will stretch forth towards you their hands and their tongues with evil, and they ardently desire that you may disbelieve" (**Qur'an 60:2**).

Abrogation—Strictly an Islamic Concept. Sometimes Allah's revelation through Gabriel put Muhammad and his desires in an unfavorable position. However, Muhammad revealed that "unchangeable" Allah, when he chose, could change his mind.

To justify the apparent changeability of Allah, Muhammad came up with the concept of *abrogation*—the changeable, repealing word of Allah. For Muslims, this only represents Muhammad's

29

shear "genius" and vision. For the Jewish and Christian believer who believe that God's word is unchangeable, abrogation is purely the self-serving creation of Muhammad.

This convenient idea is what often constitutes the verses of the Qur'an and hadith. *Nothing, no one* can change the word of Allah proclaimed Muhammad and all the Islamic clerics since his time. "And the word of your Lord has been accomplished truly and justly; there is none who can change His words . . ." **(Qur'an 6:115; 18:27)**. **Qur'an 6:34** and **10:64**, also say that "there is none to change the words of Allah . . ." or "My word shall not be changed . . ." **(50:29)**.

But then Allah conveniently revealed to Muhammad, "Whatever communications We abrogate or cause to be forgotten, We bring one better than it or like it. Do you not know that Allah has power over all things?" **(Qur'an 2:106)**. The argument and assumption here in this verse and the verses in the previous paragraph, is that, while man cannot change Allah's words, Allah is free to do so as he wishes. It would appear from this viewpoint that Allah may not get it right the first time around, therefore he has to issue an addendum or correction so that his idea or revelation is clear.

> *And when We change (one) communication for (another) communication, and Allah knows best what He reveals, they say: You are only a forger. Nay, most of them do not know.*
> *Say: The Holy Spirit has revealed it from your Lord with the truth, that it may establish those who believe and as a guidance and good news for those who submit* **(Qur'an 16:101-102)**.

The revelation above was received by Muhammad while he was headquartered in Mecca, the town of his birth. Muhammad's ancestral tribe, the Quraysh, was pagan. While pagans dominated the area, there were also Jewish tribes and Christians living in the environs of Mecca (2).

When Muhammad started preaching the message of Islam, many of the pagans, Jews and Christians of the area refused to accept this new theology and rejected Muhammad as a prophet. The Jews and Christians saw him as a false prophet and not one sent by God. To counteract their objections, Muhammad conveniently received this preceding, indisputable revelation from Allah.

Muhammad quite often received revelations of convenience or abrogations to answer his numerous detractors and "quite often during his prophetic career," author Robert Spencer wrote, "he received revelations that answered critics, or solved a disputed question, or gave his particular perspective on a series of events" (3).

Muhammad's Mecca vs. Medina Revelations. When one is

reading or studying the Qur'an, it is important to understand that Muhammad received his revelations during three key periods of his apostolic life in the Arabian Peninsula (4).

There are 114 chapters in the Qur'an representing two very distinct periods of Muhammad's life. There were two Meccan periods (611-615 A.D. and 616-622 A.D.) and his Medina period, 623-632 A.D. (present-day Saudi Arabia). During the two Meccan periods, Muhammad was more conciliatory toward the area residents as he tried to convince them of the validity of his message from Allah. Muhammad's revelations in the Qur'an during these two periods reflect his appeasing demeanor. After the Meccans finally ran Muhammad and his followers out of town, he fled to Medina. He remained in Medina until his death in 632. While in Medina, Muhammad had one epiphany after another revealing to him how Allah wanted him to convince the people of Allah's truth. That is when Allah, through Muhammad, revealed his hatred for non-believers.

It was in Medina where Muslims started their violent rampages across the Saudi Arabian peninsula and elsewhere, taking captives to convert them to Islam or murdering those who refused to convert. The only way permitted for the vanquished to escape death or conversion to Islam, was to live as a subjugated people and pay Muslims a poll tax—a tax of submission to Islam.

"Don't be deceived, my dear brothers," wrote the Apostle James. "Every good and perfect gift is from above, coming down from the Father of the heavenly lights, who does not change like shifting shadows" (**James 1:16-17**).

"The biggest contradiction in the Qur'an," wrote Islam researcher and writer, Steve Keohane, "is that it says the Qur'an can be contradicted at any time. God can change his mind, and change verses in the Qur'an, with or without telling Muslims" (5).

As an extreme example of this "Doctrine of Abrogation", there are, according to Keohane, 125 verses in the Qur'an calling for patience and tolerance that are repealed by such injunctions as unbelievers "should be murdered or crucified or their hands and their feet should be cut off on opposite sides or they should be imprisoned . . ." (**Qur'an 5:33**) or "slay the idolaters wherever you find them, and take them captives and besiege them and lie in wait for them in every ambush . . ." (**Qur'an 9:5**). Both of these surahs (5 and 9), by the way, were received by Muhammad when he was in Medina.

Muhammad Revealed Only the Truth—But Jesus *is* the Truth. The Qur'an highlights Allah's truth through the words expressed by the prophet Muhammad. Allah's words are true and Muhammad is the messenger *of* that truth. "Surely this Islam," revealed Allah, "is your religion, one religion (only), and I am your Lord, therefore serve Me" (**Qur'an 21:92**).

To be more succinct, from a biblical view, the New Testament scriptures of the Bible present God's truth in the person of Jesus Christ. Jesus, the Son of God, *is* the truth—the *only* truth of God according to the Bible.

"Jesus said to him [the Apostle Thomas], 'I am the way, the truth, and the life. No one comes to the Father [God] except through me" (**John 14:6**, NKJV). The Apostle John expressed it this way: "For the law was given through Moses; grace and truth came through Jesus Christ (**John 1:17**).

Jesus, in addressing Jewish believers in John 8:31-32 (NKJV), assured his followers, "If you abide in My word, you are My disciples indeed. And you shall know the truth, and the truth shall make you free." The *truth* that Muhammad proclaimed was far from liberating. Rather than setting people free, it brought them into oppression and bondage—either they renounce their freedom of choice and accept Islam or die.

Islam is the final religion that Allah Most High will never lessen or abrogate until the Last Day.
Reliance of the Traveller, w4.1(3)

In sharp contrast, at the beginning of Jesus' ministry, he went into the synagogue in the city of Nazareth, the town of his upbringing, and read from the scroll of the prophet Isaiah: "The Spirit of the Sovereign Lord is on me, because the Lord has anointed me to preach good news to the poor. He has sent me to bind up the brokenhearted, to proclaim freedom for the captives and release from darkness for the prisoners" (**Isaiah 61:1**). After reading this scripture, Jesus said, "Today this scripture is fulfilled in your hearing" (**Luke 4:21**).

"Now the Lord is the Spirit," the Apostle Paul stated, "and where the Spirit of the Lord is, there is freedom" (**2 Corinthians 3:17**). Wherever Jesus went, His words, deeds and spirit embodied a sense of well-being and freedom. This was not the case with Muhammad. Once he took up residence in Medina, his "ministry" took on an atmosphere of fear, chaos, oppression and death. Those who were free were enslaved, murdered or tyrannized into Islamic bondage.

Muhammad claimed that he was the "way" and that Allah had revealed to him the "truth" and he commanded through military domination, intimidation, fear and violence, that *everyone* must follow him and the revelations from Allah or be consigned to death and hell-fire.

In **Qur'an 33:36** it recites, "And it behoves [sic] not a believing man and a believing woman that they should have any choice in their matter when Allah and His Apostle have decided a matter; and whoever disobeys Allah and His Apostle, he surely strays off a manifest straying."

Jesus did not coerce or threaten anyone to follow Him. He simply stated the truth that God the Father had given Him and demonstrated the way to freedom by His example.

The Qur'an in Light of the Bible

". . . if the Muslim rejects the Bible," wrote Gnana Pragash Suresh, a priest for the Society of St. Pius X in Southern Africa, "he must also reject the Qur'an because it appeals to the Bible as God's word. On the other hand, if he accepts the Bible, he still must reject the Qur'an because it contradicts the Bible" (6).

Islamic Teaching on the Qur'an

"Something that could have been a [Sacred] Book" refers to those like the Zoroastrians, who have remnants resembling an ancient Book. As for the psuedoscriptures of cults that have appeared since Islam (n: such as the Sikhs, Baha'is, Mormons, Qadianis, etc.), they neither are nor could be a Book, since the Koran is the final revelation.

Reliance of the Traveller, o11.2

Muslims are Commanded in the Qur'an to Read the Bible. This may come as a shock to the Western, non-Muslim world, but Muslims are commanded by their own prophet, Muhammad, to read the Bible. Muslims generally believe in the Bible, but believe that it was revealed to the Jews and Christians by Allah. In fact, although most Muslims tend to deny or downplay it, they are called to believe in the Bible, as well as in the prophets and apostles of the Bible, as commanded by the prophet Muhammad.

> *Say: We believe in Allah and (in) that which had been revealed to us, and (in) that which was revealed to Ibrahim [Abraham] and to Ismail [Ishmael] and Ishaq [Isaac] and Yaqoub [Jacob] and the tribes [their descendants], and (in) that which was given to Musa [Moses] and Isa [Jesus] and (in) that which was given to the prophets from their Lord, we do not make any distinction between any of them, and to Him do we submit* (**Qur'an 2:136**).

Muslims, however, are taught to take this verse differently. This verse, they say, proves that Abraham, Isaac, Ishmael, Jacob and even

Moses and Jesus were, indeed, Muslims. This conclusion is reached despite the fact that Abraham preceded Muhammad and the birth of Islam by about 2,500 years. "When his [Abraham's] Lord [Allah] said to him," **verse 131** of the same surah claims, "Be a Muslim, he said: I submit myself to the Lord of the worlds." In **verse 135** that follows, Jews and Christians are told to submit to the religion of Abraham, which is Islam. This was "revealed" during Muhammad's Medina period when he was getting frustrated to the point of violence because the Jews and Christians were not accepting his mandate to convert to Islam. However, in three verses of the Qur'an— **6:14, 163** and **39:12**—it is revealed that Muhammad was to be the first to submit to Allah and Islam, and thus, became the first Muslim (or submitted one).

Despite Allah's admonition for his followers to read the Bible, the Bible is forbidden in Muslim homes and banned in most Muslim countries. To even possess a Bible in some Muslim countries can result in prison or execution.

According to **Qur'an 3:49**, Jesus could do nothing without Allah's permission. Of course, Jesus' disciples were also Muslims. "But when Isa perceived unbelief on their [the disciple's] part, he said: Who will be my helpers in Allah's way? The disciples said: We are helpers (in the way) of Allah: We believe in Allah and bear witness that we are submitting ones." Muhammad even revealed that Jesus Himself proclaimed His faith in Allah. "And when Isa came with clear arguments, he said: I have come to you indeed with wisdom, and that I may make clear to you part of what you differ in; so be careful of (your duty to) Allah and obey me: Surely Allah is my Lord and your Lord, therefore serve Him; this is the right path" (**Qur'an 43:63-64**). The reader should note that **Qur'an 6 and 43** were composed during Muhammad's Meccan period when he was trying to win over the Jews and Christians in the region.

This is how easy it was for Muhammad to take what he wanted from the Jewish and Christian scriptures and adopt it to his theology and declare that Jews and Christians were to do the same. After all, how could they resist him? All the Jewish and Christian forefathers and spiritual leaders, according to Muhammad, were Muslims—even Jesus.

> *Surely We have revealed to you as We revealed to Nuh* [Noah], *and the prophets after him, and We revealed to Ibrahim* [Abraham] *and Ismail* [Ishmael] *and Ishaq* [Isaac] *and Yaqoob* [Jacob] *and the tribes, and Isa* [Jesus] *and Ayub* [Job] *and Yunus* [Jonah] *and Haroun* [Aaron] *and Sulaiman* [Solomon] *and We gave to Dawood* [David] *Psalms.*
>
> *And (We sent) apostles We have mentioned to you before and apostles we have not mentioned to you; and to Musa*

[Moses], *Allah addressed His Word, speaking (to him):*
(We sent) apostles as the givers of good news and as
warners, so that people should not have to plea against Allah after
the (coming of) apostles; and Allah is Mighty, Wise (**Qur'an
4:163-165**).

Muhammad was not happy just to convert by his word the faithful
of the Bible to Islam, but to be complete, he had to convert the Bible to that
which was revealed by Allah and not by Jehovah God of the Jews. "The
revelation of the Book [Bible] is from Allah," he decreed, "the Mighty, the
Wise" (**Qur'an 46:2**). Throughout the Qur'an there are verses that reveal
that Allah and Allah alone ordained and revealed the Torah to Moses and
the Gospel to Jesus.

"Again, We gave the Book to Musa," Allah revealed to
Muhammad, "to complete (Our blessings) on him who would do good (to
others), and making plain all things and a guidance and a mercy, so that
they should believe in the meeting of their Lord. And this is a Book We
have revealed, blessed; therefore follow it and guard (against evil) that
mercy may be shown to you" (**Qur'an 6:154-155**).

Allah further revealed that the Gospels of Jesus Christ were his.
"And We sent after them [the Old Testament prophets] in their footsteps
Isa, son of Marium, verifying what was before him of the Taurat and We
gave him the Injeel [Gospel] in which was guidance and light, and verifying
what was before it of Taurat and a guidance and an admonition for those
who guard (against evil). And the followers of the Injeel should have
judged by what Allah revealed in it; and whoever did not judge by what
Allah revealed, those are they that are the transgressors" (**Qur'an 5:46-47**).

And most certainly We gave Musa the Book [Torah] *and*
We sent apostles after him one after another; and We gave Isa, the
son of Marium [Mary], *clear arguments and strengthened him*
with the holy spirit (**Qur'an 2:87**).

**Indeed, Muhammad—as it was revealed to him by Allah—
presents a great mystery here. If Allah, the revealer of the Qur'an, was
also the one who revealed the Torah to Moses and the Gospel to Jesus,
then how come the Qur'an is in such great and constant conflict with
the word of God in both the Torah and Gospel? And if Allah revealed
the Torah and Gospel, how come Muhammad and his followers did not
honor it and follow its teachings? Allah said that those who do not
follow his teachings in the Torah and Gospel are transgressors. If so,
then Muhammad, Allah's agent of "new" revelation, was chief among
the transgressors.**

Muhammad neither believed in nor followed much of the teachings in the Torah and practically none of the teachings of Jesus in the Gospels. Even today, despite their belief *in* the Bible, the Bible is forbidden to Muslims and banned in Muslim countries. This is quite a strange state of affairs for a people that are commanded by their own holy book to believe in the Bible (the message of the prophets and apostles in **Qur'an 2:136, 285; 4:136, 163** and elsewhere). How can they believe in that which is forbidden to them? The imams of Islam know that if the truth of the Bible were revealed to the Muslim faithful, Islam could no longer be spread across the world through deception, lies and fear.

One is obliged to know four particular Books:
(1) the Tawrah (Torah), revealed to our liegelord [sovereign] *Musa (Moses);*
(2) the Injil (Evangel) [Gospel]*, revealed to our liegelord 'Isa (Jesus);*
(3) the Zabur (Psalms), revealed to our liegelord Dawud (David);
(4) and the Qur'an (Koran), revealed to our liegelord Muhammad (Allah bless them all and give them peace).
                    Reliance of the Traveller, u3.4

"Those to whom We have given the Book [Bible]," **Qur'an 2:121** directs, "read [study and follow] it as it ought to be read [studied and followed]. These [that do] believe in it [the Bible]; and whoever disbelieves in it[s truth] these it is that are the losers." The message from Muhammad and Allah could not be any clearer. Read the Bible, believe in it and follow what it says. But, hold on, the verse right before this one, **Qur'an 2:120**, presents a direct contradiction (as is so often true in the Qur'an).

> *And the Jews will not be pleased with you, nor the Christians until you follow their religion. Say: Surely Allah's guidance, that is the (true) guidance. And if you follow their desires after the knowledge that has come to you, you shall have no guardian from Allah, nor any helper.*

First Allah tells Muhammad to tell his followers that they are not only to read the Bible and believe in it as the truth, and if they do not they will be condemned ("the losers"), but then Allah says not to follow through on what you learn or you might become a Christian. How confusing is that, even though it is the truth—one who accepts the words of truth in the whole Bible cannot resist becoming a follower of Jesus.

36

The fact is that, Muhammad "borrowed" from both the Old and New Testament scriptural stories or concepts he liked and incorporated them into Islamic theology as revelations from Allah.

However, Muhammad and the Qur'an teach that the Bible was corrupted or scriptures removed by the Jews or Christians, scriptures that Allah must now reveal through Muhammad to make his (Allah's) word true again. "Islam teaches that the Qur'an is an exact word-for-word copy of God's final revelation, words inscribed on tablets that have always existed in heaven" (7).

> *Do you then hope that they* [the people of the Book] *would believe in you, and a party from among them indeed used to hear the Word of Allah, then **altered it after they had understood it**, and they know (this).*
>
> *And when they meet those who believe they say: We believe, and when they are alone one with another they say: Do you talk to them of what Allah has disclosed to you that they may contend with you by this before your Lord? Do you not then understand?*
>
> *Do they not know that Allah knows what they keep secret and what they make known?*
>
> *And there are among them illiterates **who know not the Book but only lies**, and they do but conjecture.*
>
> *Woe, then, to those who write the book with their hands and then say: This is from Allah, so that they may take for it a small price; therefore woe to them for what their hands have written and woe to them for what they earn* (**Qur'an 2:75-79**; author's emphasis).

In Islamic belief, you live, you die and are weighed on the scales of Allah's judgment of good deeds versus bad deeds—and *you will* be judged as deficient. More on this in Chapter 10.

"Many Muslims," according to the former radical Shi'a Muslim, Pastor Reza Safa, "will argue that Allah is the same God that Christians and Jews worship. But by studying the Koran one will see the vast gap of character, nature and personality that exists between the God of the Bible and the Allah of the Koran" (8).

Allah Revealed the Bible is Corrupt. Sometime during his Medina residency (623 to 632 A.D.), Muhammad had this revelation about the Qur'an's place in God's realm of truth.

> *He has revealed to you the Book* [Qur'an] *with truth, verifying that which is before it, and He revealed the Taurat* [Torah] *and the Injeel* [Gospel] *aforetime, a guidance for the*

people, and He sent the Furqan [The Criterion or Standard; the Qur'an] **(Qur'an 3:3)**.

This verse provides a curious contradiction. In **Qur'an 2:75-79**, also revealed during the Medina period, Allah made it clear to Muhammad that the Bible (the Torah and the Gospels) could not be trusted because they had been corrupted by *the people of the Book*—Jews and Christians. Yet, in **Qur'an 3**, Allah revealed that the Qur'an was given to verify the truth he had previously made known through the Torah (Old Testament) and Gospels (New Testament). So, was the Qur'an revealed by Allah to confirm old truth, present new truth or to be the only truth? Neither the Qur'an itself, nor Allah is clear on that point.

Despite such a confusing message from the Qur'an, Muhammad made it clear that, "Surely they who disbelieve in the communications of Allah—they shall have a severe chastisement; and Allah is Mighty, the Lord of Retribution" **(Qur'an 3:4)**.

According to Muhammad, only he was privileged through revelation knowledge from Allah, to know what parts of the Bible were true and what parts had been corrupted by human hands. "And when Our clear communications are recited to them [people of the Book], those who disbelieve say with regard to the truth when it comes to them [via Muhammad]: This is clear magic. Nay! They say: He has forged it. Say: If I have forged it, you do not control anything for me from Allah; He knows best what you utter concerning it; He is enough as a witness between me and you, and He is the Forgiving, the Merciful" (Qur'an 46:7-8).

Of course, since the Qur'an was revealed to Muhammad in Arabic, the Qur'an, according to Islamic teaching, can only be read and recited in Arabic in order to get the true meaning and full blessing of Allah. Other translations are suspect and viewed as faulty and unreliable. As a result, despite the rapid rise in Islam currently, the vast majority of Muslims— perhaps as many as 90 percent—have never read the Qur'an and cannot read it because they do not know the Arabic language.

Furthermore, unlike the detailed account of the life of Jesus in the Bible, "The Qur'an," Crone stated, "does not give us an account of the prophet's life   We see the world through his eyes, and the allusive style makes it difficult to follow what is going on.

"Events are referred to," Crone acknowledged, "but not narrated; disagreements are debated without being explained; people and places are mentioned, but rarely named. Supporters are simply referred to as believers; opponents are condemned as unbelievers, polytheists, wrongdoers, hypocrites and the like, with only the barest information on who they were or what they said or did.   " (9).

In comparison, the Bible is very concise and well narrated by numerous groups of actors and verifiable historical figures. The history of the time is well delineated and the context of the dialogue made clear. The faithful in God and their detractors are plainly identified. Above all, the theological message delivered is clear as to its source and its targeted audience.

To reinforce the fact that only he and believers in Allah had the truth, Muhammad had this further understanding revealed to him during his Medina residency.

> *And those who were given the Book did not become divided except after clear evidence had come to them. And they were not enjoined anything except that they should serve Allah, being sincere to Him in obedience, upright, and keep up prayer and pay the poor-rate [jizya or submission to Islamic tax], and that is the right religion. Surely those who disbelieve from among the followers of the Book and the polytheists shall be in the fire of hell, abiding therein; they are the worst of men. (As for) those who believe [in Allah] and do good, surely they are the best of men* (**Qur'an 98:4-7**).

In this revelation from Allah, Muhammad makes it clear:

- The people of the Book and polytheists have gone astray from the truth (**verse 1**).
- Muhammad is the new messenger of God's truth (**verse 2**).
- With a new law to be laid down (**verse 3**).
- When this new truth was revealed, even the Jews and Christians argued among themselves as to its truthfulness (**verse 4**).
- If Jews and Christians wanted to be in the right religion, they had to follow the right laws (**verse 5**).
- If not, they would go to hell (**verse 6**).
- But only true believers, those that followed Muhammad's teachings, were acceptable to God (**verse 7**).

There is No Common Ground with the Bible and the Qur'an. The Qur'an is a very difficult book to follow (for the reasons cited in the Introduction). What does the reader of the Qur'an actually encounter in the theology of the Qur'an? According to Professor Crone, "some kind of combination of Biblical-type monotheism and Arabian paganism . . ." (10). Despite these difficulties and in spite of the *corrupted Bible* stance of Muslims, some "moderate" Muslims and Christian apologists (on behalf of Islam) maintain that there is much common ground in the scriptures of the Qur'an and the Bible. To which the Apostle Paul, who was very familiar with the pagan cultures of his day, would likely add:

> *Do not be yoked together with unbelievers. For what do righteousness and wickedness have in common? Or what fellowship can light have with darkness? What harmony is there between Christ and Belial* [Satan]? *What does a believer have in common with an unbeliever? What agreement is there between the temple of God and idols? For we are the temple of the living God. As God has said: "I will live with them and walk among them, and I will be their God, and they will be my people"* (**2 Corinthians 6:14-16**).

There can be no common ground between the Qur'an and the Bible; and there is no common ground among Muslims and Christians. The scriptures and message of both are fundamentally and spiritually diametrically opposed to each other. The Qur'an's message is one of darkness, oppression and death. The message of the New Testament Bible is one of light, freedom and life.

When Islamic apologists say terrorists quote the Qur'an on jihad 'out of context,'" author Robert Spencer noted, "they neglect to mention that the Qur'an itself often offers little context. Frequently it makes reference to people and events without bothering to explain what's going on" (11). The Bible, in contrast, is full of collaborating stories, full of detail that thoroughly inform the reader of the context in which the event occurred or the message was given.

To fill in this contextual void, Muslims have relied primarily on two early sources of additional information: the *tafsir* (or Qur'an commentary) and the *hadith* (or traditions of Muhammad). Another written tradition, the *sunnah*, follows the example of the Prophet Muhammad. It mostly consists of the hadith. Both the hadith and sunnah attempt to elaborate on the meaning of Qur'anic verses and/or Muhammad's teachings and commandments. Next to the Qur'an, either the hadith or sunnah are considered the most sacred to the Muslim. It is the sunnah that provides the legal foundation for Islamic *shari'a* law (12, 13).

"From the vantage point of fourteen hundred years later," Spencer asserted, "it is virtually impossible to tell with any certainty what is authentic in this mass of information and what isn't. Muslims themselves acknowledge that there are a great many forged *hadith* (the plural form of hadith), which were written to give the Prophet's sanction to the views or practices of a particular party in the early Muslim community. This makes the question of what the historical Muhammad actually said and did well-nigh insoluble" (14).

Surprisingly, the Qur'an itself has a solution for Muslims who really want to know the truth. "But if you are in doubt as to what We [Allah] have revealed to you, ask those [Jews and Christians] who

read the Book [Bible] before you; certainly the truth has come to you from your Lord, therefore you should not be of the disputers [doubters]" (Qur'an 10:94).

Again, this surah was "revealed" during Muhammad's conciliatory Meccan period when he was trying to win over the Jews and Christians of Saudi Arabia.

One God vs. The Triune God

According to their respective scriptures, Jews, Muslims and Christians claim to worship the one and only God. Jews and Muslims, however, due to the Christians belief in the Triune God (three revelations of God in One), believe that Christians are not monotheistic—worshipping only one God. The concept of the Triune God or Trinity, along with the crucifixion and resurrection of Jesus and that Jesus is the Son of God, are the three most difficult aspects of Christianity with which Muslims have the greatest conflict.

Through Moses in the Torah of the Old Testament and the prophets, the God of the Jews made it clear that He was their One and Only God; the God of all creation and that He would dwell among them and the Jews would be His people (**Exodus 25:8; Jeremiah 31:1**).

"'This is the covenant I will make with the people of Israel after that time,' declares the LORD. 'I will put my law in their minds and write it on their hearts. I will be their God, and they will be my people'" (**Jeremiah 31:33**). Again, through the prophet Ezekiel, God proclaims: "I will make a covenant of peace with them; it will be an everlasting covenant. I will establish them and increase their numbers, and I will put my sanctuary among them forever" (**Ezekiel 37:26**).

"You shall have no other gods [besides] me" (**Exodus 20:3**). Yahweh, Jehovah, Elohiym, the great God of the Jews, spoke through the great prophet Isaiah thirteen centuries before the birth of Islam:

> *"You are My witnesses,"* declares the Lord [Jehovah, the self-Existent or Eternal God], *"and My servant whom I have chosen, that you may know and believe Me and understand that I am He. Before Me there was no God formed, nor shall there be after Me. I, even I, am the Lord. And besides me there is no savior. I have declared* [revealed] *and saved, I have proclaimed, and there was no foreign god among you; therefore you are my witnesses,"* says the Lord, *"that I am God. Indeed before the day was, I am He; and there is no one who can deliver out of My hand; I work, and who will reverse it?"* (**Isaiah 43:10-13**, NKJV).

41

This same revelation—*And you shall know no God but Me; for there is no Savior besides Me*—was revealed through the prophet Hosea a few years earlier (**Hosea 13:4b**, NKJV). In the eyes and mind of Muhammad, this admonition was compounded by the revelation in all four Gospels that Jesus was the *Son of God.* Jesus acknowledged that He was, indeed, the Son of the Most High God (**John 3:16-18; 10:36; 11:4**).

To further complicate the issue for monotheists, Jesus said, "I am the way and the truth and the life. No one comes to the Father [God] except through me" (**John 14:6**). Such professions were enough to convince Muhammad that Christians worshipped more than one god.

> *O followers of the Book! do not exceed the limits in your religion, and do not speak (lies) against Allah, but (speak) the truth; the Messiah, Isa son of Marium is only an apostle of Allah and His Word which He communicated to Marium and a spirit from Him; believe therefore in Allah and His apostles, and say not, Three. Desist, it is better for you; Allah is only one God: far be it from His glory that He should have a son; whatever is in the heavens and whatever is in the earth is His; and Allah is sufficient for a Protector* (**Qur'an 4:171**).

Muhammad had no concept of the Triune God or Trinity, and, in fact, included Mary, the mother of Jesus in the Trinity instead of the Holy Spirit. "And when Allah will say: O Isa son of Marium! Did you say to men, Take me and my mother for two gods besides Allah, he will say: Glory be to Thee, it did not befit me that I should say what I had no right to (say) . . ." (Qur'an 5:116).

However, it is strange, that in numerous places in the Qur'an Allah reveals himself in the plural as *We, Our* or *Us.*

The Triune God of Christians Explained. The concept of the *Trinity* or the *godhead, three in one,* is a difficult perception even for the Christian to grasp, much less the non-believer; and it is especially sensitive to the Muslim that firmly believes there can only be ONE God.

However, a Muslim could agree that he or she and all mankind is comprised of a *spirit,* a *body* and a *soul* as the Apostle Paul stated in **1 Thessalonians 5:23**. Each human being is *one* person but created in three entities: spirit, body and soul. The Christian God is the same as what He created: body, soul and spirit or God the Father, Son and Holy Spirit.

May God himself, the God of peace, sanctify you through and through. May your whole spirit, soul and body be kept blameless at the coming of our Lord Jesus Christ.
1 Thessalonians 5:23

The Apostle John explains it this way: "In the beginning was the Word, and the Word was with God, and the Word was God. He was with God in the beginning   The Word became flesh and made his dwelling among us. We have seen his glory, the glory of the One and Only, who came from the Father, full of grace and truth" (**John 1:1, 14**).

A simplified way to explain the Christian God is to look to His creation, the sun. The sun, the fireball in the sky, is a molten body of fire. It produces both heat and light. The molten body would be nothing without heat and light. Without heat and light there would be no life. The indescribable heat is not the sun—it cannot be seen, it can only be felt. Likewise, the sun's brightness can only be seen, it cannot be felt except through its production of heat. All *three* make up the *one* sun— the molten body, the heat and the light. By itself, the light is not the sun; nor is the heat. All three must function together to be the sun.

Now, if God can create the sun as three separate entities, is it so difficult to believe that HE could choose to express Himself as three revelations in One?

Christians are not Polytheists. Despite Muhammad's assertions in the Qur'an and what Muslims have always been taught, Christians are not polytheists. They do not worship more than one god.

"Hear, O Israel: The Lord our God, the Lord is one!" (**Deuteronomy 6:4**) and "   besides him there is no other" (**Deuteronomy 4:35**). Jesus would not disagree, for He quoted this scripture when asked by one of the teachers of the law, "Of all the commandments, which is the most important?"

"'The most important one,' answered Jesus, 'is this: Hear, O Israel, the Lord our God, the Lord is one" (**Mark 12:28, 29**).

The prayer of Hezekiah, the king of Judah, echoes what the Jewish sages believed and taught. "O Lord Almighty, God of Israel, enthroned between the cherubim, you alone are God over all the kingdoms of the earth. . ." (**Isaiah 37:16**).

The Old Testament prophets, Jesus Christ and His apostles never claimed anything else than God Almighty, the God of the Jews and Christians, was indeed one God and one only. But Muslims believe that because Christians believe in the concept of the Trinity (God in three persons, the Father, Son and Holy Spirit (or Mary, according to Muhammad), that Christians are polytheistic. Nothing is further from the truth. For Christians to worship and serve more than God alone would be heretical and not faithful to the scriptures they have been given through the ages.

". . . We believe in that which has been revealed to us and revealed to you, and our God and your God is One, and to Him do we submit" (**Qur'an 29:46**). **Qur'an 32:4** reaffirms that there is no God but

Allah and that there is no "guardian or any intercessor" besides him. Allah revealed to Muhammad that the Christians were polytheists, worshipping more than one god and that Allah would not and could not have any "associates" (**Qur'an 4:48** and **31:13**).

"Allah, (there is) no god but He, the Everliving, the Self-subsisting by Whom all things subsist" (**Qur'an 3:2**). Other **Qur'an** verses, such as **3:18, 6:102** and **59:23**, also proclaim that Allah is the only god or that he is one god and one only. The Islamic mantra or *Shahada* (to bear witness to) is, "There is no god but Allah, Muhammad is the messenger of Allah (or Muhammad is his Prophet)." They are the first words spoken in the ears of a new born baby boy," noted the Caner brothers. "The creed is repeated at times of prayer, during rights [sic] of passage in life and throughout the life of the faithful Muslim (15).

"Certainly they disbelieve," Allah disclosed in **Qur'an 5:72-73**, "who say: Surely Allah, He is the Messiah, son of Marium; and the Messiah said: O children of Israel! Serve Allah, my Lord and your Lord. Surely whoever associates (others) with Allah, then Allah has forbidden to him the garden [of paradise], and his abode is the fire; and there shall be no helpers for the unjust.

"Certainly they disbelieve who say: Surely Allah is the third (person) of the three; and there is no god but the one God, and if they desist not from what they say, a painful chastisement shall befall those among them who disbelieve." Of course, like many Qur'anic quotes associated with Jesus, there is no corresponding Bible reference citing that Jesus said this to His followers. This was just another attempt of Muhammad to meld the two faiths—Islam and Christianity—together, thus consolidating and elevating his power.

The Death and Crucifixion of Christ

Jesus died an excruciatingly painful death of His choosing at the hands of His accusers and oppressors just as the prophets of old foretold (**Psalm 22:15-18; Isaiah 53:1-12; Zechariah 12:10**). Only He had the power and the will to freely choose the time, place and method of His atoning death (**Matthew 26:3-5; John 13:1**). Jesus died as a true martyr— one who gave His life so that all could live. He was only 33. Muhammad, despite all his calls for others to die as martyrs in Allah's cause, died a quiet, peaceful death of a non-martyr in the arms of his beloved 18-year old Aisha, the girl he had married when she was only nine and Muhammad was 53. He lived a full life and died at 62.

Jesus not only had power over death as He demonstrated in the raising of Lazarus (**John 11**), but He also had power over His own death. Jesus knew exactly when His death would occur, how it would occur and the events leading up to it. Yet, He freely chose to surrender the power He had over His own death in strict obedience to God the Father for the sake of all.

"I am the good shepherd;" Jesus said, "I know my sheep and my sheep know me—just as the Father knows me and I know the Father—and I lay down my life for the sheep. I have other sheep that are not of this sheep pen. I must bring them also. They too will listen to my voice, and there shall be one flock and one shepherd. The reason my Father loves me is that I lay down my life—only to take it up again. No one takes it from me, but I lay it down of my own accord. I have authority to lay it down and authority to take it up again. This command I received from my Father" (**John 10:14-18**).

Not only did Jesus have power over His own death, but He also had the freedom to relinquish that power to the Father so that in His death it would be a loving sacrifice for all mankind—the death of a true and faithful martyr. To accomplish this all-encompassing atoning surrender of His life for others, Jesus also knew when and how He must die. As the sacrificial *Lamb of God, who takes away the sin of the world!* (**John 1:29**), Jesus could die at no other time than the Jewish Passover. "When Jesus had finished saying all these things, he said to his disciples, 'As you know, the Passover is two days away—and the Son of Man will be handed over to be crucified'" (**Matthew 26:1-2**).

Almost 500 years before the birth of Jesus, the Jewish prophet Zechariah prophesied that the King of the Jews, the promised Messiah, would not be an ordinary king or a king in the class of Solomon. He would not only be a king of humble beginnings, but one of humble endings. "Rejoice greatly, O Daughter of Zion! Shout, Daughter of Jerusalem! See, your king comes to you, righteous and having salvation, gentle and riding on a donkey, on a colt, the foal of a donkey" (**Zechariah 9:9**). This prophecy too was fulfilled by Jesus as recorded in the Gospel of Matthew (**Matthew 21:1-11**).

When Jesus went to the cross, he fulfilled yet another of the Old Testament prophecies revealed through David. "You know how I am scorned, disgraced and shamed;" David wrote, "all my enemies are before you. Scorn has broken my heart and has left me helpless; I looked for sympathy, but there was none, for comforters, but I found none. They put gall in my food and gave me vinegar for my thirst" (**Psalm 69:19-21**).

"Later, knowing that all was now completed, and so that the Scripture would be fulfilled, Jesus said, 'I am thirsty.' A jar of wine vinegar was there, so they soaked a sponge in it, put the sponge on a stalk of the hyssop plant, and lifted it to Jesus' lips" (**John 19:28-29**).

The purpose of Christ's crucifixion according to the Apostle Paul was to have "canceled the charge of our legal indebtedness [to sin], which stood against us and condemned us; he has taken it away, nailing it to the cross. And having disarmed the powers and authorities, he

made a public spectacle of them, triumphing over them by the cross" (Colossians 2:14-15). **Allah, Islam and the Qur'an have no such concept of God's forgiveness for our sins; nor freedom from God's condemnation.**

Right before He died, Jesus fulfilled one more Old Testament prophecy from **Psalm 22:1** (written by King David), when He cried out in agony, ". . . with a loud voice, saying, 'Eli, Eli, lama sabachthani?' that is, 'My God, My God, why have You forsaken Me?'" (**Matthew 27:46**; NKJV. See also, **Mark 15:34**).

Islam's Version of Christ's Crucifixion. In **Qur'an 19** there arises another Qur'anic mystery: the crucifixion of Jesus and his subsequent resurrection. The official Islamic position and belief today, as in Islam's entire history, is that Jesus was not crucified, did not die as the Bible states and was not raised from the dead.

When Bani Isra'il [the Israelites] *wanted to kill him* [Jesus], *Allah Most High saved him . . . "They did not slay him or crucify him, but thus was it made to seem to them"* [the onlookers] *(Koran 4:157), referring to when Yahuda* (Judas Iscariot], *chief among the Jews, met with a band of his people to kill 'Isa out of fear of his message, but Allah sent Gabriel to 'Isa to lead him to a covered alley-way that had a skylight, through which he was taken up to the sky. When Yahuda, in pursuit, ordered one of his companions to follow him into the passageway and murder him, Allah cast the likeness of 'Isa upon the man as he entered, and when he came out again after a fruitless search, the Jews attacked and killed him, thinking him to be 'Isa, and hung him upon a cross.*

Reliance of the Traveller, x189

"And their [the Jews] saying: Surely we have killed the Messiah, Isa [Jesus] son of Marium [Mary], the apostle of Allah; and they did not kill him nor did they crucify him, but it appeared to them so (like Isa) and most surely those who differ therein are only in a doubt about it; they have no knowledge respecting it, but only follow a conjecture, and they killed him not for sure" (**Qur'an 4:157**). Allah, through Muhammad, proclaims that Christ's crucifixion and resurrection never happened, but that Allah took Jesus to heaven himself. In addition, all those who believe in the crucifixion and resurrection of Christ shall be condemned with Jesus as a witness against them.

"Nay!" – The crucifixion and resurrection is not true.—"Allah took him up to Himself; and Allah is Mighty, Wise.

"And there is not one of the followers of the Book but most certainly believes in this before his death, and on the day of resurrection he (Isa) shall be a witness against them" (**Qur'an 4:158-159**).

Qur'an 4:157 is the only verse in the Qur'an that mentions the crucifixion of Jesus, even though Muslims protest the reality of it with vigor. However, it is the verse that Muslims point to as proof that Jesus was no more than a mere prophet and was not crucified and raised on the third day as the Bible says. It was all a hoax of the first century Christians, Muslims claim. In spite of such Islamic claims, a closer examination of the verse is warranted. First, the verse *does not* say that Jesus was not crucified. It only says that the Jews "did not kill him nor did they crucify him." Second, that analysis would be a correct statement according to the biblical witness. While Jewish leaders conspired to have Jesus killed, they themselves did not kill or crucify Jesus. Jesus, through the false witness of certain Jews, was tried and condemned by Pilate, the Roman governor and consigned to scourged by the Roman soldiers and then delivered for the Roman death by crucifixion.

However, in **Qur'an 19**, Muhammad provides a different revelation about Jesus.

"And peace on him [Jesus] on the day he was born, and on the day he dies, and on the day he is raised to life" (**vs. 15**). This view is repeated in **verses 33 and 34**: "And peace on me [Jesus] the day I was born, and on the day I die, and on the day I am raised to life. Such is Isa [Jesus], son of Marium [Mary]; (that is) the saying of truth about which they dispute."

Muhammad believed and the Islamic faith continues to propagate, that Jesus did not die on the cross as the Bible says, but someone that Allah made to look like Jesus took his place and that Jesus continued to spread the Gospel beyond the year of his supposed crucifixion. The fact that the Qur'an mentions Jesus' bodily resurrection should not be seen as an admission of his resurrection three days after his crucifixion. Muhammad and Muslim adherents, while believing that Jesus was not crucified, do believe that he will be raised from the dead, as will Muhammad and other prophets in the last days.

This apparent conflict in theology could also be explained by Muhammad's changing revelations over his lifespan as "The Prophet" of Allah. **Qur'an 19** was received during Muhammad's second Mecca period (616-622 A.D.) when many of the doctrines of the faith were being established—a period during which Muhammad was more conciliatory toward the Jews and Christians. **Qur'an 4**, however, was revealed during the last ten years of Muhammad's life when he lived in Medina (623-632 A.D.), a period when he and his followers became militant and intolerant of Jews and Christians and anyone who refused to accept Islam as the only true religion.

As Muhammad lay dying, he reportedly said: "I have been sent with the shortest expressions bearing the widest meanings, and I have been made victorious with terror (cast in the hearts of the enemy), and while I was sleeping, the keys of the treasures of the world were brought to me and put in my hand" (16).

Muhammad's Hatred for the Cross of Christ. Hadith, volume 3, book **43:656** of Sahih Bukhari, narrated by Abu Huraira, states: "Allah's Apostle said, 'The Hour will not be established until the son of Mary (i.e. Jesus) descends amongst you as a just ruler, he will break the cross, kill the pigs [Jews], and abolish the Jizya tax. Money will be in abundance so that nobody will accept it (as charitable gifts).'"

Muhammad, according to Muslim history and traditions, had a hatred for the cross or anything that resembled it (17). Not only did Muhammad hate the cross, but Muslims claim that Christ himself not only hates the cross but will destroy it (that is, Christianity) when He returns.

A similar hadith from Sunan Abu Dawud and narrated by Abu Hurayrah, says this: "The Prophet (peace be upon him) said: 'There is no prophet between me and him, that is, Jesus (peace be upon him). He will descent (to the earth). When you see him, recognize him: a man of medium height, reddish [h]air, wearing two light yellow garments, looking as if drops were falling down from his head though it will not be wet. He will fight the people [infidels] for the cause of Islam. He will break the cross, kill swine, and abolish jizyah. Allah will perish all religions except Islam. He will destroy the Antichrist [whom the Jews follow] and will live on the earth for forty years and then he will die. The Muslims will pray over him.'"

"Islam," according to the Caners, "in order to resolve the matter of the Resurrection, teaches that Judas, not Jesus, was crucified, allowing Jesus to appear three days later" (18).

According to this new Qur'anic revelation to Muhammad, God decided that mankind was not worthy of such a loving sacrifice through Christ's crucifixion on the cross, and the only way to reach man would be through unrelenting persecution and bloodshed, which Muhammad was more than willing to carry out on a regular basis—as have jihadist Muslims for the past fourteen centuries.

For the message of the cross is foolishness to those who are perishing, but to us who are being saved it is the power of God.
1 Corinthians 1:18

It was essential to Muhammad's theology and self-serving revelations as Allah's prophet, that he discredit the crucifixion story and Christ's sacrifice for the sins of the world. To acknowledge the crucifixion and the shedding of Christ's blood as atonement for sin would mean there would be no need for Muhammad as God's new and last prophet. No new revelations would be needed. For as Jesus said on the cross, "It is finished" (**John 19:30**).

"Islam says that Jesus did not die," wrote Keohane. "So, again— Islam has proven to be false; because Muhammad claimed the Gospel is true, and all 4 Gospels (Injils) testify that Jesus died and rose from the dead" (19).

For, as I have often told you before and now tell you again even with tears, many live as enemies of the cross of Christ.
Philippians 3:18

"Jews demand miraculous signs and Greeks look for wisdom," Paul wrote, "but we preach Christ crucified: a stumbling block to Jews and foolishness to Gentiles" (**1 Corinthians 1:22-23**). The Apostle Paul and the apostles that walked with Jesus had no doubt that Jesus was crucified. They were either a witness to it or knew it happened from the testimony of other eye-witnesses, and had no reservations in preaching the Gospel of Jesus Christ crucified. In His death and resurrection, Jesus fulfilled yet another Messianic prophecy—this one by David. "Therefore my heart is glad and my tongue rejoices; my body also will rest secure, because you will not abandon me to the grave, nor will you let your Holy One see decay" (**Psalm 16:9-10**).

"The Messiah, son of Marium is but an apostle;" Muhammad revealed, "apostles before him have indeed passed away; and his mother was a truthful woman; they both used to eat food. See how We make the communications clear to them, then behold, how they are turned away" (**Qur'an 5:75**).

In spite of the overwhelming proof of the crucifixion of Jesus, Muhammad could conveniently and easily wipe it from history with a self-serving revelation from Allah.

"Anyone," the Apostle John said, "who runs ahead and does not continue in the teaching of Christ does not have God; whoever continues in the teaching has both the Father and the Son. If anyone comes to you and does not bring this teaching, do not take him into your house or welcome him. Anyone who welcomes him shares in his wicked work" (**2 John 9-11**).

Although He was the Son of God, Jesus followed in the footsteps of the men of God before Him. His message was built upon the foundation of those who went before Him. Muhammad did not build on that godly foundation, but rather tried to destroy it as a false gospel. Instead, it was Muhammad's gospel that was false and not in

49

keeping with the foundation of love, peace and forgiveness laid down so firmly by Christ and His apostles.

"The Spirit," the Apostle Paul wrote to Timothy, "clearly says that in later times some will abandon the faith and follow deceiving spirits and things taught by demons" (**1 Timothy 4:1**). Six hundred years after the death of Jesus, it is apparent, those who chose to follow the teachings of Muhammad did just that.

". . . every ritual and belief in Islam," writes Fr. Suresh, "can be traced back to pre-Islamic pagan Arabian culture. Muhammad did not preach anything new. Everything he taught had been believed and practiced in Arabia long before he was ever born. Even the idea of 'only one God' was borrowed from the Jews and the Christians.

"This irrefutable fact casts to the ground the Muslim claim that Islam was revealed from heaven.   we have to conclude along with the Middle East scholars that Allah is not God, Muhammad was not his prophet, and the Qur'an is not the Word of God" (20).

Chapter Conclusion

Muslims, since the days of Muhammad, have had a convenient way to cast aside the many contradictions and controversies in the Qur'an, it is called "abrogation". It is a uniquely Islamic concept. If a verse in the Qur'an contradicts one before it, it is just because Allah thought up a better revelation to overturn the previous one. The main purpose of abrogation was to provide Muhammad with some timely self-serving revelation that he needed to gain the upper hand on a detractor or enemy.

Although the Qur'an makes it clear that the followers of Allah are to read and believe in the Bible, possession of the Bible is condemned in many Muslim societies and for a Muslim to read it can bring harsh penalties and even death. Even for a Christian to have or read the Bible in a Muslim country can bring severe punishment, imprisonment or execution.

Christians are not polytheists, as Muhammad falsely claimed throughout the Qur'an, and Muslim clerics and scholars throughout the centuries have falsely propagated. Christians worship one God—the One and only God of creation. The fact that Jesus came into the world, sent by God, as His only begotten Son, does not detract from God's Oneness as the sole true deity of the universe. God chooses to express His nature in the presence of His Son and the Holy Spirit does not nullify His completeness as the One and only God.

While there are over 300 Bible prophecies about the coming of Jesus Christ, there are none foretelling of the birth and life of Muhammad. The Jews and Christians of Muhammad's era were not expecting another prophet and considered Muhammad to be a false prophet.

During his time in Mecca, where Muhammad first started preaching the tenets of Islam, his revelations from Allah were conciliatory as he tried to win over Jews and Christians to his theology. When that failed and Muhammad was run out of Mecca and had to flee to Medina, his revelations from his god turned more hostile and vengeful toward those who would not accept him or his revealed word.

Islam proclaims to have a new truth by negating the real truth that endured for centuries, and continues to endure through the willingness of millions of Christians to suffer persecution for the love of Christ. Real martyrs die for the love of God; false martyrs die because of their hate for others.

Although there is a wealth of biblical and historical evidence to back-up the stories and message of the Bible, there is little evidence to support the claims made by Muhammad in the Qur'an or elsewhere. Muhammad's claim that Allah was the true god and the God of the Jews and Christians who had gone astray, and thus warranted persecution by true Muslims rings hollow when the message of the Bible is compared to that of the Qur'an. The dysfunctional message of the Qur'an completely contradicts and overturns God's plan of personal redemption and salvation in the Bible and makes it null and void. The fact that Muhammad hated the cross is no surprise when the source of his revelations is revealed as satanic.

References

1. Caner, Ergun Mehmet and Emir Fethi Caner. *Unveiling Islam*, 2002. Kregel Publications, div. of Kregel. Inc., p. 35.
2. Spencer, Robert. *The Truth About Muhammad, Founder of the World's Most Intolerant Religion*, 2006. Regnery Publishing, Inc., Washington, DC., p. 34.
3. Ibid, p. 59.
4. Caner and Caner, p. 85.
5. Keohane, Steve. *Muhammad: Terrorist or Prophet?* BibleProbe.com, 200402007. Http://bibleprobe.com/ muhammad.htm. Accessed April 1, 2007.
6. Suresh, Fr. Gnana Pragash, *Understanding Islam, Part II.* Society of St. Pius X – Southern Africa, 2001. http://www.sspxafrica.com/ documents/2001_ September/Understanding_Islam.htm. Accessed March 11, 2003.
7. Caner & Caner, p. 83.
8. Safa, Reza F. *Inside Islam: Exposing and Reaching the World of Islam*, 1996. Charisma House, p. 23.
9. Crone, Patricia. *What Do We Actually Know About Mohammed?* Open Democracy, August 31, 2006. Source: http://www.openDemocracy.net. Accessed June 2, 2007.
10. Ibid.

11. Spencer, p. 21
12. Caner & Caner, p. 95-96.
13. Spencer, p. 24.
14. Ibid, p. 25.
15. Caner & Caner, p. 122.
16. Spencer, p. 165.
17. Keohane, p. 23.
18. Caner & Caner, p. 18.
19. Keohane, p. 5.
20. Suresh.

Chapter 3

Israel and the Middle East

I will bring them back to live in Jerusalem; they will be my people, and I will be faithful and righteous to them as their God.
Zechariah 8:8
(circ. 520-518 B.C.)

<u>Author's Note</u>. Some of this section draws upon an article the author wrote in 2002 for his former website and later posted on his blog on December 31, 2008 (1).

bram (Abraham) Seeks an Heir. We can gain some insight into this generation old conflict between Muslims and the Jews; between Israel and the Arab nations by picking up the story in Genesis 16 where Abraham and his wife Sarah were first known as Abram and Sarai. Abram was 86 years old and Sarai had never bore him any children, yet God had promised Abram that he would have a male descendent who would bring forth descendants as numerous as the stars of heaven (**Genesis 15:3-5**).

Frustrated and impatient with the lack of God's immediate fulfillment of His promise, Abram decided (with Sarai's encouragement) to take matters into his own hands.

He took unto himself Hagar, Sarai's Egyptian pagan maidservant, and she bore him a son.

> *And the Angel of the Lord said to her* [Hagar]*:*
> *"Behold, you are with child, and you shall bear a son. You shall call his name Ishmael* [viz., God shall hear]*, because the Lord has heard your affliction. He shall be a wild man; his hand shall be against every man, and every man's hand against him. And he shall dwell in the presence of all his brethren"* **Genesis 16:11-12** (NKJV).

The Destiny of Ishmael and His Descendants. Several things should be noted at this point about Ishmael and his relationship to Abraham and Abraham's God.

First, **Abram chose to disbelieve God's promised covenant with him and establish his own covenant <u>by the flesh</u>. *Second*, his partner in this <u>fleshly covenant</u> was the pagan, Hagar (meaning one who takes flight), the Egyptian. *Third*, it was God, not Abram, who chose the name of Ishmael for this son to be born <u>outside</u> of God's chosen covenant with His people. *Fourth*, it was God who said at**

Ishmael's conception, that he would "be a wild man;" and that "his hand shall be against every man, and every man's hand against him." At the same time "he shall dwell in the presence of all his brethren."

God's Plan and Covenant. An estimated 2,500 years before the arrival of Muhammad, the God of the Bible promised the Land of Canaan to Abraham and his descendants (c. 1918 B.C.). When Abram was 99 years old, he was still without a true heir by Sarai's womb. God then spoke to Abram and made this covenant with him:

> *As for Me, behold, My covenant is with you, and you shall be a father of many nations. No longer shall your name be called Abram, but your name shall be Abraham; for I have made you a father of many nations. I will make you exceedingly fruitful; and I will make nations of you, and kings shall come from you. And I will establish My covenant between Me and you and your descendants after you in their generations, for an everlasting covenant, to be God to you and your descendants after you. Also I give to you and your descendants after you the land in which you are a stranger, all the land of Canaan, as an everlasting possession; and I will be their God.* **Genesis 17:4-8** (NKJV; author's emphasis)

Remember this preceding scripture for later on in this chapter. It is significant to both biblical and Qur'anic citations about the land of Canaan, otherwise known as the Holy Land.

Fourteen years after the birth of Ishmael, God fulfilled His intended covenant with Abram (now Abraham) with the birth of Isaac to Sarah who was no longer called Sarai. God's promise and covenant with Abraham was three-fold: 1). God promised to multiply Abraham and his descendants greatly (**Genesis 17:2**); 2). God promised that through Abraham all the nations on earth would be blessed (**Genesis 18:18, 22:18**) and 3). God promised to give Abraham and his descendants the land of Canaan as an *everlasting possession* (**Genesis 17:8**). As you will see later in this chapter, the Qur'an corroborates this biblical version.

Ishmael was not in God's Plan for His People. Several times God makes it clear to Abraham that He (God) does not acknowledge Ishmael as Abraham's son or heir. "Then the word of the LORD came to him: 'This man [Ishmael] will not be your heir, but a son who is your own flesh and blood will be your heir'" (**Genesis 15:4**).

God never intended to establish His covenant with Ishmael, because Ishmael was not the child of the promise, but of the flesh. While God blessed Ishmael with fruitfulness, He never made a covenant with him. God's covenant was with Abraham and him only. Unlike Abraham and Isaac, God never promised Ishmael and his seed

that He would be their God.

God reiterated in **Genesis 28:13** that He was the God of Abraham, Isaac and Jacob. Ishmael was not God's chosen covenant child with Abraham, nor was he part of God's plan that would eventually bring forth God's fulfilled covenant of salvation through Jesus Christ.

Muslims are not Descendants of Abraham. Although Arabic Muslims claim Abraham as their heir, biblically they are descendants of pre-covenant Abram, the one who disobeyed God and disbelieved His promise of an heir through Sarah. God could bless Ishmael, but He could never establish His covenant with a sinful seed of the flesh.

Ishmael's sons initially inhabited an area from Egypt and the Sinai Desert, the Arabian peninsula to Assyria (which includes present day Saudi Arabia, Iran, Iraq, Jordan, Syria and the lesser Arab kingdoms). Remember, God said that Ishmael and his descendants would be wild men whose hand would be "against every man."

After the death of Abraham, some Bible translations of **Genesis 25:18** state that the descendants of Ishmael "lived in hostility toward" or "in defiance of" all their brethren (New International Version, New Living Translation and North American Standard). Other versions (including the King James, New King James and Amplified Bibles) state only that Ishmael's descendants lived "close to" or "in the presence of" their relatives.

Over 25 centuries later, Muhammad and his followers have found a simple solution to this dilemma of a negative biblical image and how to expropriate God's promise and covenant with the Jewish people. Muhammad simply revealed that Allah told him that it was Ishmael, not Isaac, that Allah chose to test Abraham's faith; and therefore it was Ishmael and all those who are descendants of him that are the true chosen people to fulfill Allah's covenant.

Remember, in **Genesis 22:2**, God called Abraham to sacrifice his son Isaac on a makeshift altar on Mount Moriah in Jerusalem. However, Muhammad ignored that biblical reality and declared that Allah called Abraham to sacrifice Ishmael on Mount Mina outside Mecca. It was that simple to change historical truth and create an alternate reality that Muslims have believed for 14 centuries.

According to the Qur'an, Abraham prayed to Allah: "'My Lord! Grant me [a son who shall be] of the doers of good deeds [that is, righteous].' So We gave [Abraham] the good news of a boy, possessing forbearance. And when [Ishmael] attained to working with him, [Abraham] said: O my son! Surely I have seen in a dream that I should sacrifice you; consider then what you see.

"He said: O my father! Do what you are commanded; if Allah please, you will find me of the patient ones. So when they both submitted and [Abraham] threw [Ishmael] down upon his forehead, and We called out to him saying: O Ibrahim! You have indeed shown the truth of the vision; surely thus do We reward the doers of good: Most surely this is a manifest trial" (**Qur'an 37:100- 106**).

God did not Recognize Ishmael as Abraham's Son. The preceding version in the Qur'an of Abraham's call to sacrifice his son strongly contradicts the biblical story. "Then God said, 'Take your son, *your only son*, Isaac, whom you love, and go to the region of Moriah. Sacrifice him there as a burnt offering on one of the mountains I will tell you about'" (**Genesis 22:2**; author's emphasis). Notice that God refers to Isaac as Abraham's *only* son. That is because only Isaac was God's choice to fulfill His covenant with Abraham—not Ishmael, the son of the flesh.

In Genesis 22, God told Abraham three times that he (Abraham) only had one son, Isaac. "Then God said, 'Take your son, *your only son*, whom you love—Isaac—and go to the region of Moriah. Sacrifice him there as a burnt offering on a mountain I will show you'" (Genesis 22:2, author's emphasis).

Because of Abraham's willingness to sacrifice his only son and not withhold him from God, God promised Abraham that "through your offspring all nations on earth will be blessed, because you have obeyed me" (**Genesis 22:18**).

From the present day and historical perspective of the daily violence against mankind by the followers of Islam, it is hard to see that this was God's plan for blessing the nations of the earth through the descendants of Ishmael. Among the descendants of Isaac, however, was Jesus, the sacrificial lamb who brought salvation to the world by the shedding of His blood and not that of another human being—truly a blessing to all who will receive Him.

The Apostle Paul affirmed that descendants of Isaac are the true heirs of God. "It is not as though God's word had failed," he asserted. "For not all who are descended from Israel are [of] Israel. Nor because they are his descendants are they all Abraham's children. On the contrary, 'It is through Isaac that your offspring will be reckoned' [**Genesis 21:12**]. In other words, it is not the natural children who are God's children, but it is the children of the promise who are regarded as Abraham's offspring" (**Romans 9:6-8**).

Paul makes it clear in **Galatians 4:22-30**, that Ishmael was the pre-covenant seed of a slave and therefore could not represent God's covenant with His people. Isaac, on the other hand, was a freeman, born of a freewoman as the fulfillment of God's promise to His people. Those who are heirs to the bondswoman of the flesh (viz., Ishmael), will remain in bondage until set free by the salvation of Christ, who is heir to the covenant of the freeman, Isaac.

Paul also pointed out that the descendants of Ishmael will always be persecuting the descendants of Isaac, the freeman, and that

the heirs of the two can never share in the inheritance of the freeman. The only hope of sharing this inheritance that the descendants of Ishmael have is to be grafted in through the salvation of Christ.

Despite the clarity from both the Old and New Testaments of the Bible and testimony from God's own mouth, Muslims, some Christian leaders and other ignorant or uninformed individuals continue to claim that Muslims—or at least Arabic Muslims—are descendants of Abraham, therefore, Islam can lay claim to being an "Abrahamic faith." Muslims also claim that the Old Testament prophets, the Apostles and Jesus Himself were Muslims.

It is important to recognize, from an Islamic viewpoint, it was necessary to supplant Isaac with Ishmael as the one God called Abraham to sacrifice. Why? Because it was through Isaac's lineage that Jesus the Messiah would be born (2).

Allah Says that Palestine is for the Jews

What does the Bible and the Qur'an say about Palestine and Palestinians? In a word: *Nothing!* The two words do not appear anywhere in the Bible or the Qur'an. As you will see later in this chapter, the terminology is a fairly recent invention of militant Arabs living in the Jewish Promised Land in an effort to corrupt and hijack both biblical and traditional history.

Throughout Islamic history, Arabic Muslims, following the teaching and example of Muhammad, have relentlessly persecuted the Jews—not only in what Muslims consider Palestine, but throughout the world. The claim of Arabic Muslims is that Palestine—that is, Canaan or the "Holy Land"—was always the inherited land of Muslims and that the Jews have no right to it and are to be driven out. Yet, the Qur'an—and this will be a shocker to both Muslims and infidels—states that Allah promised Moses and the Jews the land of Canaan or the *Holy Land.*

> *And when Musa said to his people: O my people! Remember the favor of Allah upon you when He raised prophets among you and made you kings and gave you what He had not given to any other among the nations.*
>
> *O my people! Enter the holy land which Allah has prescribed for you and turn not on your backs for then you will turn back losers* (**Qur'an 5:20-21**).

Four things are noteworthy in these Qur'anic verses: <u>First</u>, it is revealed that God (*not* Allah) did, indeed, promise the Jews that they would occupy the Holy Land or Canaan.

Second, there were no kings ruling over the Jews during Moses' lifetime. Moses died before the Jews entered Canaan and almost 200 years before the prophet Samuel anointed Saul as the first king of the Israelites.

Third, Allah tells his followers that he gave the Holy Land to the Jews and no other nation among them.

Fourth, God (*not* Allah) commands the Jews to never give up the land of Canaan that he has *prescribed* for them. It is important to note that Allah *never* spoke to the Jews, but the Qur'an claims that he did. Despite this revelation of the Jews' right to Palestine in perpetuity in the Muslim's own holy book, Muslims are bent on annihilating or forcing the Jews from their rightful homeland as guaranteed to them by God in the Bible and Allah in the Qur'an. Nevertheless, in surah 7:157, Allah commands his followers to follow that which is written in the Torah and the Gospel.

There is, however, another convoluted possibility when considering Muhammad's mindset and theology. Remember, Muhammad claims that Allah revealed that all the prophets of the Bible were indeed Muslims. Therefore, in **Qur'an 5:20** when Allah is talking about Moses and his people, maybe Muhammad believed that Allah was proclaiming the *holy land* was for Muslims.

When it comes to the Jews, Allah is apparently very changeable. "And certainly you have known those [Jews] among you who exceeded [profaned] the limits of the Sabbath, so We said to them: Be (as) apes, despised and hated" (**Qur'an 2:65**). This derogatory view of Jews by Allah is repeated in **Qur'an 7:166**. In **Qur'an 5:60**, Jews are referred to by Allah not only as apes but as swine, as well, thus giving Muslims the perceived right to habitually dehumanize Jews by referring to them as pigs and monkeys to this day.

Historical and Archeological Evidence that Jerusalem Belongs to the Jews. Muslims claim that Jerusalem belongs to them just like the rest of the Holy Land, Canaan or Palestine, whatever they choose to call it.

So, if Jerusalem belongs to them, what is their proof? How many times does the Qur'an mention Jerusalem as belonging to the followers of Allah?

NONE! How many times does the Qur'an mention Jerusalem at all? NONE! That's right, absolutely no mention of Jerusalem occurs anywhere in the Qur'an.

Now, if Jerusalem is supposed to be so important to the followers of Allah and it belongs to them, would not Allah have known that and revealed it to Muhammad?

So, how many times is Jerusalem mentioned in the Bible? It depends on the translation—767 (King James) to 1,027 (New Living), as examples.

The real fact is that Jerusalem has been continuously occupied for over 5,000 years—and not by Muslims—but not by Jews

either. However, historical record outside the Bible indicates that the Jews first fully occupied Jerusalem with the establishment of King David's dynasty around 1,000 B.C. or 1,600 years before the birth of Islam.

Archeological digs over the years have produced numerous ancient biblical sites and thousands of artifacts that support the Old Testament claims of the Bible, as well as the known history of the Jews in the Land of Canaan (3).

In the past several years, two important archeological finds support the Jewish claim to Jerusalem. On the hills of Hebron, just south of Jerusalem, archeologists led by Professor Avraham Faust of Bar-Ilan University in Israel unearthed stone structures in 2013 that they believe represent the City of David (4, 5). Radiocarbon dating of the ruins dated the site at about 1,000 B.C., the era of King David. The ruins appear to be built upon the ancient city of Eglon mentioned in **Joshua 15:39**. According to **Joshua 15**, the Tribe of Judah's inheritance included over 100 cities in the Promised Land of Canaan, including Gaza and Jerusalem. Although the Israelites could not completely dislodge the Canaanite tribe of Jebusites from Jerusalem (**Joshua 15:63**), King David was able to conquer it in 1003 B.C. and co-habit the city for many generations.

According to Professor Faust, "Hundreds of artifacts were unearthed within the debris, including a wide range of pottery vessels, loom weights, many metal objects, botanical remains, as well as many arrowheads, evidence of the battle which accompanied the conquest of the site by the Assyrians." Although the name of King David was not associated with any of the findings, Faust insists that the debris discovered is consistent with the cultural changes that occurred during the conquest of the area by King David.

Among the discoveries on the excavated site was a large residence dubbed the "Governor's Residence." Since it occupies a prominent position in the Judean foothills and is well constructed, it has been postulated that it could be the home of King David. The structure at the Tel 'Eton archeological site has been carbon dated at 1000 B.C.

Richard Elliot Friedman, in an article for Aish.com, wrote on the uniqueness of the historical Jewish experience in the confines of Israel.

"In the first place," Friedman wrote, "the land is filled with Hebrew inscriptions, so I begin with that. These are not just an occasional inscription on a piece of pottery or carved in a wall. Nor should we even start with one or two of the most famous archaeological finds. Rather, there are thousands of inscriptions. They come from hundreds of excavated towns and cities. They are in the Hebrew language. They include people's names that bear forms of the name of their God: YHWH. This means names like:

- Hoshaiah, which means "YHWH Saved"
- Ahijah, which means "YHWH is My Brother"
- Shemariah, which means "YHWH Watched"

"The inscriptions also refer to their kings. They include stamps and seals from official documents. They come from tombs where that land's people were buried. They name people who are mentioned in the Hebrew Bible. They include wording that also appears in the Hebrew Bible. They reflect a widespread community whose dominant language was Hebrew, who didn't eat pork and who worshipped a God named YHWH" (6).

In stark contrast, despite Islamic proclamations to the contrary, there is no archeological evidence of an Islamic presence in Jerusalem or within the confines of the Old Testament Holy Land or Canaan or present-day Israel before the 7th century A.D.

Two exceptional artifacts have been discovered in Israel to further support the Jews' claim to Israel or what the Arabs refer to as Palestine.

The Tel Dan Stele (an inscribed stone) was discovered in northern Israel in 1993. The inscription on the stele describes the victories over the King of Israel and the House of David (7).

"The Tel Dan Stele absolutely one hundred percent proves that King David existed," stated AnaRina Heymann, Director of Jerusalem Watch. "It refutes any claim that King David was merely a story."

Early in 2018, the Israel Antiquities Authority put on public display a recovered 2,700 year old papyrus artifact that had been stolen. The inscription clearly states, "From the king's maidservant, from Naharta, jars of wine, to Jerusalem." This demonstrates that Jerusalem was under the control of the Jews 1300 years before the establishment of Islam (8).

The Origin of Palestine and the Palestinians

Prior to 1920, an Arab people known as the "Palestinians" living in "Palestine" did not exist (9). No one from the Arab community in the Middle East referred to the region as Palestine. To do so would imply a Jewish and Christian possession. The concept of Arab nation-states did not occur until Iraq gained its independence in 1936 after the British Mandate of 1920 ended. In 1932, Saudi Arabia became an independent country, followed by Jordan, Lebanon and Syria in 1946. Smaller Arab nation-states eventually followed, with Kuwait, Yemen, Oman and United Arab Emirates in 1961, 1967, 1970 and 1971, respectively.

The Palestinian people does not exist. The creation of a Palestinian state is only a means for continuing our struggle against the state of Israel for our Arab unity. In reality today there is no difference between Jordanians, Palestinians, Syrians and Lebanese. Only for political and tactical reasons do we speak today about the existence of a Palestinian people, since Arab national interests demand that we posit the existence of a distinct "Palestinian people" to oppose Zionism. Yes, the existence of a separate Palestinian identity exists only for tactical reasons, Jordan, which is a sovereign state with defined borders, cannot raise claims to Haifa and Jaffa, while as a Palestinian, I can undoubtedly demand Haifa, Jaffa, Beer-Sheva and Jerusalem. However, the moment we reclaim our right to all of Palestine, we will not wait even a minute to unite Palestine and Jordan.

Zuheir Mohsen, Executive Committee Member of the PLO

March 31, 1977

Source: https://en.wikiquote.org/wiki/Zuheir_Mohsen

Origin of the Name "Palestine." As indicated in the above enclosure, prior to 1948, when the term "Palestinians" was used, it referred to the Jews in the Holy Land, not the Arabs. "Arabs never referred to themselves as 'Palestinians'" noted Joseph Farah, founder and editor-in-chief of WorldNetDaily (10). It was not until a few years after Israel's "Six Day War" with the Arabs in 1967 that the Egyptian, Yasser Arafat, who founded the Palestinian Liberation Organization in 1964, in an attempt to legitimize the PLO movement, decided to identify the Arabs living in the Holy Land as "Palestinians."

"Palestine has never existed—before or since—as an autonomous entity," Farah, an Arab-American, proclaimed. "It was ruled alternately by Rome, by Islamic and Christian crusaders, by the Ottoman Empire and, briefly, by the British after World War I. The British agreed to restore at least part of the land to the Jewish people as their homeland.

"There is no language known as Palestinian. There is no distinct Palestinian culture. There has never been a land known as Palestine governed by Palestinians. Palestinians are Arabs, indistinguishable from Jordanians (another recent invention), Syrians, Lebanese, Iraqis, etc.

"Keep in mind that the Arabs control 99.9 percent of the Middle East lands. Israel represents one-tenth of 1 percent of the landmass."

Though the definite origins of the word Palestine have been debated for years and are still not known for sure, the name is believed to be derived from the Egyptian and Hebrew word peleshet. Roughly translated to mean rolling or migratory, the term was used to describe the inhabitants of the land to the northeast of Egypt - the Philistines. The Philistines were an Aegean people - more closely related to the Greeks and with no connection ethnically, linguisticly [sic] or historically with Arabia - who conquered in the 12th Century BCE the Mediterranean coastal plain that is now Israel and Gaza.

A derivative of the name Palestine first appears in Greek literature in the 5th Century BCE when the historian Herodotus called the area Palaistin? (Greek - Παλαιστ?νη). In the 2nd century CE, the Romans crushed the revolt of Shimon Bar Kokhba (132 CE), during which Jerusalem and Judea were regained and the area of Judea was renamed Palaestina in an attempt to minimize Jewish identification with the land of Israel.

Under the Ottoman Empire (1517-1917), the term Palestine was used as a general term to describe the land south of Syria; it was not an official designation. In fact, many Ottomans and Arabs who lived in Palestine during this time period referred to the area as Southern Syria and not as Palestine.

After World War I, the name Palestine was applied to the territory that was placed under British Mandate; this area included not only present-day Israel but also present-day Jordan.

Leading up to Israel's independence in 1948, it was common for the international press to label Jews, not Arabs, living in the mandate as Palestinians. It was not until years after Israeli independence that the Arabs living in the West Bank and Gaza Strip were called Palestinians.

The word Palestine or Filastin does not appear in the Koran. The term peleshet appears in the Jewish Tanakh [Hebrew Bible or OT] no fewer than 250 times (11).

The Balfour Declaration of 1917. On November 2, 1917, a full year before the end of World War I, the British government voted to re-establish a Jewish homeland in what was then referred to as "Palestine" by the British. Under a League of Nations mandate the British were to administer the re-settlement of Jewish people in the region that became known as Palestine or the national homeland for the Jews (12). By 1939 the British wanted to limit Jewish migration to the region to 75,000 per year and stop migration of the Jews altogether by 1944 unless Arabs in the region consented to further immigration of Jews. With the outbreak of World War II in 1939, the Jewish migration became a moot point and the State of Israel was established in 1948.

Foreign   Office
November 2nd, 1917

Dear Lord Rothschild,

I have much pleasure in conveying to you. on behalf of His Majesty's Government, the following declaration of sympathy with Jewish Zionist aspirations which has been submitted to, and approved by, the Cabinet His Majesty's Government view with favour the establishment in Palestine of a national home for the Jewish people, and will use their best endeavors to facilitate the achievement of this object, it being clearly understood that nothing shall be done which may prejudice the civil and religious rights of existing non-Jewish communities in Palestine or the rights and political status enjoyed by Jews in any other country.

I should be grateful if you would bring this declaration to the knowledge of the Zionist Federation.

Yours,

Arthur James Balfour (13)

In 1922, the newly established League of Nations, set the borders for Israel of the Jordan River on the east, the Mediterranean Sea on the west, Lebanon on the north and Egypt on the south. Although the original Mandate included a significant land mass east of the Jordan River, the British were given the administrative option of adjusting the territory. In an effort to appease Arabs in the region, the British decided to carve off the land east of the Jordan River—77% of the total mandated—and gave it to the Arabs in the region, dubbing it Trans-Jordan (14). This left the Jewish people with only 23% of the land originally mandated for their homeland.

The Two State Solution. In 1946, the League of Nations was absorbed into the newly organized United Nations. Article 80 of the UN Charter specifically recognizes the original mandate for Palestine:

> *As a direct result of Article 80, the UN cannot transfer these rights over any part of Palestine, vested as they are in the Jewish People, to any non-Jewish entity, such as the 'Palestinian Authority'* (15).

However, not content with stripping away three-fourths of Israel's new homeland, the concept of a "Two State" solution, dividing up Israel's homeland to accommodate Arabs (now referred to as Palestinians) was devised in the 1947 U.N. Partition Plan. This chopped up Israel to the point it was not only unrecognizable, but administratively unattainable and indefensible.

Interestingly, it was not the Jews in Israel that rejected the "Two State Solution", but the Arabs resisted it. The Arabs in the region rioted in protest. On May 14, 1948, Israel proclaimed itself to be an independent State of Israel and the British withdrew from Palestine.

The Oslo Accord (16). On September 13, 1993, there was reason for hope and optimism as Israel's Prime Minister, Yitzhak Rabin, and the Palestinian Liberation Organization (PLO) Negotiator, Mahmoud Abbas met at the President Clinton White House to sign the "Declaration of Principles on Interim Self-Government Arrangements" otherwise known as the "Oslo Accord". (Abbas would later be elected the Chairman of the PLO in 2004 and the President of the State of Palestine and the Palestinian National Authority in 2005).

Both Israel and the PLO, as representative of the Palestinians, "agreed that a Palestinian Authority (PA) would be established and assume governing responsibilities in the West Bank and Gaza Strip over a five-year period." Although the United States facilitated this meeting, it had little to do with establishing the Accord or its ratification. By the time Bill Clinton left office in January 2001, the Accord had collapsed and a new series of violent Israeli-Palestinian conflicts were well entrenched.

After the signing of the Oslo Accord, Israel negotiated a peace treaty with Jordan in October 1994. Once again, although the U.S. did not play a role in the negotiations, President Clinton hosted the signing event between King Hussein of Jordan and Prime Minister Rabin. A few months earlier, in May 1994, Israel and Egypt had negotiated Israel's withdrawal from most of Gaza and Jericho in what was known as the "Cairo Agreement". In September 1995, Israel also signed the "Taba Agreement" ("Oslo II") with the PA, dividing the West Bank into Palestinian and Israeli sectors. This Agreement also "spelled out provisions for elections, civil/legal affairs, and other bilateral Israeli-Palestinian cooperation on various issues."

Two months later Prime Minister Rabin was assassinated by a disgruntled Israeli who disagreed with the Oslo Accords and the ongoing renewal of Hamas terror attacks. With Rabin's death, the Oslo Accord eventually collapsed and Israeli-Palestinian conflict reignited with a vengeance. With the election of Abbas in 2005 and his ascension to Chairman of Fatah (largest political faction of the PLO) in 2009, the PA took on a more rigid and violent approach to Israeli-Palestinian relations.

The more I read the Bible, the more clearly I saw this single truth: Loving and forgiving one's enemies is the only real way to stop the bloodshed.

Mosab Hassan Yousef, "The Green Prince"
Author of *Son of Hamas*, p. 148

With Abbas in control of the PA and his continuous incendiary rhetoric, Hamas rockets and terror attacks have once again become the daily reality for both Israelis and Palestinians.

Hamas Covenant to Destroy Israel (17). Many wonder why Israel and the Palestinians or Israel and Hamas cannot just sit down together and "hammer" out a reasonable peace agreement that all concerned can feel good about and keep. A number of such agreements have been brokered over the years to no avail. Why?

The answer is quite simple: Hamas drafted a Covenant—supported by the majority of Palestinians—with an unending commitment to destroy Israel, no matter what it takes or how many innocent lives must be sacrificed. Although former U.S. Secretary of State, Condoleezza Rice, and other political leaders have often referred to Hamas as a "resistance movement," the truth is, that Hamas and other Islamic terrorists are committed to unprovoked acts of aggression and violence.

However, despite its clear violent nature and desire to exterminate Israel, in December 2014, the General Court for the European Union ruled that Hamas should not be listed by the EU as a terrorist organization (18). Of course, Deputy Hamas Chief, Moussa Abu Marzouk, applauded the decision and stated, "The decision is a correction of a historical mistake the European Union had made. Hamas is a resistance movement and it has a natural right according to all international laws and standards to resist the occupation."

The Hamas Covenant starts with a quote from **Qur'an 3:110-112**:

> *You are the best nation that has been brought out for mankind. You command good and forbid evil and believe in Allah. If only the people of the Book [i.e., Jews and Christians] had believed, it would have been well for them. Some of them believe, but most of them are iniquitous. They will never be able to do you serious harm, they will only be an annoyance. If they fight you, they will turn their backs and flee, and will not be succored. Humiliation is their lot wherever they may be, except where they are saved from it by a bond with Allah or by a bond with men. They incurred upon themselves Allah's wrath, and wretchedness is their lot, because they denied Allah's signs and wrongfully killed the prophets, and because they disobeyed and transgressed.*

Drafted on August 18, 1988, the Preamble to the Covenant of thirty-six articles offers this insight (19):

> *The covenant of the Islamic Resistance Movement (Hamas) reveals its face, presents its identity, clarifies its stand,*

makes clear its aspiration, discusses its hopes, and calls out to help it and support it and to join its ranks, because our fight with the Jews is very extensive and very grave, and it requires all the sincere efforts. It is a step that must be followed by further steps; it is a brigade that must be reinforced by brigades upon brigades from the vast Islamic world, until the enemies are defeated and Allah's victory is revealed.

The *Preamble* says it all, Hamas and other Islamic terrorist groups have no intention of pursuing peace with Israel. Once Israel is defeated they will turn their full attention toward other non-Islamic countries, principally the United States and Europe.

Article One of the Covenant makes it clear where Hamas draws its inspiration for violence and the annihilation of the Jews (and all non-Muslims).

The Islamic Resistance Movement: Islam is its way. It is from Islam that it derives its ideas, concepts, and perceptions concerning the universe, life, and man, and it refers to Islam's judgment in all its actions. It is from Islam that it seeks direction so as to guide its steps.

The "Movement" as represented by Hamas in Palestine is part of a much larger Islamic terrorist group known as the Muslim Brotherhood which was founded in 1928 by Hasan Al-Banna. Although the "Brotherhood" is technically defunct, its ideals and precepts persist throughout the world in the largest Muslim terrorist network, including massive representation in the United States and other Western countries.

Article Two reveals the intensity of the beliefs of Islamic Resistance Movement (IRM) followers:

[IRM] is distinguished by its profound understanding and its conceptual precision and by the fact that it encompasses the totality of Islamic concepts in all aspects of life, in thought and in creed, in politics and in economics, in education and in social affairs, in judicial matters and in matters of government, in preaching and in teaching, in art and in communications, in secret and in the open, and in all other areas of life.

For followers of the Covenant there is no room for freedom of thought or democratic principles. Islam is all and governs all.

66

In **Articles Three, Six and Seven** there is a call upon all Muslims worldwide to raise the banner of jihad or holy war against all filthy, impure and evil unbelievers worldwide.

Article Nine makes it clear that Islam is to rule, not only in Israel but throughout the world.

> *The Islamic Resistance Movement has found itself in a period when Islam is absent from everyday life. Consequently, the balance has been disturbed, concepts have been confused, values have been altered, evil people have come into power, injustice and darkness have prevailed, the cowardly have become tigers, the homeland has been ravished, the people have been driven away and have been wandering in all the countries of the world. The rule of righteousness is absent, and the rule of falsehood prevails. Nothing is in its proper place. Thus, when Islam is absent, everything is transformed. These are the causes.*
>
> *As for the goals, they are to fight falsehood, vanquish it and defeat it so that righteousness shall rule, the homeland shall return [to its rightful owner], and from the top of its mosques, the [Muslim] call for prayer will ring out announcing the rise of the rule of Islam, so that people and things shall all return to their proper place. From Allah we seek succor.*

In **Article Eleven** all of Palestine (Canaan to the Jews) is declared to be an Islamic religious endowment. This is an interesting position, since the Islamic holy book, the Qur'an, clearly states that Allah promised the holy land (i.e., Palestine), not to Muslims, but to the Jews.

> *And when Musa [Moses] said to his people: O my people! Remember the favor of Allah upon you when He raised prophets among you and made you kings and gave you what He had not given to any other among the nations. O my people! Enter the holy land which Allah has prescribed for you and turn not on your backs [that is, give it up] for then you will turn back losers* (**Qur'an 5:20-21**).

While God in the Bible and Allah in the Qur'an promise the Jews Palestine, Arabic Muslims continue to fight for its possession and domination. For the Muslim, the answer is simple: Moses was not a Jew but a Muslim.

Article Thirteen of the Covenant is particularly revealing. It states that ALL "peace" initiatives or solutions for Palestine are null and void *before* they are implemented because they "stand in contradiction to the principles of the Islamic Resistance Movement" and that the *only* solution is for its members is to "wage jihad in order to raise the banner of Allah over the homeland." In the last paragraph of this Article, it concludes with: *There is no solution to the Palestinian problem except jihad.* To read the full Covenant, the student is encouraged to visit the website of Reference #19.

There is hope for peace in the Middle East, but it does not begin with political solutions or negotiations; it begins with the changing of individual hearts.

Mosab Hassan Yousef, "The Green Prince"
Author of *Son of Hamas*, p. 266

Chapter Conclusion

The Bible, the Qur'an, and ancient and recent history, as well as the constant declarations of aggression and violence by Muslims against Israel, Jews and the world's infidels, clearly illustrates that there will never be peace in the Middle East between Muslims and Jews or Muslims and Christians, or Muslims and anyone else living there. However, it is also clear that Islamic hostility is not limited to the Middle East, but has now spread worldwide as you will discover in Chapters 14 and 15 and elsewhere throughout this *Compendium*.

Despite Islamic claims to the contrary, the Holy Land, Canaan or Palestine have never belonged to the Muslims in the region. Historical, Biblical and a wealth of archeological evidence indisputably demonstrate that the region now referred to as "Palestine," which includes God's promised land of Canaan for the Jews, pre-dates the birth of Islam by at least 1600 years. No Muslim or Palestinian society existed at the time the Jews first settled in Canaan. The term "Palestine" or "Palestinian" that was coined hundreds of years later, more often than not, referred to the Jews living there, not the Arabs.

After the State of Israel was officially founded in 1948, the Arabs in the region declared war against Israel in an attempt to annihilate the Jews. With the establishment of the Palestinian Liberation Organization, Yasser Arafat declared that it was the Arabs that were the true Palestinians and the rightful heirs to Palestine. According to the Covenant of the Hamas terrorist group, no peace will exist until Israel is no more. In addition, the Muslims in the Middle East have found an all too willing ally in members of the UN General Assembly and the UN Human Rights Council, thus putting Israel on the political and military defensive on a daily basis.

References

1. Gauss, James F. *Islam and the Middle East*, December 31, 2008. Source: https://ampatriot.wordpress.com/2008/12/31/islam-and-the-middle-east/

2. Hadian, Pastor Shahram. *The Trojan Horse of Interfaith Dialogue Between Christians and Muslims*, Speech, November 27, 2018.

3. Bassett-Brody, Lisette. *Etched in Stone: Archeological Discoveries that Prove the Bible*, 2017. WND Books.

4. Rogers, James. *King David's city discovered? Ancient site linked to biblical kingdom, archaeologists say*, Fox News, May 3, 2018. Source: http://www.foxnews.com/science/2018/05/03/king-davids-city-discovered-ancient-site-linked-to-biblical-kingdom-archaeologists-say.html

5. Zaimov, Stoyan. *Archaeological Discovery: King David City Found Near Jerusalem, Excavations Align With Bible Events*, The Christian Post, May 2, 2018. Source: https://www.christianpost.com/news/archaeological-discovery-king-david-city-found-near-jerusalem-excavations-align-with-bible-events-223580/

6. Friedman, Richard Elliot. *Evidence of the Jewish People's Roots in Israel*, aish.com, October 28, 2012. Source: http://www.aish.com/jw/me/Evidence-of-the-Jewish-Peoples-Roots-in-Israel.html (accessed Sept. 24, 2018)

7. Berkowitz, Adam Eliyahu. *New Archaeological Find is Helping Settle Academic Dispute Over Historical King David*, Breaking Israel News, April 30, 2018. Source: https://www.breakingisraelnews.com/106811/new-archaeological-find-confirms-sophisticated-davidic-kingdom/

8. *Jerusalem Jewish? Yes, says 2,700-year-old relic*, WorldNetDaily, February 25, 2018. Source: http://www.wnd.com/2018/02/jerusalem-jewish-yes-says-2700-year-old-relic/

9. Pipes, Daniel. *Pre-state Israel: The Origins of the Palestinian Arabs.* Jewish Virtual Library. Source: https://www.jewishvirtuallibrary.org/the-origins-of-the-palestinian-arabs (accessed Sept. 9, 2018).

10. Farah, Joseph. *Is Newt Wrong About 'Palestinians'?* WorldNetDaily, December 11, 2011. Source: http://www.worldnetdaily.com/index.php?pageId=376613

11. *Israel: Origins of the Name "Palestine".* Jewish Virtual Library. Source: https://www.jewishvirtuallibrary.org/origin-of-quot-palestine-quot

12. *Balfour Declaration.* Encyclopaedia Britannica. Source: https://www.britannica.com/event/Balfour-Declaration (accessed September 25, 2018).

13. *Balfour Declaration: Text of the Declaration*, Jewish Virtual Library. Source: http://www.jewishvirtuallibrary.org/jsource/History/balfour.html

14. *Israel's Legal Borders in International Law.* Source: http://www.factsaboutisrael.uk/ israels-legal-borders/ (accessed Sept. 9, 2018).

15. Ibid.
16. *The Oslo Accords and the Arab-Israeli Peace Process.* Office of the Historian, Department of State, United States of America. Source: https://history.state.gov/ milestones/1993-2000/oslo (accessed October 25, 2018).
17. Gauss, James F. *Hamas Covenant to Destroy Israel*, January 12, 2009. Source: https://ampatriot.wordpress.com/2009/01/12/hamas-covenant-to-destroy-israel/
18. Malm, Sara. *Hamas should NOT be listed as a terrorist group, European Court rules, because decision to include it on EU list was based on media reports not facts*, Daily Mail, December 17, 2014. Source: https://www.dailymail.co.uk/news/article-2877291/EU-court-says-Hamas-removed-terror-list.html (accessed September 25, 2018).
19. *The Covenant of the Islamic Resistance Movement – Hamas*, 1988. Posted by Memri (The Middle East Media Research Institute) on February 14, 2006. Source: https://www.memri.org/reports/covenant-islamic-resistance-movement-%E2%80%93-hamas

Chapter 4

The Deceptions of Islamic, Christian
& Political Leaders

Jesus answered: "Watch out that no one deceives you."
Matthew 24:4

Deception #1
Allah is Just Another Name for Jehovah God

*O*n Sunday, February 16, 2014, U.S. Secretary of State, John Kerry, *was visiting Indonesia, the largest Muslim populated nation in the world. With over 200 million Muslim adherents, Indonesia is home to about 13 percent of the world's Muslims. While visiting the Istiqlal Mosque that accommodates 130,000 Muslim faithful in Jakarta, Kerry obligingly agreed to beat the mosque drum in the call to prayer.*

*Was Kerry there to encourage Indonesian and Muslim leaders to get a better handle on the growing radical Islamists who attack, suppress and persecute Christians and other non-Muslims? No, he was there to push his and the Obama Administration's controversial "climate change" agenda and to proclaim that, "**We are all bound to one God and the Abrahamic faiths tie us together in love for our fellow man and honor for the same God.**" By "we" it is assumed that he was including Muslims, Jews and Christians in one happy family of faith* (1; author's emphasis).

Mr. Kerry is not alone in his erroneous belief, as has been demonstrated with former presidents George W. Bush and Barack Hussein Obama. Even some noted theologians, such as Pastor James David Greear, who became the 62nd President of the Southern Baptist Convention in March 2018 believes that Christians and Muslims worship the same god. More on his reasons a little later.

One thing is perfectly clear from history and biblical scriptures, that while Allah is the god of Muslims, he IS NOT the Jehovah God of the Jews and Christians as represented in the Bible and history of those two bodies of believers. For centuries Muslim clerics and scholars have tried to re-write biblical and world history and claim that ALL the Old Testament prophets and Jewish patriarchs were really Muslims and that even Jesus was a Muslim. Muslims have tried for centuries to give their pagan religion legitimacy by claiming that it is an Abrahamic religion, meaning that it originated from Abraham, the Jewish patriarch who lived 2,800 years before Islam was ever conceived by Muhammad in what he considered was a satanic vision (2).

In a complete study of this *Compendium*, it will be abundantly clear to the student that Christians and the Jewish people <u>do not</u> pray to, worship or honor the same god as do Muslims. Nor do Christians and Jews have the same affection, understanding and viewpoint of mankind and human nature that Muslims do and that Islam is the most threatening ideology to Judeo-Christianity and Western societies.

Billy Graham Evangelistic Association vs. the Roman Catholic View. In December 2013, Dr. Richard Albert Mohler, Jr., the current president of The Southern Baptist Theological Seminary, in Louisville, Kentucky penned an article for the Billy Graham Evangelistic Association, titled: *Do Christians and Muslims Worship the Same God?* (3).

"We are to use the names God has given for Himself," Dr. Mohler contended, "and we are to recognize that God takes His name seriously because He desires to be rightly known by His human creatures."

Mohler argued his point using the scriptures from **Exodus 3:13-15**. This is when Moses had an encounter with God and Moses asked God, "If I come to the people of Israel and say to them, 'The God of your fathers has sent me to you,' and they ask me, 'What is his name?' what shall I say to them?"

God answered Moses, "I AM WHO I AM" (or "I WILL BE WHAT I WILL BE"). God also told Moses, "Say to the Israelites, 'The LORD the God of your fathers—the God of Abraham, the God of Isaac and the God of Jacob—has sent me to you.' This is my name forever, the name you shall call me from generation to generation."

"Any confusion about the name of God will lead to confusion about the nature of God, if not to idolatry," Dr. Mohler wrote.

A number of things should be noted in the above scripture. <u>First</u>, it is God Himself who gives Himself a name by which He is to be known. Moses did not give God His name. <u>Second</u>, note who among Abraham's lineage is left out. It is Ishmael. God never claims to be Ishmael's God as was pointed out in the previous chapter. <u>Third</u>, God said that the name He gave Himself, I AM WHO I AM (YAHWEH or YHWH in Hebrew) shall be used by all generations. God, the only true God, by any other name, is not acceptable to the God of the Jews. The Jews did give God other names to describe His character or nature, such as ELOHIM (God, The Creator, Mighty and Strong, Genesis 17:7); EL SHADDAI (God Almighty, Genesis 49:24); YAHWEH-JIREH (God Will Provide, Genesis 22:14) and many more. In the Greek New Testament, "YAHWEH" was translated "JEHOVAH."

In 2007, the Catholic News Agency reported that a Roman Catholic Bishop in the Netherlands, Martinus Muskens, recommended that Christians should refer to God as Allah. The bishop's reasoning: to promote better relations with Muslims (4). The aged bishop believes that God does not care what He is called.

"Someone like me", the bishop was quoted as saying, "has prayed to Allah yang maha kuasa (Almighty God) for eight years in Indonesia and other priests for 20 or 30 years. In the heart of the Eucharist, God is called Allah over there, so why can't we start doing that together?"

Dr. Mohler disagrees. "In the Bible, God reveals Himself to us in many names. These names are His personal property. We did not invent these names for God. To the contrary, God revealed these names as His own." Mohler noted that in the Gospels Jesus taught His followers to call God, "Father." Jesus even taught the disciples how to pray by starting with, "Our Father."

"Islam denies what Christianity takes as its central truth claim: the fact that Jesus Christ is the only begotten of the Father," stated Mohler. "If Allah has no son, then Allah is not the God who reveals Himself through the Son."

Dr. Mohler makes his position clear. "Muslims and Christians do not only use different names for God; in reality, these different names refer to different gods.

"Our challenge is to speak truthfully about God, and the only way we can do that is to use the names God gave Himself. The God of the Bible is not Allah, and Allah is not the God of the Bible. Any confusion about that undermines the very Gospel we preach" (5).

However, James David (J.D.) Greear, who was elected the 62nd President of the Southern Baptist Convention in March 2018 would disagree. Greear is also the author of *Breaking the Islam Code*. In his book and in an interview for *The Gospel Coalition* in September 2010, Greear made it clear that he felt Muslims and Christians do worship the same God, but Muslims just have a different understanding of God than Christians (6).

When interviewed by Trevin Wax of *The Gospel Coalition*, Wax asked the following:

> It's helpful to lay these misconceptions on the table and to talk honestly about our differences. You make the case that Muslims do worship the same God as Christians, although with obvious errors in understanding. Can you elaborate on how you came to this conclusion and how you would maintain major distinctions between Muslim and Christian understandings of God?

Pastor Greear responded: ". . . I think the question of whether or not you use the Arabic name for God—Allah—is more of a practical question than a theological one." He went on to build his case using the story of Jesus and the Samaritan woman in **John 4**. In **verse 21** Jesus acknowledges that the woman and the Samaritan people worship God but that they do not understand the God that they worship. Using this example of Jesus, Greear concluded that, "A better, and more Biblical approach (in my view) [in witnessing to Muslims] is to take the God that they claim to understand and show them what His true revelation is like."

Greear, a Southern Baptist pastor of a mega-church in North Carolina, would likely concur with the Roman Catholic view espoused by Bishop Muskens. But he would not be alone since the official view of the Roman Catholic Church and its papacy since at least 1964, is that Muslims and Christians do, indeed, worship the same God.

Muslims Claim Allah is Jehovah God. Muslims claim that Allah is their god, but Jesus said: "If God were your Father, you would love Me, for I proceeded forth and came from God; nor have I come of Myself, but He sent Me" (**John 8:42**, NKJV). The Islamic faith, because it is not a covenant faith with Jehovah God, cannot accept Jesus as the Son of God and therefore denies the existence of God the Father. If Allah was the One and Only true God, then he would acknowledge Christ as his son, just like the God of the Bible does.

Followers of Islam are taught through the Qur'an, to persecute and kill the infidels or non-believers—principally Christians and Jews. While they accept Jesus as a prophet to the Jews, they are taught to despise and hate all followers of Christ and Jehovah God. The question is: If Muslims accept Christ as a prophet of Allah as they claim, then why is it that Jesus, his teachings and his followers are not welcome in any Muslim religious circle?

Yet, Jesus said, "I and the Father are one" (**John 10:30**).

"I am the way, the truth, and the life. No one comes to the Father except through Me" (**John 14:6**, NKJV).

The Apostle John, who was the only one to use the term "antichrist" in the Bible, made it abundantly clear that, "Who is a liar but he who denies that Jesus is the Christ? He is antichrist who denies the Father and the Son. Whoever denies the Son does not have the Father either; he who acknowledges the Son has the Father also" (**1 John 2:22-23**, NKJV). Although some Muslims can accept that Jesus was the Jewish Messiah, they are forbidden to believe in Him as the Son of God. In the Qur'an Jesus is presented mostly as a miracle-working messenger of Allah.

And (make him) [Jesus] an apostle to the children of Israel: That I [Jesus] have come to you with a sign from your

Lord, that I determine for you out of dust like the form of a bird, then I breathe into it and it becomes a bird with Allah's permission and I heal the blind and the leprous, and bring the dead to life with Allah's permission and I inform you of what you should eat and what you should store in your homes; most surely there is a sign in this for you, if you are believers (**Qur'an 3:49**).

In his second letter, John wrote: "For many deceivers have gone out into the world who do not confess Jesus Christ as coming in the flesh. This is a deceiver and an antichrist   Whoever transgresses and does not abide in the doctrine of Christ does not have God. He who abides in the doctrine of Christ has both the Father and the Son. If anyone comes to you and does not bring this doctrine, do not receive him into your house nor greet him; for he who greets him shares in his evil deeds" (**2 John 7, 9-11**, NKJV).

Muhammad, as many before him and after Jesus, definitely brought forth a new and dramatically divergent doctrine or "gospel" than that which was preached by Jesus and His Apostles. It was a doctrine that so conflicted with Judaism and Christianity, that early converts could only be won over by the threat of the sword.

Deception #2
Islam is an Abrahamic Faith Like Judaism and Christianity

Fourteen months after the horrific attack on America on September 11, 2001, by Islamic terrorists, President George W. Bush, at the White House Iftar Dinner, was quick to assert that, "We see in Islam a religion that traces its origins back to God's call on Abraham. We share your belief in God's justice, and your insistence on man's moral responsibility" (7).

Once again, Islam *is not* an Abrahamic faith as presented in the previous chapter, nor does Islam teach or believe in the justice of a loving God, but rather in Allah's unrelenting vengeance upon non-Muslims, as will be presented in following chapters.

To link Islam with the seed of Abraham was Muhammad's attempt to gain favor with Jewish and Christian communities. In an effort to usurp the Abrahamic lineage for Islam, Muslim clerics and scholars have proclaimed for centuries that it was not Isaac—the Jewish patriarch that spawned the 12 tribes of Israel and that Abraham sought to sacrifice on Mount Moriah in Jerusalem—but rather it was Ishmael that God called Abraham to sacrifice on Mount Mina outside Mecca in Saudi Arabia.

"In other words," the Apostle Paul wrote to the Christians in Rome, "it is not the children by physical descent who are God's children, but it is the children of the promise who are regarded as Abraham's offspring" (**Romans 9:8**). The Jews were and are *the children of the promise* from God through Abraham's legitimate seed of Isaac, not Ishmael. This was addressed in Chapter 3, but worth some repetition here. Ishmael could not be the heir of Abraham since he was the product of a pagan union and therefore born outside God's covenant with Abraham. Remember, God did not even recognize Ishmael as Abraham's son (**Genesis 22:2, 12, 16**).

Show me just what Mohammed brought that was new, and there you will find things only evil and inhuman, such as his command to spread by the sword the faith he preached....

Faith is born of the soul, not the body. Whoever would lead someone to faith needs the ability to speak well and to reason properly without violence and threats   To convince a reasonable soul, one does not need a strong arm, or weapons of any kind, or any other means of threatening a person with death   (8)
Byzantine Emperor Michael Paleologos II, 1261-1280 A.D.

The Apostle Paul reiterated this point in his letter to the Church in Galatia. "If you belong to Christ," he asserted, "then you are Abraham's seed, and heirs according to the promise" (**Galatians 3:29**).

In his second letter to his protégé, Timothy, Paul warned, "For the time will come when people will not put up with sound doctrine. Instead, to suit their own desires, they will gather around them a great number of teachers to say what their itching ears want to hear. They will turn their ears away from the truth and turn aside to myths" (**2 Timothy 4:3-4**). That certainly came true with the advent of Muhammad.

The Apostle Paul's warning echoed that of Jesus:

Watch out for false prophets. They come to you in sheep's clothing, but inwardly they are ferocious wolves. By their fruit you will recognize them. Do people pick grapes from thornbushes, or figs from thistles? Likewise, every good tree bears good fruit, but a bad tree bears bad fruit. A good tree cannot bear bad fruit, and a bad tree cannot bear good fruit. Every tree that does not bear good fruit is cut down and thrown into the fire. Thus, by their fruit you will recognize them (**Matthew 7:15-20**).

Deception #3
Jews, Christians and Muslims Pray to the Same God

Jesus made it clear that He and the Father God were one (**John 10:30**) and that no one could reach God the Father without going through Him (**John 14:6**). This is a hard thing for non-Christians and even some nominal Christians to accept, that the only way to the God of the universe is through faith in Jesus Christ.

I and the Father are one. **John 10:30**

Jesus answered, "I am the way and the truth and the life. No one comes to the Father except through me." **John 14:6**

Is Jesus the only way to God? The world and other religions say, *No!*

The Roman Catholic Position. According to Roman Catholic Bishop Marinus Muskens (cited earlier), Muslims and Christians do, indeed, pray to the same God. In fact, the official position of the Vatican and the Roman Catholic Church since 1964 is that Muslims and Christians worship the same God and therefore pray to the same God (9).

Francis J. Beckwith, a Professor of Philosophy and Church-State Studies at Baylor University, wrote an article for *The Catholic Thing* on January 7, 2016, that agreed with the Catholic position.

> *On December 17 on this page I addressed the question of whether Muslims and Christians worship the same God. I gave the same answer given by Vatican II, and by the Catholic Church since the Council: yes. Muslims and Christians do worship the same God, even though Islam holds an imperfect understanding of the divine, since it denies Christ's divinity and thus, by implication, God's triune nature (10).*

Beckwith's article, according to his own confession, drew considerable outrage—not from Catholic readers—but from non-Catholic readers and mostly evangelical Christians. This acceptance of Muslims and Christians praying to the same God appears to be mostly a Roman Catholic belief. But what does Jesus and the Bible have to say on the issue of prayer.

What Does Jesus Say? What does Jesus, the "author and finisher" of the Christian faith (**Hebrews 12:2**; NKJV), have to say about prayer? As already noted, Jesus said that *no one* can come to God except

77

through Him, which is Jesus. That may be hard to accept for some, but that *is* what the Apostle John recorded in his Gospel.

Jesus also said that public, repetitive prayers are worthless and unacceptable to God and go unheard.

> *And when you **pray**, do not be like the hypocrites, for they love to **pray standing in the synagogues and on the street corners to be seen by others.** Truly I tell you, they have received their reward in full. But when you **pray, go into your room, close the door and pray to your Father,** who is unseen. Then your Father, who sees what is done in secret, will reward you. And when you **pray, do not keep on babbling like pagans, for they think they will be heard because of their many words** (**Matthew 6:5-7**; author's emphasis).*

Jesus is making a few key points here. First, prayer is mostly a private matter between a believer and God. Second, Jesus criticized the Pharisees and Jewish religious leaders (*the hypocrites*) for their pious, public display while in prayer. This would be analogous to certain Muslim groups who take over the streets of New York City and elsewhere during their Friday call to prayer in an apparent effort to demonstrate solidarity and perhaps present an image of intimidation to non-believers and city officials.

However, Jesus does acknowledge the need for His followers to come together in unified prayer. "For where two or three gather in my name, there am I with them" (**Matthew 18:20**).

Jesus even instructed His followers on how to pray; how to start one's prayer to God, The Father. If Jesus, the One and Only Son of the Most High God told His followers how to pray an effective prayer that God will hear, who are we to argue with Him?

Like the Apostle Paul instructed:

> *. . . and his [Jesus] incomparably great power for us who believe. That power is the same as the mighty strength he exerted when he raised Christ from the dead and seated him at his right hand in the heavenly realms, far above all rule and authority, power and dominion, and every name that is invoked, not only in the present age but also in the one to come. And God placed all things under his feet and appointed him to be head over everything for the church, which is his body, the fullness of him who fills everything in every way.* **Ephesians 1:19-23**

Paul re-emphasized his point to the Philippians when he wrote, "Therefore God exalted him to the highest place and gave him the name that is above every name, that at the name of Jesus every knee should bow, in heaven and on earth and under the earth, and every tongue acknowledge that Jesus Christ is Lord, to the glory of God the Father" (**Philippians 2:9-11**).

It pleased God, the God of Christians, to seat Jesus on high, at the right hand of the Father and give *him the name that is above every name . . . the name of Jesus.* It is through Jesus and only Him to which *every knee should bow . . . every tongue acknowledge that Jesus Christ is Lord.* That is God's final decision—that is, if you are a follower of Christ—or desire to be one.

The Holy Spirit, Whom Muslims Deny, Directs the Prayers of Christ Followers. Jesus did not leave His followers without help in their prayers and supplications. "And I will ask the Father," Jesus told His disciples, "and he will give you another advocate [*Helper*, NKJV] to help you and be with you forever – the Spirit of truth. The world cannot accept him, because it neither sees him nor knows him. But you know him, for he lives with you and will be in you. In the same way, the Spirit helps us in our weakness" (**John 14:16-17**). Remember, Muhammad, Allah of the Qur'an and Muslims reject the Holy Spirit of God. In fact, Muhammad in the Qur'an (**Qur'an 5:116**) replaced the Holy Spirit with Mary, the mother of Jesus, as the third member of the Trinity that Christians follow.

Christ and the Apostle Paul made it clear that it is impossible to pray effective prayers unless one is guided by the Holy Spirit. "But the Advocate [Helper, NKJV], the Holy Spirit," Jesus shared with His disciples, "whom the Father will send in my name, will teach you all things and will remind you of everything I have said to you" (John 14:26). Paul further elaborated in Romans 8:26, when he wrote, "We do not know what we ought to pray for, but the Spirit himself intercedes for us through wordless groans."

"So what shall I do?" Paul surmised rhetorically, "I will pray with my spirit, but I will also pray with my understanding; I will sing with my spirit, but I will also sing with my understanding" (**1 Corinthians 14:15**). Praying repetitive prayers without understanding and without the presence and assistance of the Holy Spirit are meaningless. Although, as Paul stated to the Roman church, sometimes we just do not know what to pray and that is when the Holy Spirit assists the Christian believer (**Romans 8:26**).

The Apostle Peter who told Jesus he would die for Him but then abandoned Christ in His hour of need, had an amazing transformation during the outpouring of the Holy Spirit on Pentecost (**Acts 2**). After his infilling of the Holy Spirit, Peter began to preach boldly and without fear about Christ.

In his first letter, Peter wrote, "For the eyes of the Lord are on the righteous and his ears are attentive to their prayer, but the face of the Lord is against those who do evil" (**1 Peter 3:12**).

Prayer in almost any religion is essential and a core belief, but prayer to the One and Only True God in Jesus Christ has its guidelines and rewards. Why Muslims pray at all is a mystery. According to Islamic teaching Allah is too high and mighty to be reached. According to Qur'an 6:39, 13:27, 14:4 and others, *whom Allah pleases He causes to err* **[sin],** *and whom He pleases He puts on the right way.* **So, why pray? For forgiveness? No, Allah's not listening, he has already determined your path. For intervention in your life and circumstances? No, Allah is too high and mighty to care about you.**

Deception #4
Islam is a Religion of Peace

Less than a week after the Islamic attack of September 11, 2001, President George W. Bush put out a press release after his speech at the Islamic Center in Washington, D.C. (11). The objective of the release did not appear to truly sooth the soul of the survivors, the families of those who lost loved ones or the American public. It was, perhaps, an attempt to placate the Muslim community or protect them from backlash or an attempt to replicate Islam's propaganda that was foisted upon a confused, grieving, angry and ignorant American public—the deception that *Islam is a religion of peace*. This same mantra which is repeated by Muslims, America's political leaders, the American media and some church leaders, has done nothing to increase the *peace* between Muslims and their avowed enemy (Christians and Jews), as clearly set out in the Qur'an and by Islam's current scholars and preachers. All it has done is to continue to perpetrate the false narrative that Islam is a great religion and a way of life that brings peace to one's soul and society.

Shortly after the proclamation on the following page, President Bush met with King Abdullah of Jordan at the White House on September 28. Apparently none of his staff, or anyone else, saw the need to correct the error of his ways eleven days earlier. Once again, President Bush reasserted that, "the Muslim faith is based upon **peace and love and compassion**. The exact opposite of the teachings of the al Qaeda organization, which is based upon evil and hate and destruction" (12; author's emphasis).

On November 19, 2001, President George W. Bush, at the Iftaar (Iftar) Dinner in The State Dining Room, in Washington, D.C., stated that, "The Islam that we know is a faith devoted to the worship of one God, as revealed through The Holy Qur'an. It teaches the value and the importance of **charity, mercy, and peace**" (13; author's emphasis). However, the facts are that the Qur'an and Islam's "prophet" Muhammad teach and taught no such virtues.

President Bush was unrelenting in his effort to convince the American people—in the midst of hundreds of jihadist attacks worldwide—that Islam was truly a religion devoted to peace. On November 15, during Ramadan 2001, he proclaimed once again, "The Islam that we know is a faith devoted to the worship of one God, as revealed through The Holy Qur'an. It teaches the value and the importance of charity, mercy, and peace" (14).

A little over a year after the 9/11 attack, on November 13, 2002, President Bush was still proclaiming that the tenets of Islam stood for peace.

"Islam, as practiced by the vast majority of people, is a peaceful religion," the President declared emphatically in a meeting with then U.N. Secretary General, Kofi Annan at the White House, "a religion that respects others" (15).

In his 2009 Cairo speech, President Obama upped the ante another notch in presenting Islam as a forerunner of peace.

"Islam is not part of the problem in combating violent extremism, it is an important part of promoting peace," the President asserted (16).

In the same speech, President Obama also proclaimed, "Because we reject the same thing that people of all faiths reject: the killing of innocent men, women, and children."

Present Obama was unyielding in pushing his "Islam is peace" agenda, and it was a clear objective of his eight year administration.

"Let's start with this fact: For more than a thousand years, people have been drawn to Islam's message of peace," President Obama once again insisted at the Islamic Society mosque in Baltimore on February 3, 2016 (17).

For over 1400 years Islam has brought nothing but misery and death to all those who refuse to accept its teachings.

Deception #5
Islam is a Religion of Tolerance

"No Compulsion in Religion." The Qur'an verse that Muslims love to quote to unsuspecting infidels is **2:256**, which starts out stating, "There is no compulsion in religion . . ." The implication and rational imposed upon the non-Muslim is that Islam is open-minded and that there is no discrimination against those who chose not to follow Islam. The truth is far from the reality of Islamic teaching.

First, let's take a full look at the verse and the one that follows it.

> ***There is no compulsion in religion***; *truly the right way has become clearly distinct from error; therefore, whoever disbelieves in the Shaitan [Satan] and believes in Allah, he indeed has laid hold on the firmest handle, which shall not break off, and Allah is Hearing, Knowing.*
>
> *Allah is the guardian of those who believe. He brings them out of the darkness into the light; and (as to) those who disbelieve, their guardians are Shaitans who take them out of the light into the darkness; they are the inmates of the fire, in it they shall abide* (**Qur'an 2:256-257**; author emphasis).

However, in the same chapter, 63 verses before, Allah revealed, "And fight with them [non-believers] until there is no persecution, and **religion should be only for Allah**, but if they desist, then there should be no hostility except against the oppressors" (**Qur'an 2:193**; author emphasis). Again, **Qur'an 8:39** reaffirms Allah's position. "And fight with them until there is no more persecution and religion should be only for Allah; but if they desist, then surely Allah sees what they do."

"Surely this Islam is your religion," Muhammad proclaimed, "one religion (only), and I am your Lord, therefore serve Me" (**Qur'an 21:92**).

So, in summation, non-Muslims are "free" to believe what they want, but if they do not believe in Allah they will suffer persecution at the hands of Allah's true believers and go to hell in the end.

Of course, Jews, Christians and others believe that their way of belief in God is the only true way. The difference, at least among Jews and Christians, is that they do not persecute or force others into believing their way. Judaism and Christianity are beliefs of personal choice; not of compulsion or persecution.

Surrendering to Islam is not an Option. Not only is Islam not a religion of tolerance and acceptance of others, it is an all-encompassing belief system and way of life that will not and does not accept any other form of belief or way of life. When Muslims immigrate to a non-Muslim country, the majority do not seek, nor are they interested in assimilation into that country's culture, politics, religion or way of life. What they seek and work toward is creating the *ummah*, the Islamic community within the host country. The end goal is for the *ummah* to become large enough and influential enough to transform the local and native society to their liking and demands.

"Humankind has suffered horrific wars in the past," wrote Amil Imani, an Iranian-American who fled Iran with his parents during the 1979 Iran revolution. "Yet the present multi-form and multi-front war waged by Muslims has the potential of inflicting more suffering and destroying more lives than ever before. Ruthless Islamic forces advance rapidly in their conquests while those of freedom are acquiescing and retreating. Before long, Islam is poised to achieve its Allah-mandated goal of cleansing the earth of all non-Muslims through 'grand Jihad' and establishing the Islamic *Ummah"* (18).

In the past few decades, a culture of "tolerance" has invaded the American psyche and educational system. On the surface, its goals seem simplistic enough: to wipe out intolerance. However, the subtle and often direct intent is to do away with socially accepted norms or established Judeo-Christian beliefs. While being tolerant and accepting of another's culture, background, ethnicity, etc. is understood to be a good thing, demanding that those of a particular faith persuasion accept certain lifestyles as normal in opposition to what they consider sinful, is not tolerance, it is oppression and intolerance.

Prior to the wave of Muslim immigrants/refugees from the Horn of Africa that started in the 1990s, most Muslim-Americans sought to assimilate into American society. They lived quietly within their communities, contributing to the broader American society. However, since the surge in refugees, most notable from war-torn Somalia, Muslim immigrants have been less willing to assimilate into American culture and have been very vocal and demanding about their rights to live separately and under different laws within American society.

Dig Deeper. *Visit this site,* https://www.tolerance.org/magazine/ publications/what-is-the-truth-about-american-muslims/american-muslims-in-the-united *(*jointly produced by the Religious Freedom Education Project of the First Amendment Center and the Interfaith Alliance Islamic Understanding*). The goal is to teach "tolerance" in America's schools, including tolerance of Muslims and Islam. Also, this Muslim site,* http://theamericanmuslim.org, *tries to portray the positive aspects of Islam for unsuspecting non-Muslim Americans and lists all those they consider "Islamophobes" who raise justifiable concerns about the overall mission of Islam and its message of intolerance. See,* http:// theamericanmuslim.org/tam.php/features/articles/a_whos_who_of_the_an ti-muslim_anti-*arabislamophobia_industry.*

The seven-page list of "Islamophobes" in the above referenced website and prepared by the site's originator, Sheila Musaji in 2012, is quite informative and includes just about every person and organization in America that has ever said anything negative about Islam.

Of course, labeling people and organizations who have legitimate questions and concerns about Islam and Islamic mandates and teaching as "Islamophobes" is a demonstration of intolerance to real debate and discussion by Muslims and the political left in America.

Amil Imani, who has been alerting the West and the world to the evils of Islam and who is surprisingly not on the list of Islamophobes, stated that, "Humanity, with the Muslims in the lead, must stop deluding themselves and abandon Islam altogether. It is really nothing more than an infested corpse that needs be properly disposed of" (19).

The most often reported statistic on various Muslim websites on Islamic terrorism is that only 6 percent of terrorist attacks worldwide are committed by Muslims. This, despite conventional knowledge and reality to the contrary, that demonstrate an overwhelming majority of the world's terrorist attacks are perpetrated by Muslims. While the majority of Muslims are peaceful, the ideology of Islam is not and terrorism is its centerpiece. Since September 11, 2001 there have been at least 36,000-plus Islamic terrorist attacks around the world accounting for over 235,000 deaths and hundreds of thousands maimed or psychologically impacted for life.

A 2015 study of 452 Middle East suicide attacks found that 450 or 99.56 percent were motivated by Islam (20). Daily, throughout the world, Muslim imams, scholars, academics, politicians and other leaders and their minions demonstrate their true lack of tolerance as they preach and spew forth their hatred of Jews, Christians and anyone else who does not accept their way of thinking and living.

"Islam is at war with us [Americans] and the free people of the world," wrote Imani in April, 2018. "We are saying we shouldn't surrender. We should reject in no uncertain terms their historical ultimatum of *aslam taslam* (surrender, become Muslim, and you will have peace). . . . We should do all we can to defeat this menace" (21).

In the same article, Imani continued with, "Many Muslims invade the country of largely Christian people with epithets such as worshipers of the cross and *al-kilab* (dogs, the most disparaging name-calling in Islam, since dogs specifically are designated *najes*—unclean or untouchable) and Jews descendants of pigs and monkeys, according to their Quran itself. Yet they have no qualms about making themselves right at home, accepting all kinds of benefits handed to them by dogs and descendants of monkeys and pigs" [see **Qur'an 5:60; 7:166**] (22).

Deception #6
Islamic Terrorism & Terrorists Do Not Represent True Islam

On February 23, 1998, Osama bin Mohammed bin Awad bin Laden or Osama bin Laden, a member of the wealthy Saudi Arabian bin Laden family and founder of the infamous al Qaeda Islamic terrorist organization, issued a *fatwah* (Islamic law proclamation) against America and the West.

"'But when the forbidden months are past, then fight and slay the pagans wherever ye find them, seize them, beleaguer them, and lie in wait for them in every stratagem (of war)' [surah 9:5]; and peace be upon our Prophet, Muhammad Bin-'Abdallah, who said: 'I have been sent with the sword between my hands to ensure that no one but Allah is worshipped, Allah who put my livelihood under the shadow of my spear and who inflicts humiliation and scorn on those who disobey my orders'" (23). It was a World Islamic Front statement on behalf of jihadi groups in the Middle East, Egypt, Pakistan and Bangladesh.

An Islamic Apologist. Not long after the September 11 2001 Islamic terrorist attack on the U.S. homeland, "moderate" Muslims rushed forward into the U.S. media in an attempt to portray a more sedate face of cultural Islam as the true Islam of Peace. One of the foremost from the American Muslim community that has become a mainstay of the American media—both conservative and liberal—is Dr. M. Zuhdi Jasser. Born in Dayton, Ohio and educated at the University of Wisconsin, Dr. Jasser is a well-respected American medical doctor in Phoenix, Arizona; a former U.S. naval lieutenant commander and is a devout Muslim who is often sought after for his Islamic views as a "moderate" Muslim. There is no doubt of Dr. Jasser's sincerity to present Islam's best face and that "moderate" Muslims are the answer to Islam's transformation into an acceptable Western society participant.

In May 2004, Dr. Jasser wrote a lengthy piece for his website proclaiming that it was not true Muslims that were the problem in the world, but the *Islamists* (advocates or supporters of Islamic militancy or fundamentalism). "At times," he wrote, "there is only a binary choice in the public either between the voices who say that *Islam is the problem* and the tired voices of the Islamists who provide endless apologetics, denial, victimization, and every deflection possible short of responsibility or actual ideological solutions for a counter-jihad and reformation. Certainly, the Islamists, no matter how peaceful, who look at the world through the lens of political Islam are at the core of the ideological problem" (24). The trouble with Dr. Jasser's logic here is that *it is* the Islamists, a.k.a. Islamic terrorists, that are following the very teaching presented by Muhammad in the Qur'an, hadith and elsewhere. While these jihadists may be labelled *fundamentalist* or not the true face of Islam, the reality is that they see people like Dr. Jasser and "cultural" Muslims as mere infidels and apostates just like other non-believers.

Fighting is enjoined on you, and it is an object of dislike to you; and it may be that you dislike a thing while it is good for you, and it may be that you love a thing while it is evil for you, and Allah knows, while you do not know.

Qur'an 2:216

85

"Most should understand," Dr. Jasser continued, "that strategically, identifying 'Islam as the problem,' immediately alienates upwards of one quarter of the world's population and dismisses our most powerful weapon against the militant Islamists—the mantle of religion and the pulpit of moderate Muslims who can retake our faith from the Islamists. The majority voices in the middle, the non-Islamist and anti-Islamist Muslims who understand the problem, have to be on the frontlines. They cannot be on the frontlines in an ideological battle being waged, which demonizes the morality of the faith of Islam and its founder, the Prophet Mohammed.   we cannot win this ideological war without the leadership of Muslim anti-Islamists. The radical and political ideologies of Islamism, Wahhabism, Salafism, Al Qaedism, Jihadism, and Caliphism, to name a few, cannot be defeated without anti-Islamist, anti-Wahhabi, anti-Salafist, anti-Al Qaedist, anti-Jihadist, and anti-Caliphist devout Muslims."

The challenge with this line of thought is that there really are no *anti-Islamists* stepping up to the plate (Dr. Jasser is the exception rather than the rule) to do battle with the Islamic scourge. When was the last time Muslims in the Middle East, Europe or the United States rise up in mass indignation and protest against the atrocities of the barbaric Islamists? Devout Muslims are, indeed, the Islamists and *are the true* Qur'an followers and devotees of Muhammad.

The other issue here is, it is Islam and its teachings and history that is the problem. There are hundreds of verses in Islamic holy texts and over 1400 years of Islamic history that support today's vile hatred against Jews, Christians and other non-Muslims. What we see today around the world is not some new uprising by a select few Islamists, jihadists or anti-colonialists. In the 21st century we see a new boldness of hatred toward the West that was birthed in the foundational teachings of Islam 14 centuries ago.

Entrenchment of the Muslim Brotherhood. In Cairo, Egypt, on June 4, 2009, President Obama tried to rationalize the explosion in Islamic violence the world over. "They [al Qaeda] have killed people of different faiths—more than any other, they have killed Muslims. Their actions are irreconcilable with the rights of human beings, the progress of nations, and with Islam. The Holy Koran teaches that whoever kills an innocent, it is as if he has killed all mankind; and whoever saves a person, it is as if he has saved all mankind. The enduring faith of over a billion people is so much bigger than the narrow hatred of a few. Islam is not part of the problem in combating violent extremism—it is an important part of promoting peace" (25). There is a lot of deception and misrepresentation of the truth in the forgoing quote.

First, the verse in the Qur'an that Obama was trying to so deftly quote was not fully quoted. The partial quote comes from **Qur'an 5:32**.

But let us look at the full verse and the one that follows it. Keep in mind that the verse is a culmination of Muhammad's retelling of the Bible story of Cain slaying his brother Abel (**Genesis 4:8**). Muhammad's recitation starts in verse 27 of the surah, but we will look at verse 32 in its entirety.

> *For this reason* [the slaying of an innocent person] *did We prescribe to the children of Israel that whoever slays a soul, unless it be for manslaughter or for mischief in the land, it is as though he slew all men; and whoever keeps it alive, it is as though he kept alive all men; and certainly Our apostles came to them with clear arguments, but even after that many of them certainly act extravagantly in the land* (**Qur'an 5:32**).

In the above verse, who is Muhammad talking about? It is not the followers of Allah, it is the Jews. This is made clear in the statement, *We prescribe to the children of Israel.* It is also apparent in the reference to *Our apostles came to them.* Israel had many apostles or prophets, Islam has one. No, this is not a verse admonishing Muslims for killing innocent people, but the Jews. That is made clear in the very next verse that prescribes what Muslims are to do by contrast.

> *The punishment of those who wage war against Allah and His apostle and strive to make mischief in the land is only this, that they should be murdered or crucified or their hands and their feet should be cut off on opposite sides or they should be imprisoned; this shall be as a disgrace for them in this world, and in the hereafter they shall have a grievous chastisement* (**Qur'an 5:33**).

This *is the verse* of instruction for all Muslims to follow, not the previous one that Obama took out of context and misquoted. However, it is the verse Islamic scholars and religious leaders and other deceivers try to pass off on unsuspecting non-Muslims.

They desire that you should disbelieve as they disbelieved, so that you might be (all) alike; therefore take not from among them friends until they fly [flee] *(their homes) in Allah's way; but if they turn back, then seize them and kill them wherever you find them, and take not from among them a friend or a helper* (**Qur'an 4:89**).

There are no civilians in Israel. The population—males, females and children—are the army reserve soldiers, and thus can be killed.
Sheikh Rashid Ghannouchi
Tunisia's "moderate" Islamist Ennahda Movement

> *What is apparent is that it is allowed for us to kill their women and children, even if that were to cause us to miss taking them as wealth (slaves), due to its breaking the hearts of the enemy.*
> Shaykh Ibn Uthaymins (dec.)
> Salafi Islam scholar, Saudi Arabia

No, Islamic terrorism is not an aberration of Islam, it is the core and spirit of Islam—the message of its holy writ and its prophet.

Deception #7
True Islam has been Hijacked and can be Reformed

"So often," Dr. Jasser pined, "attempts by anti-Islamist Muslims to claim that our faith has been hijacked or our faith has been twisted are dismissed by non-Muslims" (26). The faith has not been hijacked, it is just that the rhetoric of true Islam has boiled to the surface and with the full support of the modern technology it is now exposed for all the world to see that which non-Muslims have endured in Muslim countries for centuries.

Despite what former President Obama said, that *the United States is not at war with Islam*, the truth is, it is Islam that the West and the rest of the non-Muslim world is battling. Islam's teaching, hatred, oppression, persecution and goal of world domination are diametrically opposed to world democracies of freedom and self-determination. It is not a religion seeking equal voice and freedom of worship in non-Muslim societies. It is an ideology that seeks only to oppress and dominate those who refuse to accept its dictates. No, Islam has not been hijacked by fundamentalists or Islamists, it only has been fully exposed for the free world to see.

Amil Imani, an Iranian born American and pro-democracy advocate, cites six key reasons why Islam cannot be reformed (27).

1. **The first problem is Islam's own holy book**, the Qur'an, viewed by every true Muslim as Allah's holy, unchangeable word directly delivered to Muhammad by the angel Gabriel. Although Allah repeatedly changed or abrogated his word to Muhammad multiple times, mere humans are forbidden to do so. In Judaism and Christianity, true adherents would not think of changing God's word either. In Christianity, various translations might attempt to improve a translation to help with the understanding, however, the foundational verse and meaning are retained.
2. **Islam is** considered by its adherents as **the perfect religion and ideology**—there is no other. If it is perfect in its current form as

Islamic followers have had drilled into their beings repeatedly, why change it? Changing it would be admitting that it was not the true religion and that Muhammad was either a fraud or a figment of someone's very active imagination. There is no room for fallibility of the faith or its leaders.

3. **Islam is entirely a male-dominated**, male-controlled ideology— it is misogynist. Despite a few female activists in non-Muslim countries or those Muslim women who risk everything to speak out about Islam's abuses, the basic tenets of Islam are anti-women. That will never change; it is a core structure of Islam that makes the ideology different from all others.

4. **Islam is a racist ideology** that seeks to subjugate all others and still condones slavery. Although Islam is racist, it is not a race of people despite what the West's useful non-Muslim deceivers try to perpetrate upon unsuspecting U.S. citizens. The resounding cry against anyone who questions or confronts Islam and Islamic beliefs is that one is a "racist."

5. **Islam cannot and will not accept other belief systems.** While the official daily Islamic mantra is against Jews and Christians, the reality is that Islamic teaching does not accept any belief system other than Islam. To "reform" it would mean that it is not perfect and that other ideological beliefs have merit. According to Islamic teaching and holy texts, Allah abrogated all other religious beliefs when he revealed Islam to Muhammad and what is left is only cults that refuse to accept the only true religion of Islam.

6. **Islam was birthed in violence and subjugation** of people and remains so to this day. Islam has only existed for 14 centuries and grown because of its central belief of forcing people to believe in Allah and his prophet, Muhammad. Without that core precept of violence and submission Islam would have died an ignominious death many centuries ago as a false and seriously deficient dogma.

Truth, the unadulterated truth, is the new "hate speech" in America and the West, that handcuffs everyone—politicians, journalists, church leaders, law enforcement—anyone who submits to its spell of political correctness.

". . . Islam is a socio-cultural viral disease," Imani has come to believe, "that invades any vulnerable host with its malignancy, while simultaneously devouring its own adherents.

"... Once it invades the mind of its victim, this debilitating disease is capable of transforming him or her to a helpless pawn that has no choice but to execute what he or she is directed to do" (28).

Although individual Muslims can be redeemed through a professing faith in Jesus Christ, the religion of Islam is not capable of being reformed or redeemable. Why? Because it is adverse to God's Word and has its very roots anchored in the foundations of Satan and satanic thought, beliefs and actions.

"The founder of Islam, Mohammad," Imani asserts, "insured the faith would remain on its intended mission by providing it with its manual of murder and mayhem, the Quran. The Quran is the incubator of the virus of Islam, and Muslims are the carriers of this disease who communicates it to others while they themselves simultaneously are devoured by it" (29).

Deception #8
There are Moderate Muslims

Once again, Dr. Jasser proclaimed that moderate Muslims not only exist but are the majority of Allah-fearing believers.

"Some Muslims," Jasser wrote, "may behave, interpret, and express ideologies which are not from God but contrarily evil and from Satan, but they are still Muslim. I cannot deny that. We have no church to excommunicate them.

"However, we also should remember that every God-fearing Muslim believes that the religion of Islam as a faith comes from God in the same way as Judaism and Christianity" (30).

If Dr. Jasser is trying to convince his readers that Islam comes from the same God as Judaism and Christianity, then that is a fundamental lie that Islam uses to gain equal footing with Jews and Christians. While he may believe that is true—since Islamic teaching has always stated so—it is still a lie of the devil. Islam cannot possibly have its roots in the same soil as the God of the Jews and Christians.

"... a central morality of individual Islam (the personal character of most Muslims) has generally demonstrated synergy with Judaism and Christianity," Jasser asserted in his editorial. Again, this is typical Islamic deceptive jargon. There is nothing synergistic among the beliefs of Muslims, Jews and Christians.

Apostle Paul has this warning for Christ-followers, "What harmony [accord] is there between Christ and Belial? Or what does a believer have in common with an unbeliever?" (**2 Corinthians 6:15**). *Belial* is Satan or a person of wickedness. Paul is not advocating that Christians not associate with non-believers. Otherwise how would believers be able to share the Gospel with the unsaved world? What Paul is communicating and what Christians need to understand is that there is no agreement, synergy or common ground with those who are of the source of wickedness. Can one still reach out and befriend a Muslim? Sure! Can one express Christ's love and compassion to individual Muslims? Of course! But one must understand that we come from diametrically opposed mindsets and worldviews that are not compatible. At that juncture there is no common ground.

The Myth of the "Moderate Muslim." "It is important to be academic about this assessment [of political Islam] and not assume that what appears to be the silence of the majority of Muslims equates to agreement with the Islamist leadership who exerts a stranglehold over the community," Dr. Jasser penned. "We are doing our national counterterrorism efforts and Muslims a disservice if we assume that the 'lowest hanging fruit,' which comprise all currently Islamist organizations (CAIR, MPAC, or ISNA—to name a few) and their proportionally limited membership speak for all American Muslims" (31).

So, the question is, "Where are all of these moderate Muslims that supposedly are opposed to and working against the allegedly misrepresentation of true Islam?" Muslim Brotherhood organizations like CAIR and ISNA would appear to have a free reign for representing all American-based Muslims. There have been no protests or push-back against these well-entrenched radical, hate mongers by the so-called "moderate" Muslims.

When the West looks at Islam it tends to see the adherents of the faith in terms of *black and white*: they are either "radical" or "peaceful", "terrorist" or "non-terrorist", "fundamentalist" or "moderate." However, in the Muslim world, among Islamic clerics and the teachings of the Qur'an and the prophet Muhammad, there is *only* one form of Islam—radical and fundamental—that strictly follows the words of the Qur'an and the teaching of Muhammad. ALL Muslims are called to believe in the fundamental (basic, original, elemental) truths of their faith as embodied in the Qur'an and the teachings of their prophet, Muhammad. There are no exceptions or deviations permitted. You are not likely to see a "moderate" Muslim like Dr. Jasser debating a "radical," fundamental Islamist on nationwide television or anywhere else. What would they debate? Qur'anic interpretation? The validity of the biography or words of Muhammad? Whether or not all Muslims are called to both lesser jihad (warfare against infidels) and greater jihad (inner spiritual self-examination)?

When it comes to debate on these topics, there is no debate. There can be no deviation. The Qur'an and the words of Muhammad are cast in stone and cannot be reinterpreted or modified to suit one Islamic faction or view over another. With jihad—both lesser and greater—every Islamic believer is called to commit themselves to those commandments in the Qur'an, the hadith and in Islamic law.

Unlike the Christian faith, in which there are many interpretations of scripture and the teachings of Jesus that have resulted in numerous denominations over the centuries, Islam is seen as one size fits all and all must believe in the same things. Hence, the ongoing blood baths between Islamic sects, such as the Sunni versus the Shi'a, etc. Each believes that they and they only are the followers of true Islam.

A moderate Muslim is actually more dangerous than a fundamentalist, however, because he appears to be harmless, and you can never tell when he has taken the next step toward the top [jihad]. Most suicide bombers began as moderates.
Mosab Hassan Yousef, "The Green Prince"
Author of *Son of Hamas*, p. 12

In religion, a fundamentalist is one who takes the holy scriptures of their faith literally as the divinely inspired and infallible word of their god. Christian fundamentalists, for example, believe that the Bible—in every detail—is the divinely inspired word of God and is free from any human error. Although fundamentalist Christians are sometimes ridiculed, they are not typically persecuted or murdered, nor do they assault non-fundamentalist Christians. It is different within Islam.

All **Muslims are called to believe in the Qur'an as the undeniable and infallible word of Allah as revealed through Muhammad—despite the fact that there are numerous historical errors and contradictions throughout the Qur'an. Historical or scientific proof aside, the Qur'an cannot be disputed or challenged.**

Therefore, all Muslims are called to and commanded to follow a fundamentalist faith of Islam. There can be no moderation or moderate Muslims, only fundamentalists or "radical" believers. "Moderate" Muslims, if the West chooses to use such a moniker, in the reality of the Muslim world, do not exist. If they do in practicality, they are viewed as *akafir* or infidels just like the rest of the unbelievers outside of Islam.

Seventeen years since the September 11, 2001 terrorist attack and still there has been no massive repentant outcry from the Muslim clerical community throughout the world. No repudiation of the terrorists or their dastardly acts. America still waits. However, in October, 2007, a group of 138 Muslim leaders from around the world sent a 17-page open letter to the Christian community titled, *A Common Word between Us and You* (this is explored in Chapter 14). It was presented as an olive branch based on a "common ground" of Islam, Judaism and Christianity. Among the deceptive rhetoric was the insistence that Muslims, Jews and Christians worship the same God and that all three stand for peace. No apology or asking forgiveness for the thousands of Christians persecuted and slaughtered by Muslims worldwide every year just because they are Christians that refuse to submit to Islam.

Instead, six years after the 2001 attack, despite overwhelming evidence to the contrary, the vast majority of Muslims in the United States and worldwide believe that the terrorist attacks were either carried out by Israel or the United States. The Pew Research Center survey, *Muslim Americans*, released May 22, 2007, found that only 40 percent of Muslims living in the U.S. thought that the September 11 attacks were carried out by Arab Muslims (32). In the rest of the world it is worse. Only 35 percent of Muslims living in Germany believe the terrorists were Muslim. In Egypt, 32 percent; Turkey, 16 percent and Pakistan, only 15 percent thought Muslims did it.

"If a band of Americans," wrote noted late author and columnist, William F. Buckley, Jr in 2002, "proclaiming their devotion to the faith, assaulted a Muslim center, we would not need to wait very long for disavowals by Christian leaders. When John Brown [the Kansas abolitionist] carried his faith to unreasonable lengths, we hanged him [in 1859]. What we are waiting for . . . is an apology from Muslim leaders . . . an explicit disavowal, as contrary to acceptable teachings of the Koran, of the acts of the terrorists" (33). Sixteen years after the Buckley editorial, America and Americans are still waiting for an apologetic response from the worldwide Muslim community.

On the concept of the *moderate* Muslim, Mark Steyn, NY Times best-selling author, wrote in 2006 that "the most prominent 'moderate Muslims' would seem to be more accurately designated as apostate or ex-Muslims . . . It seems likely that the beliefs of Mohammed Atta [leader of the September 11, 2001 attack on America] **are closer to the thinking of most Muslims . . ."** (34).

Ibn Warraq (pseudonym), author of *Why I Am Not a Muslim*, believes there are moderate Muslims but that Islam, itself, is *not* moderate. Interviewed on Australian Radio National a month after the attack on the World Trade Center in New York, Warraq stated that, "both [President George W.] Bush and [Prime Minister] Tony Blair are the two leaders who have introduced religion into political life, and now they're the ones who refuse to use the word 'Islam' when talking about terrorism. They just won't understand what is happening; they will repeat the same old mistakes. If they cannot analyze the situation and see that Islam is the motivating factor behind all this [the September 11, 2001 attack], then how on earth are they going to tackle the problem?" (35).

Can True Muslims Adapt to the West? "Islam as practiced and held by Muslims fits into the predominant moral framework of American spirituality," Dr. Jasser asserted in his op ed, "and values of the

God of Abraham (a Judeo-Christian-Islamic morality, if you will)." Once again Jasser is perpetrating a myth and fallacy—either purposefully or out of lack of true understanding and knowledge. As pointed out in Chapter 3 and earlier in this chapter, Muslims are not descendants of Abraham although they desperately want to be for various reasons. This is a continued false narrative foisted on an unsuspecting populace, especially upon Western societies.

To "bring political Islam into this mix, and one is left with many questions," Jasser continued.

"Is Islam compatible with democracy?

"Can Muslims separate mosque and state?

"Can Muslims be anti-theocratic?

"Can Muslim behavior and thought today be consistent with modernity while so many current Muslim legal constructs enacted in the name of *sharia* law seem not to be?

"How do Muslims reconcile their history of an empire ruled by a Muslim Caliphate, an empire which had varying rules for its citizens based upon faith with today's more pluralistic universal laws of American society blind to one faith?

"How do Muslims reconcile the plight of women's rights in 'Muslim' societies with their faith and the West? (36).

All of these are good and probing questions and can easily be answered in one word if one assumes moderate Muslims are lumped into the same stew as non-believing infidels by Islamists, i.e., radical, fundamentalist Muslims. The answer to all those questions would simply be, "No" or "They can't."

Again, Amil Imani, a non-Muslim Iranian-American, who fled Iran with his parents during the 1979 Iranian revolution, is a frequent critic of Islam. In an opinion piece in September, 2018, he asked the rhetorical question: "Can a Muslim be a loyal American?" (37). In the article, he cited several areas he believed would be significant stumbling blocks for true Muslims to become fully absorbed into American culture and societal beliefs.

The first issue referenced by Imani **is loyalty**. Can a Muslim pledge loyalty to the United States of America? "A Muslim's loyalty," noted Imani, "is to the Islamic ummah [Muslim community] that recognizes nothing other than one worldwide ummah of Islam, with no allowance for independent nationalities."

The second challenge is submitting to Islamic Law. "A Muslim is required to abide by and live under the laws of Sharia," Imani declared, "and not by the Constitution of the United States of America." Of course, the majority of U.S. Muslims and resident imams would vehemently deny that, but Imani is right. True, Allah-fearing Muslims must abide by Islamic law, not the law of the land in which they reside.

While they are an insignificant minority they will abide by U.S. law. However, where and when they develop a sizeable ummah like in Dearborn, Michigan it would not only be tempting but very possible to develop Islamic shari'a law. It has happened throughout Europe and in Canada.

The third problem is the outright obedience to Allah. "The Pledge of Allegiance says, 'one nation under God,'" Imani pointed out, "while a Muslim is required to be part of the ummah under Allah. It is critically important to realize that Allah is not the same as the Judeo-Christian God. The two are vastly different beings." Here, again, Muslims will insist, along with some American religious leaders and politicians, that Muslims, Jews and Christians worship the same god. As the reader has discovered up to this point in the *Compendium* and throughout, such an assertion is not only the deception, but the often repetitive willful lie of practicing Muslims, as well as the blatant ignorance of non-Muslims, no matter how intelligent.

A fourth test for Muslims in America is **justice and liberty.** "The shield of justice and the life-sustaining air of liberty are constricted in Islam and their beneficence reserved primarily for Muslim men," Imani stated. "Muslim women are excluded from the same rights   And since Islam is impervious to reformation and Muslims view their belief as the best and immutable faith of their Allah, slavery is permissible. Treating even non-slave women as chattel is part and parcel of Allah-ordained law." Once more, while Muslims are a small minority, they will give the impression of compliance with local law until the balance of power shifts into their favor. However, as can be seen in Europe where Muslims only represent 5-10% of the population in many European Union countries, chaos can rule the day.

"To be a loyal and faithful Muslim, one must adhere to and perform many rituals, as specified in the Quran by Allah and the Hadiths/Sunna, every waking moment of his entire life. Disobeying these rituals does not make one a moderate Muslim, but rather it would make him a non-Muslim, facing an uncertain future.

". . . a Muslim can never be both a Muslim and an American at the same time.

"Hence, a Muslim is, first and foremost, an *ummaist:* a citizen of international Islam" (38).

In 2015, the Center for Security Policy published a poll done by The Polling Company of 600 U.S. Muslims. Among the findings were that 33% of those surveyed want shari'a law, not U.S. constitutional law to govern over their conflicts. Only 39% want U.S. courts to rule. Even more disturbing, 29% believe violence is an acceptable option when dealing with someone who insults their prophet Muhammad, the Qur'an or Islam. A staggering 25% believe that jihad violence against Americans is justified (39). If one believes the U.S. Muslim population estimate by Pew Research of 3.3 million in 2015, then that translates into a potential 825,000 jihadists in America right now—men women and children.

This is extremely problematic for the future of the United States of America. Where are these so-called "moderate" Muslims?

It seems wishful thinking on the part of non-Muslims to believe that one can be a moderate Muslim, given that Islam is radical at its very core. To be a moderate Muslim demands that the person explicitly renounce much of the violent, exclusionary, and radical teachings of the Quran. By so doing, the individual issues his own death warrant in Islamic countries and is condemned as apostate. And if he lives in a non-Islamic land, he may even earn a fatwa on his head—Amil Imani (40).

Dr. Jasser wrote, "As a Muslim, my faith as I see it and as it has been taught to me in its most devotional expression is simply—my personal relationship with a moral God—the God of Abraham" (41). However, if his faith is that basic, then Dr. Jasser, by the definition of the Qur'an and Islamic Law, is an infidel, an apostate of Islam. "The stronger and more personal is that relationship, the more pious an individual may be," he continued. "Thus piety is not measured by others or by outward actions or expressed beliefs, but rather piety is dependent upon the intensity and purity of that internal relationship with God." That sentiment, however, is not according to the Qur'an and Hadith where both explicitly call believers to jihad as the highest calling for Allah. The *Reliance of the Traveller*, the book of Islamic law, also makes it clear that violent jihad for the cause of Allah is the Muslim's highest calling.

"It is this inherent human tendency toward good and away from evil," Jasser insisted, "which is the central notion of Islam as it is for Judaism and Christianity." No disrespect meant to Dr. Jasser, but every Muslim who has converted to Christianity would likely and strongly disagree with him.

"It is the corruption, tribalism, and ignorance of so many in the Muslim world," Jasser claimed, "which has poisoned any moves towards enlightenment. But this conflict between good and evil is one, which will be won by the righteous when pious Muslims who fear God, and respect universal humanitarian principles are empowered to stand up to evil under the moral courage of the inspired principles of the God of Abraham" (42). Unfortunately, that will never happen as long as they remain in Satan's oppressive grasp. As pointed out earlier, it is not possible to reform Islam. To reform it would take rejecting the Qur'an, hadith and other Muslim scared texts as the true and unchangeable word of Allah.

> *Dozens of jihads are presently raging in the world, aided and abetted by a "moderate Muslim" majority. The so called moderate Muslims, even if they do exist, are complicit in the crimes of the radicals, either by providing them with funds, logistics, and new recruits, or by simply failing to actively confront and unequivocally renounce them* (43).

"While so-called peaceful Muslims are generally silent, either out of fear, lack of organization, or apathy, violent and supremacist Muslims work around the clock and around the world to further their agenda   The rank-and-file Islamic clergy, for their part, transmit these fatwas and edicts to their flock in mosques and hammer them into the minds of impressionable children in madrassahs [Islamic schools]. Through this grassroots process, Islam is recruiting greater and greater numbers of adherents   Muslims engage in acts of violence to disrupt the functioning of societies, while on the other they cleverly exploit the freedom they enjoy in non-Islamic lands to subvert them from within" (44).

The Question Remains: If Muslims in America someday become a significant minority of only 5-10%, whose side will the "moderate" Muslims drift toward? Will they be staunch and loyal Americans submitted to U.S. Constitutional law and American culture or will they submit to the Islamic will of the imams and ummah as in Europe?

Chapter Conclusion

That the Muslim peoples of the earth have been forever a warring people, especially afflicting the people of the Bible (Christians and Jews) was prophesied by the God of the Bible (revisit Chapters 2 and 3). Muhammad, in establishing Islam as the faith of the Arabic people, facilitated the fulfillment of this prophecy. Islam was birthed in violence and wickedness and has continued in that vein for fourteen centuries. The sin of hatred runs so deep that even Muslims slaughter other Muslims the world over. Nothing will change until the bondage to this satanic religion is broken and the captives are set free.

Leaders in the West, including Muslims, Christians, political leaders and the media at-large, have become complicit in propagating false truths about Islam in order to placate societal resistance in the West and in the Christian church. Christians and Jews do not serve, worship or pray to the same god as Muslims; nor can Muslims truthfully lay claim to being an Abrahamic faith.

Islam is not a religion of peace and has been dominated by acts of violence and terror since its inception and throughout its 14 century history. It cannot be reformed as some "moderate" Muslim pundits suggest. To reform Islam would be admitting that Allah is a false god and Muhammad was a false, self-serving prophet.

References

1. Gauss, James F. *Allah IS NOT God!* March 4, 2014. Source: https://ampatriot. wordpress.com/2014/03/04/allah-is-not-god/
2. Ibid.
3. Mohler, Albert. *Do Christians and Muslims Worship the Same God?* Billy Graham Evangelistic Association, December 1, 2013. Source: https://billygraham.org/decision-magazine/december-2013/do-christians-and-muslims-worship-the-same-god/ (accessed October 1, 2018).
4. *Dutch bishop says Christians should call God 'Allah'.* Catholic News Agency, August 15, 2007. Source: https://www.catholicnewsagency. com/news/dutch_bishop_says_christians_should_call_god_allah (accessed Oct. 2, 2018).
5. *Do Christians and Muslims Worship the Same God?* The Catholic News, Archdiocese of Singapore, October, 2006. Source: http://catholicnews.sg/index.php?option=com_content&view=article&id=1547:do-christians-and-muslims-worship-the-same-god&catid=119&lang=en&Itemid=473 (accessed Sept. 18, 2018)
6. Wax, Trevin. *Reaching Muslims for Christ: A Conversation with J.D. Greear.* The Gospel Coalition, September 30, 2010. Source: https://www. thegospelcoalition.org/blogs/trevin-wax/reaching-muslims-for-christ-a-conversation-with-j-d-greear/ (accessed Oct. 2, 2018)
7. *Backgrounder: The President's Quotes on Islam.*
8. *Faith, Reason and the University Memories and Reflections: Benedict XVI Speeches*, September 12, 2006. Source: http://w2.vatican.va/content/benedict-xvi/en/speeches/2006/september/documents/hf_ben-xvi_spe_20060912_ university-regensburg.html (accessed Oct. 2, 2018)
9. *Vatican Council and Papal Statements on Islam*, United States Conference of Catholic Bishops. Source: http://www.usccb.org/beliefs-and-teachings/ecumenical-and-interreligious/interreligious/islam/vatican-council-and-papal-statements-on-islam.cfm (accessed Oct. 3, 2018).
10. Beckwith, Francis J. *Why Muslims and Christians Worship the Same God.* The Catholic Thing, January 7, 2016. Source: https://www.thecatholicthing.org/2016/01/07/why-muslims-and-christians-worship-the-same-god/ (accessed Oct. 3, 2018).
11. *"Islam is Peace" Says President.* The White House, Press Release, September 17, 2001. Source:
12. *Backgrounder: The President's Quotes on Islam.*
13. Ibid.
14. Ibid.

15. Ibid.
16. *Text: Obama's Speech in Cairo.* New York Times, June 4, 2009.
17. Trifkovic, Srdja, *Obama's Mosque Visit: Wrong Message, Wrong Venue.* Chronicles, February 4, 2016. Source: https://www. chroniclesmagazine.org/obamas-mosque-visit-wrong-message-wrong-venue/ (accessed Sept. 28, 2018).
18. Imani, Amil. *A Metaphor about Islam,* Geller Report, September 12, 2018. Source: https://gellerreport.com/2018/09/metaphor-about-islam.html/
19. Ibid.
20. Issacharoff, Avi. *450 of 452 suicide attacks in 2015 were by Muslim extremists, study shows,* The Times of Israel, January 8, 2016. Source: http://www.timesofisrael.com/450-of-452-suicide-attacks-in-2015-were-by-muslim-extremists-study-shows/ (accessed November 21, 2018).
21. Imani, Amil. *Islam contra the West: Surrender is not an option,* American Thinker, April 29, 2018. Source: https://www.americanthinker.com/blog/2018/04/islam_contra_the_west_surrender_is_not_an_option.html
22. Ibid.
23. *Osama bin Laden's 1998 fatwa.* The Federation of American Scientists. Source: http://www.fas.org/irp/world/para/docs/980223-fatwa.htm
24. Jasser, M. Zuhdi. *Islamism, not Islam is the Problem,* May 18, 2004. Source: http://www.mzuhdijasser.com/3279/islamism-not-islam-is-the-problem (accessed Sept. 14, 2018).
25. *Text: Obama's Speech in Cairo.*
26. Jasser, M. Zuhdi.
27. Imani, Amil. *Will Islam Ever Reform?* Geller Report, August 18, 2018. Source: https://gellerreport.com/2018/08/islam-ever-reform.html/
28. Imani, Amil. *The Virus of Islam: Can It Be Cured?* Source: http://www.amilimani.com/index.php/archives/post/the-virus-of-islam-can-it-be-cured (accessed Sept. 15, 2018)
29. Ibid.
30. Jasser, M. Zuhdi.
31. Ibid.
32. *Muslim Americans: Middle Class and Mostly Mainstream.* Pew Research Center, May 22, 2007. Source: http://www.pewresearch.org/2007/05/22/muslim-americans-middle-class-and-mostly-mainstream/
33. Buckley, Jr., William F. *Are We Owed an Apology?* Townhall.com, August 19, 2002. Source: https://townhall.com/columnists/williamfbuckley/2002/08/19/are-we-owed-an-apology-n1318467 (accessed August 21, 2002).
34. Steyn, Mark. *America Alone: The End of the World as We Know It,* 2006. Regnery Publishing, Inc., p.19.
35. *Ibn Warraq; Why I Am Not A Muslim.* The Religion Report, ABC Radio National (Australia), October 10, 2001. Source: http://www.abc.net.au/rn/talks/8:30/relrpt/stories/S386913.htm (accessed May 22, 2007).
36. Jasser, M. Zuhdi.
37. Imani, Amil. *Can a Muslim be a Loyal American?* September 18, 2018. Source: https://gellerreport.com/2018/09/muslim-loyal-american.html/

38. Ibid.
39. *Poll of U.S. Muslims Reveals Ominous Levels Of Support For Islamic Supremacists' Doctrine of Shariah, Jihad.* Center for Security Policy, June 23, 2015. Source: https://www.centerforsecuritypolicy.org/2015/06/23/nationwide-poll-of-us-muslims-shows-thousands-support-shariah-jihad/ (accessed December 14, 2018).
40. Imani, Amil. *The Myth of the Moderate Muslim*, Geller Report, September 14, 2018. Source: https://gellerreport.com/2018/09/myth-moderate-muslim.html/
41. Jasser, M. Zuhdi.
42. Ibid.
43. Imani, Amil. *The Myth of the Moderate Muslim.*
44. Imani, Amil. *A Metaphor About Islam*, Geller Report, September 12, 2018. Source: https://gellerreport.com/2018/09/metaphor-about-islam.html/

Chapter 5

Muhammad vs. Prophets of the Bible

Then the LORD said to me, "The prophets are prophesying lies in my name. I have not sent them or appointed them or spoken to them. They are prophesying to you false visions, divinations, idolatries and the delusions of their own minds.

Jeremiah 14:14

Of the world's major religions, Islam is one of the most recent, even though it was birthed over 1400 years ago. Despite that indisputable fact, the official position of Muslim clerics and scholars is that Islam always existed because Allah has always existed, and therefore Christians and Jews are really Allah worshippers that have gone astray. Islam's followers also maintain that the Jewish prophets, from Adam through Malachi, as well as John the Baptist and Jesus, were really Muslims and prophets of Allah. Of course, the official explanation is that the word "Islam" means "submission" to be "submitted to God," which, of course, all the prophets, including Jesus were submitted to God—just not the god of Islam.

True Prophets Know the Voice of God

In Chapter 1, it was pointed out that when Muhammad received his first revelation he believed that he had been visited by a demon. He had no recognition or understanding of the voice of God. The future revelations he claimed to receive from God, particularly those he claimed to receive when he was in Medina, were clearly anti-Jew and anti-Christian, and undoubtedly not from the God of the Jews and Christians. By stark contrast, the prophets of the Bible had no doubt whatsoever that God was speaking to them—either in person or through an angel. They knew His voice; they knew His character and they did not question His word.

Moses, an Ordinary Man. Chapter 3 of Exodus describes the story of Moses' first encounter with God on Mount Horeb. Prior to his visit from God, Moses was a common man and a criminal. It was the time of Jewish enslavement in Egypt. Moses came upon an Egyptian beating a fellow Jew and Moses came to the defense of his brethren and killed the Egyptian (**Exodus 2:11-12**). In fear, Moses fled to Midian in northwest Arabia (**Exodus 2:15**). In Midian, he was befriended by Reuel, and Moses tended Reuel's flocks. Moses settled down to an ordinary life. He married a daughter of Reuel (also known as Jethro) and they had a son. Moses was not looking to do God's work, but God would seek him out.

"During that long period [of Jewish captivity], the king of Egypt died. The Israelites groaned in their slavery and cried out and their cry for help because of their slavery went up to God. God heard their groaning and he remembered his covenant with Abraham, with Isaac and with Jacob. So God looked on the Israelites and was concerned about them" (**Exodus 2:23-25**).

One day Moses was pasturing Reuel's flock on Mount Horeb. "There the angel of the LORD appeared to him in flames of fire from within a bush. Moses saw that though the bush was on fire it did not burn up" (**Exodus 3:2**). At this point most men would have fled in fear, but Moses was curious.

"When the LORD saw that he had gone over to look, God called to him from within the bush, 'Moses! Moses!' And Moses said, 'Here I am'" (**Exodus 3:4**). Moses was spooked by the voice coming from the burning bush, but knew it was the voice of God, and responded with, *Here I am.* The voice from the burning bush identified itself: "'I am the God of your father, the God of Abraham, the God of Isaac and the God of Jacob.' At this, Moses hid his face, because he was afraid to look at God'" (**Exodus 3:6**). Moses knew without a doubt that he was in the presence of Almighty God, the God of his ancestors; the God of the Hebrews.

> *And now the cry of the Israelites has reached me, and I have seen the way the Egyptians are oppressing them. So now, go. I am sending you to Pharaoh to bring my people the Israelites out of Egypt."*
> *But Moses said to God, "Who am I that I should go to Pharaoh and bring the Israelites out of Egypt?"*
> *And God said, "I will be with you. And this will be the sign to you that it is I who have sent you: When you have brought the people out of Egypt, you will worship God on this mountain* (**Exodus 3:9-12**).

Moses, an ordinary, God-fearing man, knew God's voice and responded to God's call upon his life. He followed God's instructions, boldly proclaimed God's word, led the Jews out of Egyptian captivity and toward the Land of Canaan, that God had promised the Jews through Abraham.

Samuel, the Boy. "The boy Samuel ministered before the LORD under Eli [a priest of the Lord]. In those days the word of the LORD was rare; there were not many visions" (**1 Samuel 3:1**). Samuel also came from humble circumstances. His mother, Hannah, was barren, but God blessed her with the birth of Samuel. Because of this blessing Hannah dedicated her son to God (**1 Samuel 1:28**) and he "ministered before the Lord under Eli the priest" (**1 Samuel 2:11**).

As Eli's health began to fail, God spoke to Samuel as he laid down in the temple of the Lord. "Now Samuel did not yet know the LORD: The word of the LORD had not yet been revealed to him" (**1 Samuel 3:7**). God called Samuel by name three separate times, but Samuel thought it was Eli calling him. After the third time, Eli realized that it was God speaking to Samuel. *So Eli told Samuel, "Go and lie down, and if he calls you, say, 'Speak, LORD, for your servant is listening.'" So Samuel went and lay down in his place* (**1 Samuel 3:9**).

"The LORD came and stood there, calling as at the other times, 'Samuel! Samuel!' Then Samuel said, 'Speak, for your servant is listening'" (**1 Samuel 3:10**). Because of Samuel's obedience to God's call he would become instrumental in God's plan to anoint David king of Israel. It was through David's lineage that the Jewish Messiah, Jesus Christ, would be born.

Isaiah, the Messianic Prophet. Like Moses, Isaiah was initially reluctant to be called of God.

> *In the year that King Uzziah died* [ca. 736 B.C.], *I saw the Lord, high and exalted, seated on a throne; and the train of his robe filled the temple. Above him were seraphim, each with six wings: With two wings they covered their faces, with two they covered their feet, and with two they were flying. And they were calling to one another:*
> *"Holy, holy, holy is the LORD Almighty; the whole earth is full of his glory."*
> *At the sound of their voices the doorposts and thresholds shook and the temple was filled with smoke.*
> *"Woe to me!" I cried. "I am ruined! For I am a man of unclean lips, and I live among a people of lips, and my eyes have seen the King, the LORD Almighty."* (**Isaiah 6:1-5**).

Isaiah initially felt he was unworthy of God's calling. However, God revealed to him that "your guilt is taken away and your sin atoned for" (**Isaiah 6:7**). "Then", Isaiah said, "I heard the voice of the Lord saying, 'Whom shall I send? And who will go for us?'

"And I said, "Here am I. Send me!" (**Isaiah 6:8**).

Isaiah was not a popular prophet because he continually called the Israelites, and their kings, to turn from their sins. He was Israel's greatest prophet for 60 years and repeatedly prophesied of the coming savior of the world, Jesus Christ (**Isaiah 9:1-7, 11:1-12, 40:1-13, 49:1-8, 53:1-12, 61:1-2**). It was through Isaiah that God would repetitively reveal that He was the *first and the last*, that there were no other Gods before or after Him, and that He was mankind's only savior (**Isaiah 41:4, 43:10-11, 44:6, 45:5-6, 48:12**).

103

Jeremiah, the Weeping Prophet. God had plans for Jeremiah, the son of a Jewish priest, before he was even conceived or born. "The word of the LORD came to me, saying, 'Before I formed you in the womb I knew you, before you were born I set you apart; I appointed you as a prophet to the nations'" (**Jeremiah 1:4-5**). Jeremiah tried to get out of his calling because he thought he was too young and not a good orator. "'Alas, Sovereign LORD,' I said, 'I do not know how to speak; I am too young.' But the LORD said to me, 'Do not say, *I am too young.* You must go to everyone I send you to and say whatever I command you. Do not be afraid of them, for I am with you and will rescue you,' declares the LORD" (**Jeremiah 1:6-8**).

Bible scholars often refer to Jeremiah as the "Weeping Prophet" because he wept over Israel's disobedience and witnessed the demise and destruction of Jerusalem and the captivity and deportation of the Jews to Babylon.

Ezekiel, Prophet of the Captivity. The prophetic ministry of Ezekiel overlapped the end of Jeremiah's calling. God called him when he was a priest among the Jews held captive in Babylon.

In my thirtieth year, in the fourth month on the fifth day, while I was among the exiles by the Kebar River, the heavens were opened and I saw visions of God. On the fifth of the month—it was the fifth year of the exile of King Jehoiachin – the word of the LORD came to Ezekiel the priest, the son of Buzi, by the Kebar River in the land of the Babylonians. There the hand of the LORD was on him (**Ezekiel 1:1-3**).

God called Ezekiel to be His prophet to the Jews who were in captivity in Babylon. "And he said to me, 'Son of man, listen carefully and take to heart all the words I speak to you. Go now to your people in exile and speak to them. Say to them, *This is what the Sovereign LORD says,* whether they listen or fail to listen'" (**Ezekiel 3:10-11**). God's mission for Ezekiel was two-fold:

First, to call the Israelites held in captivity to repentance and back to faith in their God. Second, to let them know that God planned to restore them back to their homeland in Israel.

There are many other prophets in the Old Testament, each of them called by God for a particular purpose and ministry to God's people. Each and every one of them knew God's voice and that God had called them to speak His truth, unlike Muhammad.

John the Baptist. The calling and ministry of John the Baptist was foretold by God through the prophet Isaiah. "A voice of one calling: 'In the wilderness prepare the way for the LORD; make straight in the desert a highway for our God'" (**Isaiah 40:3**). John also had a two-fold ministry: First, to call the people to repentance. Second, to prepare them for the coming of Jesus Christ.

> *In those days John the Baptist came, preaching in the wilderness of Judea and saying, "Repent, for the kingdom of heaven has come near." This is he who was spoken of through the prophet Isaiah: "A voice of one calling in the wilderness, 'Prepare the way for the Lord, make straight paths for him.'"*
> *John's clothes were made of camel's hair, and he had a leather belt around his waist. His food was locusts and wild honey. People went out to him from Jerusalem and all Judea and the whole region of the Jordan. Confessing their sins, they were baptized by him in the Jordan River* (**Matthew 3:1-6**).

John the Baptist never doubted God's calling for his life. He was fervent in preaching repentance and the coming of the Lord at all cost. In fact, he eventually was imprisoned and beheaded for preaching God's truth (**Matthew 14:6-8**). However, when John was in prison, he apparently did have some doubts about Jesus as the promised Messiah. "When John, who was in prison, heard about the deeds of the Messiah, he sent his disciples [3] to ask him, 'Are you the one who is to come, or should we expect someone else?'" (**Matthew 11:2**).

Jesus, the Christ. Jesus Christ, the proclaimed "Son of God" (see Chapter 9), knew He was called and sent by God the Father, and He announced His calling in a formal and vivid way in the synagogue in Nazareth, His hometown. As He stood before the congregation He read from the prophet **Isaiah 61:1-2**:

> *The Spirit of the Lord is on me, because he has anointed me to proclaim good news to the poor. He has sent me to proclaim freedom for the prisoners and recovery of sight for the blind, to set the oppressed free, to proclaim the year of the Lord's favor* (**Luke 4:18**).

After Jesus recited this passage of Old Testament scripture, he calmly sat down and then said, "Today this scripture is fulfilled in your hearing" (**Luke 4:21**). Later in His ministry, Jesus would further complicate matters for His hearers by claiming to be the "Son of God" and that He and the Father God were One and the same.

Jesus not only knew the voice of God, unlike Muhammad, He knew when it was Satan speaking to Him. Chapter 4 of the Gospel of Matthew discloses when Jesus was led by the Spirit of God into the wilderness for forty days and nights of fasting (Matthew 4:1-2). During His fast, the devil came to Jesus three times in an effort to tempt

Him (Matthew 4:3-11). "If You are the Son of God", the devil would say, then do this . . . . Each time, Jesus would resist the devil's temptation and quote God's Word to the devil. Jesus clearly knew the difference between the Word of God and Satan's perversion of God's Word. Muhammad could not distinguish between the devil's voice and that of his god.

The Changeable Allah vs. the Unchangeable God

For the word of God is alive and active. Sharper than any double-edged sword, it penetrates even to dividing soul and spirit, joints and marrow; it judges the thoughts and attitudes of the heart (Hebrews 4:12).

The Purpose of Prophecy. In the Old Testament, all the prophets, first of all, provided proof of God's inspiration, inerrancy and authority of His word. The purpose of every prophecy is its fulfillment, either in the near or distant future. All the prophets in the Old Testament, as well as, John the Baptist and Jesus in the New Testament, brought words of warning, of repentance; of hope or of things to come. Throughout the Bible, the prophets of God made it clear, the word of God is unchangeable because God is unchangeable.

Even with a superficial examination of the Qur'an, it becomes abundantly clear, Allah is an indecisive and changeable god. The concept of abrogation in the Qur'an was reviewed in Chapter 2. There is the notion that Allah will change any previous revelation to a more current one when it suits his needs, or, more precisely, when necessary to rectify a wrong doing by Muhammad or one of his followers, or to gain the upper hand over some perceived enemy.

God, who is enthroned from of old, who does not change— he will hear them and humble them, because they have no fear of God.
Psalm 55:19

"I know", wrote King Solomon, "that everything God does will endure forever; nothing can be added to it and nothing taken from it. God does it so that people will fear him" (**Ecclesiastes 3:14**).

By comparison, prophets and sages of the Bible, and Jesus and His Apostles, all warned those who would seek to add or take away from the word of God in the Bible. "Every word of God is flawless [pure]; he is a shield to those who take refuge in him. Do not add to his words, or he will rebuke you and prove you a liar" (**Proverbs 30:5-6**).

In the Qur'an, Allah says that all the prophets before Muhammad testified to the existence of Allah. "And We did not send before you any apostle but We revealed to him that there is no god but Me, therefore serve Me" (**surah 21:25**).

If Muhammad was a prophet in the tradition of the Old Testament prophets, he apparently was uninformed or unaware of the prophets that came before him. He neither followed their example, nor circulated their truths, as revealed to them by Jehovah God.

Although, all the prophets of the Bible knew that God had called them to be prophets, Muhammad did not know that Allah had called him to be his prophet until someone else told him that he was a prophet. As far as Muhammad's message being in keeping with biblical prophets before him, Muhammad did not meet the same standards. Instead of proving the inerrancy and authority of God's word, he presented a contradiction of God's word and authority. Muhammad did not bring words of encouragement, nor call for repentance, nor prophesy anything about future events that were to be fulfilled. He spoke only in his own authority and not that of the Judeo-Christian God.

The ministry and calling of every prophet in the Old Testament pointed to God's fulfillment of His covenant with Israel and the promised coming of their Messiah. Muhammad prophesied nothing. He only repeated what he had heard elsewhere. There was no new truth that Muhammad brought to the world. To the contrary, he consistently contradicted the One and Only true God and His Son, Jesus Christ.

Old Testament Prophecies About Jesus

Before we explore the issue of Muhammad in Bible prophecy, let us first review some of the Old Testament scriptures that foretold of the coming of Jesus Christ as the Messiah (The Anointed One). There are well over one hundred names in the Old and New Testament used to describe Jesus Christ—there are none to describe Muhammad.

According to the website, *According to the Scriptures.org*, there are 353 prophecies in the Old Testament that Jesus fulfilled (http://www.accordingtothescriptures.org/prophecy/). We will take a look at just a handful of some of the most memorable ones.

Seed of David. God promised King David that his kingdom would live on forever. "Once for all, I have sworn by my holiness—and I will not lie to David—that his line will continue forever and his throne endure before me like the sun; it will be established forever like the moon, the faithful witness in the sky" (**Psalm 89:35-37**).

In the first verse of chapter one of the Gospel of Matthew, the author confirms that, "This is the genealogy of Jesus the Messiah the son of David, the son of Abraham" (**Matthew 1:1**). In **Luke 3:23-38**, Luke

107

traces Jesus' ancestors all the way back to Adam. How far back does the Qur'an trace Muhammad's lineage?—Only back to his father, one generation.

Son of God. In **1 Chronicles 17:12-13**, God said in reference to Jesus, "He is the one who will build a house for me, and I will establish his throne forever. I will be his father, and he will be my son. I will never take my love away from him, as I took it away from your predecessor." Once again, God confirmed to David that He (God) will bring forth a Son. I will proclaim the LORD's decree: He said to me, "You are my son; today I have become your father" (**Psalm 2:7**).

This prophecy about Jesus as the Son of God was fulfilled as reported in the Gospel of Luke. "He will be great and will be called the Son of the Most High. The Lord God will give him the throne of his father David" (**Luke 1:32**).

"And a voice from heaven said, 'This is my Son, whom I love; with him I am well pleased'" (**Matthew 3:17**).

The Apostle Paul reaffirmed this fulfillment in his letter to the Christians in Rome: "regarding his Son, who as to his earthly life was a descendant of David, and who through the Spirit of holiness was appointed the Son of God in power by his resurrection from the dead: Jesus Christ our Lord" (**Romans 1:3-4**).

The letter to the Jews put it all together: "For to which of the angels did God ever say, 'You are my Son; today I have become your Father'? Or again, 'I will be his Father, and he will be my Son'"? (**Hebrews 1:5**).

The Mediator Between Man and God. In the Book of Job, Job lamented that there was no one to intervene between him and God. "He [God] is not a mere mortal like me that I might answer him, that we might confront each other in court. If only there were **someone to mediate between us**, someone to bring us together, **someone to remove God's rod** [condemnation] from me, so that his terror would frighten me no more. Then I would speak up without fear of him, but as it now stands with me, I cannot" (**Job 9:32-35**; author's emphasis). With Christ's birth, God provided this mediator between man and God; one who would take away the sins (condemnation) of all mankind.

In Isaiah, the prophet penned, "Truth is nowhere to be found, and whoever shuns evil becomes a prey. The LORD looked and was displeased that there was no justice. He saw that there was no one, he was appalled that there was **no one to intervene**; so his own arm achieved salvation for him, and his own righteousness sustained him. He put on righteousness as his breastplate, and the helmet of salvation on his head; he put on the garments of vengeance and wrapped himself in zeal as in a cloak" (**Isaiah 59:15-17**; author's emphasis).

The Apostle Paul confirmed that it was Jesus and only Him that was God's sent mediator; one who brought justice, righteousness and salvation to man. "For there is one God and one mediator between God and mankind, the man Christ Jesus" (**1 Timothy 2:5**).

The Anointed One—The Messiah. The kings of the earth rise up and the rulers band together against the LORD and against his anointed" (**Psalm 2:2**).

"Know and understand this: From the time the word goes out to restore and rebuild Jerusalem until the **Anointed One**, the ruler, comes, there will be seven 'sevens,' and sixty-two 'sevens.' It will be rebuilt with streets and a trench, but in times of trouble. After the sixty-two 'sevens,' the **Anointed One** will be put to death and will have nothing. The people of the ruler who will come will destroy the city and the sanctuary. The end will come like a flood: War will continue until the end, and desolations have been decreed" (**Daniel 9:25-26**; author's emphasis).

In the Gospel of Matthew, Matthew started by listing the genealogy of Jesus, "and Jacob the father of Joseph, the husband of Mary, and Mary was the mother of Jesus who is called the Messiah" (**Matthew 1:16**).

Andrew, who was the brother of Simon Peter, was one of the first to follow after Jesus. "The first thing Andrew did was to find his brother Simon and tell him, 'We have found the Messiah' (that is, the Christ)" (**John 1:41**).

At one point in His ministry Jesus asked His disciples, "Who do people say the Son of Man is?" (**Matthew 16:13**). Various disciples responded that people thought Jesus was the reincarnation of Elijah, Jeremiah or John the Baptist. Then Jesus asked His disciples, "'But what about you?' he asked. 'Who do you say I am?'" (**Matthew 16:15**).

"Simon Peter answered, 'You are the Messiah, the Son of the living God'" (**Matthew 16:16**).

"Jesus replied, 'Blessed are you, Simon son of Jonah, for this was not revealed to you by flesh and blood, but by my Father in heaven'" (**Matthew 16:17**).

Born of a Virgin. "Therefore the Lord himself will give you a sign: The virgin will conceive and give birth to a son, and will call him Immanuel" [God with us] (**Isaiah 7:14**).

Again, in **Isaiah 9:6**, Isaiah prophesied, "For to us a child is born, to us a son is given, and the government will be on his shoulders. And he will be called Wonderful Counselor, Mighty God, Everlasting Father, Prince of Peace."

The Gospels of Matthew and Luke provide testimony to the virgin birth of Jesus Christ.

109

> *Then the angel said to her, "Do not be afraid, Mary, for you have found favor with God. And behold, you will conceive in your womb and bring forth a Son, and shall call His name JESUS. He will be great, and will be called the Son of the Highest; and the Lord God will give Him the throne of His father David. And He will reign over the house of Jacob forever, and of His kingdom there will be no end."*
>
> *Then Mary said to the angel, "How can this be, since I do not know a man?"*
>
> *And the angel answered and said to her, "The Holy Spirit will come upon you, and the power of the Highest will overshadow you; therefore, also, that Holy One who is to be born will be called the Son of God* (**Luke 1:30-35**).

In Matthew it is reported that the angel also visited Joseph to whom Mary was betrothed.

> *Now the birth of Jesus Christ was as follows: After His mother Mary was betrothed to Joseph, before they came together, she was found with child of the Holy Spirit. Then Joseph her husband, being a just man, and not wanting to make her a public example, was minded to put her away secretly. But while he thought about these things, behold, an angel of the Lord appeared to him in a dream, saying, "Joseph, son of David, do not be afraid to take to you Mary your wife, for that which is conceived in her is of the Holy Spirit. And she will bring forth a Son, and you shall call His name JESUS, for He will save His people from their sins."*
>
> *So all this was done that it might be fulfilled which was spoken by the Lord through the prophet, saying: "Behold, the virgin shall be with child, and bear a Son, and they shall call His name Immanuel," which is translated, "God with us"* (**Matthew 1:18-23**).

Born in Bethlehem. About 750 years before the birth of Jesus, the prophet Micah prophesied that the Jewish Messiah would be born in Bethlehem. "But you, Bethlehem Ephrathah, though you are small among the clans of Judah, out of you will come for me one who will be ruler over Israel, whose origins are from of old, from ancient times" (**Micah 5:2**).

Both Matthew and Luke (**Luke 2:4-7**) record the birth of Jesus in Bethlehem just as Micah had prophesied.

> *After Jesus was born in Bethlehem in Judea, during the time of King Herod, Magi from the east came to Jerusalem and*

asked, "Where is the one who has been born king of the Jews? We saw his star when it rose and have come to worship him."

When King Herod heard this he was disturbed, and all Jerusalem with him. When he had called together all the people's chief priests and teachers of the law, he asked them where the Messiah was to be born. "In Bethlehem in Judea," they replied, "for this is what the prophet has written:

"'But you, Bethlehem, in the land of Judah, are by no means least among the rulers of Judah; for out of you will come a ruler who will shepherd my people Israel'" (**Matthew 2:1-6**).

A Man Without Sin. Once again, Isaiah revealed, "He was assigned a grave with the wicked, and with the rich in his death, though he had done no violence, nor was any deceit in his mouth" (**Isaiah 53:9**). The Apostle Peter confirmed that Jesus was this sinless, non-violent man of God. "He committed no sin, and no deceit was found in his mouth.

"When they hurled their insults at him, he did not retaliate; when he suffered, he made no threats. Instead, he entrusted himself to him who judges justly. 'He himself bore our sins' in his body on the cross, so that we might die to sins and live for righteousness; 'by his wounds you have been healed'" (**1 Peter 2:22-24**).

Betrayed by a Friend. In **Psalm 41:9**, David foretold of Christ's betrayal. "Even my close friend, someone I trusted, one who shared my bread, has turned against me."

Jesus would make reference to this scripture on the day of His last supper. "I do not speak concerning all of you. I know whom I have chosen; but that the Scripture may be fulfilled, 'He who eats bread with Me has lifted up his heel against Me'" (**John 13:18**). Jesus was referring to Judas Iscariot, one of His twelve disciples who would betray Him to the Roman and Jewish authorities that night.

Crucified and Pierced for Our Sake. In his 22nd Psalm, David wrote about the crucifixion of Christ. "Dogs surround me, a pack of villains encircles me; they pierce my hands and my feet" (**Psalm 22:16**)

The prophet Zechariah also prophesied about the coming death of Christ. "And I will pour out on the house of David and the inhabitants of Jerusalem a spirit of grace and supplication. They will look on me, the one they have pierced, and they will mourn for him as one mourns for an only child, and grieve bitterly for him as one grieves for a firstborn son" (**Zechariah 12:10**). Jesus was the firstborn of the Father and the only begotten Son of God.

The Apostle John recorded the fulfillment of this scripture in Zechariah. "Instead, one of the soldiers pierced Jesus' side with a spear, bringing a sudden flow of blood and water   and, as another scripture says, 'They will look on the one they have pierced'" (**John 19:34, 37**).

The Apostle Peter, after the outpouring of the Holy Spirit on Pentecost, preached to all those gathered and said, "Therefore let all Israel be assured of this: God has made this Jesus, whom you crucified, both Lord and Messiah" (**Acts 2:36**).

Jesus was Resurrected and Did Not Die. "You, LORD, brought me up from the realm of the dead; you spared me from going down to the pit" [of death] (**Psalm 30:3**). Since all flesh dies and is no more, it is clear that God, through David, is talking about one in the future who will not see death and that One was and is Jesus Christ.

The psalmist David, again wrote, "For You will not leave my soul in Sheol [place of the dead], nor will You allow Your Holy One to see corruption" [decay] (**Psalm 16:10**, NKJV).

In numerous places in the New Testament, it was confirmed that Jesus Christ was the One that the prophecies of Old Testament talked about as the One who would not see death. Jesus also foretold of the manner of His death and His resurrection. "When they came together in Galilee, he [Jesus] said to them, 'The Son of Man is going to be delivered into the hands of men. They will kill him, and on the third day he will be raised to life.' And the disciples were filled with grief" (**Matthew 17:22-23**).

After Jesus' crucifixion He was laid in the tomb of Joseph of Arimathea. After the Sabbath day, two women identified as Mary Magdalene and the "other Mary" came to the tomb where Jesus was laid (**Matthew 28:1**).

"And behold, there was a great earthquake; for an angel of the Lord descended from heaven, and came and rolled back the stone from the door, and sat on it. His countenance was like lightning, and his clothing as white as snow. And the guards shook for fear of him, and became like dead men" (**Matthew 28:2-4**).

The angel then gave testimony to the women that Jesus had risen from the grave. "Do not be afraid, for I know that you are looking for Jesus, who was crucified. He is not here; he has risen, just as he said. Come and see the place where he lay. Then go quickly and tell his disciples: 'He has risen from the dead and is going ahead of you into Galilee. There you will see him.' Now I have told you" (**Matthew 28:5-7**).

The Apostle Peter, after the Day of Pentecost, would proclaim boldly, "God has raised this Jesus to life, and we are all witnesses of it" (**Acts 2:32**).

The Apostle Paul, although not likely present at Christ's crucifixion, gave a vibrant testimony of it. Perhaps because of the enthusiastic and vivid testimony of those that had witnessed it or perhaps through Jesus' revelation to Paul on the Damascus Road (**Acts 9**). In his letter to Roman Christians, Paul wrote, "and who through the Spirit of holiness was appointed the Son of God in power by his resurrection from the dead: Jesus Christ our Lord" (**Romans 1:4**).

The Apostle Peter would also become a bold proclaimer of Christ's crucifixion and resurrection. He was a witness, although perhaps at a distance, since he abandoned Jesus (as the other disciples did) in His hour of suffering. "For Christ also suffered once for sins," Peter wrote, "the righteous for the unrighteous, to bring you to God. He was put to death in the body but made alive in the Spirit. After being made alive, he went and made proclamation to the imprisoned spirits" (**1 Peter 3:18-19**).

As presented in Chapter 2, there were numerous witnesses to Christ's crucifixion and His resurrection. Not just His followers, but non-believers as well.

Prophet of Justice and Good News. Jesus was God's messenger of "Good News" about whom Isaiah foretold. "You who bring good news to Zion, go up on a high mountain. You who bring good news to Jerusalem, lift up your voice with a shout, lift it up, do not be afraid; say to the towns of Judah, 'Here is your God!'" (**Isaiah 40:9**).

Throughout the Gospels and the Acts of the Apostles, the scriptures relate how Jesus and His disciples preached the "Good News" of the Kingdom of God; that God had brought salvation to mankind through the sacrificial work of Christ on the cross. To demonstrate the reality of the Good News, Jesus healed the sick, cast out demons from the possessed, calmed the storms, gave sight to the blind and bound up the brokenhearted.

"Jesus went throughout Galilee, teaching in their synagogues, proclaiming the good news of the kingdom, and healing every disease and sickness among the people" (**Matthew 4:23**).

"After John was put in prison, Jesus went into Galilee, proclaiming the good news of God" (**Mark 1:14**).

"But he [Jesus] said, 'I must proclaim the good news of the kingdom of God to the other towns also, because that is why I was sent'" (**Luke 4:43**).

Jesus' preaching of the Good News brought freedom and release from bondage—whether spiritual, psychological, mental or physical—for a people living under both religious and political tyranny. The Israelites had not experienced such a salvation since King David. However, Jesus brought true salvation, not just for the Jews who would believe, but also for all those who would receive His Good News message of freedom from sin and bondage, to a redemptive life of saving grace based on faith and forgiveness.

Lord and Savior. God, through the prophet Isaiah made it clear that salvation would come from no other god but Him, Jehovah God of the Jews. "I, even I, am the LORD, and apart from me there is no savior" (**Isaiah 43:11**).

113

*Declare what is to be, present it – let them take counsel together. Who foretold this long ago, who declared it from the distant past? Was it not I, the LORD? And there is no **God apart from me**, a righteous God and a Savior; **there is none but me**.*
*"Turn to me and be saved, all you ends of the earth; for **I am God, and there is no other**. By myself I have sworn, my mouth has uttered in all integrity a word that will not be revoked: Before me every knee will bow; by me every tongue will swear. They will say of me, 'In the LORD alone are deliverance and strength.'" All who have raged against him will come to him and be put to shame* (**Isaiah 45:21-24**; author's emphasis).

In the above scripture, God repeatedly makes it clear that He is the only true God and there is none but Him.   Apart from Him there is no salvation for mankind.   Eventually, *every knee will bow; . . . every tongue will swear* that, *In the Lord alone are deliverance and strength.*   God continues and states that everyone who opposes Him will *be put to shame.*
The prophet Jeremiah also prophesied about the coming of Jesus as the *Lord Our Righteous Savior.* "In those days and at that time I will make a righteous Branch sprout from David's line; he will do what is just and right in the land. In those days Judah will be saved and Jerusalem will live in safety. This is the name by which it [Judah] will be called: The LORD Our Righteous Savior" (**Jeremiah 33:15-16**). Notice, once again, that this *Righteous Savior* will arise from the seed of David.
When Jesus was born, an angel of God announced His birth by saying, "Today in the town of David a Savior has been born to you; he is the Messiah, the Lord" (**Luke 2:11**).
The Apostle Peter later confirmed that: "Salvation is found in no one else [except Jesus], for there is no other name under heaven given to mankind by which we must be saved" (**Acts 4:12**).
The Apostle Paul also affirmed that, "From this man's [David's] descendants God has brought to Israel the Savior Jesus, as he promised" (**Acts 13:23**).
Source of the Holy Spirit (see also Chapter 10). Throughout the Old Testament there are numerous examples of God pouring out or anointing His chosen servants with His Spirit to empower them for some task or calling. "For I will pour water on the thirsty land," God told Isaiah, "and streams on the dry ground; I will pour out my Spirit on your offspring, and my blessing on your descendants" (**Isaiah 44:3**). Earlier, God told Isaiah, "The Spirit of the Lord will rest on him [the coming Messiah]—the **Spirit of wisdom and of understanding**, the **Spirit of counsel and of might**, the **Spirit of the knowledge and fear of the Lord**" (**Isaiah 11:2**; author's emphasis).

114

Once again, in **Isaiah 42:1**, God spoke to Isaiah, "Here is my servant, whom I uphold, my chosen one in whom I delight; I will put my Spirit on him, and he will bring justice to the nations" (**Isaiah 42:1**). Jesus was and is that Servant of God whom God endowed with His Holy Spirit. Jesus acknowledged the presence of God's Spirit when He quoted from **Isaiah 61:1**, "The Spirit of the Sovereign Lord is on me, because the Lord has anointed me to proclaim good news to the poor   "

It was this same Spirit of God that Jesus would promise His followers, but not until after His death. "Whoever believes in me," Jesus stated, "as Scripture has said, 'rivers of living water will flow from within them.' By this he meant the Spirit, whom those who believed in him were later to receive. Up to that time the Spirit had not been given, since Jesus had not yet been glorified" (**John 7:38-39**).

Jesus repeated this assurance of the Holy Spirit in **John 14:16-17**, when He said, "And I will ask the Father, and he will give you another advocate to help you and be with you forever—the Spirit of truth. The world cannot accept him, because it neither sees him nor knows him. But you know him, for he lives with you and will be in you."

"When the Advocate [Holy Spirit] comes, whom I will send to you from the Father—the Spirit of truth who goes out from the Father—he will testify about me" (**John 15:26**). The purpose of God's gift of the Holy Spirit is to reveal the truth—the truth of the Gospel of Jesus Christ—and to give testimony of Jesus Christ as Lord and Savior.

> *But very truly I tell you, it is for your good that I am going away. Unless I go away, the Advocate will not come to you; but if I go, I will send him to you. When he comes, he will prove the world to be in the wrong about sin and righteousness and judgment: about sin, because people do not believe in me;*
> *about righteousness, because I am going to the Father, where you can see me no longer; and about judgment, because the prince of this world now stands condemned.*
> *"I have much more to say to you, more than you can now bear. But when he, the Spirit of truth, comes, he will guide you into all the truth. He will not speak on his own; he will speak only what he hears, and he will tell you what is yet to come. He will glorify me because it is from me that he will receive what he will make known to you* (**John 16:7-14**).

There are numerous other prophecies in the Old Testament that point to the coming of Jesus Christ, the Messiah, the Redeemer, the first and the last and many other names conferred on Jesus by His Father God. Far too many to continue to address here.

Does the Bible Prophesy About Muhammad's Coming?

In the review of the foregoing prophecies about God's chosen deliverer, it is clear that Muhammad could not have fulfilled any of them. However, Muslims, their religious leaders and scholars claim that both the Old and New Testament foretold of Muhammad's coming and point specifically to **Deuteronomy 18:15 and 18; John 14:16** and other nebulous biblical scriptures as concrete proof.

If the Bible did originally contain verses that foretold of Muhammad's coming as the last and most important of God's prophets, they would also contain a description of the character and ministry of such a significant messenger of God. The scriptures would have had to foretell that this special messenger of God would be identified, not by signs and wonders, but by butchery, thievery and deception; by immorality and adultery; by the omen that he killed his own people and the Jews, God's own chosen people.

Jesus' Wisdom vs. Muhammad's. Jesus' wisdom, knowledge and understanding far exceeded that of all the prophets that preceded Him (**Isaiah 9:6-7**). Muhammad's wisdom and knowledge was often confused, ignorant and erroneous. He often had his historical facts wrong and frequently contradicted himself and the revelations he claimed to have received by Allah.

"For to us a child is born," Isaiah prophesied, "to us a son is given, and the government will be on his shoulders. And he will be called Wonderful Counselor, Mighty God, Everlasting Father, Prince of Peace. Of the greatness of his government and peace there will be no end. He will reign on David's throne and over his kingdom, establishing and upholding it with justice and righteousness from that time on and forever. The zeal of the LORD Almighty will accomplish this." Only the coming of Jesus Christ, and no other, could fulfill this prophecy. Muhammad, in fact, represented the dead opposite. He was not a *Wonderful Counselor*; he was not *Mighty God* in the flesh; he did not represent the *Everlasting Father* and certainly was not the *Prince of Peace*; nor did he descend from *David's throne* or bring forth *justice and righteousness*. He was the antithesis of everything Jesus stood for and demonstrated.

Qur'an 61:6 makes the radical claim that Jesus foretold of Muhammad's coming.

> *And when Isa* [Jesus] *son of Marium said: O children of Israel! Surely I am the apostle of Allah to you, verifying that which is before me of the Taurat* [Torah] *and giving good news of an Apostle who will come after me, his name being Ahmad* [variation of Muhammad]*; but when he came to them with clear arguments they said: This is clear magic.*

116

The Bible, of course, records no such revelation by Jesus. No wonder the Jews and Christians of Muhammad's era responded to his claims of God's apostle as *clear magic*. It was not only magic but complete fabrication inspired by satanic sources. And Jesus NEVER referred to Himself as a prophet of Allah.

Many of the one hundred names and titles conferred on Jesus were done so by prophets before him, but mainly by those who knew him intimately and who walked with him on earth during his ministry. None of these monikers ascribed to Jesus would describe Muhammad or his "ministry." Muhammad claimed and Islamic tradition has affirmed that there are 99 names for Allah and whoever can recite them all is guaranteed a place in Paradise (3). Some of the names attributed to Allah are not very flattering for the deity. Among others, Allah is known as the Afflicter (*Ad-Darr*), the Humiliator (*Al-Mudhill*) and the Killer at His Will (*Al-Mumit*). Most of the names refer to Allah's all-powerful attributes, but none give him the image of a personal, intimate god. However, only one name has been conferred on Muhammad, the *Prophet (Messenger) of Allah*—which was not given to him by Allah, nor acknowledged by Muhammad himself.

An Examination of Deuteronomy 18:15 and 18. While Muslims believe in the Bible and the Old Testament prophets, they have been taught since the days of Muhammad that the Bible has been corrupted and therefore cannot be fully relied on as God's word. This, they believe, despite a thunderous silence of any historical proof from any quarter that the Bible has been corrupted in any form, by any person, at any time in history. This, they choose to believe, despite the thousands of historical biblical manuscripts that have been discovered and preserved that fully collaborate the scriptures, stories, prophecies, the people of the Bible and the historical records.

In stark contrast, there are no collaborating works that can verify or support the words supposedly revealed to Muhammad in the Qur'an. The Qur'an is strictly the words of one man who claimed they came from God. There were no witnesses, no subsequent revelations or prophecies from others to confirm or support these one-man revelations – many of which were conveniently self-serving for the Prophet himself.

However, there is one biblical verse, in particular, Muslims do rely on as a testimony of Muhammad's coming. They cite **Deuteronomy 18:15** as evidence that the coming of Muhammad as God's prophet was foretold by Moses about 2,000 years before Muhammad's birth. There are a number of problems with this assertion. First, the full context of the scripture carries through verse 22.

117

*The Lord your God will raise up for you **a prophet like me** [Moses] **from among your own brothers**. You must listen to him. For this is what you asked of the Lord your God at Horeb on the day of the assembly when you [the Israelites] said, 'Let us not hear the voice of the Lord our God nor see this great fire anymore, or we will die.'*

*The Lord said to me: 'What they say is good. I will raise up for them a **prophet like you from among their brothers**; I will put **my words in his mouth**, and he will tell them everything I command him. If anyone does not listen to my words that the prophet speaks in my name, I myself will call him to account. But **a prophet who presumes to speak in my name anything I have not commanded him to say, or a prophet who speaks in the name of other gods, must be put to death.'***

You may say to yourselves, 'How can we know when a message has not been spoken by the Lord?' **If what a prophet proclaims in the name of the Lord does not take place or come true, that is a message the Lord has not spoken.** *That prophet has spoken presumptuously. Do not be afraid of him* (**Deuteronomy 18:15-22**; author's emphasis).

The particulars of this prophecy of Moses should shed some light on the claim of Islam, that this prophecy refers to the coming of Muhammad.

- First, the prophet is to represent the God of the Jews. The word "Lord" in the first verse refers to the self-Existent Jehovah God of the Jews.
- Second, the prophet foretold is to be like Moses. Moses was a Jew born to the house of a Levite (Jewish high priest). Muhammad was neither a Jew nor born of the house of Levi.
- Third, the prophet was to be *from among your own brothers*, that is, from among the Israelites themselves. This does not fit Muhammad either, since he was an Arab, a descendant of Ishmael.
- Fourth, this prophet is to speak only the words of Jehovah God, not Allah or a god by any other name. Muhammad spoke the words of an unknown god, and initially believed that it was a demon who spoke to him and that he was demon-possessed.

Jesus, on the other hand, made direct reference to this prophecy by Moses. As He was speaking to the Jews, Jesus said, "If you believed Moses, you would believe me, for he wrote about me" (**John 5:46**).

Unlike Muhammad, Jesus proved His divinity and calling as God's prophet upon His death and resurrection. "So Jesus said, 'When you have lifted up the Son of Man, then you will know that I am he and that I do nothing on my own but speak just what the Father has taught me'" (**John 8:28**).

If Muslims want to point to **Deuteronomy 18:15** as God's unadulterated word and prophecy about Muhammad, then they also must accept **Deuteronomy 18:20** as God's unadulterated word. That verse says: *But **a prophet who presumes to speak in my name anything I have not commanded him to say, or a prophet who speaks in the name of other gods, must be put to death.***'

Unlike the prophets of the Old Testament and Jesus, where God chose to speak directly to them, Allah did not or would not speak directly to Muhammad. Allah's revelation or *wahy* came to Muhammad in various forms—dreams, trances, visions, angelic visitation, foaming fits, etc.—but never face-to-face or by personal revelation direct from Allah.

The reason Allah did not speak to Muhammad personally is explained by Muhammad in **Qur'an 42**.

> *And it is not for any mortal that Allah should speak to him except by revelation or from behind a veil, or by sending a messenger and revealing by His permission what He pleases; surely He is High, Wise.*
>
> *And thus did we reveal to you an inspired book by Our command. You did not know what the Book was, nor (what) the faith (was), but We made it a light, guiding thereby whom We please of Our servants; and most surely you show the way to the right path:*
>
> *The path of Allah, Whose is whatsoever is in the heavens and whatsoever is in the earth; now surely to Allah do all affairs eventually come* (**Qur'an 42:51-53**)

This surah above clearly eliminates Muhammad as the prophet spoken of in **Deuteronomy 18:15** that would be like Moses. There are three distinct characteristics of Moses' ministry that would have to be met by the foretold prophet to come.

- First, he would have to know God *face-to-face* as Moses did. The above surah states clearly that Allah would not reveal himself to Muhammad. Jesus, on the other hand, descended from the Father and knew God face-to-face because He was one with God.
- Second, Moses was the mediator of God's covenant with the Jews. The prophet to come would also have to mediate God's covenant. Allah made no covenant with Muhammad or his followers

and therefore Muhammad could not be the mediator of any covenant. Jesus, however, was the mediator of the *New Covenant*, a covenant based on *better promises*. "But the ministry Jesus has received is as superior to theirs [the Jewish high priests] as the covenant of which he is mediator is superior to the old one, and it is founded on better promises" (**Hebrews 8:6**).

- <u>Third</u>, the prophet foretold in **Deuteronomy 18:15** would have to be a miracle worker just like Moses. Muhammad never performed a miracle throughout his lifetime as a prophet. In fact, in response to a request that he perform a miracle, he confessed that he could do none. Jesus' life (which was far shorter than Muhammad's) was differentiated by signs and wonders everywhere he went.

Only Muhammad and the traditions of Islam lay claim that Deuteronomy 18 was a prophecy that foretold of the coming of Muhammad. None of the Jews or Christians of Muhammad's era believed, in the least, that he was the fulfillment of this prophecy. However, when Jesus performed the great miracle of the feeding of the five thousand (John 6:1-15), the Jewish witnesses readily proclaimed, *"Surely this is the Prophet who is to come into the world"* (John 6:14, author's emphasis). The Jews had been waiting for centuries for the coming of The Prophet and Messiah prophesied by Moses, David, Isaiah, Daniel, Micah, Zechariah, Malachi and others. Some knew what to look for and how they could identify him, and without doubt, saw Jesus as the fulfillment of the long-awaited prophet. No such acceptance was ever accorded Muhammad during his lifetime.

Although the Jews were expecting *the* Prophet and Messiah—and many of them were beginning to accept Jesus as the fulfillment of that expectation—the Jewish leaders turned against Him when He proclaimed Himself to be the Son of God, a claim the religious leaders saw as blasphemy.

Stephen, one of the seven deacons of the first Christian church and the first martyr of the Church—right before his martyrdom—gave testimony before the Jewish Sanhedrin, the prophet of whom Moses foretold was, indeed, Jesus. Stephen told the Jews, just as they had rejected Moses, they were rejecting Jesus, whose coming was prophesied through Moses.

This is the same Moses they had rejected with the words,
"Who made you ruler and judge?" He was sent to be their ruler
and deliverer by God himself, through the angel who appeared

to him in the bush. He led them out of Egypt and performed wonders and signs in Egypt, at the Red Sea and for forty years in the wilderness.

This is the Moses who told the Israelites, "God will raise up for you a prophet like me from your own people" (**Acts 7:35-37**).

Robert Spencer, author of the best-selling book, *The Truth About Muhammad* (2006), noted that, "as a matter of history, that there is no record of Christians expecting a prophet in Arabia 540 years after the death of Jesus; nor is there any record of any Christian book with signs marking out an Arabian prophet . . . nor is there any record of any Christian heresy that held such beliefs . . ." (4).

After the Apostle Peter healed the lame beggar, all the onlookers were amazed. He then gave the following testimony pointing to Jesus as the fulfillment of biblical prophecy:

*Now, brothers, I know that you acted in ignorance, as did your leaders. But this is how God fulfilled what he had foretold through all the prophets, saying that his Christ would suffer. Repent, then, and turn to God, so that your sins may be wiped out, that times of refreshing may come from the Lord, and that he may send the Christ, who has been appointed for you – even Jesus. He must remain in heaven until the time comes for God to restore everything, as he promised long ago through his holy prophets. For **Moses said**, "The Lord your God will raise up for you a **prophet like me from among your own people**; you must listen to everything he tells you. Anyone who does not listen to him will be completely cut off from among his people."*

Indeed, all the prophets from Samuel on, as many as have spoken, have foretold these days. And you are heirs of the prophets and of the covenant God made with your fathers. He said to Abraham, "Through your offspring all peoples on earth will be blessed."

When God raised up his servant, he sent him first to you to bless you by turning each of you from your wicked ways (**Acts 3:17-26**; author's emphasis).

"On hearing his words, some of the people said, '**Surely this man is the Prophet**.' Others said, 'He is the Messiah.' Still others asked, 'How can the Messiah come from Galilee? Does not Scripture say that the Messiah will come from David's descendants and from Bethlehem, the town where David lived?'" (**John 7:40-42**; author's emphasis). Jesus did indeed come from Galilee and the lineage of David and was born in Bethlehem.

Many of the Jews who heard Jesus preach and saw the miracles He performed, believed that He was the fulfillment of the prophecy spoken to Moses by God and recorded in **Deuteronomy 18:15**.

After John the Baptist was imprisoned he heard from his followers about the many miracles Jesus performed. He sought to reassure himself that Jesus was the promised Messiah. "When John heard in prison what Christ was doing, he sent his disciples to ask him, 'Are you the one [the Prophet] who was to come, or should we expect someone else?' Jesus replied, 'Go back and report to John what you hear and see: The blind receive sight, the lame walk, those who have leprosy are cured, the deaf hear, the dead are raised, and the good news is preached to the poor. Blessed is the man who does not fall away on account of me'" (**Matthew 11:2-6**).

In His own words Jesus assured John the Baptist that He was, indeed, the fulfillment of the prophecy that Moses received over 1400 years before Christ's birth.

At the beginning of His ministry Jesus recruited the brothers Peter and Andrew. He then called Philip to follow Him. All three were from the town of Bethsaida, near the north shore of the Sea of Galilee. "Philip found Nathanael and told him, 'We have found the one Moses wrote about in the Law, and about whom the prophets also wrote— Jesus of Nazareth, the son of Joseph'" (John 1:45).

After Jesus' resurrection, He appeared to two of His followers as they walked along the road to Emmaus. "He said to them, 'How foolish you are, and how slow of heart to believe all that the prophets have spoken! Did not the Christ have to suffer these things and then enter his glory?' And beginning with Moses and all the Prophets, he explained to them what was said in all the Scriptures concerning himself' (**Luke 24:25-27**).

If Muhammad was *the prophet* the Jews were expecting, why did they not recognize him or accept him as such? Why was Muhammad unable to get his biblical history and Old Testament prophecies correct? It is simple! Muhammad *was not* the fulfillment of any biblical prophecy, nor was he the prophet foretold in the Bible—in either the Old or New Testament. Only Jesus could and did fulfill all that was prophesied about the coming Messiah, *the* Prophet.

Once again, it was the Apostle Peter, in his testimony about Jesus as he preached to the Jews at Solomon's Colonnade, who confirmed Jesus' fulfillment of this Old Testament prophecy. "For Moses said, 'The Lord your God will raise up for you a prophet like me from among your own people; you must listen to everything he tells you. *Anyone who does not listen to him will be completely cut off from among his people'"* (**Acts 3:22-23**; author's emphasis).

    An Examination of John 14:16. Historically, Muslims have claimed that Muhammad was the foretold *Comforter* or *Counselor* promised by Jesus in **John 14:16**. "... I will ask the Father, and he will give you another Counselor [Helper; Comforter] to be with you forever."

    To fully understand this verse it must be put into the context of the verse preceding and following. "If you **love me**," Jesus said, "you will **obey what I command**. And I will ask the Father, and he will give you another Counselor [Helper; Comforter] to be with you **forever**—the **Spirit of truth**. The world cannot accept him, because it neither sees him nor knows him. But **you know him**, for he lives with you and **will be in you**" (**John 14:15-17**, author's emphasis).

    Despite Muslim assertions and hope upon hope, Muhammad cannot possibly be the promised *Comforter* or *Counselor*. Muhammad met absolutely none of the criteria for such a fulfillment.

- First, the Counselor or Comforter will come only to those who *love* Jesus and *obey* His *command*. Neither Muhammad nor any of his followers love and obey the commands of Jesus.
- Second, the Counselor *is* the *Spirit of Truth* who will be with the believers in Jesus *forever*. Muhammad was not a spirit, he was flesh and bone like every other mortal being and he did not live forever. He died a human death, was buried, never to rise again, and he certainly did not personify the truth of Almighty God.
- Third, the followers of Jesus, and Him only, will know the Counselor—the Spirit of Truth whom the world cannot see—because He resides within them. Muhammad, being flesh and bone, could not and does not live within any living soul. Likewise, he was far from personifying a "spirit of truth." Instead he embodied lies and fabrications to suit his ungodly purposes.

    Jesus' further description of the coming Counselor/Comforter in John 15:26 and John 16:7-15 thoroughly eliminate Muhammad from being even remotely considered as the person Jesus was talking about. "When the Counselor comes," Jesus said, "whom I will send to you from the Father, the Spirit of truth who goes out from the Father, *he will testify about me*" (John 15:26, author's emphasis). Muhammad could not and would not *testify* to the true purpose of Jesus' coming. While he recognized Jesus as a prophet, he refused to accept Him as the Son of God; as the vehicle of God's salvation for mankind;

as the source of redemption from sin; or that He was crucified, died, was buried and rose again. Truly, only the Holy Spirit, the Spirit of Truth, the Counselor and Comforter could give testimony to such things and bear witness within the soul of every believer.

> But I tell you the truth: It is for your good that I am going away. Unless I go away, the Counselor will not come to you; but if I go, I will send him to you. When he comes, **he will convict the world of guilt** in regard to sin and **righteousness and judgment**: in regard to sin, because men do not believe in me; in regard to righteousness, because I am going to the Father, where you can see me no longer; and in regard to judgment, because the prince of this world now stands condemned.
>
> I have much more to say to you, more than you can now bear. But when he, the Spirit of truth, comes, he will **guide you into all truth**. He will not speak on his own; he will speak only what he hears, and he will **tell you what is yet to come**. He will **bring glory to me** by taking from what is mine and making it known to you. All that belongs to the Father is mine. That is why I said the Spirit will **take from what is mine and make it known to you** (**John 16:7-15**, author's emphasis).

Once again, Jesus makes it abundantly clear that the Counselor/Comforter is the Holy Spirit of God who will *convict the world of guilt* (sin) with all *righteousness and judgment*. He will *guide* the followers of Jesus *into all truth. He will tell you what is yet to come* and *bring glory* to Jesus and *make known* the birthright of Jesus to His disciples. Muhammad, of course, could do none of this. He had no power to convict the world of sin; no God-given righteousness and judgment; possessed no indisputable truth; could not predict anything of the future; did not bring any glory to Christ and made nothing known about the true ministry and purpose of Jesus' life on earth.

"This is the one who came by water and blood—Jesus Christ. He did not come by water only, but by water and blood. And it is the Spirit who testifies, because the Spirit is the truth" (**1 John 5:6**).

God's Unchangeable Word. Allah revealed to Muhammad that He guided all the prophets of old and their descendants, including Jesus and John the Baptist, along the right path of truth. The Jews, both during the age of the Jewish patriarchs and during the time of Jesus, relied on the *spoken* word of the prophets and the *written* word of the Law (the Torah or Pentateuch) for God's guidance in the path of righteousness. Therefore, if Allah guided them in all truth through the spoken and written word, then the Torah and the Gospel must be Allah's true and faithful word.

However, **Qur'an 2:75** states that the Torah and Gospel of "the people of the Book" was corrupted or altered by Jews and Christians. If it was altered, then how could Allah guide the Jews of both the Old and New Testament era along the right path?

Do you then hope that they would believe in you, and a party from among them indeed used to hear the Word of Allah, then altered it after they had understood it, and they know (this).
Qur'an 2:75

If Allah is All-Knowing and All-Powerful, then why did he let someone alter his word that he had given to Moses, the Prophets and Jesus? If Allah is the same God as that of the Christians and Jews, then God is reversing His promised word, which the Bible says God cannot and will not do.

Here are some of the Bible scriptures that confirm God cannot lie or change.

1. *God is not human, that he should lie, not a human being, that he should change his mind. Does he speak and then not act? Does he promise and not fulfill?* (**Numbers 23:19**).

2. *Do not add to what I command you and do not subtract from it, but keep the commands of the LORD your God that I give you* (**Deuteronomy 4:2**).

3. *See that you do all I command you; do not add to it or take away from it* (**Deuteronomy 12:32**).

4. *He who is the Glory of Israel does not lie or change his mind; for he is not a human being, that he should change his mind* (**1 Samuel 15:29**).

5. *but I will not take my love from him, nor will I ever betray my faithfulness. I will not violate my covenant or alter what my lips have uttered* (**Psalm 89:33-34**).

6. *But you [God] remain the same, and your years will never end* (**Psalm 102:27**).

7. *The LORD has sworn and will not change his mind: "You [Christ Jesus] are a priest forever, in the order of Melchizedek"* (**Psalm 110:4**).

8. *Every word of God is flawless; he is a shield to those who take refuge in him. Do not add to his words, or he will rebuke you and prove you a liar* (**Proverbs 30:5-6**).

9. *I know that everything God does will endure forever; nothing can be added to it and nothing taken from it. God does it so that people will fear him* (**Ecclesiastes 3:14**).

10. *The LORD Almighty has sworn, "Surely, as I have planned, so it will be, and as I have purposed, so it will happen"* (**Isaiah 14:24**).

11. *From the east I summon a bird of prey; from a far-off land, a man to fulfill my purpose. What I have said, that I will bring about; what I have planned, that I will do* (**Isaiah 46:11**).

12. *so is my word that goes out from my mouth: It will not return to me empty, but will accomplish what I desire and achieve the purpose for which I sent it* (**Isaiah 55:11**).

13. *Therefore the earth will mourn and the heavens above grow dark, because I have spoken and will not relent, I have decided and will not turn back* (**Jeremiah 4:28**).

14. *Who can speak and have it happen if the Lord has not decreed it?* (**Lamentations 3:37**).

15. *Therefore say to them, 'This is what the Sovereign LORD says: None of my words will be delayed any longer; whatever I say will be fulfilled, declares the Sovereign LORD.'* (**Ezekiel 12:28**).

16. *I the LORD do not change. So you, the descendants of Jacob, are not destroyed* (**Malachi 3:6**).

17. *For truly I tell you, until heaven and earth disappear, not the smallest letter, not the least stroke of a pen, will by any means disappear from the Law until everything is accomplished* (**Matthew 5:18**).

18. *for God's gifts and his call are irrevocable* (**Romans 11:29**).

19. *in the hope of eternal life, which God, who does not lie, promised before the beginning of time* (**Titus 1:2**).

20. *People swear by someone greater than themselves, and the oath confirms what is said and puts an end to all argument. [17] Because God wanted to make the unchanging nature of his purpose very clear to the heirs of what was promised, he confirmed it with an oath. [18] God did this so that,*

21. *by two unchangeable things in which it is impossible for God to lie, we who have fled to take hold of the hope set before us may be greatly encouraged* (**Hebrews 6:16-18**).

22. *Every good and perfect gift is from above, coming down from the Father of the heavenly lights, who does not change like shifting shadows* (**James 1:17**).

23. *I warn everyone who hears the words of the prophecy of this scroll: If anyone adds anything to them, God will add to that person the plagues described in this scroll. And if anyone takes words away from this scroll of prophecy, God will take away from that person any share in the tree of life and in the*

Holy City, which are described in this scroll. He who testifies to these things says, "Yes, I am coming soon." Amen. Come, Lord Jesus. (**Revelation 22:18-20**).

True Prophets Know Their History

As stated previously, both Muhammad and Islamic leaders proclaim that every word of the Qur'an was delivered to Muhammad from Allah—either personally or through the angel Gabriel—and therefore is perfect and without error. The same proclamation of perfection is put forth for the *hadith* (the sayings and examples of Muhammad). When it came to recounting biblical stories, it seems that either Muhammad or Allah erred about biblical history. The Jewish prophets of the Old Testament, as well as John the Baptist, Jesus and His apostles knew the history about which they preached and prophesied.

"Prophets must be students of history," penned McKenzie. "They must also be students of contemporary events. The whole of a nation's history is a record of God's dealings with his people. The prophetic message must be spoken in this context" (5).

In an apparent effort to elevate himself among the prophets of old, Muhammad frequently retold a biblical story in the Qur'an or hadith with a distorted version of the truth or important diversions from the biblical account.

"If a prophet has no personal history with God," wrote Brogden, "no spiritual depth to draw from, no deep root in firm soil established over many seasons of [religious] experience, how can the prophet presume to speak from a position of revelation into what God is telling the [people] . . .? Furthermore, if a prophet cannot accurately interpret and read the signs of the present times; if a prophet cannot correctly judge and precisely discern his own generation; if a prophet cannot relate to what God is saying and doing in terms of present truth, how can the prophet presume to speak of future events?" (6).

Not only did Muhammad ignore the centuries of God's revealed truth to previous prophets, but confused the history of God's people, and even went against that which was revealed in the Qur'an that was entrusted to him.

Was Muhammad the Last Prophet?

According to Islam, Muhammad is the last prophet. "Muhammad is not the father of any of your men, but he is the Apostle of Allah and the Last of the prophets . . ." (**Qur'an 33:40**).

The official teaching of Islam is, "Allah Most High sent Muhammad . . . to deliver His inspired message to the entire world . . .

127

superseding and abrogating all previous religious systems with the Prophet's Sacred Law, except for the provisions of them that the new revelation explicitly reconfirmed. Allah has favored him above all the other prophets and made him the highest of mankind . . ." (*Reliance of the Traveller*, v2.1). "Muhammad . . . is the last prophet and messenger" [*ROT*, w4.1(1)].

Muhammad's Claims to Prophethood
Messengerhood and prophethood have ceased. There will be no messenger or prophet after me   through me the line of the prophets . . . has been brought to completion.

I have been favored above the prophets in six things: I have been endowed with consummate succinctness of speech, made triumphant through dread, war booty has been made lawful for me, the whole earth has been made a purified place of worship for me, I have been sent to all created beings, and the succession of prophets has been completed in me.

Reliance of the Traveller, w4.2(1)(2)(3)

Muhammad's self-adulation, not withstanding, Islam also recognizes 24 other prophets, of which 21 are taken from the Bible. The biblical ones include Adam, Enoch, Noah, Lot, Abraham, Ishmael, Isaac, Jacob, Joseph, Aaron, Moses, David, Solomon, Job, Ezekiel, Jonah, Elijah, Elisha, Zechariah, John the Baptist and Jesus. Biblical history and tradition do not mention Adam, Lot or Ishmael as prophets. Islam claims three Arabian "prophets" that lived before Moses (over 2,000 years before the birth of Islam). They are Hud, Salih and Shu'ayb. Prophets in both the Old and New Testament—those considered "major" and "minor" but also those used by God to prophesy one or more times—include over 70 individuals. In the list of acceptable Islamic prophets it is noteworthy that the major prophet Isaiah—the Messianic Prophet—is absent.

It is obligatory for Muslims to know the 25 prophets of Islam. The majority—20—are taken from the Bible, although some, such as Lot and Ishmael are not deemed prophets in Judeo-Christian faiths.

The 25 Prophets of Islam (Allah's Messengers)
Adam, Enoch, Noah, Hud, Salih, *Lot, Abraham, Ishmael, Isaac, Jacob, Joseph,* Shu'ayb, *Aaron, Moses, David, Solomon, Job, Ezekiel, Jonah, Elias* (Elijah), *Elisha, Zacharias* (Zechariah, father of John the Baptist), *John* (the Baptist), *Isa* (Jesus) and Muhammad (Biblical characters are in *italics*).

Reliance of the Traveller, u3.5.

128

Muhammad died in 632 A.D. Interestingly, according to Islamic scholar Professor Patricia Crone, "a Greek text written during the Arab invasion of Syria between 632 and 634 mentions that 'a false prophet has appeared among the Saracens [Muslims of the Syro-Arabian desert]' and dismisses him as an imposter on the grounds that prophets do not come 'with sword and chariot'" (7).

Despite Islam's proclamation that Muhammad was to be God's last and most important prophet, Muhammad himself, according to the Qur'an never referred to himself as the prophet of Allah. Nor did Allah in the Qur'an call Muhammad his prophet. To the contrary, Muhammad only acknowledged that he was a mere *warner*.

Although Muhammad's followers, then and since, claimed he brought new and important revelation knowledge for both Jews and Christians, the people of the *Book* and the *polytheists* did not recognize him as such, nor would they have anything to do with him and his incantations and moralistic disclosures. The only way that Jews and Christians submitted to his revelations of "truth" was under the severe oppression from Islamic followers. If they survived Muhammad's murderous raids and submitted to Islamic domination, then they could live as secondary citizens if they paid Muhammad the *jizyah* or *poor-rate*—the tax of submission.

At the end of the Apostle John's revelation on the Isle of Patmos, Jesus made it clear, "I am the Alpha and the Omega, the First and the Last, the Beginning and the End" (**Revelation 22:13**).

> *"This is what the Lord says – Israel's King and Redeemer, the Lord Almighty: I am the first and I am the last; apart from me there is no God. Who then is like me? Let him proclaim it. Let him declare and lay out before me what has happened since I established my ancient people, and what is yet to come* (**Isaiah 44:6-7**).

"When I saw him [the son of man]," the Apostle John wrote, "I fell at his feet as though dead. Then he placed his right hand on me and said: 'Do not be afraid. I am the First and the Last. I am the Living One; I was dead, and behold I am alive for ever and ever! And I hold the keys of death and Hades'" (**Revelation 1:17-18**). Jesus was the first and the last to reveal God's final and only plan for mankind. There can be no other plan of salvation and no other prophet to reveal a different plan. Any prophet to come after Jesus is sent by God only to confirm what He has already put into motion through Christ, the anointed Messiah.

"Listen to me, O Jacob, Israel, whom I have called: I am he; I am the first and I am the last. My own hand laid the foundations of the earth, and my right hand spread out the heavens; when I summon them, they all stand up together" (**Isaiah 48:12-13**).

Only Jesus could and did fulfill the Messianic prophecies of Isaiah and other Old Testament prophets. "I will also make you a light for the Gentiles, that you may bring my salvation to the ends of the earth" (**Isaiah 49:6b**). Only Jesus brought the light of God's truth to both the Jews and the Gentiles (non-believers or infidels). None of the prophets before Him did so. Muhammad brought only persecution, oppression and death to non-believers.

ALL the prophets of the Old Testament foretold of the coming of Jesus, the Messiah, not of Muhammad. As the Apostle Peter testified, "And [Jesus] commanded us to preach to the people, and to testify that it is He who was ordained by God to be Judge of the living and the dead. To Him all the prophets witness that, through His name, whoever believes in Him will receive remission of sins" (Acts 10:42-43, NKJV).

> *"I have heard what the prophets have said who prophesy lies in My name, saying, 'I have dreamed, I have dreamed!'*
>
> *"How long will this be in the heart of the prophets who prophesy lies? Indeed they are prophets of the deceit of their own heart, who try to make My people forget My name by their dreams which everyone tells his neighbor, as their fathers forgot My name for Baal"* (**Jeremiah 23:25-27**).

If Muhammad fulfilled anything, it was this prophecy. He convinced many that he had dreamed of a new revelation from the god he called Allah. The new revelations he spoke of greatly contradicted previous revelations, turning the truth of God into a lie, deceiving many and turning them away from the only true God—the God of the Jews and Christians.

Signs of a False Prophet

"Above all," the Apostle Peter asserted, "you must understand that no prophecy of Scripture came about by the **prophet's own interpretation**. For prophecy never had its origin in the will of man, but men spoke from God as they were carried along by the Holy Spirit" (**2 Peter 1:20-21**, author's emphasis).

A true prophet of Almighty God must meet the following criteria:

- They must know God's voice.
- Their word must conform to God's previous word and build upon it.
- Their prophecies, if in the near future, must be fulfilled to prove their authenticity.
- If necessary, they can perform miracles according to God's command.
- They must be empowered by the Holy Spirit of God.

Muhammad failed miserably in all five categories. He did not know the voice of the true God; the revelations he received contradicted God's previous word; he did not receive any authentic prophecies from God; he admittedly could not perform any signs or miracles and he certainly was not empowered by the Holy Spirit whom he denied.

Muhammad did not believe in the Holy Spirit, the One who reveals all truth according to Jesus (John 16:13). To believe in the Holy Spirit would mean that Muhammad would have to confirm the crucifixion and resurrection of Jesus was real, because the Holy Spirit could not come until Jesus' glorification was accomplished according to God's plan.

"On the last and greatest day of the Feast" [of Tabernacles], the Apostle John wrote, "Jesus stood and said in a loud voice, 'If anyone is thirsty, let him come to me and drink. Whoever believes in me, as the Scripture has said, streams of living water will flow from within him.' By this he meant the Spirit, whom those who believed in him were later to receive. Up to that time the Spirit had not been given, since Jesus had not yet been glorified" [that is crucified and resurrected] (**John 7:37-39**).

"This is what the Lord Almighty says: 'Do not listen to what the prophets are prophesying to you;' Jeremiah the prophet warned, 'they fill you with false hopes. They speak visions from their own minds, not from the mouth of the Lord'" (**Jeremiah 23:16**). Despite the numerous world religions worshiping different gods, there can only be one true God. The source of Muhammad's revelations are debatable and highly suspicious because they strongly contradicted the word of God that went before him. His revelations directly opposed the known and accepted truth of the God of the Jews and Christians. His proclamation of new "truth" provided only false hope to a desperate people.

"'Therefore behold, I am against the prophets,' says the Lord, 'who steal My words every one from his neighbor. Behold, I am against the prophets,' says the Lord, 'who use their tongues and say, *He says.* Behold, I am against those who prophesy false dreams,' says the Lord, 'and tell them, and cause My people to err by their lies and by their recklessness. Yet I did not send them or command them; therefore they shall not profit [benefit] this people at all,' says the Lord" (**Jeremiah 23:30-32**, NKJV).

God's prophets did not and do not oppress the poor and needy; deprive people of their rights; make widows their prey or steal from the fatherless. As the Lord God of Israel spoke through the prophet Isaiah: "Woe to those who make *unjust laws*, to those who issue *oppressive decrees*, to *deprive the poor* of their rights and *withhold justice* from the oppressed of my people, making *widows their prey* and *robbing the fatherless*. What will you do on the day of reckoning, when disaster comes from afar? To whom will you run for help? Where will you leave your riches?" (**Isaiah 10:1-3,** author's emphasis).

Muhammad did all that the Almighty God commanded one not to do. He made unjust laws and decrees to oppress the people. He stole from anyone he was against—rich or poor. He was not a man of his word or justice, and meted out cruel and savage punishment. He made widows out of his enemies and then took their wives captive, often giving their wives and daughters to his fighting men to rape or enter into a three-day marriage of convenience to satisfy their sexual desires. By pillaging and destroying the property of his enemies, he left the fatherless abandoned and destitute—unless he took them as his captives and slaves.

Muhammad was very familiar with the story of Jesus' birth and the appearance of Gabriel to Mary. The Qur'an repeats the story several times. Is it possible that because of Muhammad's acquaintance with this story, that it was not Gabriel that chose Muhammad to deliver Allah's message, but rather Muhammad chose Gabriel to reveal Allah's word?

"The spirit that raised Islam has three main objectives," wrote Reza Safa: "1. To challenge Christ, His Word and His church. 2. To hinder the end-time world revival. 3. To oppose the Jewish people and take over their God-given land" (8).

"I believe," Safa continued, "Islam is Satan's weapon to oppose God, His plan and His people" (9).

> *"But a prophet who presumes to speak in my name anything I have not commanded him to say, or a prophet who speaks in the name of other gods, must be put to death."*
>
> *You may say to yourselves, 'How can we know when a message has not been spoken by the LORD ?' If what a prophet proclaims in the name of the LORD does not take place or come true, that is a message the LORD has not spoken. That prophet has spoken presumptuously. Do not be afraid of him* (**Deuteronomy 18:20-22**).

The real test as to whether a self-proclaimed prophet was sent by God is in the truth of his word and actions. No true prophet of Almighty God can bring forth a new revelation that would contradict or make false a previous revelation of God. "Then the LORD said to me, 'The prophets are prophesying lies in my name. I have not sent them or appointed them or spoken to them. They are prophesying to you false visions, divinations, idolatries and the delusions of their own minds'" (**Jeremiah 14:14**).

"Watch out for false prophets," Jesus advised. "They come to you in sheep's clothing, but inwardly they are ferocious wolves. **By their fruit you will recognize them**. Do people pick grapes from thornbushes, or figs from thistles? Likewise every good tree bears good fruit, but a bad tree bears bad fruit. A good tree cannot bear bad fruit, and a bad tree cannot bear good fruit. Every tree that does not bear good fruit is cut down and thrown into the fire. Thus, by their fruit you will recognize them.

"Not everyone who says to me, 'Lord, Lord,' will enter the kingdom of heaven, but only he who does the will of my Father who is in heaven" (**Matthew 7:15-21**, author's emphasis).

Clearly, when the ministry of Muhammad is compared to that of Jesus, John the Baptist and the prophets of the Old Testament it fell way short of bearing *good fruit*. To the contrary, it bore extremely *bad fruit*. It led people to accept false and satanic teaching that led them to oppress and kill their neighbors; rape women and children; pillage and destroy whole communities and cause havoc wherever they went. Beyond doubt, by the fruit of Muhammad and his followers, anyone can see and conclude that he and his followers were driven by anti-God, anti-Christ, demonic influences.

"Dear friends," the Apostle John wrote, "do not believe every spirit, but test the spirits to see whether they are from God, because many false prophets have gone out into the world. This is how you can recognize the Spirit of God: Every spirit that acknowledges that Jesus Christ has come in the flesh is from God, but every spirit that does not acknowledge Jesus is not from God. This is the spirit of the antichrist, which you have heard is coming and even now is already in the world" (**1 John 4:1-3**).

The same Moses who supposedly foretold of Muhammad's coming also made it clear that the Jews were not to believe in or follow any prophet *or one who foretells by dreams*, trying to get them to *follow other gods*. The Jews were to adhere to the commandments of the one and only true God, Jehovah.

If a prophet, or one who foretells by dreams, appears among you and announces to you a miraculous sign or wonder, and if the sign or wonder of which he has spoken takes place, and he says, "Let us follow other gods" (gods you have not known) "and let us worship them," you must not listen to the words of that prophet or dreamer. The LORD your God is testing you to find out whether you love him with all your heart and with all your soul. It is the LORD your God you must follow, and him you must revere. Keep his commands and obey him; serve him and hold fast to him. That prophet or dreamer must be put to death, because he preached rebellion against the LORD your God, who brought you out of Egypt and redeemed you from the land of slavery; he has tried to turn you from the way the LORD your God commanded you to follow. You must purge the evil from among you (**Deuteronomy 13:1-5**).

Once again, God Almighty, through the prophet Jeremiah, warned about lying false prophets who were not sent by Him. False prophets are ones who reveal only *false hopes. They speak visions from their own minds* and not from the word of God (**Jeremiah 23:16**). Muhammad often spoke convenient "truths" that benefited only him but insisted they were from the mind of Allah. Muhammad spoke of peace as long as everyone followed his commands.

Nearly twelve centuries before the birth of Muhammad, the God of the Jews spoke through the prophet Jeremiah concerning false prophets.

"I have heard what the prophets say **who prophesy lies in my name**. *They say, 'I had a dream! I had a dream!' How long will this continue in the hearts of these lying prophets,* **who prophesy the delusions of their own minds**? *They think the dreams they tell one another will make my people* **forget my name**, *just as their fathers forgot my name through Baal worship. Let the prophet who has a dream tell his dream, but let the one who has my word speak it faithfully. For what has straw to do with grain?" declares the LORD. "Is not my word like fire," declares the LORD, "and like a hammer that breaks a rock in pieces?*

*"Therefore," declares the LORD, "***I am against the prophets who steal from one another words supposedly from me.** *Yes," declares the LORD, "I am against the prophets who* **wag their own tongues** *and yet declare, 'The LORD declares.' Indeed,* **I am against those who prophesy false dreams**,*" declares the LORD. "***They tell them and lead my people astray with their reckless lies, yet I did not send or appoint them.** *They do not benefit these people in the least," declares the LORD* (**Jeremiah 23:25-32**, author's emphasis).

False prophets, according to the words of God spoken through the prophet Micah, were ones who proclaimed *'peace'* as long as the people gave them what they wanted. "This is what the LORD says: 'As for the prophets who lead my people astray, if one feeds them, they proclaim 'peace'; if he does not, they prepare to wage war against him. Therefore night will come over you, without visions, and darkness, without divination. The sun will set for the prophets, and the day will go dark for them. The seers will be ashamed and the diviners disgraced. They will all cover their faces because there is no answer from God'" (**Micah 3:5-7**). This was frequently Muhammad's ploy. If people cooperated with him, he would proclaim peace; if they opposed him, he would declare war against them and do his best to destroy them.

Another characteristic of a false prophet is that they have *a different spirit* within them and profess a different *gospel* or word of God then previously revealed or preached (see Chapter 10).

There is no question that Muhammad had a different spirit within him than Jesus or any of God's apostles or prophets before him. His spirit was obsessed with coercion and violence against all people who refused to follow him. He continually preached a different gospel or word of God then that which had been preached for centuries before him. His message came against those who were considered to be God's chosen—Jews by covenant; Christians by the blood of Christ and the New Covenant.

Finally, "Who is the liar?" the Apostle John affirmed. "It is the man who denies that Jesus is the Christ. Such a man is the antichrist – he denies the Father and the Son. No one who denies the Son has the Father; whoever acknowledges the Son has the Father also" (**1 John 2:22**). Once more John made it clear: "Many deceivers, who do not acknowledge Jesus Christ as coming in the flesh, have gone out into the world. Any such person is the deceiver and the antichrist. Watch out that you do not lose what you have worked for, but that you may be rewarded fully. Anyone who runs ahead and does not continue in the teaching of Christ does not have God; whoever continues in the teaching has both the Father and the Son. If anyone comes to you and does not bring this teaching, do not take him into your house or welcome him. Anyone who welcomes him shares in his wicked work" (**2 John 7-11**).

Chapter Conclusion

Despite the centuries of assertions by the Muslim clerics and scholars, the coming of Muhammad was not foretold in either the Old or New Testament scriptures. However, the birth and ministry of Jesus fulfilled over 300 prophecies in the Old Testament about the coming Messiah and *the Prophet*. Muhammad fulfilled none of the prophecies of the Old Testament prophets, nor that of Jesus. In fact, Muhammad met none of the characteristics associated with the prophets of the Bible. If Muhammad was not *the* false prophet spoken of in the biblical book of Revelation, he certainly was *a* false prophet that Jesus (**Matthew 7:15**) and the Apostle John (**1 John 4:1**) warned about.

The ministry of the prophets of the Bible was normally associated with signs and wonders. No miracles were associated with Muhammad's life. The prophets of Jehovah God never persecuted, oppressed or killed people that disagreed with their message. Muhammad frequently planned and/or carried out murderous raids against those who refused to accept him or his message. Prophets often foretold of future events; Muhammad foretold nothing of the future. Prophets of the Bible knew their history and understood the context of their ministry. Muhammad was repeatedly confused or wrong about biblical history and frequently offered little current context for his message to be understood.

Most importantly, Muhammad's revelations completely contradicted the consistent message that God had revealed through His prophets throughout the ages—a message of hope and redemption. The message Muhammad brought from Allah offered no hope, no redemption, and no plan of salvation to relieve mankind of its sin. If Muhammad was a prophet, he was not a prophet of the same God that Jews and Christians worshipped during his time or since.

Muhammad, as a false prophet, should be put to spiritual death as prescribed by God in **Deuteronomy 18:20** (and elsewhere). During his era, he was considered a false prophet by those who heard him preach the tenets of Islam. He provided no new revelations from God, and, in fact, what he did reveal contradicted what God had brought forth before him. He never claimed to be a prophet, nor did he demonstrate the signs of a true prophet. It is past time to set the Islamic captives free to seek out and worship the One and Only True God of Abraham, Isaac and Jacob—the Father God incarnate in Jesus Christ that was prophesied in the Old Testament and in whom over 300 prophesies were fulfilled.

References

1. Safa, Reza F. *Inside Islam: Exposing and Reaching the World of Islam,* 1996. Charisma House, p. 17.
2. Ibid.
3. Caner, Ergun Mehmet and Emir Fethi Caner. *Unveiling Islam,* 2002. Kregel Publications, div. of Kregel. Inc., p. 110.
4. Spencer, Robert. *The Truth About Muhammad, Founder of the World's Most Intolerant Religion,* 2006. Regnery Publishing, Inc., p.38.
5. Mckenzie.
6. Brogden, Chip, *Prophetic Dissonance.* Source: http://www.reconciliation.com/n_brogden01.htm. Accessed July 14, 2007.

7. Crone, Patricia. *What Do We Actually Know About Mohammed?* Open Democracy, August 31, 2006. Source: http://www.openDemocracy.net. Accessed June 2, 2007.
8. Safa, p. 18.
9. Ibid.

Chapter 6

Prince of Peace vs. Warrior Prophet
Blessed are the peacemakers, for they will be called sons of God.
Jesus Christ
Sermon on the Mount
Matthew 5:9

What the Qur'an Says About Peace

Undoubtedly, most Muslims desire peace, both outwardly and inwardly. However, for those Muslims who strictly follow the teachings of the Qur'an, the concept of being a person of peace as Jesus calls His followers to emulate, is a sign of weakness of which Muslims are to take advantage. A peaceful person is an emotional and psychologically disarmed one and an easy prey, one to be controlled.

In the 114 chapters of the Qur'an, only 56 verses mention the concept of "peace." The majority of the verses, however, refer to the Qur'anic greeting, "peace be unto you," or similar salutation. Others deal with the "peace" that Allah brings after a military conflict.

In contrast to the Qur'an, the New International Version of the Bible provides 249 verses with the mention of "peace". The New Living Translation lists 362, while the King James Version offers 420 verses on the subject of "peace."

How Muhammad and the Qur'an View Peace. After the difficult Battle of Hunayn in Arabia in 630 A.D.—in which Muhammad and his army were initially overrun, but subsequently prevailed—Muhammad received this revelation from Allah (1):

> *Then Allah sent down His tranquility* [peace] *upon His Apostle and upon the believers, and sent down hosts which you did not see, and chastised those who disbelieved, and that is the reward of the unbelievers* (**Qur'an 9:26**).

In **Qur'an 48:18** and **26** a similar blessing of peace from Allah after conflict is offered.

> *Certainly Allah was well pleased with the believers when they swore allegiance to you under the tree, and He knew what was in their hearts, so He sent down tranquility on them and rewarded them with a near victory. . . . When those who disbelieved harbored in their hearts (feelings of) disdain, the disdain of (the days of) ignorance, but Allah sent down His tranquility on His Apostle and on the believers, and made them*

keep the word of guarding (against evil), and they were entitled to it and worthy of it; and Allah is Cognizant of all things.

In the above citation, Allah's *tranquility* or peace seems to be available only at certain times for a select number of believers and is conditional.

There are also some interesting references to peace in other verses of the Qur'an. In **Qur'an 2:248**, the verse reflects on how God brought peace to the children of Israel and King Saul before an impending battle.

> *And the prophet said to them: Surely the sign of His kingdom is, that there shall come to you the chest in which there is tranquility* [peace] *from your Lord and residue of the relics of what the children of Musa* [Moses] *and the children of Haroun* [Aaron] *have left, the angels bearing it; most surely there is a sign in this for those who believe.*

Allah, according to the Qur'an, also bestowed peace upon Nuh (Noah, in **Qur'an 37:79**), Ibrahim (Abraham, **37:109**), Musa and Haroun (**37:120**), Ilyas (Elijah, **37:130**) and all of Allah's apostles (**37:181**).

In an interesting aside, while Muslims revere Elijah as a prophet of Allah, Elijah's name literally means, "his God is Jehovah," the name that Jews attribute to God Almighty and the name for God that Muslims refuse to use.

The Qur'an even exclaims that God's peace was upon Jesus the day he was born. "And peace on him [Jesus] on the day he was born, and on the day he dies, and on the day he is raised to life . . . And peace on me [Jesus] on the day I was born, and on the day I die, and on the day I am raised to life" (**Qur'an 19:15, 33**).

This peace of God that was bestowed on Jesus was something that Muhammad could never claim or aspire to throughout his entire life—nor did most of his life exhibit peace.

I have been sent with the sword between my hands to ensure that no one but Allah is worshipped, Allah who put my livelihood under the shadow of my spear and who inflicts humiliation and scorn on those who disobey my orders.

Osama bin Laden
(Quoting Muhammad)
February 23, 1998

Other verses of the Qur'an state that Allah offers a *word* of peace to believers (**Qur'an 36:58**); that Muslims are never to beg for peace in the midst of battle (**Qur'an 47:35**); that Allah dispenses peace to increase faith (**Qur'an 48:4**) but only to select believers (**Qur'an 10:25**).

Does the follower of Allah have any assurance of peace in this life or the next? Is peace—real inner peace of the soul—offered by or guaranteed by Allah to the faithful? No, not really. Faithful Muslims are only offered the illusion or possibility of peace from Allah if they do what is right in the eyes of Allah (**Qur'an 6:127**). The problem is, not even the most faithful Muslim can be assured he or she has done what is right. An adherent to the faith might receive inner peace – and, perhaps it is the only way in this life – if he makes the pilgrimage to the Ka'bah (site of Abraham's supposed offering of Ishmael to Allah) in Mecca. This offer is not available to females or children, only to adult male believers. If one misses out on this opportunity to receive peace from Allah, then there is always the possibility that Allah will bestow peace on the believer after they get to Paradise (**Qur'an 19:62; 50:34**). However, it is only the *possibility* of peace.

Noticeably missing from the teachings of the Qur'an are references that Allah grants peace to all those who accept him, or that he is the source of inner peace, or that he is the God of peace. Muhammad, as Allah's prophet, certainly did not demonstrate the presence of inner peace throughout his lifetime; nor did he teach or model peace for his followers. One thing the annals of history and the Qur'an <u>cannot</u> attribute to Muhammad, was that he was a *man of peace*.

God of Peace and the Prince of Peace

Twenty centuries of secular and religious history attest to Jesus Christ as the "Prince of Peace." No other deity or human being has or can claim that title. It solely and indisputably belongs to Christ, in the past, present and forever.

Around 740 B.C., the Old Testament prophet Isaiah heralded the coming of the Jewish Messiah with this revelation from God:

> *For unto us a Child is born, unto us a Son is given; and the government will be upon His shoulder. And His name will be called Wonderful, Counselor, Mighty God, Everlasting Father, Prince of Peace* (**Isaiah 9:6**, NKJV).

"Surely," the prophet Isaiah testified, "he [the promised Messiah] took up our infirmities and carried our sorrows, yet we considered him stricken by God, smitten by him, and afflicted. But he was pierced for our transgressions, he was crushed for our iniquities; the punishment that brought us peace was upon him, and by his wounds we are healed" (**Isaiah 53:4-5**). **Certainly, this type of self-sacrifice for others is not something that Muhammad could lay claim to as Allah's last and most important prophet. Muhammad never took upon himself anyone's sicknesses or sins. He never suffered torture or extreme punishment and pain for the sake of his follower's inner peace and spiritual freedom.**

According to Mark Gabriel, when he was a freshman Islamic student at the prestigious Al-Azhar University in Cairo, Egypt in 1980, the blind sheikh, Omar Abdel Rahman, was lecturing 500 students on "Quranic Interpretation." In opposition to teachings on peace, love and forgiveness, the sheikh told the students that, "there is a whole surah [chapter 8] called the 'Spoils of War.' There is no surah called 'Peace.' Jihad and killing are the head of Islam. If you take them out, you cut off the head of Islam" (2).

That radical Muslim leader, (Sheikh) Omar Abdel Rahman, you might recall, was caught and convicted of being the architect behind the February 26, 1993 World Trade Center bombing in New York City that killed six people and wounded over one thousand. Despite his disability since near age one, Rahman had a long history of Islamic terrorist activity--even against other Muslims he disagreed with. In 1981 he issued a *fatwa* that resulted in the assassination of Egyptian President Muhammad Anwar Sadat on October 6, 1981. Sadat was only the third president in Egypt's history after the 1952 Egyptian Revolution that overthrew King Farouk.

In 1995, the blind sheikh was convicted for his role in the WTC bombing and sentenced to life in the Federal Medical Center prison in Butner, North Carolina. Despite his incarceration, his followers continued to carry out terrorist activities including the 1997 tourist massacre in Egypt killing 58. The Sheikh died in prison February 18, 2017 but still has a wide following in America and abroad.

Unfortunately, Sheikh Rahman was and is right in his assessment of the Qur'an's mostly silence on the subject of peace. While the Bible has much to say about and teach about peace at all levels of human existence, the Qur'an offers little guidance to the wayward, sinful man.

The God of Peace. The God of the Christians and Jews is known in scripture and life as the *God of Peace*. The Apostle Paul, ended his letter to the Jewish and Gentile Christians in Rome and elsewhere in Asia Minor with, "The God of peace be with you all" (**Romans 15:33**).

Paul's closing blessing to the church in Corinth ended similarly with: "Finally, brothers and sisters, rejoice! Strive for full restoration, encourage one another, be of one mind, live in peace. And the God of love and peace will be with you" (**2 Corinthians 13:11**).

Not only is the Judeo-Christian God known as the God of Peace, but He sent His Son to be the example of His peace on earth. Christ established a new covenant built upon the old promises of God, restoring God's peace to mankind through His shed blood on the cross. The Apostle Paul, in his letter to the church at Ephesus, put it this way:

> *For he himself is our peace*, *who was made the two one and has destroyed the barrier, the dividing wall of hostility, by abolishing in his flesh the law with its commandments and regulations. His purpose was to create in himself one new man out of the two, thus making peace, and in this one body to reconcile both of them to God through the cross, by which he put to death their hostility* (**Ephesians 2:14-16**; author's emphasis).

It was Almighty God's intention from the beginning to bring His Son into the world to abolish the old covenant that brought enmity between God and His creation. Through Jesus' sacrifice and shedding of blood on the cross, God installed a new covenant of reconciliation and peace. Allah, on the other hand, according to his revelations to Muhammad, used Muhammad to bring about discord and blood shed – not the sacrificial blood of Muhammad, his chosen prophet – but the shed blood of all those deemed to be the *enemies of Allah*.

Jesus taught his followers to demonstrate peace to the world; even toward ones' enemies. "Blessed are the peacemakers," He preached in the Sermon on the Mount, "for they will be called sons of God" (**Matthew 5:9**).

By comparison, Muhammad taught his followers to carry out a "holy war" or jihad against anyone who refused to accept Islam or have faith in Allah. According to the Qur'an, adherents to Islam are to fight against all who stand in the way of the spread of Islam and to fight against anyone who refused to enter into the Islamic faith.

> *And fight with them* [the unbelievers] *until there is no more persecution and religion should be only for Allah; but if they desist, then surely Allah sees what they do* (**Qur'an 8:39**).

Muhammad's revealed message from Allah brought about extreme conflict and bloodshed between families and among neighbors, both near and far, especially after Muhammad's flight to Medina and by his followers ever since.

Jesus, throughout His ministry, continually shared with His disciples and those who would hear Him, about God's love and reconciliation and the coming of God's Holy Spirit to dwell within those who chose to follow Him. "I have told you these things," Jesus told His disciples shortly before His arrest, "so that in me you may have peace. In this world you will have trouble. But take heart! I have overcome the world" (**John 16:33**).

Note that Jesus did not command His followers to go forth and conquer the world for His sake. But, rather, He had already conquered the world in the spiritual realm through His coming and future sacrifice on the cross for all mankind. Allah, by contrast, revealed to Muhammad, that he and those who chose Islam were to go forth and violently subdue the world through bloody conquest.

In the letter to the Jewish-Christians, written in the first century, A.D., the author re-assures the believers who were struggling with their faith under persecution and doubts with these parting words: "May the God of peace, who through the blood of the eternal covenant brought back from the dead our Lord Jesus, that great Shepherd of the sheep, equip you with everything good for doing his will, and may he work in us what is pleasing to him, through Jesus Christ, to whom be glory forever and ever. Amen" (**Hebrews 13:20-21**).

Christ's Guarantee of Peace. Jesus, however, as the *Prince of Peace* and the incarnation of His Father, Almighty God, on earth, overtly and without reservation offered and guaranteed God's inner peace to His disciples. "Peace I leave with you," He said; "my peace I give you. I do not give to you as the world gives. Do not let your hearts be troubled and do not be afraid" (**John 14:27**). While Jesus offered this clear message of God's peace – because He was the source of peace – the significance of Allah's peace appears to get lost in the overall message of the Qur'an and Muhammad's murderous exploits.

It is hard to see or interpret Allah as a god of peace when the Qur'an is full of verses that command the followers of Islam to "kill [the unbelievers] wherever you find them . . ." (Qur'an 2:191, as an example). Muhammad, in the name of Allah, the As-Salam, sought to conquer his foes, near and far, and force them into submission to Allah. Christ, through words and deeds of peace and love, sought to reconcile both Jews and Gentiles – believers and non-believers; those who were near and far from God in spirit and distance – with God's saving grace.

But now in Christ Jesus you who once were far off have been brought near by the blood of Christ. For He Himself is our

> *peace, who has made both* [Jews and Gentiles] *one, and has broken down the middle wall* [of the law] *of separation, having abolished in His flesh the enmity, that is, the law of commandments contained in ordinances, so as to create in Himself one new man from the two, thus making peace, and that He might reconcile them both to God in one body through the cross, thereby putting to death the enmity* (**Ephesians 2:13-16**, NKJV).

The Apostle Paul made it clear that the mission of Jesus was to bring about peace and reconciliation. "For God was pleased to have all his fullness dwell in him [Jesus], and through him to reconcile to himself all things, whether things on earth or things in heaven, by making peace through his blood, shed on the cross" (**Colossians 1:19-20**). If we are to assume and accept, as the Qur'an and Islam teaches, that Jesus was a great prophet of God (Allah), but *not* the Son of God, then Allah must be one confused and changeable deity. First, he sends Jesus to clearly bring a message and example of peace and reconciliation. Then, 600 years later, he changes his mind, and sends Muhammad, one whose message was the dead opposite – one of conflict, chaos and inner turmoil.

"Let the peace of Christ rule in your hearts," the Apostle Paul wrote, "since as members of one body you were called to peace. And be thankful" (**Colossians 3:15**). While followers of Christ are called to peace and are called to be peacemakers by Christ (**Matthew 5:9**), Muslims are called, not to peace, but to jihad, that is, a *continuous* holy war against the infidels, all those who do not accept Allah as God (see chapters 8, 11-16). The Apostle Paul, taking from Jesus' example, called upon all Christians to, "Pursue peace with all people . . ." (**Hebrews 12:14**, NKJV). Something the prophet Muhammad did not exemplify or encourage his followers to practice.

Even the psalmist, King David, reminded the Jews to, "Turn from evil and do good; seek peace and pursue it" (**Psalm 34:14**). And again, to "Consider the blameless, observe the upright; there is a future for the man of peace" (**Psalm 37:37**).

The biography of Muhammad and the many historical accounts of his persona and exploits do not give way to him being a man of peace. Nor does the history of Islam paint a pretty picture of a people or religion of peace. Yes, there are periods and incidents in the history of the Christian faith that paint a dark picture that is contrary to a religion of peace. But, unlike Islam, the teachings of Christ and the Apostles command and demand that His followers take the road of peace wherever possible.

"You will keep him in perfect peace, whose mind is stayed on You, because he trusts in You" (**Isaiah 26:3**, NKJV). This was and is the promise of God through His prophet, Isaiah. "The fruit of righteousness will be peace; the effect of righteousness will be quietness and confidence forever. My people will live in peaceful dwelling places, in secure homes, in undisturbed places of rest" (**Isaiah 32:17-18**).

Is Allah a Peacemaker? While Allah is said to offer peace at times to his followers, only one verse in the entire Qur'an identifies Allah as a god of peace (*As-Salam*). But the Qur'an does not refer to Allah as the source of inner or eternal peace. As-Salam designates Allah as the "embodiment of peace" or one who makes peace (3, 4). It is by implication in this name associated with Allah, that Allah brings inner peace to a believer, but nowhere in the Qur'an does it say that Allah explicitly or irrevocably offers or secures inner peace for those that follow him. In fact, the explanation for this name describing Allah is: "The One who is free from every imperfection" (4). Although *salam* means peace in Arabic, the Islamic explanation for this name for Allah draws up short of identifying him as a god of peace or one who brings peace to the believer or to the world. The surah below tries to make that connection.

He is Allah, besides Whom there is no god; the King, the Holy, the Giver of peace [or peacemaker], *the Granter of security, Guardian over all, the Mighty, the Supreme, the Possessor of every greatness . . .* (**Qur'an 59:23**).

However, other names by which Allah is known seem to circumvent his designation as *As-Salam*. Because Allah is also known as (4):

- *Al-Khaafid*, The Reducer—"The Abaser, The One who lowers whoever He willed by His Destruction and raises whoever He willed by His Endowment."
- *Al-Muzil*, The Abaser —"The Dishonourer, The Humiliator, He gives esteem to whoever He willed, hence there is no one to degrade Him; And He degrades whoever He willed, hence there is no one to give Him esteem."
- *Al-Mumeet*, The Inflictor of Death —"The Creator of Death, The Destroyer, The One who renders the living dead."
- *Al-Muntaqim*, The Retaliator —"The Avenger, The One who victoriously prevails over His enemies and punishes them for their sins. It may mean the One who destroys them."
- *Ad-Daarr*, The Distressor—"The One who makes harm reach to whoever He willed and benefit to whoever He willed."

Dig Deeper: Visit this website, https://99namesofallah.name/, to view all 99 names for Allah and their explanation.

The Religion of Peace? According to Open Doors USA, a Christian persecution watchdog ministry, in 2018, the Top 10 countries for persecution of Christians included nine Muslim dominated nations (in order 2-10 with % Muslim population): Afghanistan (99), Somalia (99), Sudan (71), Pakistan (96), Eritrea (36), Libya (97), Iraq (99), Yemen (99) and Iran (100). North Korea topped the list (5).

In commenting on his latest book, *The History of Jihad: From Muhammad to ISIS* (2018), prolific author, Robert Spencer, noted, "What I found is that through 14 centuries, without any break, without any let-up, without any reformation or reconsideration, without any period of tolerance—although there are a lot of historical myths about that—Islam has been responsible for conflict between Muslims and non-Muslims for 14 uninterrupted centuries.

". . . I think a lot of people take for granted the idea that there was some kind of mass conversion to Islam, that people were converting to it because they were convinced that it was true and that this is what was responsible for the Islamization of the Middle East and North Africa. That's actually not the case. It was all done by conquest (6)."

According to *The Religion of Peace* website (https://www.thereligionofpeace.com), since the horrific Islamic attack on the United States homeland on September 11, 2001 that killed 2,976 people, there have been 53 additional Islamic terror attacks on the U.S. homeland (through October 23, 2018) that have killed 158 Americans. (NOTE: This site only keeps track of known attacks as reported in the media or elsewhere. There are likely hundreds of attacks every year that go unreported for various reasons.)

However, this does not tell the whole story of Islam's war against Americans. The first acknowledged attack against U.S. citizens by members of the Islamic community occurred on April 14, 1972 when ten members of a New York City Nation of Islam Mosque No. 7 in Harlem called in a false alarm and then ambushed the responding police officers, killing one and wounding three more. Since that fatal attack there have been a total of 80 Muslim-led terror attacks on American soil (through October 23, 2018). In total, since the Harlem Mosque attack, Muslims in the United States of America have killed 3,175 and wounded untold thousands of U.S. citizens in their own homeland for no other reason than their faith in Allah commands them to do so.

The worst of these attacks prior to September 11, 2001 was the first attempt to blow up the **World Trade Center twin towers on February 26, 1993**. The horrendous explosion killed six and injured 1,040 innocent people who likely knew very little if anything about Islam or Muslims.

Islamic attacks on U.S. citizens, of course, is not limited to U.S. soil. Some of the most notable attacks on Americans abroad by Muslim adherents include the attack by the Islamic Jihad on the multinational peacekeeping barracks in Beirut, Lebanon on October 23, 1983 during the Lebanese Civil War. Two powerful suicide truck bombs exploded killing 241 U.S. marines and 58 French peacekeepers. Almost four years later, on May 17, 1987, the USS Stark was struck by Iraqi jet missiles during the war between Iraq and Iran. Thirty-seven U.S. Navy personnel were killed and 21 injured. On October 12, 2000 another U.S. Navy vessel, the USS Cole, was hit by an Islamic guided missile as it was refueling in Yemen's Aden harbor. Al Qaeda claimed responsibility for the killing of 17 sailors and injuring 39.

Worldwide the cost of Islamic terror has been incalculable. Since September 11, 2001 alone, there have been an estimated *34,025 Islamic terror attacks* throughout the globe (this author calculated 36,322 such attacks on *The Religion of Peace* site through October 23, 2018). These attacks resulted in the untimely deaths of 235,037 men, women and children and the wounding of another 313,784 from bombings, stabbings, beheadings, drownings, and all forms of gross and unimaginable horrors. A total of 548,821 lives snuffed out or forever changed—not counting the tens of thousands of families affected—by the followers of Allah. The people killed, maimed or whose lives were forever changed were not military combatants, but were innocent adults and children who just happened to be in the wrong place at the wrong time. Every year 50-60 countries experience the inhumane horror of Islam's teachings and its followers. Few countries have escaped the scourge of Islamic terror.

Ramadan, the holiest month or time of the year for Muslims, seems also to be a favored time to commit terror and mayhem. In 2017, 1,627 were killed in the name of Allah during Ramadan (www.brcitbart.com). During the first week of the celebration and fasting in 2018 (May 17-25) Muslims ad already killed 218 innocents in 53 separate attacks around the world (7).

According to the Clarion Project (https://clarionproject.org/ montenegro) **U.S. embassies** abroad have been attacked by Muslims since 1924. On July 18 that year a group of Muslim clergy and Persian military stormed the embassy in Tehran and beat to death the U.S. Consul, Robert W. Imbrie.

Since that time there have been an additional 30 more attacks on U.S. embassies by Muslims in 18 countries.

The most recent and notable one was the terrible Islamic attack on the U.S. consulate compound in Benghazi, Libya where four U.S. citizens were killed, including U.S. Consul Christopher Stevens. In a delayed reaction to that attack this author posted a blog on October 31, 2012,

Was Ambassador Stevens Assassinated? You can read it here: https://ampatriot.wordpress.com/ 2012/10/31/was-ambassador-stevens-assassinated/. I present no proof, just a hypothesis based on the timeline of events and the Obama Administrations refusal to send aid to the beleaguered compound.

In the 1400+ years of the history of Islam on earth an estimated 270 million non-Muslims have been slaughtered in the "Cause of Allah" by Muslims (http://markhumphreys.com/ islam.killings.html). This, of course, does not include the millions of people over the centuries that Muslims have enslaved, or forced into being sex slaves, destroyed businesses and livelihoods or forced into second class existence. Nor does it include the millions of fellow Muslims that have been attacked and murdered just because they believed differently than their attackers.

One might tend to argue or point out that Christians have also been responsible unimaginable horrors as swell over the centuries and I would agree that is true. However, there is one big difference. When Muslim adherents carry out their violence and death, they are following the dictates of their god. When Christians do the same they are violating the dictates of the One they proclaim to follow, Jesus Christ.

Peace—a Gift from God

Peace, true inner, personal peace that also manifests itself in expressions of outer peace, can only come from God. It is a gift from God. Man cannot manufacture it. It is impossible to have a real sense of inner peace without the presence of God and the knowledge of His presence in the life of one who believes in Him.

The word used for *peace* in both the Old Testament and New Testament parts of the Bible describes a person who is *happy; has a sense of wellbeing; feels safe; is prosperous, healthy and at rest.*

That is, a person who experiences to the depth of his or her soul, a state of peace. For the Muslim believer, this state of existence does not and cannot occur. In every Muslim nation in the world there is extreme unrest, turmoil and bloodshed. While Muslim leader after Muslim leader cry out that "Islam is a religion of peace," the worldwide current events and wealth of Islamic history tell the truth of the matter.

Once again, King David, who was no stranger to inner turmoil or outer conflict with his enemies, wrote, "The Lord gives strength to his people; the Lord blesses his people with peace" (**Psalm 29:11**). While David defended against and in some cases pursued his enemies, he knew God would have him strive for peace.

The Apostle Paul put it this way: "The mind of a sinful man is death, but the mind controlled by the Spirit is life and peace" (**Romans**

8:6). Man cannot create his own peace; he can only create in his own mind the illusion of peace. He can build walls of defense, train great armies, earn great wealth or do whatever he may imagine will bring him peace, and it will all deceive him. It will not bring him the inherent desire to know true inner peace.

The Apostle Paul, who prior to his conversion to Christianity was a persecutor of the followers of Christ, understood this inner peace concept well. Prior to his meeting Jesus on the road to Damascus (the current capital of Syria), Paul's life was one of inner and outer chaos. Yes, he was an educated Roman citizen and a Pharisee, a Jew by birth, yet he knew nothing of God's peace. He was obsessed with persecuting the followers of Christ and destroying the fledgling Christian Church.

After his conversion he became committed to following Christ, his newfound Lord and Savior. It was then that Paul found true inner peace that was expressed in outer deeds of personal sacrifice and love. "May god himself, the God of peace," he wrote to the church in Thessalonica (a coastal city along the Aegean Sea of ancient Greece), "sanctify you through and through. May your whole spirit, soul and body be kept blameless at the coming of our Lord Jesus Christ" (**1 Thessalonians 5:23**). Paul now understood what it meant to experience the God of Peace and the inner presence of peace, a peace that only Jesus Christ could bring to him. In an effort to encourage the believers in this Roman-controlled city, he once again wrote: "Now may the Lord of peace himself give you peace at all times and in every way. The Lord be with you all" (**2 Thessalonians 3:16**).

This peace of God was a conscious part of Paul daily. So much so, that he desired for all of God's children to experience it. He did not presume to understand it. He just knew it existed, was available and he basked in its presence every day of his life. "Do not be anxious about anything," he wrote to the believers in Philippi (another coastal city in ancient Greece), "but in everything, by prayer and petition, with thanksgiving, present your requests to God. And the peace of God, which transcends all understanding, will guard your hearts and your minds in Christ Jesus" (**Philippians 4:6-7**). Even for the great Apostle Paul, God's peace rose beyond his personal understanding. All he knew was that through the grace and sacrifice of Jesus Christ, it became available to him and he wanted everyone else to know about it.

The Gospel of Peace

"How beautiful upon the mountains are the feet of him who brings good news," the prophet Isaiah wrote, "who proclaims peace, who brings glad tidings of good things, who proclaims salvation, who says to Zion, 'Your God reigns!'" (**Isaiah 52:7**, NKJV). The people of the world, both ancient and modern, have sought the message and reality of peace for thousands of years. And, just like in the days of old, it continues to elude them.

Not long after Jesus' crucifixion and resurrection, the Apostle Peter preached, "You know the message God sent to the people of Israel, telling the good news of peace through Jesus Christ, who is Lord of all" (Acts 10:36). That was and is "good news." Throughout the history of the world, one thing the peoples of the earth have had in common – they all yearned for peace. A similar gospel of peace cannot be found in the Qur'an or among the teachings of Muhammad.

While Jesus was a "prophet" of peace, Muhammad was a "prophet" of war. "O Prophet! Urge the believers to war" (**Qur'an 8:65**). Again, "It is not fit for a prophet that he should take captives unless he has fought and triumphed in the land" (**Qur'an 8:67**). The contrast of prophethood could not be any clearer: Jesus offered the world peace; Muhammad offered the world confrontation and hostility. Jesus and His Apostles preached peace and were examples of peace. Muhammad and his disciples proclaimed and carried out war against the infidels.

Once again, Jesus, in His Sermon on the Mount, declared that "Blessed are the peacemakers, for they will be called sons of God" (**Matthew 5:9**). There is nothing in the world like proclaiming a message of peace as an illustration of God's love.

"On the evening of that first day of the week [after Jesus' crucifixion], when the disciples were together, with the doors locked for fear of the Jews, Jesus came and stood among them and said, 'Peace be with you!' . . . Again Jesus said, 'Peace be with you! As the Father has sent me, I am sending you'" (**John 20:19, 21**). Upon seeing His disciples for the first time since His resurrection, Jesus could not have said anything more reassuring than, "Peace be with you!" The disciples were fearful for their lives. Jesus wanted to reassure them, that despite their fear and circumstances, His peace was with them. So much so, that He was sending them out into their hostile surroundings to continue to preach His redemptive message of God's peace and love.

"But the wisdom that comes from heaven is first of all pure;" wrote James, the brother of Jesus, "then peace-loving, considerate, submissive, full of mercy and good fruit, impartial and sincere. Peacemakers who sow in peace raise a harvest of righteousness" (**James 3:17-18**). The early followers of Jesus understood His message of peace and were willing to die for it; and many of them did.

By comparison, one of Muhammad's most flamboyant and fortunately past disciples preached a quite different message. In a religious ruling (fatwa) of February 23, 1998, Osama bin Laden (Shaykh Usamah Bin-Muhammad Bin-Ladin) and the leaders of four

other Islamic jihad groups, called for the wanton killing of Americans, both civilian and military. In doing so, bin Laden quoted the Prophet Muhammad to support their justification. "I have been sent with the sword between my hands to ensure that no one but Allah is worshipped, Allah who put my livelihood under the shadow of my spear and who inflicts humiliation and scorn on those who disobey my orders" (8).

The Apostle Paul reiterated time and again, that Jesus "came and preached peace to you who were far away and peace to those who were near" (**Ephesians 2:17**). Isaiah prophesied about such a messenger of peace when he said: "'I create the fruit of the lips: Peace, peace to him who is far off and to him who is near,' says the Lord. 'And I will heal him'" (**Isaiah 57:19**, NKJV).

Allah instructs Muhammad to do otherwise. "O Prophet! Strive hard against the unbelievers and the hypocrites and be unyielding to them; and their abode is hell, and evil is the destination" (**Qur'an 9:73**). The Apostle Paul, however, as God's anointed Apostle, reminds the faithful, "If it is possible, as far as it depends on you, live at peace with everyone" (**Romans 12:18**). Again, how can Allah and the God of the Jews and Christians be one and the same? God cannot tell the followers of Jesus *to live at peace with everyone* and then tell Muhammad and his followers to, *Strive hard against the unbelievers . . . and be unyielding to them*. Certainly, this is not a message of peace, nor would it demonstrate a god of consistency.

For the kingdom of God is not a matter of eating and drinking, but of righteousness, peace and joy in the Holy Spirit,
Romans 14:17

"Flee the evil desires of youth," Paul admonishes the faithful, "and pursue righteousness, faith, love and peace, along with those who call on the Lord out of a pure heart" (**2 Timothy 2:22**). Christians – true followers of the Lord Jesus Christ – are not only called to live in peace, but they are to pursue peace at every opportunity.

The Qur'an instructs the followers of Allah to do just the reverse: Not only to not live in peace but to pursue the destruction and murder of those who disbelieve in Allah.

"And kill them [the unbelievers] wherever you find them, and drive them out from whence they drove you out, and persecution is severer than slaughter, and do not fight with them at the Sacred Mosque until they fight with you in it, but if they do fight you, then slay them; such is the recompense of the unbelievers" (**Qur'an 2:191**). Two verses later, this instruction is repeated. "And fight with them until there is no persecution, and religion should be only for Allah, but if they desist, then there should be no hostility except against the oppressors" (**Qur'an 2:193**).

"Some of these so called 'peaceful' campaigns documented," wrote Islamic researcher, Steve Keohane, **"were the massacre of the Jews of Medina, attack and enslavement of the Jews of Khayber, rape of women and children, sale of these victims after rape, trickery, treachery and bribery employed to their fullest extent to grow the numbers of [Muhammad's] new Islamic religion which ironically was supposed to mean 'Peace'! Muhammad organized no less than 86 expeditions of rape, plunder and murder; 27 of which he led himself. In 9 of these, he fought himself on the battlefield"** (9).

Peter, one of Jesus' twelve Apostles, provides a contrary view of God's word. "'Whoever would love life and see good days must keep his tongue from evil and his lips from deceitful speech. He must turn from evil and do good; he must seek peace and pursue it. For the eyes of the Lord are on the righteous and his ears are attentive to their prayer, but the face of the Lord is against those who do evil'" [**Psalm 34:12-16**] (**1 Peter 3:10-12**).

Lest the reader think that the verses of the Qur'an above are isolated quotations, they pretty much mirror a theme throughout much of the Qur'an. "And let not those who disbelieve think that they shall come in first; surely they will not escape. And prepare against them what force you can and horses tied at the frontier, to frighten thereby the enemy of Allah and your enemy and others besides them, whom you do not know (but) Allah knows them . . ." (**Qur'an 8:59,60**). *The Noble Qur'an* (an English translation of the Qur'an published by King Fahd of Saudi Arabia in 1998) has this take on **Qur'an 8:60**: "And make ready against them all you can of power, including steeds of war (tanks, planes, missiles, artillery) to threaten the enemy of Allah . . ." (10).

"So when the sacred months have passed away, then slay the idolaters wherever you find them, and take them captives and besiege them and lie in wait for them in every ambush, then if they repent and keep up prayer and pay the poor-rate, leave their way free to them . . ." (**Qur'an 9:5**). This is what Mark Gabriel, an Islamic scholar and former radical Muslim, calls the Jihad Stage of the Muslim movement – the antithesis of peace. "This stage is when Muslims are a minority with strength, influence and power. At this stage every Muslim's duty is to actively fight the enemy, overturning the system of the non-Muslim country and establishing Islamic authority" (11).

This verse of the Qur'an is clear, according to Gabriel, "Muslims are commanded to kill anyone who chooses not to convert to Islam . . . There are no geographic limits" (12).

God cannot be a peacemaker on the one hand and a warmonger on the other. He cannot be divided among Himself. "For God is not the author of confusion but of peace . . ." (**1 Corinthians 14:33**) and the followers of Jesus are to preach the Gospel of Peace to the world (**Romans 10:15**).

False Prophets of Peace

Muhammad and the modern day imams of Islam are clear examples of what and who the Old Testament prophets warned the Jews about. They cry out that Islam is a religion of peace and that Muhammad was a messenger of peace. They shout, "Peace, Peace!" where there is no peace.

> "Therefore this is what the Sovereign LORD says: Because of your false words and lying visions, I am against you, declares the Sovereign LORD. My hand will be against the prophets who see false visions and utter lying divinations. They will not belong to the council of my people or be listed in the records of the house of Israel, nor will they enter the land of Israel. Then you will know that I am the Sovereign LORD.
>
> "'Because they lead my people astray, saying, 'Peace,' when there is no peace, and because, when a flimsy wall is built, they cover it with whitewash, therefore tell those who cover it with whitewash that it is going to fall. Rain will come in torrents, and I will send hailstones hurtling down, and violent winds will burst forth (**Ezekiel 13:8-11**).
>
> "To whom can I speak and give warning? Who will listen to me? Their ears are closed so they cannot hear. The word of the LORD is offensive to them; they find no pleasure in it. But I am full of the wrath of the LORD, and I cannot hold it in. . . .
>
> "From the least to the greatest, all are greedy for gain; prophets and priests alike, all practice deceit. They dress the wound of my people as though it were not serious. 'Peace, peace,' they say, when there is no peace (**Jeremiah 6:10-11a, 13-14**).

The Apostle Paul warned his protégé, Timothy, about such men. "But evil men and imposters will grow worse and worse, deceiving and being deceived" (**2 Timothy 3:13**, NKJV). We live in an evil and dangerous time. Men still clamor for peace and are willing to do almost anything to achieve or receive it. And evil men are only too willing to say what the ear of the peace-hungry populace wants to hear.

Peace Denied to the Wicked

Islam throughout the centuries gives the distinct impression that it is a religion that is in constant conflict within itself and with its neighbors near and far. Its most outspoken religious leaders neither preach peace nor encourage peace among their followers. "There is no peace," says the Lord, "for the wicked" (**Isaiah 48:22**). Those who preach and instigate evil deeds cannot know peace.

As God spoke through the prophet Isaiah, He said, "But the wicked are like the tossing sea, which cannot rest, whose waves cast up mire and mud. 'There is no peace,' says my God, 'for the wicked'" (**Isaiah 57:20-21**).

It has been several years since the horrible day of unprovoked attacks on innocent life on September 11, 2001, and there has yet to be a universal outcry from the leaders of Islam to denounce this wicked deed in the name of Islam and issue a call for peace. Men who know no inner peace—the peace of God—are helpless when a call for peace is required.

The Apostle Paul, in his letter to the church in Rome, recounts the mindset and fate of those who do not know God by citing Old Testament scriptures.

> *As it is written:*
> *"There is no one righteous, not even one; there is no one who understands, no one who seeks God. All have turned away, they have together become worthless; there is no one who does good, not even one"* [**Psalm 14:1-3**].
> *"Their throats are open graves; their tongues practice deceit"* [**Psalm 5:9**].
> *"The poison of vipers is on their lips"* [**Psalm 140:3**].
> *"Their mouths are full of cursing and bitterness"* [**Psalm 10:7**].
> *"Their feet are swift to shed blood; ruin and misery mark their ways, and the way of peace they do not know"* [**Isaiah 59:7-8**].
> *"There is no fear of God before their eyes"* [**Psalm 36:1**] (**Romans 3:10-18**).

Once again, the prophet Isaiah spoke vehemently against those of his day that had nothing but evil intent in their thoughts and actions. His words have rung true throughout the centuries and for today.

> *Surely the arm of the LORD is not too short to save, nor his ear too dull to hear. But your iniquities have separated you from your God; your sins have hidden his face from you, so that*

he will not hear. For your hands are stained with blood, your fingers with guilt. Your lips have spoken lies, and your tongue mutters wicked things. No one calls for justice; no one pleads his case with integrity. They rely on empty arguments and speak lies; they conceive trouble and give birth to evil   Their feet rush into sin; they are swift to shed innocent blood. Their thoughts are evil thoughts; ruin and destruction mark their ways.

The way of peace they do not know; there is no justice in their paths. They have turned them into crooked roads; no one who walks in them will know peace. So justice is far from us, and righteousness does not reach us. We look for light, but all is darkness; for brightness, but we walk in deep shadows. Like the blind we grope along the wall, feeling our way like men without eyes. At midday we stumble as if it were twilight; among the strong, we are like the dead. We all growl like bears; we moan mournfully like doves. We look for justice, but find none; for deliverance, but it is far away (**Isaiah 59:1-4, 7-11**).

Parting Words

Muhammad's last words to his followers before his death, according to **hadith 5:716**, were, "Turn the pagans out of the Arabian Peninsula" (13, 14). Muhammad wanted Arabia to be for none other than Muslims. No matter what it took, non-Allah worshippers were to be wiped off the peninsula of Arabia.

Nearing death, these words were also spoken by Muhammad, according to **hadith 4:52:220**, narrated by Abu Huraira:

Allah's Apostle said, "I have been sent with the shortest expressions bearing the widest meanings, and I have been made **victorious with terror** *(cast in the hearts of the enemy), and while I was sleeping, the keys of the treasures of the world were brought to me and put in my hand." Abu Hiraira added: Allah's Apostle has left the world and now you, people, are bringing out those treasures (i.e. the Prophet did not benefit by them).* [Author's emphasis.]

In another hadith, Aisha, Muhammad's favorite wife, stated:

Allah's Apostle in his fatal illness said, "Allah cursed the Jews and the Christians, for they built the places of worship at the graves of their prophets." And if that had not been the case, then the Prophet's grave would have been made prominent before the people. So (the Prophet) was afraid, or the people were

155

afraid that his grave might be taken as a place for worship (**Volume 2, Book 23, Number 472**).

In stark contrast, Jesus' last recorded words before he ascended into heaven, as reported in the Gospel of Matthew were: ". . . All authority in heaven and on earth has been given to me. Therefore go and make disciples of all nations, baptizing them in the name of the Father and of the Son and of the Holy Spirit, and teaching them to obey everything I have commanded you. And surely I am with you always, to the very end of the age" (**Matthew 28:18-20**).

The Gospel of Mark records these last words of Jesus: ". . . Go into all the world and preach the gospel to every creature. He who believes and is baptized will be saved; but he who does not believe will be condemned. And these signs will follow those who believe: In My name they will cast out demons; they will speak with new tongues; they will take up serpents; and if they drink anything deadly, it will by no means hurt them; they will lay hands on the sick, and they will recover" (**Mark 16:15-18**, NKJV).

In addition, when Jesus knew His crucifixion was drawing near, He spoke these reassuring words to His disciples:

> *Peace I leave with you; my **peace** I give you. I do not give to you as the world gives. Do not let your hearts be troubled and do not be afraid* (**John 14:27**, Author's emphasis.

A wider divergence in messages and messengers is hard to imagine. In the life and words of Jesus we have a human being preaching and conveying acts of peace from the first to the last day of His ministry on earth. In Muhammad, we have a self-serving, power-hungry warrior who sought to destroy his neighbors under the guise of Allah's good will and design for mankind. If man desires peace, would not his god also desire and grant peace? If a man's theology causes him to seek conflict instead of peace, then his god must be a god of war and not the God of Peace portrayed in the Bible and throughout Judeo-Christian history.

". . . Islam does in fact have an essential and indispensable tenet of militaristic conquest," wrote the Caner brothers (15). These two American-born brothers should know. Raised in a strict Muslim home, when they converted to Christianity, their father disowned them. Today, as Christian theologians, they educate people on the true tenets of the Islamic faith. "Military warfare," they added, "is an absolute necessity if Allah is to be honored and worshipped" (16).

156

Chapter Conclusion

Is it possible, as Muhammad and the Qur'an attest, that Jesus Christ, the Prince of Peace, was sent by Allah and gave testimony to Allah? Or, from the opposite viewpoint, that Muhammad was the spokesperson or prophet for the god, known to the Jews and Christians as the God of Peace? Could two lives be more diametrically opposed to each other than the lives of Jesus and Muhammad? If they were both messengers of the same god, how could one preach and live peace and the other preach and live a life of military aggression?

Clearly, Allah is not the God of Peace that the prophets and sages of the Bible talk about and followed. Muhammad, in the furthest stretch of one's imagination, could not be the Prince of Peace prophesied by Isaiah. Only Jesus could and did fulfill that image of the unseen God, the God of the Jews and Christians only. The harsh character of Allah portrayed in the Qur'an and demonstrated in the barbaric life of Muhammad and his followers would prevent those who have a personal knowledge of the God of the Bible in declaring that He and Allah are one. It is both a theological and practical impossibility.

References
1. Spencer, Robert. *The Truth About Muhammad, Founder of the World's Most Intolerant Religion*, Regnery Publishing, Inc., Washington, DC., 2006, p. 151.
2. Gabriel, Mark A. *Islam and Terrorism*, published by FrontLine, a Strang Company, Lake Mary, Florida, 2002, p. 24.
3. *The Beautiful Names of Allah.* Source: http://wahiduddin.net/words/99_pages/salam_5.htm.
4. *99 Names of Allah.* Source: https://99namesofallah.name/.
5. Winston, Kimberly. *North Korea is worst place for Christian persecution, group says*, January 10, 2018. Source: http://religionnews.com/2018/01/10/north-korea-is-worst-place-for-christian-persecution-group-says/#
6. Corombos, Greg. *1,400 years of uninterrupted conflict laid on Islam's doorstep*, WorldNetDaily, July 27, 2018. Source: http://www.wnd.com/2018/07/1400-years-of-uninterrupted-conflict-laid-on-islams-doorstep/
7. Spencer, Robert. *Ramadan Jihad 2018 Death Toll So Far Is 218*, Geller Report, May 26, 2018. Source: https://gellerreport.com/2018/05/ramadan-jihad-218.html/
8. *Jihad Against Jews and Crusaders: World Islamic Front Statement*, February 23, 1998. http://www.fas.org/irp/world/para/docs/980223-fatwa.htm. Accessed December 11, 2006.
9. Keohane, Steve. *Muhammad: Terrorist or Prophet?* BibleProbe.com, 200402007. Http://bibleprobe.com/muhammad.htm. Accessed April 1, 2007.

10. Gabriel, Mark A., p. 87.
11. Ibid.
12. Ibid.
13. Caner, Ergun Mehmet and Emir Fethi Caner. *Unveiling Islam*, Kregel Publications, div. of Kregel. Inc., 2002, p. 189.
14. Spencer, Robert, p. 165.
15. Caner and Caner, p. 184.
16. Ibid, p. 185.

Chapter 7

The Duplicity of Faith

. . . for all have sinned and fall short of the glory of God,

Romans 3:23

No one is exempt from sin or immorality. However, there is a distinct difference between the higher standard that Jesus called His followers to emulate than that which Muhammad demonstrated and called his followers to imitate.

When Christians follow the teachings of Jesus, they will be acting morally and in accordance with God's moral law. That moral law is often expressed as the "Golden Rule" articulated by Jesus in **Matthew 7:12**, "So in everything, do to others what you would have them do to you, for this sums up the Law and the Prophets."

There is, however, a duplicity of faith among human beings. Some profess one thing and do another. Others do things that contradict what their faith demands of them, while still others will deflect their faith responsibility upon others.

"The eye is the lamp of the body. If your eyes are healthy," Jesus taught, "your whole body will be full of light. But if your eyes are unhealthy, your whole body will be full of darkness. If then the light within you is darkness, how great is that darkness!

"No one can serve two masters. Either you will hate the one and love the other, or you will be devoted to the one and despise the other. You cannot serve both God and money (**Matthew 6:22-24**). Although the last verse applies to those who seek wealth, it is also a spiritual principle for all areas of life. After all, one cannot serve God and Satan, that is, serve both the concepts of good and evil. While a person claims to not believe in a certain type of evil, but encourages or endorses it, that person is complicit with evil and is accountable to God.

It is evident that America has been in a steep precipitous moral decline for decades. Despite America's distinct Christian foundation and principles, today's America can easily be defined by its citizens' propensity for immorality, debauchery and a culture of death.

> *For the wrath of God is revealed from heaven against all ungodliness and unrighteousness of men, who suppress the truth in unrighteousness, because what may be known of God is manifest in them, for God has shown it to them. For since the creation of the world His invisible attributes are clearly seen, being understood by the things that are made, even His eternal*

power and Godhead, so that they are without excuse, because, although they knew God, they did not glorify Him as God, nor were thankful, but became futile in their thoughts, and their foolish hearts were darkened. Professing to be wise, they became fools, and changed the glory of the incorruptible God into an image made like corruptible man—and birds and four-footed animals and creeping things.

Therefore God also gave them up to uncleanness, in the lusts of their hearts, to dishonor their bodies among themselves, who exchanged the truth of God for the lie, and worshiped and served the creature rather than the Creator, who is blessed forever. Amen.

For this reason God gave them up to vile passions. For even their women exchanged the natural use for what is against nature. Likewise also the men, leaving the natural use of the woman, burned in their lust for one another, men with men committing what is shameful, and receiving in themselves the penalty of their error which was due.

And even as they did not like to retain God in their knowledge, God gave them over to a debased mind, to do those things which are not fitting; being filled with all unrighteousness, sexual immorality, wickedness, covetousness, maliciousness; full of envy, murder, strife, deceit, evil-mindedness; they are whisperers, backbiters, haters of God, violent, proud, boasters, inventors of evil things, disobedient to parents, undiscerning, untrustworthy, unloving, unforgiving, unmerciful; who, knowing the righteous judgment of God, that those who practice such things are deserving of death, not only do the same but also approve of those who practice them (**Romans 1:18-32**).

"America has no excuse for its predicament and darkened future. It was founded on biblical principles and Godly vision. Yes, it still gave way to many sins of oppression and other ungodly acts, but it still had the foundational beliefs to repent, led by a God-centered church. However, today, even much of the church and its members have fallen into depravity and worldly ways so that it no longer stands out as a light in darkness; as a city of God on a mountain in the midst of heathenism" (1).

Perhaps this is why Islam seems like a plausible option for some. Islam claims to stand against many of the very ills that afflict American society: abortion, alcohol, lewdness in women's dress, pornography, racism, homosexuality, murder, etc. But do the proclamations of Islam hold true in action or in the Qur'an?

The prophets of God in the Old Testament led exemplary lives.

160

What example of godly living did Muhammad leave his followers? Those that the Bible refers to as prophets, such as Aaron, Amos, Daniel, Elijah, Elisha, Ezekiel, Habakkuk, Hosea, Isaiah, Jeremiah, Joel, Jonah, Malachi, Micah, Moses, Nathan, Nehemiah, Obadiah, Samuel, Zechariah and numerous others, did not have multiple wives. Most apparently did not have even one wife. They did not steal, lie, covet or lead murderous raids or personally kill anyone—except for Moses (**Exodus 2:11-12**), before he was appointed by God to rescue the Jews. They were all men of integrity and honesty with a sincere desire to communicate God's words of truth and warning. Most endured stark and harsh living conditions as a personal sacrifice to remain true to God's calling upon their lives.

Jesus Christ, as God's Son, is the only human being that led a perfect life of peace and love. He taught and prophesied about God's goodness and love for all who would call upon Him.

He taught about loving others as you would love yourself and as God loved you; about compassion and forgiveness and going the extra mile for those in need. While some of Jesus' followers assumed He had come to lead the Jews in a holy war, He rejected the assertion and admonished them for believing so.

If any of Jesus' followers so much as picked up a sword, He stiffly admonished them and set them straight as to His mission of peace. There is no record or mention that He even had a place to call home during His three year ministry. While He was called the Son of God and King of the Jews and other monikers of high honor, He walked and ministered among the poor, the dispossessed and the flagrant sinners of society.

Muhammad, by contrast, did not serve the people but only his personal lusts for power and domination over his fellow man. Yes, it is recorded that he shared the "spoils of war" with his followers (see **Qur'an 8**), but he also led a life of immorality and encouraged others to do the same. He never prophesied anything concerning God's will for the human race. No one ever gave testimony as to his veracity or the purpose of his existence. Instead of living a life of peace and personal sacrifice in service to God, he led a life of a warrior who called for the slaughter of thousands who would not submit to his will and pleasure.

Muhammad's life and example did not demonstrate love or compassion toward anyone who did not believe as he believed. To the contrary, he was ruthless and a barbarian in his teaching and practice. He lusted after women and children and had multiple wives to satisfy his urges.

"And no wonder," the Apostle Paul wrote, "for Satan himself masquerades as an angel of light. It is not surprising, then, if his servants masquerade as servants of righteousness. Their end will be what their actions deserve" (**2 Corinthians 11:14-15**).

The Righteous Man

For in the gospel the righteousness of God is revealed—a righteousness that is by faith from first to last, just as it is written: "The righteous will live by faith."
Romans 1:17

Jesus the Light vs. Muhammad of Darkness. The followers of Yahweh, the God of the Jews and Christians, are called to a life of righteousness. Although called, none can attain it as evidenced by the millions of spiritually and morally fallen Jews and Christians worldwide. The Qur'an also provides evidence that the followers of Allah are called to righteousness. "Surely those who believe and those who are Jews and the Sebeans [those who lived in the southern Arabian Peninsula] and the Christians whoever believes in Allah and the last day and does good—they shall have no fear nor shall they grieve" (**Qur'an 5:69**; also **2:62**).

"You are the best of the nations raised up for (the benefit of) men," **Qur'an 3:110** states; "you enjoin what is right and forbid the wrong and believe in Allah; and if the followers of the Book had believed it would have been better for them; of them (some) are believers and most of them are transgressors."

The theme of righteousness continues in **verses 114** and **115**: "They [followers of the Book who] believe in Allah and the last day, and they enjoin what is right and forbid the wrong, and they strive with one another in hastening to [do] good deeds, and those are among the good. And whatever good they do, they shall not be denied it, and Allah knows those who guard (against evil)."

Come to me, all you who are weary and burdened, and I will give you rest. Take my yoke upon you and learn from me, for I am gentle and humble in heart, and you will find rest for your souls. For my yoke is easy and my burden is light.
Matthew 11:28-30

Based on the violent history of Islam it would seem that the call to righteousness in the Qur'an has mostly fallen on deaf ears of its followers, much like among Christians who do not heed the call of Christ. The official proclamation of Islam and its teachings over the centuries is that "evil is good." Islam's prophet of "change" was evil and barbaric and far from a righteous leader and example. However, the position of Islam and its adherents over the centuries is that Muhammad's murderous raids, pillages, rapes and enslavements were justified, righteous and good—in fact commanded by the "loving" god, Allah. Beheadings and mutilations are also good and remain so to this day. And the Holocaust? That evil did not occur. It is a fabrication of the Jews and Christians. Therefore, evil is good and whatever evil you can deny, that also is good. Righteousness and truth? Do not expect to find them among the teachings and many followers of true Islam.

Of course, much of the same can be said about certain periods of the Jewish and Christian faiths. The Old Testament or the Jewish Torah provide ample testimony to Israel's dark times. In Christian history there was a period commonly referred to as the "Dark Ages" (ca. 500-1500 A.D.)—although some historians resist that designation—a period of mostly spiritual darkness in Western Europe. It was a period that spawned the much debated Roman Church-sponsored crusades of the 11th through the 13th centuries to push the Muslim Moors out of southern Europe and to recover the Holy Land from the Muslims. It also included periods of persecution by the Roman church against dissidents and those that chose to break away from its oppression.

Although the Qur'an states that Muhammad was sent by Allah to be an example to others in the latter days, Muhammad's life paled by comparison to that of Jesus Christ. Muhammad's example was to manipulate and control the lives of others through oppression and persecution; to destroy them if they did not accept his mandates that he claimed came from his god. Jesus, by distinct contrast, brought forth a message of God's love and compassion; of forgiveness and redemption; of God's mercy and grace—a message of freedom of choice.

"You were taught," the Apostle Paul penned, "with regard to your former way of life, to put off your old self, which is being corrupted by its deceitful desires; to be made new in the attitude of your minds; and to put on the new self, created to be like God in true righteousness and holiness" **(Ephesians 4:22-24)**. Through the ministry and teaching of Jesus and His Apostles, His followers are called to a changed life; a higher moral standard; a changed way of looking at the world and to do things God's way.

God's People are Called to Righteousness. "Righteousness exalts a nation, but sin is a disgrace to any people," wrote the wise King Solomon **(Proverbs 14:34)**. Sin never advances the cause of God or His people—only righteousness. Likewise, it is revealed in **Proverbs 29:2** that, "When the righteous thrive, the people rejoice; when the wicked rule, the people groan." This verse in the Bible is blatantly indicative of Christianity compared to Islam—those called to righteousness vs. those called to unrighteousness.

Throughout the Qur'an there are numerous verses that stipulate that *Allah loves those who do good to others.* "And what (reason) have we that we should not believe in Allah and in the truth that has come to us, while we earnestly desire that our Lord should cause us to enter with the good people" [viz., count us among the righteous] (**Qur'an 5:84**)? Whereas, Allah's call to righteousness is unmistakable here, the very same surah proclaims that Allah's followers are to punish those who resist Allah. ". . . they should be murdered or crucified or their hands and their feet should be cut off on opposite sides or they should be imprisoned; this shall be as a disgrace for them in this world . . ." (**Qur'an 5:33**). Five verses later, the following admonition: "And (as for) the man who steals and the woman who steals, cut off their hands as punishment for what they have earned, an exemplary punishment from Allah . . ." (**Qur'an 5:38**). Sadly, this type of inhumane punishment is still the practice in some Muslim countries today.

"Blessed are those who are persecuted because of righteousness," Jesus preached in His Sermon on the Mount, "for theirs is the kingdom of heaven" (**Matthew 5:10**). The Qur'an is conspicuously silent on the concept of one being persecuted for the sake of righteousness while speaking volumes on the call to persecute those who disbelieve in Allah and his Apostle.

"And kill them [the infidels] wherever you find them, and drive them out from whence they drove you out, and persecution is severer than slaughter . . . And fight with them until there is no persecution, and religion should be only for Allah   " (**Qur'an 2:191, 193**).

In clear distinction, the Apostle Paul calls the disciples of Jesus to a much higher ground. "But you, man of God, flee from all this [evil], and pursue righteousness, godliness, faith, love, endurance and gentleness" (**1 Timothy 6:11**). This higher ground of morality was also espoused by Solomon when he wrote: "Better a little with righteousness than much gain with injustice" (**Proverbs 16:8**).

Both the Bible and the Qur'an call upon its adherents to refrain from hateful speech. However, the Qur'an appears to offer a loophole. Once again, Proverbs presents an unequivocal moral ground for God's followers.

"The mouth of the righteous is a fountain of life, but violence overwhelms the mouth of the wicked.   The tongue of the righteous is choice silver, but the heart of the wicked is of little value. The lips of the righteous nourish many, but fools die for lack of judgment" (**Proverbs 10:11, 20-21**).

The Qur'an implies a similar call to morality. "Allah does not love the public utterance of hurtful speech, unless (it be) by one to whom injustice has been done. . ." (**Qur-an 4:148**). There is, however, some ambiguity in this verse. Allah's believers are called to abstain from hateful words, unless, of course, they feel they have been victimized—which the violent and abusive Muslim often claim and use as justification for hateful oratory or acts.

"The righteous hate what is false, but the wicked bring shame and disgrace. Righteousness guards the man of integrity, but wickedness overthrows the sinner" (**Proverbs 13:5-6**).

Jesus is the Example of Righteousness. The sole, and only authoritative and pure example of righteousness that God ever placed on earth was Jesus Christ. It was not Muhammad; it was not any of the prophets of the Bible; it was not the Apostles of Jesus. "Whatever happens," the Apostle Paul wrote to the church in Philippi, "conduct yourselves in a manner worthy of the gospel of Christ" (**Philippians 1:27a**).

Of course, Muslims *do* **believe that it is Muhammad that is the premier model for godly living. "Certainly you have in the Apostle of Allah an excellent exemplar** [other versions: "beautiful pattern of conduct" or "good example for everyone"] **for him who hopes in Allah and the latter day and remembers Allah much" (Qur'an 33:21).**

In response, the Apostle Paul would likely retort as he did in his second letter to the Corinthians who were being swayed by false apostles. "Do not be unequally yoked together with unbelievers. For what fellowship has righteousness with lawlessness? And what communion has light with darkness? And what accord has Christ with Belial [Satan]? Or what part has a believer with an unbeliever. And what agreement has the temple of God with idols? For you are the temple of the living God . . ." (**2 Corinthians 6:14-15**, NKJV).

Once again, while Christians are called to share God's love and compassion with all people, as well as share the Good News of the Gospel, they are not called, nor are they supposed to fellowship with those who represent the Kingdom of Darkness; those who oppose Christ and His Gospel.

This is a hard fact for the Church to accept in today's era of the social gospel, but there is very good reason for Paul's strong admonition and it dates back to the time of Moses. God revealed to Moses that he was to instruct the Israelites that they were not to intermingle with or marry those of unlike faith, "for they will turn your children away from following me to serve other gods, and the LORD's anger will burn against you and will quickly destroy you" (**Deuteronomy 7:4**).

The Apostle Paul, in his letter to the Ephesians, instructed Christ-followers, that although Christians are called to be imitators of Christ and walk in love just as Jesus did, the disciples of Christ are not to enter into such a relationship with unbelievers that will draw them away from the

Gospel of Christ. "Let no one deceive you with empty words, for because of such things God's wrath comes on those who are disobedient. Therefore do not be partners with them" (**Ephesians 5:6-7**).

This is not to say that Paul or Christ forbids contact with unbelievers. To the contrary, Christians are to demonstrate the love of Christ to all and share the Good News of salvation through Jesus Christ.

Even the Qur'an professes that Jesus is among the righteous. "And Zakariya [Zacharias] and Yahya [John the Baptist] and Isa [Jesus] and Ilyas [Elijah]; every one was of the good [viz. righteous]; and Ismail and Al-Yasha [Elisha] and Yunus [Jonah] and Lut [Lot]; and every one We made to excel (in) the worlds. And from among their fathers and their descendants and their brethren, and We chose them and guided them into the right way" (**Qur'an 6:85-870**).

Note that Jesus and many of the prophets of the Bible are listed among the righteous, but Muhammad is not.

"You see," the Apostle Paul wrote, "at just the right time, when we were still powerless, Christ died for the ungodly. Very rarely will anyone die for a righteous man, though for a good man someone might possibly dare to die. But God demonstrates his own love for us in this: While we were still sinners, Christ died for us" (**Romans 5:6-8**).

Muhammad died for no one. As an unrighteous person his death meant nothing in God's plan to save mankind. Only through the sacrificial death of a purely righteous and sinless man could God accomplish His plan of redemption for ungodly, sin-laden man.

Righteousness is by Faith. Since no one can achieve righteousness by their own thoughts or deeds, how then, can one attain such a high standard of virtue? Righteousness, according to God, can only be truly obtained through faith in the One who was truly righteous—Jesus Christ. It cannot be achieved through good deeds, right thinking, obeying the Law or righteous living.

"Therefore," the Apostle Paul instructed the church in Rome, "no one will be declared righteous in his sight by observing the law; rather, through the law we become conscious of sin. But now a righteousness from God, apart from law, has been made known, to which the Law and the Prophets testify. This righteousness from God comes through faith in Jesus Christ to all who believe. There is no difference" (**Romans 3:20-22**).

After his salutation to the church in Rome, Paul laid down the foundational relationship between righteousness and faith. "For in the gospel a righteousness from God is revealed, a righteousness that is by faith from first to last, just as it is written: 'The righteous will live by faith'" [**Habakkuk 2:4**] (**Romans 1:17**). Because God lives within believers in Jesus Christ, through the presence of the Holy Spirit, Christians are considered to be the living temple of God on earth.   Unfortunately, fewer and fewer Christians exemplify Christ's presence in their lives today.

"Don't you know," Paul wrote to the Corinthians, "that you yourselves are God's temple and that God's Spirit lives in you? If anyone destroys God's temple, God will destroy him; for God's temple is sacred, and you are that temple" (**1 Corinthians 3:16-17**).

Muslims can only represent Allah on earth through good deeds and obedience to his law. They are not the embodiment of Allah on earth. Christians, on the other hand, are presumed to be living temples of God's presence on earth through the personification of God in Christ Jesus through the indwelling of the Holy Spirit. Christians, in and of themselves are not righteous, but the Holy Spirit within them by the appropriation of faith in Christ will lead a Christian into all righteousness—if such a believer will permit that to happen.

"Do not offer the parts of your body to sin, as instruments of wickedness," Paul continued in his letter to Roman Christians, "but rather offer yourselves to God, as those who have been brought from death to life; and offer the parts of your body to him as instruments of righteousness" (**Romans 6:13**).

How Evil Works

Edmund Burke (1729-1797), an Irish born American, who was a staunch supporter of the American colonies' revolution against Britain's King George III, is credited with saying, *The only thing necessary for the triumph of evil is for good men to do nothing* (2).

The Judeo-Christian Bible is the standard of absolute truth for hundreds of millions of people in the United States and worldwide. It clearly defines right from wrong; good from evil. However, in today's world, absolute truth is quickly falling along the wayside, even among those that claim to adhere to the biblical view of good and evil. The Qur'an, on the other hand, is really murky in separating what stands for good and evil in other parts of the world, as the reader will discover in this and succeeding chapters.

Tactics/Strategies of the Evil One. There are many schemes of the one who seeks to constantly overcome good with evil. Following is a brief description of some of the most common ones (3).

Anti-Christian; Anti-Jew. Evil hates and despises Christians and Jews and would do anything to diminish their influence in the world and wipe them off the face of the earth.

Tyrannical & Intimidating. Evil is bellicose, confrontational, demanding and insisting on getting its way, no matter what the cost to others. It is dictatorial, exercising totalitarian principles.

Cunning & Deceptive. Evil is cunning, crafty and always plotting to cause disruption and chaos in the lives of others. The more unsettled it can make society, the more Evil rejoices. Evil diverts attention from its evil plans and deceives people into believing that a lie is the truth.

Treasonous. Evil denies culpability while scheming to undermine the safety and security of others. Evil puts others in harm's way, turning a blind eye to obvious threats to personal safety. It subverts what is best for others in the interest of a personal agenda, thus denying any allegiance or loyalty to others; it is treasonous.

Destroyer. Evil is a destroyer. It seeks to destroy what is good; what is ordained by God. It seeks to destroy the family unit; tear it apart and cause mayhem. It seeks to destroy innocent life and life that is still in the womb.

Lies and Deceit. Evil pontificates and proliferates outright lies, when the intelligent and wary observer can easily see and conclude that the world is going "to hell in a hand basket." Evil perpetrates the perception that all is well when it knows full well that hardship and destruction are here or on its way.

Divider & Conqueror. Evil seeks to divide and conquer; to pit one person against another; one group against another. By creating disunity and sowing discord, evil scatters, demoralizes and weakens the opposition.

Creator of Crises. Evil seeks to cause turmoil and enjoys creating constant conflict. It is all too ready to jump into the fray of a confrontation and take sides before it knows the facts and thus perverts justice and the rule of law.

Author of Confusion. Evil is the author of confusion. The more turmoil and disruption it can cause, the better in its plan to weaken society and the individual.

Lawless. Evil does not feel constrained by law. Evil is lawless. Evil is above the law. The law is for others; for fools, but not for Evil.

Enslavement. Evil seeks to enslave the populace; to take away freedoms and self-determination and self-will; to gain control over the masses by making them dependent upon sources and means that evil deems best.

Falsely Accuses and is Antagonistic. Evil accuses others of wrong-doing, but constantly and consistently makes excuses for itself. Evil blames everything and everyone else for what goes wrong in and around its life and experience.

Confuses the Truth. Evil sees no absolute truth, only shades of gray or what can be manipulated into false truth for evil to obtain its objective and get its way. Evil constantly calls evil good and good, evil.

Narcissistic and Prideful. Evil focuses on itself; is prideful and arrogant. Evil takes credit for the good, but denies responsibility for anything bad or displeasing. Prideful Evil cannot and will not admit to any culpability or take any responsibility for anything that goes wrong or is wrong under its watch.

Is a Usurper. Evil is a usurper of all that is good; all that has been established for the benefit of the whole. It seizes power by force that rightfully belongs to the people. This power grab is illegal and without the agreement of the majority and in violation of established law.

Masquerades as an Angel of Light. Evil disguises itself as an Angel of Light; a deliverer from one's woes and wants. It promises to satisfy everyone's needs, wants and desires; usually at the expense of others.

This, of course, is not a complete list of the characteristics of Evil, but it gives you an idea of how Evil slips into the life of an individual or society. This applies to all societies and ideological beliefs; it is common to all humanity.

At Enmity with Women

So the LORD God said to the serpent, "Because you have done this, cursed are you above all livestock and all wild animals! You will crawl on your belly and you will eat dust all the days of your life. And I will put enmity between you and the woman, and between your offspring and hers; he will crush your head, and you will strike his heel" (**Genesis 3:14-15**).

Women as Chattel. Without a shadow of doubt Islam was created for men to satisfy all their wants and needs. Women are not equal to men in Islam. "Muslims," wrote Amil Imani, an Iranian-born American activist, "by belief and practice, are the most blatant violators of human rights. We hardly need to detail here Muslims' systemic cruel treatment of the unbelievers, women of all persuasions, and any and all minorities across the board. " (4).

Cruelty toward women is permitted and openly practiced by many Muslim men, toward both Muslim and non-Muslim women. From the very beginning of human time Satan has been against women, and especially since a woman brought forth his chief adversary, Jesus Christ. Such a demonic adversarial relationship toward women is

one of the main indicators that Islam was birthed from the pits of hell.

Oppression of women, for one, is so systemic in Islam that to this day, women are, at best, second-class citizens under Islamic law (5).

Muhammad, and thus Allah his god, had a high level of contempt for women and demeaned them and encouraged his followers to see them the same way. In all Muslim societies women tend to be viewed as nothing more than chattel—a human possession for the man to do with as he sees fit. Betrothal or an arranged marriage, is commonplace in many Muslim societies, even in the United States. It does not matter if the girl is barely of school age or a young woman, she has no say in the selection of her husband to be.

Although, in **Hadith 7:62:67**, Muhammad gives the impression that women do have some say in who they married. "The Prophet said, 'A matron should not be given in marriage except after consulting her; and a virgin should not be given in marriage except after her permission.'"

How is one to know if the woman gives her permission? "The people asked, 'O Allah's Apostle! How can we know her permission?' He said, 'Her silence (indicates her permission).'" So, in a society where women cannot freely speak their mind, her silence (which is expected of her) is her consigned approval. If she has the nerve to protest or refuses to marry her betrothed she is seen as dishonoring her father and her family. She then can be banished or shunned, or in some cases murdered by her father, brother or uncle in order to remove the "shame" from the family.

"Your wives are your tilth [cultivated field] for you," Muhammad taught, "so go into your tilth [have intercourse] when you like, and do good beforehand for yourselves; and be careful (of your duty) to Allah, and know that you will meet Him, and give good news to the believers" (**Qur'an 2:223**).

For the Muslim woman to decline or resist her husband's sexual desires is unthinkable and forbidden. "The Prophet said, 'If a man invites his wife to sleep with him and she refuses to come to him, then the angels send their curses on her till morning'" (hadith 7:62:121).

". . . women" [in Islamic society], Imani claims, "are virtually imprinted by their parents and the clergy from birth to adopt the gender inequality, as well as the entire pathological Islamic ethos" (6). Although women have very little or no rights in many Islamic countries, some Islamic societies have eased restrictions on women in order to gain favor with Western cultures. However, there is still much discrimination—both closeted and in public—against Islamic women within their own sub-

170

culture in non-Islamic countries.

> *Men have authority over women because Allah has made the one superior to the others and because they spend their wealth to maintain them. Good women are obedient. They guard their unseen parts because Allah has guarded them. As for those from whom you fear disobedience, admonish them and send them to beds apart and beat them. Then if they obey you take no further action against them. Allah is high, supreme.*
>
> *This misogynist religion of Allah is custom-made for the savage male. A faithful follower of Allah can have as many as four permanent wives—and replace any of them at any time he wants—as well as an unlimited number of one-night or one-hour stands that he can afford to rent. But woe unto a woman if she has even a single love affair with another man. Nothing less than death by stoning is her just punishment* (7).

Wife Beating & Oppression of Women is Permissible by Allah. Striking a woman is forbidden or at the least is frowned upon by the civilized Western World and in most non-Islamic societies. However, Muhammad and the Qur'an encourage it.

"Men are the maintainers of women because Allah has made some [men] of them to excel others and because they spend out of their property;" surah 4:34 states, "the good women are therefore obedient [the truly devout ones], guarding the unseen [intimacy] as Allah has guarded; and (as to) those [women] on whose part you fear desertion, admonish them, and leave them alone in the sleeping-places and beat [scourge] them; then if they obey you, do not seek a way [of harm] against them; surely Allah is High, Great."

If [the wife] *commits rebelliousness, he* [the husband] *keeps from sleeping (and having sex) with her without words, and may hit her, but not in a way that injures her, meaning he may not (bruise her) break bones, wound her, or cause blood to flow   He may hit her whether she is rebellious only once or whether more than once....*
Reliance of the Traveller, m10.12

There is one prohibition for wife beating. Muhammad declared, "None of you should flog his wife as he flogs a slave and then have sexual intercourse with her in the last part of the day" (**hadith 7:62:132**).

According to **hadith 7:67:449**, Muhammad forbade his followers from beating animals in the face. Conversely, there is no such courtesy that is afforded Muslim women. Such mistreatment of women is permissible some Muslim scholars say because the Bible states that Job beat his wife. **Qur'an 38:44** erroneously conveys that God told Job to "take in your hand a green branch and beat her with it and do not break your oath . . ." There is no such reference in the Bible. Job, according to the Bible, "was blameless and upright; he feared God and shunned evil" (**Job 1:1**).

If a Muslim man does beat his wife, as he is expected to do if she displeases him in any way, the Prophet said, "A man will not be asked as to why he beat his wife" (Abu-Dawud **hadith 11:2142**).

Muslim clerics are not content to preach their contempt of women among their followers, but have also gained permission to preach the same in Western society, even the United States. In the spring of 2018, the radical imam, Muhammad ibn Adam Al-Kawthari, from Great Britain, began a speaking tour in the U.S. He is well known for his fundamentalist view on man-woman relationships. Although his preaching was under the benign title of "Women's Rights in Marriage", he has previously advocated for wife beating and a woman's subjugation to a man's desire for sexual gratification (8).

Sadly, incidents of abuse of women occur thousands of times a day throughout the world. However, rarely are they committed in the name of religion or in the name of one's god, except in Islam.

There are many examples of Islamic abuse toward women, but one of the sickest and most demonic was revealed in December, 2018 during a Muslim convention on "Reviving the Islamic Spirit" in Toronto, Canada. At that gathering, one of the featured speakers, Tariq Jamil, a Pakistani Islamic scholar and religious leader who administers an Islamic school in Pakistan, proffered a disgusting Islamic premise for husbands and wives (9). This author considers it too vile to report here, but the mature reader can check the reference at the end of the chapter, if so desired.

Jesus' and the Christian View of Women. Jesus taught His disciples and all who would follow Him to honor and respect women on the same level as men. He did not discriminate between male or female; Jew or Gentile; believer or non-believer. All were the same in His sight—children of the Living God in need of a *Savior*. Jesus did not even elevate His own mother above others.

> *Someone told* [Jesus], *"Your mother and brothers are standing outside, wanting to speak to you."*
> *He replied to him, "Who is my mother, and who are my brothers?" Pointing to his disciples, he said, "Here are my mother and my brothers. For whoever does the will of my Father in heaven is my brother and sister and mother"* (**Matthew 12:47-50**).

In one of the most poignant stories of the gospels is the encounter Jesus had with the Samaritan woman at Jacob's well near the town of Sychar in Samaria (about 30 miles north of Jerusalem). The Jews of Jesus' era despised the Samaritans and shunned them. Jesus engaged her in friendly conversation and asked her for a drink.

"The Samaritan woman said to him, 'You are a Jew and I am a Samaritan woman. How can you ask me for a drink?'" (**John 4:9**). Jews would not associate with Samaritans and considered them to be unapproachable.

"Jesus answered her, 'If you knew the gift of God and who it is that asks you for a drink, you would have asked him and he would have given you living water'" (**verse 10**).

The woman became confused, noticing that Jesus had nothing to use to draw water from the well, so how could He offer her water? Jesus was patient and took the opportunity for a life-saving spiritual lesson.

"Jesus answered, 'Everyone who drinks this water will be thirsty again, but whoever drinks the water I give him will never thirst. Indeed, the water I give him will become in him a spring of water welling up to eternal life'" (**verses 13** and **14**). Not understanding the spiritual analogy, the woman requested this unique water that Jesus offered. Jesus proceeded to reveal her past life to her, much to her astonishment. Although the woman had been married five times and the man she was now living with was not her husband, Jesus did not condemn her. Instead, He revealed to her the truth of worshipping the only true God.

> *Jesus declared, "Believe me, woman, a time is coming when you will worship the Father neither on this mountain nor in Jerusalem. You Samaritans worship what you do not know; we worship what we do know, for salvation is from the Jews. Yet a time is coming and has now come when the true worshipers will worship the Father in spirit and truth, for they are the kind of worshipers the Father seeks. God is spirit, and his worshipers must worship in spirit and in truth"* (**John 4:21-24**).

Jesus then disclosed that He was the Messiah that the Samaritans had also been waiting for (**John 4:25-26**). The woman became overwhelmed with joy and ran into town to announce the arrival of *the Christ* (**John 4:25-26, 28-29**).

As with men, Jesus forgave the sins of women (**Luke 7:36-48**); blessed them (**Luke 7:50**); healed them and cast evil spirits from them (**Luke 8:1-3a; 13:10-13**) and looked to them for support (**Luke 8:3b**). Jesus had equal empathy toward all, including women. A woman that touched the hem of His garment was instantly healed of chronic bleeding

(**Matthew 9:20-22**) as an example of His unreserved compassion.

Christian Headship and Servant Leadership. The Apostle Paul, who never walked with Jesus in the flesh, but knew his Master through a vision and revelation knowledge, propagated Jesus' non-prejudicial teachings. In his letter to the young church in Galatia where new Christians were under Jewish law, Paul wrote, "There is neither Jew nor Greek, slave nor free, male nor female, for you are all one in Christ Jesus" (**Galatians 3:28**).

There is quite a difference in Jesus' approach to women and that of Muhammad. In Islam the man is to dominate and control women and his wife, in Christianity the husband is to provide servant leadership as Christ leads the church.

The Apostle Paul made this clear in his letter to the church in Ephesus:

> *For the husband is the head of the wife as Christ is the head of the church, his body, of which he is the Savior. Now as the church submits to Christ, so also wives should submit to their husbands in everything.*
>
> *Husbands, love your wives, just as Christ loved the church and gave himself up for her to make her holy, cleansing her by the washing with water through the word, and to present her to himself as a radiant church, without stain or wrinkle or any other blemish, but holy and blameless. In this same way, husbands ought to love their wives as their own bodies. He who loves his wife loves himself. After all, no one ever hated his own body, but he feeds and cares for it, just as Christ does the church – for we are members of his body.*
>
> *"For this reason a man will leave his father and mother and be united to his wife, and the two will become one flesh." This is a profound mystery – but I am talking about Christ and the church. However, each one of you also must love his wife as he loves himself, and the wife must respect her husband* (**Ephesians 5:23-33**).

Paul, following the teaching of Christ, was affirming that husbands and wives should treat each other with mutual respect and love. Husbands, in particular, are called to love their wives just as Christ loves the church, the representation of His body on earth. The Apostle Peter, likewise, called male Christ followers to honor and respect their wives. "Husbands, in the same way be considerate as you live with your wives, and treat them with respect as the weaker partner and as heirs with you of the gracious gift of life, so that nothing will hinder your prayers" (**1 Peter 3:7**).

In his first letter to the Corinthians, Paul also asserted that, "For the unbelieving husband has been sanctified through his wife, and the unbelieving wife has been sanctified through her believing husband. Otherwise your children would be unclean, but as it is, they are holy" (**1 Corinthians 7:14**).

Temporary Marriage for Sexual Gratification. Muhammad also permitted women to be demeaned as sex objects through temporary contractual marriages purely of the man's desire to relieve his sexual urges. These usually one-sided sexual trysts could last for only 15 minutes or up to three days. They were then broken off by the man without any writ of divorce, no obligation of alimony or bequeath of inheritance. The marriage was one solely for immediate sexual pleasure for the man—a sort of legalized use of prostitution initiated by the male believer.

Such a contractual marriage was permitted by Muhammad when his men were away in battle without their wives.

"We were on an expedition with Allah's Messenger (may peace be upon him)," narrated Abdullah, "and we had no women with us. We said: Should we not have ourselves castrated? He (the Holy Prophet) forbade us to do so. He then granted us permission that we should contract temporary marriage for a stipulated period giving her a garment. . ." (**hadith of Sahih Muslim, 2:8:3243** and also of **Sahih Bukhari**, 7:62:13). To justify this perversion of marriage, **Qur'an 5:87** was quoted: "O you who believe! do not forbid (yourselves) the good things which Allah has made lawful for you and do not exceed the limits; surely Allah does not love those who exceed the limits."

"This marriage," wrote Egyptian pastor Dr. Saleem Almahdy, "is not bound to any of the rules set in Islam for a normal marriage. In this 15-minute marriage, the man does not write a contract of marriage or divorce after he enjoys her. The only thing the man has to do is to give the woman something, like money or food" (10).

In this *sigheh* or *mut'a* (temporary marriage), today has a much broader application in the Muslim world than Muhammad's original proclamation. Today, if a "women [is] interested in or forced by circumstances beyond their control to seek this type of 'marriage' [she] would register with a local mullah (one trained in Islamic law and theology). Men seeking a temporary wife would contact the mullah and specify what kind of woman they desired and for how long. Depending on the marketability of the candidate woman, a fee is levied on the man, and the mullah pronounces them husband and wife for a stipulated duration. Once the patron satisfies his urges, the same mullah simply annuls the marriage" (11). In reality, the mullah takes the place of what the West might call the "pimp" for sexual favors.

Rape is Permissible in Islam. Citing **Qur'an 4:3**, an Islamic scholar at Islam's prestigious Al Azhar University in Cairo, Egypt, Suad Saleh (a female professor), declared that it was permissible for a Muslim

175

man to rape a slave woman or a non-Muslim woman (12). This was not some antiquated, barbaric proclamation of 14 centuries ago, but in early 2016. That this barbarous mindset still exists—especially at the academic level—is not only appalling, but should be a huge red flag for Western societies everywhere.

And if you fear that you cannot act equitably towards orphans [widows], then marry such women as seem good to you, two and three and four; but if you fear that you will not do justice (between them), then (marry) only one or what your right hands possess [i.e., slaves]; this is more proper, that you may not deviate from the right course.
Qur'an 4:3

As a reminder, this Islamic university is the same one where the blind sheikh, Omar Abdel Rahman, taught students that there is no surah in the Qur'an that taught about peace, but that there is one (surah 8) that teaches about the "spoils of war" (see the previous chapter).

In Europe, thanks to all the Muslim refugees flooding mostly into Western Europe, many countries are experiencing an unsavory sexual revolution. Women, especially white European women, are being treated like sex slaves by young refugee Muslim men.

According to Raymond Ibrahim, an American research librarian and author of *Sword and Scimitar: Fourteen Centuries of War between Islam and the West*, and focuses on Arabic history and language, non-Muslim women (as well as pubescent teens) are seen as "impure infidels" that have one purpose only, to gratify the sexual lusts of Muslim men. This demonic mentality, Ibrahim acknowledged, "permeates the totality of Islamic culture."

Ibrahim cited a number of occurrences to prove his point. In Pakistan, three young Christian women were walking home after work and were confronted by four Muslim men. When the women refused to yield to the sexual advances and tried to run away, the men became incensed at their rebuff. "How dare you run from us," it was reported that they shouted, "Christian girls are only meant for one thing: the pleasure of Muslim men." They promptly drove their car into the women, killing one and severely injuring the other two.

In another incident, Ibrahim referred to a case of Muslim man's rape of a nine-year old girl. In response to the attack, a human rights activist was quoted as stating matter-of-factly: "Such incidents occur frequently. Christian girls are considered goods to be damaged at leisure. Abusing them is a right. According to the community's mentality it is not even a crime. Muslims regard them as spoils of war" (13).

Inside Germany, Sweden, England and other European Union

countries, sexual assaults by Muslims upon European women has become epidemic.

In Dortmund, Germany (Germany's third largest city of over 600,000), women are terrified to venture out at night because the resident Muslim refugees have declared that "German women are there for sex."

On New Year's Eve, 2017, an estimated 1,000 mostly North African Muslim refugee men went on a rampage shouting "Allahu Akhbar" (Allah is the Greatest). Hundreds of German women were raped, groped, beaten and traumatized according to police and media reports (14, 15).

In Britain, this sexual attitude seems to reside largely among Somali men, Ibrahim noted. Among this growing Muslim minority population, Somali men are taught that women are "second-class citizens, little more than chattels or possessions over whom they have absolute authority," a Muslim imam was quoted as saying. However, Ibrahim stated, "the imams preach a doctrine 'that denigrates all women, but treats whites (meaning non-Muslims) with particular contempt." In a case in Britain where a Somali man was convicted of raping a woman, his retort, Ibrahim reported, was that sex with non-Muslim women "was part of Somali culture;" a "religious requirement" nonetheless.

"Islamic culture," Ibrahim concluded "the . . . treatment and sexual degradation of non-Muslim women and children by Muslims who deem it their 'right' is apparently another 'exoticism' the West must embrace if it wishes to keep worshipping at the altar of multiculturalism" (16).

Once again, in Pakistan, it was reported that a number of Muslim men kidnapped and gang raped a Christian teen girl repeatedly throughout the night. Their reason? ". . . you are a Christian women and it's your punishment to be a Christian" (17).

Sweden's answer to the rape epidemic in their country is to protect their women by offering potential Muslim rapists video sex education. According to the Swedish news outlet, *Fria Tider*, the liberal Swedish government in 2018 decided that the best way to combat its growing reputation as the rape capital of Europe, was to spend nearly a half million Euros on migrant sex education. Imbedded in the effort is the production of a sex education video that explicitly teaches Muslim men the proper way to woo their blond haired, fair-skinned pursuits.

"The goal of the website is to teach migrants 'health, sexuality and gender equality.' On the website, sex information is illustrated, among other things, with several pictures of foreign men with blonde, Swedish women" (18).

Islam has no age barrier in marriage and Muslims have no apology for those who refuse to accept this. Ishaq Akintola, professor of Islamic Eschatology and Director of Muslim Rights Concern, Nigeria.

There is no minimum marriage age for either men or women in Islamic law. The law in many countries permits girls to marry only from the age of 18. This is arbitrary legislation, not Islamic law. Dr. Abd Al-Hamid Al-'Ubeidi, Iraqi expert on Islamic law.

There is no minimum age for marriage and that girls can be married "even if they are in the cradle. Dr. Salih bin Fawzan, prominent cleric and member of Saudi Arabia's highest religious council.

Islam does not forbid marriage of young children. Pakistan's Council of Islamic Ideology.

Robert Spencer, Jihad Watch (19)

Women are Deficient and Hellbound. The negative and inferior portrayal of women, as well as the approval of mistreatment, is a recurring theme in many hadith. To make sure that women knew their place in the male-dominated Islamic society, Muhammad taught that, "After me I have not left any affliction more harmful to men than women" (**hadith 7:62:33**). In the same hadith volume and book, **verse 30**, "Allah's Apostle said, 'Evil omen is in the women, the house and the horse.'"

Wives and children were also to be suspected of evil doing. ". . . And the Statement of Allah: 'Truly, among your wives and your children, there are enemies for you (i.e. may stop you from obedience to Allah)'" (**hadith 7:62:29**).

Even Aisha, Muhammad's youngest wife complained, "It is not good that you people have made us (women) equal to dogs and donkeys" (**hadith 1:498**). This is analogous to the Qur'an proclaiming that Jews are nothing more than pigs and monkeys (**Qur'an 5:60**).

In some verses of the Qur'an it is implied that women have equality. "Whoever does good whether male or female and he is a believer," Muhammad revealed in **Qur'an 16:97**, "We will most certainly make him live a happy life, and We will most certainly give them their reward for the best of what they did."

Although women, as child bearers, were to be accorded some respect, it's hard to imagine that happening on a daily basis when Muhammad taught that women were evil; the primary reason for men turning from Allah and that women dominated the fires of hell.

"The Prophet said, 'I stood at the gate of Paradise and saw that

178

the majority of the people who entered it were the poor, while the wealthy were stopped at the gate (for the accounts). But the companions of the Fire were ordered to be taken to the Fire. Then I stood at the gate of the Fire and saw that the majority of those who entered it were women'" (**hadith 7:62:124**).

Again, "The Prophet replied, 'I saw Paradise . . . I also saw the Hell-fire and I had never seen such a horrible sight. I saw that most of the inhabitants were women.' The people asked, 'O Allah's Apostle! Why is this so?' The Prophet replied, 'Because of their ungratefulness'" (**hadith 2:161**).

In other hadith, Muhammad continued to put women in their proper subservient place. "After finishing the prayer, [Muhammad] delivered the sermon and ordered the people to give alms. He said, 'O people! Give alms.' Then he went towards the women and said. 'O women! Give alms, for I have seen that the majority of the dwellers of Hell-Fire were you (women).' The women asked, 'O Allah's Apostle! What is the reason for it?' He replied, 'O women! You curse frequently, and are ungrateful to your husbands. I have not seen anyone more deficient in intelligence and religion than you'" (**hadith 2:541**).

Although Muhammad is admonishing the women to give alms as a command from Allah, he later (in the same hadith) reverses himself. When Zainab, the wife of Ibn Masud, came to the Prophet's house to ask if it was acceptable to give away some of her jewelry for the poor, Muhammad told her that her husband and children disserved it more than the poor.

In **hadith 1:301**, Muhammad clarifies a woman's deficiencies further. "The women asked, 'O Allah's Apostle! What is deficient in our intelligence and religion?' He said, 'Is not the evidence of two women equal to the witness of one man?' They replied in the affirmative. He said, 'This is the deficiency in her intelligence. Isn't it true that a woman can neither pray nor fast during her menses?' The women replied in the affirmative. He said, 'This is the deficiency in her religion.'" Notice that the deficiencies ascribed to women are those assigned them by Muhammad and the male-dominated society of which he was a part and that a woman's *deficiency* had nothing to do with her intelligence but with a biological function beyond her control. Once again, in **hadith 3:826**, Muhammad asserts a woman's mental lack. "The Prophet said, 'Isn't the witness of a woman equal to half of that of a man?' The woman said, 'Yes.' He said, 'This is because of the deficiency of a woman's mind.'"

Multiple Wives

In Britain, it did not take long for Muslim refugees to discover that with the generous welfare policies of the British, they hit a gold mine of which they could take full advantage. In a Muslim society where the revered leader, Muhammad, sanctioned up to four wives for every Muslim man, England represented the nirvana of benefits (20). Likewise the same is true in the ever generous United States of America.

By revelation from Allah, Muhammad was free to take as many wives as he wanted. "O Prophet!" Allah revealed to Muhammad, "surely We have made lawful to you your wives whom you have given their dowries, and those [slaves] whom your right hand possesses out of those whom Allah has given to you as prisoners of war, and the daughters of your paternal uncles and the daughters of your paternal aunts, and the daughters of your maternal uncles and the daughters of your maternal aunts who fled with you; and a believing woman if she gave herself to the Prophet, if the Prophet desired to marry her—**specially for you, not for the (rest of) believers**; We know what We have ordained for them concerning their wives and those whom their right hands possess in order that no blame may attach to you; and Allah is Forgiving, Merciful" (**Qur'an 33:50**, author's emphasis).

Allah was generous toward his prophet and messenger. Muhammad could have whatever woman he wanted in marriage and as many wives as he desired and no woman was free to resist or deny him. He had special self-serving dispensation from Allah to do as it pleased him. Partly, as a result of this freedom for a Muslim man to marry almost any woman he wanted, marrying first cousins was and is permissible among Muslims, a practice abhorred in Western culture.

A Few Islamic Rules of Marriage
Marry such women as seem good to you (surah 4:3).
Marry one another, that you may increase.
Reliance of the Traveller, m1.0

A man who needs to marry (O: because of desire for sexual intercourse) and has enough money . . . is recommended to do so   One who needs to marry but does not have enough to pay for these expenses is recommended not to marry, but rather to suppress his sexual desire by fasting.
Reliance of the Traveller, m1.1

It is unlawful for a free man to marry more than four women. It is fitter to confine oneself to just one.
Reliance of the Traveller, m6.10

In the box above are just a few of the numerous rules/laws

concerning Muslim marriage. However, note in just these few some anomalies. First, it is the man that gets to choose whom he will marry and the plural "women" is used, not woman. Second, the two primary reasons for marriage is procreation and sex—not because of love for one another, common beliefs or a sense of God's calling the two together.

In **Qur'an 33:51**, Allah certifies Muhammad's freedom of personal indulgence. "You may put off whom you please of them, and you may take to you whom you please, and whom you desire of those whom you had separated provisionally [like the wife of Muhammad's adopted son Zayd]; no blame attaches to you; this is most proper, so that their eyes may be cool and they may not grieve, and that they should be pleased, all of them, with what you give them, and Allah knows what is in your hearts; and Allah is Knowing, Forbearing."

A personal god that permits you to sin where no others are allowed. There will be *no blame* attached to you; after all it *is most proper* for you to do. Not only that, but your followers must accept it even though it is not permissible for them to do likewise.

. . . a marriage contract can be made between a female fetus and a male fetus by their respective guardians . . .
The Qur'an says so, not me.
Sheikh Saeed Numan, Egyptian cleric at Al-Azhar University
November 14, 2018
Source: https://www.memri.org/tv/egyptian-azhar-cleric-saeed-numan-fetus-marriage-okay-girls-married-nine-quran/transcript

---

Polygamy, or the taking of concubines was also practiced by some Middle Eastern Jews, although it was clearly forbidden by God in the Old and New Testament. It is recorded in **Genesis 2:22-23** that God made woman out of the rib of man and that "The man said, 'This is now bone of my bones and flesh of my flesh; she shall be called *woman*, for she was taken out of man.'"

"For this reason," the scripture states, "a man will leave his father and mother and be united to his wife, and they will become one flesh" **(Genesis 2:24)**. Now, a man can become *one* only with one woman at a time. To become *one* with multiple women at the same time or through multiple simultaneous marriages is emotionally and spiritually impossible. To convince oneself of this possibility is a complete deception from Satan.

Yahweh, the God of the Jews and Christians detests polygamy. He made this clear through the prophet Malachi.

Another thing you do: You flood the LORD's altar with

tears. You weep and wail because he no longer pays attention to your offerings or increase accepts them with pleasure from your hands. You ask, "Why?" It is because the LORD is acting as the witness between you and the wife of your youth, because you have broken faith with her, though she is your partner, the wife of your marriage covenant.

Has not the LORD made them one? In flesh and spirit they are his. And why one? Because he was seeking godly offspring. So guard yourself in your spirit, and do not break faith with the wife of your youth (**Malachi 2:13-15**).

Jesus also taught of the importance of a monogamous marriage relationship (Matthew 19:5-6 and Mark 10:7-8). Muhammad advocated multiple and simultaneous marriages. "And if you fear that you cannot act equitably towards orphans, then marry such women as seem good to you, two and three and four. . ." (surah 4:3). If the man felt he could not treat that many wives fairly, then he should only marry one.

Paul also advocated the one wife/one husband directive. "Now the overseer [deacon, elder] must be above reproach, the husband of but one wife, temperate, self-controlled, respectable, hospitable, able to teach, not given to drunkenness, not violent but gentle, not quarrelsome, not a lover of money" (**1 Timothy 3:2-3**; see also **1 Timothy 3:12**; **Titus 1:6**).

However, Allah sees marriage and fidelity differently. "O Prophet!" disclosed Allah to Muhammad, "why do you forbid (yourself) that which Allah has made lawful for you; you seek to please your wives; and Allah is Forgiving, Merciful" (**Qur'an 66:1**). Allah is telling Muhammad that he should not withhold himself from having intercourse with all his wives anytime he wanted. In the next verse, Allah annuls any oaths Muhammad might have made concerning such a matter. "Allah indeed has sanctioned for you the expiation [end] of your oaths . . ." If any of Muhammad's wives refused his sexual advances, Allah also had a word of warning for them. "Maybe, his Lord, if he divorces you, will give him [Muhammad] in your place wives better than you, submissive, faithful, obedient, penitent, adorers, fasters, widows and virgins" (**Qur'an 66:5**).

Muhammad's Multiple Wives. After 25 years of monogamous life with his first wife, Khadija, Muhammad, in 620 A.D. (a few days after Khadija's death), married his second wife, Sawda, an elderly widow. The same year, Aisha (or Aishah), the six-year old daughter of Abu Bakr, was betrothed to Muhammad. Three years later he would consummate his marriage with Aisha when she was only nine years old and he was 53 (21, 22, 23).

Probably, because of the West's distaste for an adult to marry a child, some modern Islamic web sites claim that Aisha was sixteen when

Muhammad married her (24). This contradicts the wealth of historical Islamic records and Aisha herself, who in **hadith 7:62:64** is recorded to have said, "that the Prophet married her when she was six years old and he [Muhammad] consummated his marriage when she was nine years old, and then she remained with him for nine years (i.e., till his death)." Ursa also related the same facts in **hadith 7:62:88**.

In 625, Muhammad married his fourth wife, Hafsah, a young widow of 18 or 20 years old. Muhammad was 55 at the time. A year later he married two more widows, Um Salma and Zaynab (25, 26, 27).

Muhammad's 7th, 8th and 9th marriages took place in 627. He married the 20-year old Juweiriyeh, a captive from the Banu Mustaliq tribe that Muhammad had defeated. He also married Zaynab bint Jarsh and the Jewess, Rayhana (28, 29, 30). The marriage to Zaynab has also become historically controversial. Zaynab was the beautiful wife of Zayd (or Zaid), Muhammad's adopted son. When Muhammad went to visit one day he inadvertently saw Zaynab scantily clad and from that moment lusted after her (31). Zayd knew that the Prophet wanted her and offered to divorce his wife so Muhammad could marry her. Muhammad struggled with his covetousness briefly until he got this convenient revelation from Allah giving him the go ahead to fulfill his wanton desire.

> *And when you said to him to whom Allah had shown favor and to whom you had shown a favor: Keep your wife to yourself and be careful of (your duty to) Allah; and you concealed in your soul what Allah would bring to light, and you feared men, and Allah had a greater right that you should fear Him. But when Zaid had accomplished his want* [or come to the end of his union with] *her, We gave her to you as a wife, so that there should be no difficulty for the believers in respect of the wives of their adopted sons, when they have accomplished their want of them; and Allah's command shall be performed.*
>
> *There is no harm in the Prophet doing that which Allah has ordained for him; such has been the course of Allah with respect to those who have gone before; and the command of Allah is a decree that is made absolute* (**Qur'an 33:37-38**).

It was not uncommon in Muhammad's era for fathers without sons (as Muhammad was) to adopt the sons—either minors or adults—of widows. In this surah, it appears that Allah is rewarding Muhammad for his lust and covetousness, and thus setting the example for his followers that might also have adopted sons who were married.

Yahweh, the God of the Jews and Christians says, "You shall not covet your neighbor's house. You shall not covet your neighbor's wife, or his manservant or maidservant, his ox or donkey, or anything

that belongs to your neighbor" (Exodus 20:17). The Hebrew word for "neighbor" also stands for an associate, friend, brother, husband or companion.

In 628, at age 58, Muhammad married Maryam (or Mary the Copt), Um Habeeba and Sufia, his 10th, 11th and 12th wives. Maryam was a Christian; Sufia was a Jew taken as a captive and "booty" after Muhammad had her husband and relatives slaughtered. Juweiriyeh and Sufia (or Safiya) were procured by Muhammad for his 7th and 10th wives after he attacked and killed the inhabitants of Khaibar (**hadith 5:59:512**) and attacked the Bani Mustaliq without warning, killing the men and taking the women and children captive (**hadith 3:46:717**).

In 629, Muhammad married Maimoona, his 13th and last wife (32, 33, 34). Of the 13 women, eleven were considered his wives, two his concubines.

Let me tell you that your husband is only yours 25 per cent; your husband is not your property; your only share of him is 25 per cent. The remaining 75 per cent belongs to other women.

If you want your husband 100 per cent, then you are a thief; you are going beyond the 25 per cent that is yours; the remaining 75 per cent belongs to other ladies.

Don't think that because you are wives, other women should not share your husbands.

Men are not stupid, the men are even becoming smart. It's until when some die that you know how many children they have.

I am not saying that is what happens every time; but if you think you are too smart, men are smarter.

You have never been a man before in your life, you can't imagine what goes through in the minds of men. Let us fear Allah, as much as possible.

Ustaz Abdulfattah Adeyemi, "renowned" Islamic scholar
& founder of Baynakum Family Counseling Centre in Nigeria (35)

Honor Killings

Although there is no passage in the Qur'an that sanctions honor killings, the Muslim community, in essence, does. Honor killing, or abusive behavior, to defend one's honor or that of the family, is not exclusively Muslim, but it is the one that occurs the most, and that Western society hears about most often. Although not singularly practiced by some Muslims, honor killing in some societies is a kind of human sacrifice to appease pagan gods and rid the one or ones whose honor has been offended, of the mark or sin of being dishonored.

The Honour Based Violence Awareness Network (http://hbv-awareness.com) estimates that at least 5,000 honor killings occur each year in various cultures throughout the world.

While "No passage in the Koran discusses honor killings . . . Muslim clerics justify them and secular Muslims either do not punish them or pass laws to mitigate punishment for them. With this, Muslims make honor killings a part of Islam" (36).

In 2011, in Britain, there were a reported estimate of 5,500 honor attacks and perhaps thousands more that went unreported (37). According to a Freedom of Information Act request, this number was a huge jump from Britain's near 3,600 such attacks in 2010. Jasvinder Sanghera, who is the founder of the victim support group, Karma Nirvana, estimates that the real number could be four times that estimate during that period.

"The figures are woefully underestimated," Sanhera proclaimed, "we are dealing with the tip of the iceberg, we don't know how many thousands are at risk because it is a hidden crime and there is no statutory duty to record it. . .

"This is not a cultural issue, it's an issue of abuse and while we tiptoe around it we are giving power to the perpetrators," she added.

As Muslims relocate across the world, honor killings and abusive behavior in the name of Allah and in the defense of one's honor are quick to follow. Such practices, once unknown in the West, are now becoming entrenched in Western society, including the United States and Canada.

Honor violence, in general, is a mechanism to maintain or regain a family's honor by punishing or eliminating girls and women whose actions invite rumors of sexual impropriety or disobedience. Boys and men may also be victims of honor violence if they violate sexual norms or defy patriarchal authority (38).

In a 2014 draft report by the U.S. Bureau of Justice Statistics on honor violence, the authors relied on a study by Professor Richard Curtis of John Jay College of Criminal Justice of the City University of New York. Using a survey of reported incidents in Europe and North America, Prof. Curtis postulated that in America there were between 23 and 27 honor killings per year (39). This is not a significant number to alarm law enforcement or politicians.

Although it is clear from incident reports that honor violence and killings do occur in the United States, the frequency and number has not been determined. This relatively new violent and criminal phenomenon in America has not been empirically studied or quantified. Besides, authorities and researchers are not exactly

185

rushing in to study it because of the cultural and politically incorrect stigmas attached to the issue.

In addition, according to the draft report, "Information about honor violence is held tightly within families. Victims or potential victims may not report victimization because of concern about an extremely negative family response. Moreover, victims may not report information, because in their home cultures, what has happened is not viewed as a crime."

Is Honor Violence a Threat to the West? In the twelve months leading up to April, 2011, the Metropolitan Police of London had recorded 443 occurrences of honor violence or forced marriage (40). Using Britain's Freedom of Information Act, researchers discovered that there were nearly 3,600 cases of honor violence in Britain in 2010. Although, admittedly, the number of recorded cases were seen as only the "tip of the iceberg." From 2010-2014, the British police recorded 11,744 cases of honor violence. However, this represented data from only 39 of 52 police precincts and included forced marriage and female genital mutilation (41). By June, 2014, British lawmakers had enough and passed a law banning forced marriage in Britain and Wales.

On May 11, 2017, the European Union council of member states took steps for a groundbreaking treaty for the EU to combat violence against women as well as domestic violence. The agreement, dubbed the "Istanbul Convention" or the Council of Europe Convention, required the ratification of all 28 members of the European Union (42). As of January, 2018, 46 European region countries and the 28 member states of the EU signed the agreement, with 33 countries ratifying it.

"The regime of honor is unforgiving: women on whom suspicion has fallen are not given an opportunity to defend themselves, and family members have no socially acceptable alternative but to remove the stain on their honor by attacking the woman."
Amnesty International

Granted, the number of honor killings, has not been as wide spread in the United States and Canada as in Britain, but any occurrence of this non-American cultural "phenomenon" is unsettling at the least. Part of the differential could be the concentration of Muslims. In the United Kingdom, the 2016 Muslim population was pegged at 8.2%, while in the U.S. it is estimated to be around one percent.

It is hard to know when the first honor killing occurred in America, however, its frequency seems to be increasing.

One highly publicized honor killing occurred in Texas in 2012. Jordanian immigrant, Ali Mahwood-Awad Irsan, who immigrated to the

United States in 1979, and became a naturalized citizen, killed his daughter, her husband and the daughter's close friend, Iranian-born activist, Gelereh Bagherzadeh. Why? Because he became enraged when his daughter became a Christian and married a Christian man. As a devout Muslim, he apparently did not adapt well to American culture. His attack was not random or haphazard, but it was well planned and included the collusion of several women in his household, including his wife and another daughter. He also intended on killing others who helped his daughter break free from the bondage of Islam and family oppression (43).

So, why should America and Americans be concerned? After all, this was just another few murders of thousands that are committed in the United States every year.

"'Cases of honor killings and/or violence in the U.S. are often unreported because of the shame it can cause to the victim and the victim's family,' Farhana Qazi, a former U.S. government analyst and senior fellow at the Center for Advanced Studies on Terrorism, told FoxNews.com. 'Also, because victims are often young women, they may feel that reporting the crime to authorities will draw too much attention to the family committing the crime'" (44).

Unlike some murders in society, honor killings are not committed by some wacko or on the whim of the moment. Such deeds are usually well-planned and frequently involve more than one family member who are committed to each other to keep their plans and dastardly act secret. But it is not just the outcome that is so horrific, it is the threat of such an attack— usually teen girls or young women—that hovers over the head of the potential victim every moment of their lives.

One such high profile case made headlines in July, 2009 when sixteen year old Rifqa Bary arrived in Orlando, Florida after a thousand mile bus trip from her home in Columbus, Ohio. Bary, who emigrated to the U.S. with her family from Sri Lanka in 2000, became a Christian as a young teenager.

"They have to kill me," Bary was quoted by CBN News. "My blood is now halalh [sic] which means . . . because I am now a Christian. I'm from a Muslim background. It's an honor, if they love God more than me. They have to do this" (45).

When your Lord revealed to the angels: I am with you, therefore make firm those who believe. I will cast terror into the hearts of those who disbelieve. Therefore strike off their heads and strike off every fingertip of them. This is because they acted adversely to Allah and His Apostle; and whoever acts adversely to Allah and His Apostle – then surely Allah is severe in requiting (evil) (Qur'an 8:12-13).

Whether a real or imagined threat, Bary believed she had to flee her family to escape being killed by her father. She found a temporary sanctuary in Orlando with a Christian pastor and his family until a Florida judge determined she had to return to Ohio. On October 27, 2009 Bary returned to Ohio and was placed under the protective custody of Franklin County Children Services. After a year of back and forth court battles with her parents, she turned 18 on August 10, 2010 and the county's custody ended.

In her 2015 autobiography, *Hiding in the Light: Why I Risked Everything to Leave Islam and Follow Jesus*, revealed, that while living in her native land of Sri Lanka she was molested by a family relative. She also lost an eye as a little girl when her brother threw a metal plane at her.

"In some Muslim cultures, like mine," Bary wrote, "this kind of violation is a great source of dishonor. Yet the shame is not attached to the abuser; it is cast on the victim. So not only was I viewed now in my parents' eyes as a half-blind picture of imperfection, but I was also a shameful disgrace to the Bary name. My mere presence and appearance were a stain against the most important thing of all—our family honor" (46).

In the spring of 2018, she graduated from college *cum laude* and entered her first year of law school in August. Bary claims she is still not ready to reconcile with her parents.

The official position of Islamic leadership in America for public consumption is that honor violence or killing is condemned in the Muslim community.

"Typically seen in the form of physical or emotional abuse, rape or kidnapping, honor violence also includes harmful practices such as female genital mutilation (FGM) and forced marriage," noted Stephanie Baric who serves as the executive director of the AHA Foundation, an organization founded by women's rights activist and FGM survivor Ayaan Hirsi Ali, and noted author of, *Infidel* (2006). "In extreme cases, murder" is sanctioned, Baric added.

"In sharp contrast with domestic violence, families and communities often condone honor violence, which makes it more difficult to identify and stop" (47).

Saba Ahmed, the Executive Director of the Republican Muslim Coalition in America, claims that such "barbaric acts" are in total conflict with the teachings of Islam (48). However, in truth, they are not. Although some Muslim scholars claim that honor killings are not mentioned in the Qur'an, they are enshrined in Islamic law.

When a person who has reached puberty and is sane voluntarily apostatizes from Islam, he deserves to be killed.

In such a case, it is obligatory for the caliph (A: or his representative) to ask him to repent and return to Islam. If he does, it is accepted from him, but if he refuses, he is immediately killed.
Reliance of the Traveller, o8.1-2

Honor violence or killings are not limited to any particular Muslim lifestyle or status in American or Western society. Even the highly respected—if they are strong adherents to Islamic law—can commit such heinous acts. Early in 2009, for instance, Muzzammil Hassan, a prosperous and highly respected businessman and founder of Bridges TV, murdered and then beheaded his wife. They lived in the affluent community of Orchard Park, a suburb of Buffalo, New York. His reason for his brutality: his wife had filed for divorce and requested an Order for Protection from him due to his repeated physical abuse. Ironically, Mr. Hassan had established his TV program to help dispel what he believed were stereotypical images of Muslims as terrorists and people of violence (49).

Once again, a Muslim apologist was quick to respond. Khalid J. Qazi, president of the Muslim Public Affairs Council of Western New York, put Islam's public face forward and stated: "There is no place for domestic violence in our religion—none. Islam would 100 percent condemn it" (50).

<u>Dig Deeper</u>. **Watch the award-winning *Honor Diaries* movie produced by Ayaan Hirsi Ali at: https://honordiaries.com.**

Murder

According to the *The Religion of Peace* website, (https://www.thereligionofpeace.com/pages/quran/violence.aspx), the Qur'an has at least 109 verses about war with non-believers or killing them. Unlike the Bible, where killing is related to a specific historical event, the commands to kill in the Qur'an are open-ended and apply to today as well.

If nothing else, Muslim leaders and their minions of followers are thin-skinned, unable to take any criticism or verbal assault on their beliefs. "No one has a right to criticize Islam or Islam's prophet" is their incessant mantra. However, they in turn can insult, demean, slander and say whatever they like when it comes to non-Muslims, whether they be Christians, Jews or infidels of any persuasion.

Before we explore Islamic teaching and the Muslim mindset on murder and its ramifications, let's look at a booklet that is held up as a classic in Islamic literature. In 1964, a celebrated Egyptian Muslim poet and novelist, Sayed (also spelled Syed or Sayyid) Qutb Shaheed, published his views on Islam and how to revive it in a screed titled,

Milestones.

In his Introduction Qutb begins:

> *Mankind today is on the brink of a precipice, not because of the danger of complete annihilation which is hanging over its head—this being just a symptom and not the real disease—but because humanity is devoid of those vital values which are necessary not only for its healthy development but also for its real progress. Even the Western world realises* [sic] *that Western civilization is unable to present any healthy values for the guidance of mankind. It knows that it does not possess anything which will satisfy its own conscience and justify its existence.*
>
> *Democracy in the West has become infertile to such an extent that it is borrowing from the systems of the Eastern bloc, especially in the economic system, under the name of socialism* (51).

Although this introduction brings forth an element of truth about the conditions in the West in the 1960s as well as today, it is Qutb's solutions later presented that should raise concerns for the West and the non-Islamic world.

In his first chapter, Qutb presents his case for the changing of the guard.

> *It is necessary for the new leadership to preserve and develop the material fruits of the creative genius of Europe, and also to provide mankind with such high ideals and values as have so far remained undiscovered by mankind, and which will also acquaint humanity with a way of life which is harmonious with human nature, which is positive and constructive, and which is practicable.*
>
> *Islam is the only system which possesses these values and this way of life* (52).

In light of what has been happening throughout Europe in the last decade-plus due to accelerated Muslim immigration, it is difficult to see Islam as the source of mankind's *high ideals and values* or that it presents *a way of life which is harmonious with human nature.* With the huge influx of millions of Muslims into European Union countries in the past decade, the primary benefits Europe has experienced are increased incidents of Islamic terrorism and a skyrocketing increase in sexual assaults on women.

> *Islam knows* [recognizes] *only two kinds of societies,* Qutb wrote, *the Islamic and the jahili* [pre-Islamic Arabian] (53).

Only Islam has the distinction of basing the fundamental binding relationship in its society on belief; and on the basis of this belief, black and white and red and yellow, Arabs and Greeks, Persians and Africans, and all nations which inhabit the earth become one community (54).

Milestones
by Syed Qutb Shaheed
1964

Syed was an Egyptian Islamist, author, educator and poet. The books [sic] *is presented here today because of Syed Qutb Shaheeds* [sic] *continuing influence on a number of currently active radical Islamist groups. Syed Qutb Shaheed was also the leading member of the Muslim Brotherhood in Egypt in the 1950s and 1960s. In 1966 he was convicted of plotting the assassination of Egyptian president Abdel Nasser and he was executed by hanging. His masterpiece is the 30 volume commentaries on the Qu'ran: In the Shade of the Qu'ran, which is mandatory bedtime reading for members of ISIS, Al-Qaeda, Islamic Jihad and similar groups. Milestones is one of his works on social justice and the role of Islam in politics. I post this book here, not to promote these views, but in order to help people to understand the ideology subscribed to by radical Islamist groups.*

Milestones is a modern classic works on social justice and the role of Islam in politics.

Source: https://www.holybooks.com/milestones-by-syed-qutb-shaheed/

So, how did Qutb suggest creating this utopian society of *fundamental binding relationship* into *one community?* As a devout Muslim, for Qutb, the solution was simple.

No political system or material power should put hindrances in the way of preaching Islam. It should leave every individual free to accept or reject it and if someone wants to accept it [Islam], *it should not prevent him or fight against him. If someone does this, then it is the duty of Islam to fight him until either he is killed or until he declares his submission* (55).

This sounds like the proverbial *my way or the highway* axiom. To create this great open Islamic society, Qutb recommends forcing everyone to be a part of it or die. Yet, *It should leave every individual free to accept or reject it . . .* This booklet would be nothing more than interesting and informative reading if it had been tossed on the dung heap of history. However, it is touted as an Islamic classic and promoted on the website of the North American Islamic Trust (NAIT). Who is the NAIT? NAIT, headquartered in Chicago, is the powerful Islamic financier for the Council on American-Islamic Relations (CAIR), the Islamic Society of North America (ISNA), the Muslim Student Association (MSA) and other Muslim Brotherhood associated groups across America (56). Founded in 1973 and heavily bankrolled by Saudi Arabia, NAIT also holds the title to over 300 mosques in the U.S., including some of America's largest.

Whoever intentionally kills a believer, his recompense shall be hell, abiding therein forever, and Allah shall be wroth with him, damn him, and ready for him a painful torment (Koran 4:93).
Whoever takes the life other than to retaliate for a killing or for corruption in the land is as if he had slain all mankind (Koran 5:32).
Reliance of the Traveller, p2.1(1-2)

As you will discover in Chapter 15, Qutb's position is reaffirmed in the Muslim Brotherhood manifesto or *An Explanatory Memorandum* for takeover operations in the United States.

Do not murder! The biblical admonition is simple enough but has been the subject of great debates and schisms in the Christian church since the day of Christ. Outside the context of the *just war* or self-defense, the majority of Christians around the world would agree that murder is a sinful act worthy of punishment according to biblical and/or societal laws.

To complicate this injunction, Jesus took it a major step forward. "You have heard that it was said to the people long ago, 'Do not murder, and anyone who murders will be subject to judgment.' But I tell you," Jesus declared, "that anyone who is angry with his brother will be subject to judgment" (**Matthew 5:21-22a**). Jesus is equating unrepentant anger with murder.

However, Jesus' teaching on this subject did not stop there either. Jesus called for and demanded a higher morality for His disciples.

> *You have heard that it was said, 'Eye for eye, and tooth for tooth'* [**Exodus 21:23-25**]. *But I tell you, Do not resist an evil person. If someone strikes you on the right cheek, turn to him the other also. And if someone wants to sue you and take your tunic, let him have your cloak as well. If someone forces you to go one mile, go with him two miles. Give to the one who asks you, and do not turn away from the one who wants to borrow from you* (**Matthew 5:38-42**).

Law of Retaliation (*Qisas*). Muslims reject this type of morality expressed by Jesus in the preceding scripture as simplistic and ludicrous. They completely subscribe to the pre-Christ barbarism of retaliatory vengeance of an eye-for-an-eye, life-for-a-life justice. God Almighty, through Jesus Christ, clearly repudiated such justice, calling mankind to a much higher level of responsibility and righteousness. Muhammad, in his form of castigating justice claimed to speak for the same god that Jesus represented. Obviously, he did not. God would not go back on His word and instruction that He cemented in place through His Son, Jesus.

Not only did God call the followers of Christ to reject *eye for eye* justice, but He called for the followers of His Son to reach for a higher level of response to those that attacked or persecuted them.

> *You have heard that it was said, 'Love your neighbor* [**Leviticus 19:18**] *and hate your enemy.' But I tell you: Love your enemies and pray for those who persecute you, that you may be sons of your Father in heaven. He causes his sun to rise on the evil and the good, and sends rain on the righteous and the unrighteous. If you love those who love you, what reward will you get? Are not even the tax collectors doing that? And if you greet only your brothers, what are you doing more than others? Do not even pagans do that? Be perfect, therefore, as your heavenly Father is perfect* (**Matthew 5:43-48**).

"And there is life for you in (the law of) retaliation, O men of understanding, that you may guard yourselves" (**Qur'an 2:179**). Muhammad subscribed to the ancient form of retaliatory justice as he revealed in **Qur'an 2:178**. "O you who believe! retaliation is prescribed for you in the matter of the slain; the free for the free, and the slave for the slave and the female for the female . . ." In the perverted form of justice that the Qur'an is noted for, one could not just go kill the murderous guilty party. If someone killed your slave, you would not necessarily go and kill the murderer. In the life-for-a-life mentality you more than likely kill one of his slaves—as innocent as he or she might be. The rest of **verse 178** also provides another "out" for the guilty party. If the murderer is a person of means, then he might offer the family of the one he murdered *blood money* as a form of restitution. ". . . but if any remission is made to any one by his (aggrieved) brother, then prosecution (for the bloodwit) [a fine or compensation for the killing of another] should be made according to usage, and payment should be made to him in a good manner . . ."

Although this seemed to follow the Old Testament admonition of an *eye for an eye* cited earlier, it certainly did not comply with the teaching of Jesus, but rather reversed God's plan of redemptive justice.

Qur'an 5:45 and **17:33** makes it clear that it is Allah that gives the permission for retaliatory killing and maiming.

And We prescribed to them in it that life is for life, and eye for eye, and nose for nose, and ear for ear, and tooth for tooth, and (that there is) reprisal in wounds; but he who forgoes it, it shall be an expiation for him; and whoever did not judge by what Allah revealed, those are they that are the unjust (**Qur'an 5:45**).

And do not kill any one whom Allah has forbidden, except for a just cause, and whoever is slain unjustly, We have indeed given to his heir authority [to retaliate], so let him not exceed the just limits in slaying; surely he is aided (**Qur'an 17:33**).

According to Allah, it is okay to take vengeance, but do not take it too far and kill too many. But what about suicide bombers who take innocent life indiscriminately? That type of mass murder, as described previously, falls under the privilege and grace of *jihad*. As it has been pointed out before in the Qur'an and hadith, Jews, Christians, pagans and apostates fall into a special unprotected class of past, current and future victims known as *infidels*—all those who refuse to accept Islam as the only way of life. Here, there is no justice for this Islamic prey under the commands of jihad. The *mujahidin* or holy warriors are free to take life wherever, whenever and of whomever they please without clear cause or respect for the innocent—whether female, child or otherwise.

The Law of Retaliation is also operative during the "sacred months" (i.e. Ramadan).

The Sacred month for the sacred month and all things are (under the law of) retaliation; whoever then acts aggressively against you, inflict injury on him according to the injury he has inflicted on you and be careful (of your duty) to Allah and know that Allah is with those who guard (against evil) (**Qur'an 2:194**).

"There are six things the LORD hates," King Solomon related, "seven that are detestable to him: haughty eyes, a lying tongue, **hands that shed innocent blood**, a heart that devises wicked schemes, feet that are **quick to rush into evil**, a false witness who pours out lies and a man who stirs up dissension among brothers" (**Proverbs 6:16-19**, author's emphasis).

The prophet Isaiah also is quick to reaffirm God's abhorrence of the shedding of innocent blood. "Their feet rush into sin; they are swift to shed innocent blood. Their thoughts are evil thoughts; ruin and destruction mark their ways. The way of peace they do not know; there is no justice in their paths. They have turned them into crooked roads; no one who walks

194

in them will know peace" (**Isaiah 59:7-8**). Isaiah's words, spoken some 27 centuries ago, might just as well have been directed at today's jihadists, as well as the Muslim clerics and Islamic faithful who remain silent or cheer the mujahidin on in their bloodshed.

God Almighty, the only true God of justice would have this to say: "When you spread out your hands in prayer, I will hide my eyes from you; even if you offer many prayers, I will not listen. Your hands are full of blood; wash and make yourselves clean. Take your evil deeds out of my sight! Stop doing wrong, learn to do right! Seek justice, encourage the oppressed. Defend the cause of the fatherless, plead the case of the widow" (**Isaiah 1:15-17**). Allah apparently has no such reservations about hearing the prayers of his faithful murderers killing in the *cause of Allah*.

Taqiyya: Lying & Deceit

Taqiyya, or lying and deception, is one of the most important teachings and concepts of Islam that non-Muslims need to grasp and understand. *Taqiyya* can, and often does, affect much of the communication and understanding between Muslims and non-Muslims or infidels, especially in the West, where Muslims may be in the minority.

Lying and deception starts with the numerous English translations of the Qur'an that are published by Islamic translators for politically correct consumption by non-Muslims and non-Arabic speakers.

Allah is the Best Deceiver. According to wikiislam.net, just about all of the English translations of Qur'an deliberately mistranslate the Arabic word, *makr*, to mean "planner" or "plotter."

The correct translation of *makr* or *makir* is not "planner" or "plotter" but "deception" or "schemer" (https://wikiislam.net/wiki/Allah_the_Best_Deceiver).

For example, in **Qur'an 3:54**, "And they [the Jews] planned and Allah (also) planned, and Allah is the best of planners." According to Sam Shamoun, a native of Kuwait, who immigrated to the United States with his parents, and is a renowned Christian apologist who writes articles frequently for http://answering-islam.org, Islamic scholars purposely mistranslate this verse and many others in the Qur'an. A verse such as this should correctly read: "And they *were deceptive* and Allah (also) *was deceptive*, and Allah is the best of *deceivers*."

. . . makir is never used in a positive sense—it denotes a shifty, sly person who uses deception as a means to their ends.

We see that most of the translators have taken makir (with one of its possible translations 'scheme') to mean 'a systematic plan of action', and have translated makir to mean 'planner' or 'plotter'.

However this completely disregards the accepted connotations of the word and the context of the given verses. Makir does not mean planner. Just because makir can be translated as scheme, and scheme can mean plan/plot, this does not mean that you can translate makir as planner/plotter. This is dishonesty on the part of those translators.

https://wikiislam.net/wiki/Allah_the_Best_Deceiver#Deceptive_

Translators

"*Taqiyya*—lying, or dissimulation—is not only condoned, it is recommended to Muslims in their scripture. Hence a Muslim can and would lie without any compunction, whenever it is expedient" (57).

Another deceptive translation of a Qur'anic verse occurs in **Qur'an 8:30**, which reads: "And when those who disbelieved devised plans against you that they might confine you or slay you or drive you away; and they devised plans and Allah too had arranged a plan; and Allah is the best of planners."

Again, the accurate translation according to Shamoun and https://wikiislam.net/wiki/Allah_the_Best_Deceiver, would be: "And when those who disbelieved devised *schemes* [evil plans] against you [i.e., Muhammad] that they might confine you or slay you or drive you away; and they *schemed* and Allah too had arranged a *scheme*; and Allah is the best of *schemers/deceivers*."

Writing for Arutz Sheva 7 (television) and Israel National News, Rochel Sylvetsky wrote, ". . . western concepts of truth do not exist in the Muslim world. It sometimes seems that America is being brainwashed for the kill" (58).

So you can see we were not preaching with any deceit or impure motives or trickery. For we speak as messengers approved by God to be entrusted with the Good News. Our purpose is to please God, not people. He alone examines the motives of our hearts.

1 Thessalonians 2:3-4; NLT

Another verse, **Qur'an 4:142**, also brings out the deceptive nature of Allah. "Surely the hypocrites strive to deceive Allah, and He shall requite [turn back to them] their deceit to them. . ." In this verse, it depicts Allah as one who uses deception in order to get back at those who are non-believers.

One of the most revealing scriptures in the Qur'an is **Qur'an 7:182-183**, which authorizes Allah's followers to deceive non-believers. "And (as to) those who reject Our communications, We draw them near (to destruction) by degrees [of deception] from whence they know not.

And I grant them respite [a short period of rest]; surely My scheme [deception] is effective." This concept of deceiving non-believers is practiced with abandon in the West and in the United States in order to deceive politicians, the media, church leaders, educators and the public in order to strengthen the Islamic position and power.

Our analysis, noted Shamoun, *has shown that Muhammad's deity is a deceiver who cannot be trusted since he lies without hesitation.*

A Muslim may contend that Allah only deceives unbelievers who deserve it. The problem with this assertion is that the Muslim scripture teaches that Allah doesn't merely deceive unbelievers but also his followers (59).

We reject all shameful deeds and underhanded methods. We don't try to trick anyone or distort the word of God. We tell the truth before God, and all who are honest know this   Satan, who is the god of this world, has blinded the minds of those who don't believe. They are unable to see the glorious light of the Good News. They don't understand this message about the glory of Christ, who is the exact likeness of God.

2 Corinthians 4:2, 4; NLT

Another deceptive ploy of Allah is that he deliberately leads people astray. According to **Qur'an 4:88** and **14:4**, it pleases Allah to lead people astray and if he wants to lead people astray, Muslims are forbidden to guide them on the right path. Thus, in the name of Allah, Muslims are commissioned, to lead non-believers down the wrong path in order to deceive them about Allah's true mission.

Westerners, especially those brought up in the Judeo-Christians faiths, are taught to speak the truth and therefore cherish honest communication and relationships built on trust. The saying, "a man's word is his bond," means a lot to most in Western society.

"Truth should never be sacrificed at the altar of any goal," wrote Iranian immigrant, Amil Imani, "We firmly believe that truthfulness is indeed the foundation of all virtues" (60).

Islam's, and a Muslim's rational for lying and using deception, rest on one's goals and objectives. According to the *Reliance of the Traveller* (r8.2), there are three things or conditions in which one can lie: war; settling disagreements and in husband and wife communications. The concept of deception in war is not uncommon throughout the world. Deception is a common battleground strategy employed by military leaders everywhere. However, Muslims take this strategy to a different level and understanding. When Muslims are in a non-Muslim country or in the minority, they consider themselves, per Allah's admonition, "to be at war." Therefore, lying and deception is not only permissible, but exemplary.

What! Do they then feel secure from Allah's plan [deception]*? But none feels secure from Allah's plan* [deception] *except the people who shall perish.*

Qur'an 7:99

The rational for lying and deception disclosed in the *ROT,* r8.2 is that "Speaking is a means to achieve objectives." To achieve an objective, it is therefore permissible to lie.

If a praiseworthy aim is attainable through both telling the truth and lying, it is unlawful to accomplish through lying because there is no need for it. When it is possible to achieve such an aim by lying but not by telling the truth, it is permissible to lie if attaining the goal is permissible (Reliance of the Traveller, r8.2).

It is further stated, in the same section, that it is "obligatory to lie if the goal is obligatory." Well, what is the obligatory goal of every Muslim according to the Qur'an and every imam—to war in the Cause of Allah until the whole earth is submitted to Islam.

Whether the purpose is war, settling a disagreement, or gaining the sympathy of a victim legally entitled to retaliate against one so that he will forbear to do so; it is not unlawful to lie when any of these aims can only be attained through lying. But it is religiously more precautionary . . . in all such cases to employ words that give a misleading impression, meaning to intend by one's words something that is literally true, in respect to which one is not lying . . ., while the outward purport of the words deceives the hearer, though even if one does not have such an intention and merely lies without intending anything else, it is not unlawful in the above circumstances.
. . . One should compare the bad consequences entailed by lying to those entailed by telling the truth, and if the consequences of telling the truth are more damaging, one is entitled to lie, though the reverse is true or if one does not know which entails more damage, then lying is unlawful (ROT, r8.2).

Who is the Deceiver and Master of Lies according to Jesus? "You [those who claim to be descendants of Abraham] belong to your father,

198

the devil, and you want to carry out your father's desires. He was a murderer from the beginning, not holding to the truth, for there is no truth in him. When he lies, he speaks his native language, for he is a liar and the father of lies" (**John 8:44**).

On the other hand, the writer to the Hebrews clearly stated, "God did this [fulfilled His promise to Abraham through Jesus Christ] so that, by two unchangeable things in which it is impossible for God to lie, we who have fled to take hold of the hope set before us may be greatly encouraged" (**Hebrews 6:18**). Unlike Allah, the God of the Jews and Christians cannot lie and cannot deceive, He is a speaker of truth and the fulfiller of His promises.

Masters of Deceit and Lying. While Muslims worldwide will vehemently deny it, the truth is that Muslims, in general, are masters of deceit and lying, and the teachings of their holy prophet condone and encourage it. "Do not give false testimony," Jesus taught His followers (**Matthew 19:18**). At first glance, it would appear that the command of Allah in the Quran would agree: "And do not mix up the truth with the falsehood, nor hide the truth while you know it" (**Qur'an 2:42**). However, the reality and practice of Muslims is much different in both the historic past and the present.

Honesty and truthfulness have been the hallmarks of much of Western society—especially those based in a Judeo-Christian foundation—for two millennia. "However, unlike most religions," author Abdullah Al Araby wrote, "within Islam there are certain provisions under which lying is not simply tolerated, but actually encouraged" (61). It may be hard for a Westerner to fathom the practice of habitual lying and deceit, but for the Muslim it is easy—especially before an infidel or in a non-Muslim country—to proclaim that "black" is "white" or that "darkness" is "light" or that a "lie" is "truth." Deception and lies roll off some Muslim tongues like some harmless platitude.

The Western world still does not seem to accept this presentation of reality as their diplomats enter into one "agreement" after another with Muslims in the Middle East and elsewhere, accepting their lies as the truth. Relying on or trusting a Muslim to tell the truth when your well-being depends on it, is sort of like trusting that the twenty-foot high bulging, seeping earthen dam you are standing under will not break during the deluge you are witnessing. Even when Muslims are caught in the act of lying, most will deny culpability. They will even go to the extreme of venting anger at your accusations to the point where you begin to believe they must be telling the truth since their passion of resentment has risen so high. Even the taking of an oath in a court of law can come to naught if a Muslim looks to the Qur'an for guidance. "Allah does not call you to account for what is vain [worthless] in your oaths, but He will call you to account for what your hearts have earned. . ." (**Qur'an 2:225**). A Muslim can lie under oath and have a clear conscience as long as he believes he was doing it for the cause of Allah.

"There is only cursing [that is to pronounce a curse upon someone], lying and murder, stealing and adultery [says the Lord]; they break all bounds, and bloodshed follows bloodshed. Because of this the land mourns [dries up] and all who live in it waste away; the beasts of the field and the birds of the air and the fish of the sea are dying" (**Hosea 4:2-3**).

Lying *about* Allah or Muhammad is forbidden and a grievous sin or enormity [*Reliance of the Traveller*, w52.1(49)]. "A lie about me [Muhammad] is not the same as a lie about someone else: whoever intentionally lies about me shall take a place for himself in hell" [(*Reliance of the Traveller*, p9.2(1)].

However, a Muslim can deny Allah if one's life depends on it; but cannot lie *about* Allah. "And who is more unjust than he who forges a lie against Allah," Muhammad revealed in **Qur'an 6:93**, "or says: It has been revealed to me; while nothing has been revealed to him . . . Give up your souls; today shall you be recompensed with an ignominious chastisement because you spoke against Allah other than the truth . . ."

Lying was acceptable to Muhammad, unless you were lying about him. "I heard the Prophet saying, 'Ascribing false things to me is not like ascribing false things to anyone else. Whoever tells a lie against me intentionally then surely let him occupy his seat in Hell-fire'" (**hadith 2:378**).

But Muhammad also said: "He who makes peace between the people by inventing good information or saying good things [though they be lies], is not a liar" (**hadith 3:857**).

As in the *Reliance of the Traveller*, **hadith 32:6303** of Sahih, Muslims are given permission to lie under three circumstances: 1) In the heat of battle; 2) in an effort to bring reconciliation between persons and 3) in the communication between a husband and wife if it brings about a resolution. Other Islamic traditions support telling lies if it is to save one's life; bring about peace or settlement between peoples; influence a woman or when a Muslim is on a journey or mission (62).

"Muslims believe that war means deception," acknowledged Qur'an scholar and former Muslim, Mark Gabriel, "so lying is an important element of war in Islam   it's OK to lie to non-Muslims to protect yourself when you are a minority in their country" (63). Muhammad routinely practiced deception during his military campaigns. "When the Prophet   intended to go on an expedition [of war], he always pretended to be going somewhere else, and he would say: 'War is deception'" (Dawud **hadith 14:2631**). Muhammad's practice of deception did not stop there. He advocated lying when it came to deceiving his enemies. A long hadith of Bukhari (**5:59:369**) describes Muhammad's permission for one of his cohorts, Muhammad bin Maslama, to use a lie so that Maslama could deceive an opponent of Muhammad's and kill him. "There is deceit in the hearts of those who plot evil, but joy for those who promote peace" (**Proverbs 12:20**).

According to Al Araby, ". . . Muslims' unintentional lies are forgivable and that even their intentional lies can be absolved by performing extra duties, . . . Muslims can lie while under oath and can even falsely deny faith in Allah, as long as they maintain the profession of faith in their hearts" (64). Christians, on the other hand, cannot deny their faith in Christ, not even under persecution or the threat of death. "Whoever acknowledges me before men," Jesus shared with His followers, "I will also acknowledge him before my Father in heaven. But whoever disowns me before men, I will disown him before my Father in heaven" (**Matthew 10:32-33**).

"'These *are* the things you shall do:'" God revealed to the prophet Zechariah, "'Speak each man the truth to his neighbor; give judgment in your gates for truth, justice, and peace; let none of you think evil in your heart against your neighbor; and do not love a false oath. For all these *are things* that I hate,' Says the LORD" (**Zechariah 8:16-17**, NKJV).

Unfortunately, this one permissible characteristic of the Islamic faithful makes it extremely difficult for people in the West to trust Muslims at almost any level because one can never know for sure if the truth is being told, or a lie is being perpetrated on the unsuspecting listener.

Lying and deceit are primary tools of the devil. Forget not, that ". . . lying and deceit are a part of the Islamic mind-set," warned Gabriel (65). To which the Apostle John would add: "Many deceivers, who do not acknowledge Jesus Christ as coming in the flesh, have gone out into the world. Any such person is the deceiver and the antichrist" (**2 John 7**).

Jesus said to them, "If God were your Father, you would love me, for I came from God and now am here. I have not come on my own; but he sent me. Why is my language not clear to you? Because you are unable to hear what I say. You belong to your father, the devil, and you want to carry out your father's desire. He was a murderer from the beginning, not holding to the truth, for there is no truth in him. When he lies, he speaks his native language, for he is a liar and the father of lies. Yet because I tell the truth, you do not believe me! Can any of you prove me guilty of sin? If I am telling the truth, why don't you believe me? He who belongs to God hears what God says. The reason you do not hear is that you do not belong to God (**John 8:42-47**).

Chapter Conclusion

Muhammad was not a man of high integrity and morality. He was not a righteous man after God's own heart like Noah, Abraham, David or Jesus. He was a sin-laden man in need of repentance and forgiveness for his multitude of sins against God and mankind. He was an opportunist that took advantage of the pagan lifestyle and morals of his day. Although he presented a moralistic law to offset pagan beliefs, his own self-serving way of life was no better than the murderous tribal chiefs of the Arabian Peninsula. He did not improve upon God's revelation that came through Jesus Christ. Instead, he denied the truth and moral code of conduct that was sent by God through Jesus and the Jewish prophets, making a mockery out of the Ten Commandments and all that Jesus Christ stood for and taught.

His personal lifestyle, while proclaimed by Muslims for fourteen centuries as exemplary, was anything but a model for those that seek the truth of God. Muhammad's example of murderous escapades has carried through the centuries and into the 21st century with Islamic terrorist groups like al-Qaida, Boko Haram and the Islamic State mimicking and extolling his example as a pattern for all true Muslims.

Lying, although despicable in most cultures, takes on a whole new meaning in Islam. Lying and deception are not only permissible, but obligatory when dealing with the perceived enemies of Allah. Since all non-Muslims are considered to be enemies of Allah and therefore adversaries of all Muslims, it makes it very difficult for non-Muslims to trust Muslims and their real motivations.

References

1. Gauss, James F. *Evil is Good.* Blog post, November 8, 2012. Source: https://ampatriot.wordpress.com/2012/11/08/evil-is-good/
2. Gauss, James F. *How Evil Works and Prevails.* Blog post, September 5, 2014. Source: https://ampatriot.wordpress.com/2014/09/05/how-evil-works-prevails/
3. Ibid.
4. Imani, Amil. *Islam: An Exclusive Fraternity for Men*, Geller Report, September 7, 2018.
5. Ibid.
6. Ibid.
7. Ibid.
8. Westrop, Sam. *Hardline Islamic Cleric to start U.S. Speaking Tour*, April 6, 2018. Source: https://www.rabwah.net/hardline-islamic-cleric-to-start-u-s- speaking-tour/

9. Ehrenfeld, Rachel. *Muslim scholar in Toronto: Wife should be obedient to her husband, lick his wounds, pus. . .* American Center for Democracy, December 20, 2018. Source: http://news.acdemocracy. org/muslim-scholar-visiting-toronto-wife-should-be-obedient-to-her-husband-lick-his-wounds-pus/

10. Almahdy, Dr. Saleem. *Islam Q & A, The Voice of the Martyrs*, April, 2002.

11. Imani, Amil. *Islam: An Exclusive Fraternity for Men.*

12. Ibrahim, Raymond. *Islamic Scholar: Muslims Can Rape "Legitimately-Owned Slaves,"* PJ Media, February 8, 2016. Source: https://www. meforum.org/ articles/2016/islamic-scholar-muslims-can-rape-legitimately-ow (Accessed Sept. 11, 2018).

13. Ibrahim, Raymond. *The Muslim Man's Sexual "Rights" Over Non-Muslim Women*, February 11, 2016. Source: https://www. raymondibrahim.com/ 2016/02/11/the-muslim-mans-sexual-rights-over-non-muslim-women/ (accessed November 1, 2018).

14. Hale, Virginia. *Revealed: 1,000-man mob attack police, set Germany's oldest church alight on New Year's Eve*, Breitbart, January 3, 2017. Source: https://www.breitbart.com/europe/2017/01/03/dortmund-mob-attack-police-church-alight/

15. Ibrahim, Raymond. *The Muslim Man's Sexual "Rights" Over Non-Muslim Women.*

16. Ibid.

17. Geller, Pamela. *Muslims GANG-RAPE Christian teen girl, "you are a Christian women and it's your punishment to be a Christian"*, Geller Report, August 20, 2018. Source: https://gellerreport.com/2018/08/ muslim-gang-rape-christian-teen.html/ (accessed November 1, 2018).

18. *Sweden invests millions to teach migrants how to have sex 'with blonde women'.* Voice of Europe, July 21, 2018. Source: https:// voiceofeurope.com/2018/07/sweden-invests-millions-to-teach-migrants-how-to-have-sex-with-blonde-women/ (accessed Sept. 8, 2018).

19. Spencer, Robert. *UK: Muslim convicted pedophile claims he didn't know sex with 14-year-olds was illegal*, January 20, 2018. Source: https://www. jihadwatch.org/2018/01/ uk-muslim-convicted-pedophile-claims-he-didnt-know-sex-with-14-year-olds-was-illegal (accessed November 4, 2018).

20. Wynne-Jones, Jonathan. *Multiple wives will mean multiple benefits.* The Telegraph, February 3, 2008. Source: https://www.telegraph.co.uk/ news/politics/1577395/Multiple-wives-will-mean-multiple-benefits.html

21. Spencer, Robert. *The Truth About Muhammad, Founder of the World's Most Intolerant Religion*, pp. 170-171.

22. *Muhammad's Wives.* Wikipedia. Source: http://en.wikipedia.org/ wiki/Muhammad%27s_marriages (accessed August 17, 2007).

23. Caner & Caner, p.59.

24. *Detail of Marriages of Prophet.* http://www.answering-christianity.com/ wives.htm (accessed February 1, 2007).

25. Caner & Caner, p.56.

26. *Muhammad's Wives.*

27. *Detail of Marriages of Prophet.*

28. Caner & Caner, p.56.
29. *Muhammad's Wives.*
30. *Detail of Marriages of Prophet.*
31. Spencer, Robert. *The Truth About Muhammad, Founder of the World's Most Intolerant Religion*, pp. 59-60
32. Caner & Caner, p. 56.
33. *Muhammad's Wives.*
34. *Detail of Marriages of Prophet*
35. Sanya, Agunbiade. *Your husband is meant to be shared with other women – Muslim cleric.* Lailas News, December 17, 2018. Source: https://lailasnews.com/your-husband-is-meant-to-be-shared-with-other-women-muslim-cleric/
36. Zaidi, Supna. *Does Islam Justify Honor Killings?* Pajamas Media, September 27, 2008. Source: https://www.meforum.org/articles/2008/does-islam-justify-honor-killings (accessed November 7, 2018).
37. Geller, Pamela. *5,500 Reports of Honor Attacks This Year in UK; Thousands of Others Unreported.* Atlas Shrugs, September 29, 2011 (web address no longer exists).
38. Helba Ph.D., Cynthia, Matthew Bernstein, Mariel Leonard and Erin Bauer. *Report on Exploratory Study into Honor Violence Measurement Methods* (draft). U.S. Bureau of Justice Statistics, November 26, 2014.
39. Ibid.
40. Bingham, John. *Hidden tide of 'honour' violence in Britain's communities.* Telegraph, December 28, 2011. Source: https://www.telegraph.co.uk/ news/uknews/crime/8961352/ Hidden-tide-of-honour-violence-in-Britains-communities.html (accessed November 9, 2018).
41. Talwar, Divya and Athar Ahmad. *'Honour crime': 11,000 UK cases recorded in five years.* BBC News, July 9, 2015. Source: https://www.bbc.com/news/uk-33424644 (accessed November 9, 2018).
42. Margolis, Hillary. *EU Getting Serious About Violence Against Women.* Human Rights Watch, May 12, 2017. Source: https://www.hrw.org/ news/2017/05/12/eu-getting-serious-about-violence-against-women (accessed November 9, 2018).
43. Sylvetsky, Rochel. *Honor killing – coming to a neighborhood near you.* Arutz Sheva 7, Israel National News, September 2, 2018. Source: https://www.israelnationalnews.com/ Articles/Article.aspx/22686
44. McKay, Hollie. *Honor Killing in America: DOJ report says growing problem is hidden in stats*, Fox News, May 3, 2016. Source: https://www.foxnews.com/us/honor-killing-in-america-doj-report-says-growing-problem-is-hidden-in-stats (accessed November 8, 2018).
45. Hurd, Dale. *Christian Girl Says Her Muslim Family Will Kill Her*, CBN News, August 11, 2009.
46. Cherney, Elyssa. *Rifqa Bary tells of molestation, DCF woes and Christian faith in new book*, Orlando Sentinel, May 17, 2015. Source: http://www.orlandosentinel.com/news/ local/os-rifqa-bary-islam-book-20150516-story.html (accessed December 20, 2018).
47. McKay, Hollie.

48. Ibid.
49. Williams, Fred O. and Gene Warner. *Orchard Park businessman charged in beheading of wife*, The Buffalo News, February 14, 2009. Source: Web link no longer available.
50. Ibid.
51. Qutb, Sayed. *Milestones*, 1964, p.3 (Reprinted in 2006 by Islamic Book Service).
52. Ibid, pp. 3-4.
53. Ibid, p. 75.
54. Ibid, p. 77.
55. Ibid, p. 43.
56. *Custodian of U.S. mosques promotes slaying Americans NAIT: 'It is the duty of Islam to fight him until he is killed'*. WorldNetDaily, March 7, 2010. Source: https://www.wnd.com/ 2010/03/127262/
57. Imani, Amil. *Can a Muslim be a Loyal American?* Geller Report, September 18, 2018. Source: https://gellerreport.com/2018/09/muslim-loyal-american.html/
58. Sylvetsky, Rochel.
59. Shamoun, Sam. *Allah – the Greatest Deceiver of them All*. Answering-Islam.org. Source: https://answering-islam.org/Shamoun/allah_best_deceiver.htmlImani, Amil. *Islam contra the West: Surrender is not an option*. American Thinker, April 29, 2018. Source: https://www.americanthinker.com/blog/ 2018/04/islam_contra_the_west_surrender_is_not_an_option.html#ixzz5E5IWVf8H
60. Al Araby, Abddullah, *Lying in Islam*. IslamReview.com. Source: http://www.islamreview. com/articles/lying.htm. Accessed November 11, 2006.
61. *Lying*. Answering-Islam.com. Source: http://answering-islam.org. uk/Index/ L/lying.html (accessed November 2, 2005).
62. Gabriel, Mark A. *Islam and Terrorism*, 2002. Published by FrontLine, a Strang Company, p. 91.
63. Al Araby.
64. Gabriel, p. 92

Chapter 8

God of Love vs. Allah of Hate

For God so loved the world that he gave his one and only Son,
that whoever believes in him shall not perish but have eternal life.

John 3:16

The concept of a god of unconditional love is alien to the Qur'an and the Muslim world. At best, Allah is portrayed as a god whose love is conditional. ". . . Allah loves those who fight in His way . . .," Muhammad revealed (**Qur'an 61:4**). Or, "Surely (as for) those who believe and do good deeds for them will Allah bring about love" (**Qur'an 19:96**).

The Bible, both the Old Testament and the New Testament, has much to say about love. Depending on which translation of the Bible you consult, there are between 442 (King James Version), 686 (New International Version) and 763 verses (New Living Translation) on the subject of love. The vast majority deal with God's love for man, man's love for God or man's command to love others (both believers and non-believers).

The Qur'an has little to say about love—Allah's unconditional love for all people; instructions on loving the non-believer, etc. According to Quora.com (1), an Islamic site that answers questions about Islam, an Iraqi Muslim, Baraa AlChalabi, claims there are 84 verses in the Qur'an that use the term "love" in one of three Arabic forms. However, another Muslim from Egypt, Bassel Elgohary Helal, proclaimed that the word "love" is used 190 times in the Qur'an and he cites the verses. On the other hand, Farid Malhally, discovered that the Qur'an only uses the variants of the word "love" (*hubb*) 69 times (2) and compares that to just one scripture quote from **1 John 4:7-21** which mentions "love" 27 times.

Upon looking up the verses that Helal cited in the version of the Qur'an used for this study, this author could only find 56 verses that used some form of the word "love." Of the verses cited by Helal, 23 did not use the word "love" in any form in the verse, nor was the concept of love addressed. At least another 32 verses stated clearly what Allah did not love. One verse mentions Allah's love for Moses. Seven verses warn about the love of wealth or the things of this world. Another verse states that Abraham did not love the setting stars and one that refers to man's love for a woman.

Only a few verses mention "Allah's love" for believers. "If you love Allah," Muhammad states, "then follow me, Allah will love you and forgive you your faults . . ." (**Qur'an 3:31**). Or in **Qur'an 3:76**: "Yea, whoever fulfills his promise and guards (against evil)—then surely Allah loves those who guard against evil." Allah also loves believers who do good works (**Qur'an 3:134**).

Only one verse addresses the idea of loving your neighbor: "Lo! You are they who will love them while they do not love you . . . (**Qur'an 3:119**). However, the verse right before it says, ". . . do not take for intimate friends from among others than your own people . . . (**Qur'an 3:118**).

What Allah Does Not Love. The Qur'an clearly states that Allah hates the sinner. "And fight in the way of Allah with those who fight with you, and do not exceed the limits, surely Allah does not love those who exceed the limits" [that is, those who are transgressors or sinners] (**Qur'an 2:190**). In **verse 276** of the same surah, it states, ". . . Allah does not love any ungrateful sinner." Nor does Allah love the unjust (**Qur'an 3:140**). Note that Allah not only hates the sin but he hates the sinner also.

Allah does not love:

- aggressors (**Qur'an 2:190**;
- unbelievers (**Qur'an 3:32; 30:45**);
- the unjust; the evildoers (**Qur'an 3:57, 140; 42:40**);
- the unfaithful (**Qur'an 22:38**);
- the mischief makers (**Qur'an 5:64**);
- those who act corruptly (**Qur'an 2:205; 28:77**);
- those who deny the truth (**Qur'an 3:32**);
- those who are proud or boastful; exultant (**Qur'an 4:36; 16:23; 28:76; 31:18; 57:23**);
- those who are not trustworthy (**Qur'an 4:107**);
- those who do not do what is right; exceed the limits (**Qur'an 5:87; 7:55**);
- those who are wasteful; the extravagant (**Qur'an 6:141; 7:31**);
- those who commit treachery (**Qur'an 4:107; 8:58**);
- those who are arrogant (**Qur'an 16:23**);
- those who betray his trust or are unthankful (**Qur'an 22:38**);
- and he certainly does not love those who worship idols instead of him (**Qur'an 2:165**);
- or those that love riches (**Qur'an 89:20; 100:8**);
- those who are sinful (**Qur'an 4:102**)

In that list of whom Allah does not love, it would be hard for anyone to see themselves passing Allah's test of acceptance—even the most devout Muslim.

Dig Deeper. **Go to the site, https://www.quora.com/How-many-times-does-the-word-Love-appear-in-the-Quran and look up the cited Qur'an verses on love and categorize them by topic.**

What or whom does Allah love? Apparently, Allah has little love to spare. Allah loves only those who do (unspecified) good (**Qur'an 2:195; 3:148; 5:13, 93; 19:96**), those who repent (**Qur'an 2:222**), those who somehow keep themselves pure or purify themselves (**Qur'an 2:222; 9:108**), are patient in adversity (**Qur'an 3:146**), those who trust in him (**Qur'an 3:159**), are careful of their duty to [or conscious of] him (**Qur'an 9:4, 7**), or those who act rightly (**Qur'an 49:9; 60:8**). The only way to be assured of Allah's love is to fight for him. "Surely Allah loves those who fight in His way . . .," Muhammad revealed in **Qur'an 61:4**.

Malhally points out that there are ten types of people that Allah loves (3).

- Allah loves those who do good (**Qur'an 2:195; 3:134, 148; 5:14, 96**);
- Allah loves the pure and clean (**Qur'an 2:222; 9:108**);
- Allah loves those who are righteous (**Qur'an 3:76; 9:4, 7; 19:96**). It is interesting that sandwiched in between the thoughts on righteousness is the infamous **Qur'an 9:5** where Allah calls for his followers to "slay the idolaters wherever you find them, and take them captives and besiege them and lie in wait for them in every ambush . . ."
- Allah loves those who are just and judge rightly (**Qur'an 5:45; 49:9; 60:8**);
- Allah loves those who trust him (**Qur'an 3:159**);
- Allah loves those who persevere and are patient (**Qur'an 3:146**);
- Allah loves those who love him and follow the Prophet (**Qur'an 3:31**);
- Allah will produce a people he can love (**Qur'an 5:57**);
- Allah loved Moses (**Qur'an 20:39**);
- Allah loves those who fight for his cause (**Qur'an 61:4**).

> *Allah is exalted and pleased as he sends people to hell:*
> *this is the fatalistic claim of Islam.*
> Ergun Mehmet Caner and Emir Fethi Caner
> *Unveiling Islam*, 2002, p. 31

Qur'an 11:90 implies that repentance *might* bring about Allah's love. "And ask forgiveness of your Lord, then turn to Him; surely my Lord is Merciful, Loving-Kind." While this verse implies that Allah is a source of love, it does not assure the believer that Allah will freely give his love to the repentant believer. The verse also seems to imply that Muhammad has special favor with Allah ("my Lord"). However, do other Muslim believers have favor with Allah in receiving his love?

The Apostle Paul, in his letter to the Roman church stated, "for all have sinned and fall short of the glory of God" (**Romans 3:23**). However, Paul followed this obvious factual statement with one of the most amazing and glorious verses in the Bible. "But God demonstrates his own love for us in this: While we were still sinners, Christ died for us" (**Romans 5:8**).

Think about that for a minute, and let it sink into your spirit. Unlike Allah, who makes it clear that he does not love sinners, the Judeo-Christian God, the Father of Jesus Christ, loves us—every sinner, including every Muslim—while we were still entrenched in our sins. God so loved His human creation that He could not and would not leave us trapped in our sinful condition. He has a plan of redemption; a plan of salvation through His One and Only Son, Jesus Christ. Allah has no such plan of redemption and salvation—Allah desires to save no one.

"Since we have now been justified by his [Christ's] blood," Paul continued, "how much more shall we be saved from God's wrath through him! For if, while we were God's enemies, we were reconciled to him through the death of his Son, how much more, having been reconciled, shall we be saved through his life! Not only is this so, but we also boast in God through our Lord Jesus Christ, through whom we have now received reconciliation" (**Romans 5:9-11**).

"Therefore," Paul summarized, "just as sin entered the world through one man [Adam], and death through sin, and in this way death came to all people, because all sinned" (**Romans 5:12**).

Unlike Allah, who condemns sinners and those who reject him, the God of the Bible offers every sinner a way back to Him through the shed blood of His Son, Jesus Christ.

In fact, according to Allah in **Qur'an 19:68-72**, no one initially goes to heaven, but everyone goes to hell along with the evil spirits.

So by your Lord! We will most certainly gather them together and the Shaitans [evil spirits], *then shall We certainly cause them to be present round hell on their knees.*

Then We will most certainly draw forth from every sect of them him who is most exorbitantly rebellious against the Beneficent God.

Again We do certainly know best those who deserve most to be burned therein.

*And there is **not one of you but shall come to it** [hell]; **this is an unavoidable decree** of your Lord.*

And We will deliver those who guarded (against evil), and We will leave the unjust therein on their knees (author's emphasis).

This is not very encouraging for those who chose to follow Allah or are forced to do so. More on this topic will be presented in Chapter 10.

In the Gospel of John, Jesus expands on the concept of the shepherd who makes sacrifices for his sheep and who goes after those who are not yet in the fold.

I am the good shepherd, Jesus says. *The good shepherd lays down his life for the sheep. The hired hand is not the shepherd who owns the sheep. So when he sees the wolf coming, he abandons the sheep and runs away. Then the wolf attacks the flock and scatters it. The man runs away because he is a hired hand and cares nothing for the sheep.*

I am the good shepherd; I know my sheep and my sheep know me – just as the Father knows me and I know the Father – and I lay down my life for the sheep. I have other sheep that are not of this sheep pen. I must bring them also. They too will listen to my voice, and there shall be one flock and one shepherd (**John 10:11-16**).

The Qur'an presents a works-based theology where Allah will love you if you do something for him or that he can approve. For instance, **Qur'an 19:96** states, "Surely (as for) those who believe and do good deeds for them will Allah bring about love." Allah will love those who do good works.

God is Love

While devout Muslims will shout *Allahu akbar* (God is great!) before, during or after a terror attack upon their unsuspecting foe, you are not likely to hear a Muslim proclaim *Allahu muhibba* (God is love).

210

The central theme of the Bible is that *God is love* and He loves those whom He created. Christianity can lay claim to one of the greatest and most reassuring verses of scripture of all the world religions: "For God so loved the world, that He gave His only begotten Son, that whoever believes in Him should not perish but have everlasting life. For God did not send His Son into the world to condemn the world, but that the world through Him might be saved" (**John 3:16-17**, NKJV).

God, the Almighty, the Ruler of the Universe, loved His creation so much, that He decided that the greatest gift He could ever give the world was to send into the world a human being who was without sin. A person who embodied the complete thought and presence of God; who was endowed with God's own Spirit, for the eternal and loving purpose of redeeming man from his sin and separated him from God and God's love. What an earth-shaking concept that exists in no other religion but Christianity—a concept, which on the surface of man's intellect, seems so preposterous that it could only be true. Man could never have conceived of such an act by any god. Man can only conceive that he must work his way into his god's good graces through fulfilling laws or doing good works that will somehow make him worthy of his god's love and acceptance.

Allah, however, revealed through his prophet, Muhammad, that all those that refused to follow him were condemned to hell. Either follow Muhammad's teachings, or be persecuted, or experience a horrible "chastisement," i.e., death.

God Loves You! "God loves you! . . . Yet in the Qur'an, no such statement is to be found" (4).

Jesus' testimony in **John 3:16-17** is such a striking contrast to the message that Muhammad brought to the world. Muhammad, according to the Qur'an, was Allah's mouthpiece to condemn the world for not believing in him in the first place. Muhammad was the messenger, procurer and consummator of Allah's hate and wars upon the unbelieving Arabian world (as well as the rest of the world today). Muhammad did not come into the world as Allah's messenger of love and salvation. He came forth as Allah's apostle to persecute those who would not accept the tenets of Islamic faith as laid down by Muhammad.

"Islam is full of discrimination—against women, against non-Muslims, against Christians and most especially against Jews. Hatred is built into the religion.

"The history of Islam, which was my special area of study," wrote former Muslim, Mark Gabriel, "could only be characterized as a river of blood" (5).

One must ask: If God spent so much effort in the Bible and through various messengers in the Bible, as well as His own Son, to convince the world of His unconditional love for mankind, why would He send the opposite message some 600 years later? Was not the message of His love getting through, thus He had to repent and reveal His true feelings of hate for mankind? God, according to biblical scripture, cannot lie about what He says or what He feels.

The Apostle Paul, in the salutation of his letter to Titus, wrote, we have "a faith and knowledge resting on the hope of eternal life, which God, who does not lie, promised from the beginning of time" (**Titus 1:2**). Similarly, the writer to the Hebrews emphatically stated, "it is impossible for God to lie" (**Hebrews 6:18**).

God *could not* and *would not* go against His covenant of love and salvation that He established through the blood and sacrifice of His dear Son some 600 years prior to the appearance of Muhammad.

The Apostle John, the one that Christ loved, makes it abundantly clear, that God is love, that love is from God and that His love abides with us through Jesus Christ. Muhammad could make no such claim—that Allah's love abided with him. The life and times of Muhammad were the antithesis of Jesus and His ministry during His short time on earth.

The Apostle John makes it profusely apparent the purpose and all-inclusiveness of God's love.

> *Beloved, let us love one another, for love is of God; and everyone who loves is born of God and knows God. He who does not love does not know God, for God is love. In this the love of God was manifested toward us, that God has sent His only begotten Son into the world, that we might live through Him. In this is love, not that we loved God, but that He loved us and sent His Son to be the propitiation* [atoning sacrifice] *for our sins. Beloved, if God so loved us, we also ought to love one another. No one has seen God at any time. If we love one another, God abides in us, and His love has been perfected in us   And we have known and believed the love that God has for us. God is love, and he who abides in love abides in God, and God in him* (**1 John 4:7-12, 16,** NKJV).

Muhammad did not know Allah's Love. The concept and reality of a loving God escaped Muhammad's perception of the real God. Such an intimate and assured understanding of God's love was neither a part of Muhammad's experience, nor a part of his revelation of the nature of his god. Therefore, as Allah's apostle, he could not assure his followers that they would experience or have a time in their life when they could be guaranteed of Allah's unmitigated love and compassion.

It is ironic, that all the prophets that Muhammad looked to in the Bible, including Abraham, Moses, Jacob, Noah, David, John the Baptist, Jesus and others, all had an intimate understanding and assurance of

God's unconditional love for them. This understanding and experience of a personal love evaded Muhammad throughout his entire lifetime—as it does the followers of Islam today.

The Apostle Paul was so assured of God's love—not only for himself, but for those he called brothers in Christ—that he ended his letters with confident reassurance such as he did in his letter to the church in the wealthy seacoast city of Corinth in ancient Greece.

"Finally, brethren, farewell. Become complete [aim for perfection]. Be of good comfort, be of one mind, live in peace; and the God of love and peace will be with you" (**2 Corinthians 13:11**, NKJV).

To the church in Ephesus, an ancient large port city in Asia Minor near the Aegean Sea, Paul also guaranteed the faithful that God loved them. This, he was able to do, despite that he was in a Roman prison at the time, and the city of Ephesus was the location of the Great Temple of Diana (a Greek goddess). The city was overflowing with idol worshippers and the commerce of the city was largely dependent on silversmiths that made icons for the worship of this false god. Yet, Paul encouraged this small group of believers with these words: "But because of his great love for us, God, who is rich in mercy, made us alive with Christ even when we were dead in transgressions—it is by grace you have been saved" (**Ephesians 2:4-5**).

Toward the end of his first letter to the believers in Corinth, Paul made it clear how important God's love was in his eyes.

If I speak in the tongues [languages] of men and of angels, but have not love, I am only a resounding gong or a clanging cymbal. If I have the gift of prophecy and can fathom all mysteries and all knowledge, and if I have a faith that can move mountains, but have not love, I am nothing. If I give all I possess to the poor and surrender my body to the flames, but have not love, I gain nothing.

Love is patient, love is kind. It does not envy, it does not boast, it is not proud. It is not rude, it is not self-seeking, it is not easily angered, it keeps no record of wrongs. Love does not delight in evil but rejoices with the truth. It always protects, always trusts, always hopes, always perseveres.

Love never fails (**1 Corinthians 13:1-8a**).

God's Love Covenant

God's love is a covenant love. It is a love that has been sealed and delivered through the shed blood of Jesus Christ, and no other. Moses, a prophet of God that Muhammad revered, reminded the Israelites, after

God rescued them from the slavery of the Egyptians, that God was faithful and they could count on His unfailing love.

> *Know therefore that the Lord your God is God; he is the faithful God, keeping his covenant of love to a thousand generations of those who love him and keep his commands* (**Deuteronomy 7:9**).

Likewise, King Solomon, as he knelt and prayed before the whole assembly of Israel in front of the altar of the Lord, proclaimed, "O Lord, God of Israel, there is no God like you in heaven or on earth—you keep your covenant of love with your servants who continue wholeheartedly in your way" (**2 Chronicles 6:14**).

The prophet Nehemiah and Daniel also prayed a similar prayer about God's "covenant of love."

"LORD, the God of heaven, the great and awesome God, who keeps his covenant of love with those who love him and keep his commandments," (**Nehemiah 1:5**).

"I prayed to the LORD my God and confessed: 'Lord, the great and awesome God, who keeps his covenant of love with those who love him and keep his commandments'" **Daniel 9:4**).

God's Love is Irreversible. God's covenant love is unbreakable and irreversible; it cannot be revoked. In **Psalm 89**, God, through the Psalmist, expresses His faithfulness to David and his lineage.

> *My faithful love will be with him, and through my name his horn* [strength] *will be exalted. I will set his hand over the sea, his right hand over the rivers. He will call out to me, 'You are my Father, my God, the Rock my Savior.'*
>
> *I will also appoint him my firstborn, the most exalted of the kings of the earth.*
>
> *I will maintain my love to him forever, and my covenant with him will never fail. I will establish his line forever, his throne as long as the heavens endure.*
>
> *If his sons forsake my law and do not follow my statutes, if they violate my decrees and fail to keep my commands, I will punish their sin with the rod, their iniquity with flogging; but I will not take my love from him, nor will I ever betray my faithfulness. I will not violate my covenant or alter what my lips have uttered. Once for all, I have sworn by my holiness—and I will not lie to David—that his line will continue forever and his throne endure before me like the sun; it will be established*

forever like the moon, the faithful witness in the sky (**Psalm 89:24-37**).

It is important to make a note of the fact that God's love is a <u>covenant</u> **love—a promise or a contract that cannot be broken (nor will God break it). God's love is** *forever* **and it** *will never fail.* **God will not even withhold or violate His covenant of love when one sins against Him. God solidified this love contract with man by sending His only begotten Son into the world to reconcile man with God through the Son's death on the cross.**

Unfortunately, for the Muslim believer, Allah offers no such covenant of love or remedy of reconciliation between himself and his followers. Allah's love is conditional; it's reversible and he can withhold his love at any time for any reason. There is no way for a Muslim to reconcile himself to Allah or to bridge this great divide to assure himself of Allah's love.

Jesus, according to the Gospel of Luke, made it clear to His followers that everyone was important to God. "Are not five sparrows sold for two pennies?" he asked. "Yet not one of them is forgotten by God. Indeed, the very hairs on your head are all numbered. Don't be afraid; you are worth more than many sparrows" (**Luke 12:6-7**). Again, in **verses 22-26** in the same chapter, Jesus affirms God's provision for His children: "'Therefore I tell you, do not worry about your life, what you will eat; or about your body, what you will wear. Life is more than food, and the body more than clothes. Consider the ravens: They do not sow or reap, they have no storeroom or barn; yet God feeds them. And how much more valuable you are than birds! Who of you by worrying can add a single hour to his life? Since you cannot do this very little thing, why do you worry about the rest?"

This love covenant was part of God's plan from the beginning. He reaffirmed it through the institution of the Passover in Egypt. He confirmed it with the Israelites in the Sinai Desert during the forty years of wandering in the wilderness. Then He solidified it for the entire world through the shed blood of His beloved Son, Jesus Christ.

The Sealed Covenant. The Holy Spirit within the Christian believer seals God's love covenant with them. "Now hope does not disappoint, because the love of God has been poured out in our hearts by the Holy Spirit who was given to us" (**Romans 5:5**, NKJV).

While God loves us, He loves us for a reason. He loves us because we are His creation, but He also loves us so that we will love Him and share His love with others. Despite His love so freely given, God knows that we are powerless to love others, even with our best efforts and intentions. Therefore, He seals His covenant with those who accept His Son as Lord and Savior, with the inner presence of

215

His Holy Spirit. It is God's presence within the believer that empowers them to act upon and fully share God's unconditional love.

The Apostle Paul proclaimed this when he wrote: "For all the promises of God in Him [Christ] are Yes, and in Him Amen, to the glory of God through us. Now He who establishes us with you in Christ and has anointed us is God, who also has sealed us and given us the Spirit in our hearts as a guarantee" [of His covenant] (**2 Corinthians 1:20-22**, NKJV).

The eternal reward of accepting the redemptive work of Christ on the cross and receiving Him as your personal Lord and Savior is the adoption into God's family as His very own son or daughter.

"And because you are sons [of God], God has sent forth the Spirit of His Son into your hearts, crying out, 'Abba, Father!' Therefore you are no longer a slave but a son, and if a son, then an heir [to the covenant] of God through Christ" (**Galatians 4:6-7**, NKJV).

Allah has no sons. Nowhere in the Qur'an is the word *son* used in any connection with Allah. Allah has no sons—spiritual, adopted or otherwise. It is beneath Allah to have such an intimate or personal relationship with mankind. Allah does not even accept "adopted" sons as real sons of his followers (**surah 3:4**). For more information on this topic, see the next chapter.

There is no covenant in Islam: no children; no shed blood; no Holy Spirit to seal a covenant. The old or first covenant God made with the Jews in the Old Testament was sealed with the shed, sacrificial blood of animals. In the New Testament, God made a new covenant, a second and lasting covenant with His people through the shed blood of His Son.

In the Old Testament, it was the priests who were the mediators between the people and God. The Israelites had no access to God other than through the sacrifices of the priests. There was no remission for sins except through the shed blood sacrifice of animals by the priests once per year.

Jesus Christ is the only mediator, the intermediary through which man can receive God's unconditional love. There is no other go-between; no other agent or liaison. Jesus Christ, crucified, and Him only.

"But in fact the ministry Jesus has received is as superior to theirs [the priests] as the covenant of which he is mediator is superior to the old one, since **the new covenant is established on better promises.**

"For if there had been nothing wrong with that first covenant, no place would have been sought for another. But God found fault with the people and said" [**Exodus 25:40**] (**Hebrews 8:6-7**; author's emphasis):

> *The days are coming, declares the Lord, when I will make a new covenant with the people of Israel and with the people of Judah. It will not be like the covenant I made with their*

ancestors when I took them by the hand to lead them out of Egypt, because they did not remain faithful to my covenant, and I turned away from them, declares the Lord.

This is the covenant I will establish with the people of Israel after that time, declares the Lord. I will put my laws in their minds and write them on their hearts. I will be their God, and they will be my people.

No longer will they teach their neighbor, or say to one another, 'Know the Lord,' because they will all know me, from the least of them to the greatest. For I will forgive their wickedness and will remember their sins no more. [**Jeremiah 31:31-34**] (**Hebrews 8:8-12**).

"By calling this covenant 'new,'" the writer to the Hebrews concluded, "he has made the first one obsolete; and what is obsolete and outdated will soon disappear" (**Hebrews 8:13**).

This is yet another proof that Allah is not the God of the Bible. The God of the Bible cannot and would not renege on His sworn covenant with His people—especially when it was sealed with the shed blood of His One and Only Son, Jesus Christ.

"And the Jews and the Christians say: We are the sons [children] of Allah and His beloved ones. Say: Why does He then chastise you for your faults? Nay, you are mortals from among those whom He has created; He forgives whom He pleases and chastises [causes to suffer] whom He pleases . . ." (**Qur'an 5:18**). This surah illustrates Muhammad's pure ignorance of God's relationship with His chosen people, the Jews and the Christians through Christ, the Jewish Messiah. Perhaps, because Muhammad himself was an orphan early in life, he had a hard time grasping the concept of sonship. Muhammad could not conceive of such a familial, personal relationship with the god of his affections (more on this in the next chapter).

What a dim view of one's god. No compassion, no rhyme or reason as to who Allah will forgive or who he will punish. Allah has no children, so how could he show compassion to those who are so distant and removed from him? Muhammad's rational was, if the Christians and Jews were God's "children" then why did He "chastise" them so much? The Bible makes it clear.

The loving God of the Jews and Christians so loves them as His children that He guides and corrects them when they err or go astray. "My son, do not despise the Lord's discipline and do not resent his rebuke, because the Lord disciplines those he loves, as a father the son he delights in" (**Proverbs 3:11-12**).

"If you endure chastening, God deals with you as with sons; for what son is there whom a father does not chasten? But if you are without chastening, of which all have become partakers, then you are illegitimate and not sons" (**Hebrews 12:7-8**, NKJV).

The Good News for Muslims and anyone else, is that the God of the Bible eagerly awaits everyone to freely chose Him through His Son, Jesus Christ, and be a partaker in the family of God as His beloved sons and daughters.

The stark contrast here is this: Allah chastises those whom he hates; God chastises those whom He loves. Why the difference? It is the difference between a distant, detached god and a God who is also a loving Father—a God who has children that He loves and cares about in a very personal, intimate way.

"And you also were included in Christ when you heard the word of truth, the gospel of your salvation. Having believed, you were marked in him with a seal, the promised Holy Spirit, who is a deposit guaranteeing our inheritance until the redemption of those who are God's possession— the praise of his glory" (**Ephesians 1:13-14**).

There is no place in the theology of Islam for the presence of God's spirit dwelling among and in men or women. Without the pouring out of God's spirit to dwell within a man or a woman, there can be no sealing— no assurance—of His love covenant.

Once again, "God demonstrates His own love toward us," the Apostle Paul wrote, "in that while we were still sinners, Christ died for us" (**Romans 5:8,** NKJV). The Apostle Paul's statement is all inclusive. No one is left out, since *all* have sinned. God could not have demonstrated any greater love for His human creation than to allow His own perfect Son to be crucified for the sins of all mankind. Allah, on the other hand, is quite selective in whom he decides to accept, for "Allah makes whom He pleases err [sin] and He guides whom He pleases . . ." (**Qur'an 14:4**).

Jesus said, "Greater love has no one than this, than to lay down one's life for his friends" (**John 15:13**, NKJV). While Muhammad was undoubtedly a brave and courageous man in battle, he never laid down his life for another human being. To the contrary, he only took life away from those that opposed him.

Not only does God love us and has established a covenant of His love with us, but in times of trouble we can take refuge in Him. "He who dwells in the shelter of the Most high will rest in the shadow of the Almighty. I will say of the Lord, 'He is my refuge and my fortress, my God, in whom I trust'" (**Psalm 91:1-2**).

God's Revolutionary Love. Although the Qur'an teaches that the followers of Allah should only love those who love them, Jesus taught a different perspective. Jesus Christ, and only Him, truly revealed the heart of God. "You have heard that it was said," Jesus commanded, "'Love your neighbor [**Leviticus 19:18**] and hate your enemy.' But I tell you: Love your enemies and pray for those who persecute you, that you may be sons

218

of your Father in heaven. He causes his sun to rise on the evil and the good, and sends rain on the righteous and the unrighteous. If you love those who love you, what reward will you get? (**Matthew 5:43-46a**)."

This proclamation by Jesus was not only revolutionary, it was audacious and unheard of, not only for His time, but for any age. No one had ever heard of such a concept, nor had it ever been practiced. How could one love their enemy? There were likely thousands of ears listening to Jesus' Sermon of the Mount and assuredly just about every one of them must have perked up at such a profound statement. Not only did Muhammad not believe in this or preach it as the revealed word of Allah, but Christ followers throughout history and today have a hard time swallowing this provocative discourse of Jesus.

However, the Apostle John, the one who possibly was the closest to Jesus and referred to himself, not too candidly, as *the one whom Jesus loved*, would later give testimony to this type of love. "Whoever does not love does not know God, because God is love. This is how God showed his love among us: He sent his one and only Son into the world that we might live through him" (**1 John 4:8-9**).

We are commanded to love God, but we are also commanded to love others as God loves them. That is the full circle purpose of God loving His children—so that they will love Him and love others.

Moses made this clear to the Israelites during their journey out of the bondage in Egypt.

> *And now, O Israel, what does the Lord your God ask of you but to fear the Lord your God, to walk in all his ways, to love him, to serve the Lord your God with all your heart and with all your soul, and to observe the Lord's commands and decrees that I am giving you today for your own good?*
> *. . . For the Lord your God is God of gods and Lord of lords, the great God, mighty and awesome, who shows no partiality and accepts no bribes. He defends the cause of the fatherless and the widow, and loves the alien, giving him food and clothing* (**Deuteronomy 10:12-13, 17-18**).

n an effort to trap Jesus on the issue of love, "One of them [a Pharisee], an expert in the law, tested him with this question: 'Teacher, which is the greatest commandment in the Law?'

"Jesus replied: 'Love the Lord your God with all your heart and with all your soul and with all your mind' [**Deuteronomy 6:5**]. This is the first and greatest commandment. And the second is like it: 'Love your neighbor as yourself' [**Leviticus 19:18**]. All the Law and the Prophets hang on these two commandments" (**Matthew 22:35-40**).

As Jesus was nearing the time of His crucifixion, He re-emphasized the commandment to love with a slight twist. "A new command I give you: Love one another. As I have loved you, so you must love one another. By this all men will know that you are my disciples, if you love one another" (John 13:34-35).

Notice that Jesus said this is the one distinguishing trait of His followers by which the rest of the unbelieving world will know that Jesus was truly sent by God. Unfortunately, for many centuries since, Christians the world over have been struggling to demonstrate to the rest of the world their love for one another.

Although, the Qur'an admonishes Muslims to love Allah, there is no such commandment in the Qur'an that requires Muslims to love their neighbors. Who is a neighbor according to Jesus? It is not necessarily someone who lives nearby. In the Parable of the Good Samaritan (**Luke 10:25-37**), Jesus demonstrates that the *neighbor* can also be a foreigner, one who is not of like beliefs, but yet someone that shows mercy to a complete stranger.

Allah's revelation to Muhammad in **Qur'an 60:1** forbids the followers of Islam to love anyone who is not a believer in Allah. To offer one's love to someone outside the faith invites Allah's wrath.

Christians, conversely, are called to "Be imitators of God," commanded the Apostle Paul, "therefore, as dearly loved children and live a life of love, just as Christ loved us and gave himself up for us as a fragrant offering and sacrifice to God" (**Ephesians 5:1-2**). The followers of Christ are not to withhold love from anyone—friend or foe. Because God has so freely showered us with His love, we ought to share this abundance with others.

The Apostle Paul knew what he was talking about because he had many opportunities to demonstrate Christ's forgiving love. Paul, the only apostle that was a former persecutor of Christians, experienced great hardships and persecution himself. Five times, he received 40 lashes as punishment for his new convictions and peaching about Christ. Three times, he was beaten with rods. He was pelted with stones in an effort to kill him. Three times, he was shipwrecked, and once he spent a night and a day in the sea. He was in constant danger from bandits and his fellow Jews who hated his preaching about the love of Christ as the Son of God. Often, he wrote, he was hungry and thirsty; naked and cold (see **2 Corinthians 11:24-29**). If anyone had a reason to be angry, unforgiving and unloving, Paul was the one. Yet, he never expressed anything but the forgiving love of Christ toward all those who sought his demise.

The Qur'an, however, orders the followers of Islam to attack and kill their enemies, even if there is no provocation to do so. "True" Muslims are required by Allah, as revealed in the Qur'an, to carry out a one-sided offensive and violent war of attrition against all those who do

220

not accept Allah as God and follow his "commandments." This Islamic directive will be fully presented in Chapters 11-13 in *The Mission* section.

"O you who believe! fight those of the unbelievers who are near to you and let them find in you hardness [harshness]; and know that Allah is with those who guard (against evil)" [or are *Al-Muttaqun* (the pious)] (**Qur'an 9:123**).

Muhammad believed, taught and commanded the followers of Islam to religiously follow the will of Allah, which he believed was to persecute, plunder and kill all non-believers. "It is not fit for a prophet that he should take captives [of war] unless he has fought and triumphed [or until he has made a great slaughter] in the land" (Qur'an 8:67). Again, this is a harsh contrast to the ministry, life and call of Jesus to His followers. The same god cannot and would not call his followers to seek out and kill unbelievers while at the same time commanding believers to love their enemies.

"And let not those who disbelieve think that they shall come in first [that is, can get the better (of the godly)]; surely they will not escape. And prepare against them what force you can [or make ready your strength to the utmost of your power] and horses [of war] tied at the frontier, to frighten [or strike terror] thereby [into the hearts of] the enemy of Allah and your enemy and others besides them, whom you do not know (but) Allah knows them . . ." (**Qur'an 8:59-60**).

God's Love is Everlasting

God's love is everlasting because His covenant is everlasting; it never ends. "Give ear and come to me;" said God through the prophet Isaiah, "hear me, that your soul may live. **I will make an everlasting covenant with you, my faithful love promised to David**" (**Isaiah 55:3**; author's emphasis). Jesus made it clear right before His crucifixion that the shedding of His blood would permanently seal God's love covenant with His children (**Matthew 26:28**).

Nowhere in the Qur'an does it state that Allah has any kind of covenant with his followers. The word covenant occurs, but only when referencing God's covenant with Moses (**Qur'an 7:134**), with Abraham (**Qur'an 2:124**) and with the Israelites (**Qur'an 20:80**). If one is to assume that Allah was the one making the covenant with Moses, Abraham and the Jews, then **Qur'an 9:111** implies that Muslims, by default, have a covenant with Allah. Exactly what kind of covenant is left wide open for interpretation.

> *Surely Allah has bought of the believers their persons and their property for this* [paradise], *that they shall have the garden; they fight in Allah's way, so they slay and are slain; a*

221

promise which is binding on Him in the Taurat [Torah] *and the Injeel* [Gospel] *and the Qur'an; and who is more faithful to his covenant than Allah? Rejoice therefore in the pledge which you have made; and that is the mighty achievement* (**Qur'an 9:111**).

If, indeed, by the implication in this verse, Allah has made a covenant with his followers, it is a covenant of death—*fight* and *slay*. It is not the blood covenant of God's love that God has bound Himself to with both the Jews and Christians. Muhammad apparently had a very scant understanding of such a covenant as it was prophesied and laid down in both the Old and New Testaments—texts to which Muhammad referred to frequently but had little understanding as to their uniqueness and significance.

Once again, the Apostle Paul made it clear that for those who have accepted Christ it is impossible to be separated from God's love.

Who shall separate us from the love of Christ? Shall trouble or hardship or persecution or famine or nakedness or danger or sword? As it is written:

"For your sake we face death all day long; we are considered as sheep to be slaughtered" [**Psalm 44:22**].

No, in all these things we are more than conquerors through him who loved us. For I am convinced that neither death nor life, neither angels nor demons, neither the present nor the future, nor any powers, neither height nor depth, nor anything else in all creation, will be able to separate us from the love of God that is in Christ Jesus our Lord (**Romans 8:35-39**).

Those Who Hate Christians & Jews, Hate God

In **Qur'an 3:119**, Allah revealed that Muslims are to exercise conditional love—loving only those who love them. "Lo! You are they who will love them while they do not love you, and you believe in the Book (in) the whole of it; and when they meet you they say: We believe, and when they are alone, they bite the ends of their fingers in rage against you. Say: Die in your rage; surely Allah knows what is in the breast."

Jesus said, "But small is the gate and narrow the road that leads to life, and only a few find it. Watch out for false prophets. They come to you in sheep's clothing, but inwardly they are ferocious wolves ....Not everyone who says to me, 'Lord, Lord,' will enter the kingdom of heaven, but only the one who does the will of my Father who is in heaven" (**Matthew 7:14-15, 21**).

"If anyone does not love the Lord," Paul confessed, "let that person be cursed! Come, Lord!" (**1 Corinthians 16:22**). The Greek word used here for "cursed" is *anathema*, which means to be banned; excommunicated; accursed. The Apostle Paul was directing his admonishment to fellow believers, who were not really committed to Christ because their actions demonstrated that they did not love the Lord they professed to follow. To be an unbeliever is one thing, but to be a professed believer who did not love Jesus was the same as being an infidel—a non-believer.

There is a way that appears to be right, but in the end it leads to death.

Proverbs 14:12

"Remember the word that I said to you," Jesus instructed His disciples, "'A servant is not greater than his master.' If they persecuted Me, they will also persecute you. If they kept My word, they will keep yours also. But all these things they will do to you for My name's sake, because they do not know Him who sent Me. If I had not come and spoken to them, they would have no sin, but now they have no excuse for their sin. He who hates Me hates My Father also" (**John 15:20-23**, NKJV).

No one, Jesus said, can profess to know and love God and deny Him as the Son of God. No one can love God without loving Jews and Christians whom God loves. No one can love God without loving all those whom He has created.

Muhammad had access to the truth of God's word. It is clear from passages in the Qur'an that he availed himself of certain teachings from both Jewish and Christian sources. However, he decided to turn the truth of God into a lie that has misled billions astray for over 14 centuries.

"These things I have spoken to you," Jesus shared with His followers, "that you should not be made to stumble. They will put you out of the synagogues; yes, the time is coming that whoever kills you will think that he offers God service. And these things they will do to you because they have not known the Father nor Me" (**John 16:1-3**, NKJV).

The Apostle John would later confirm, "Whoever denies the Son does not have the Father either; he who acknowledges the Son has the Father also" (**1 John 2:23**, NKJV).

In the Gospel of John, when Jesus was brought before Pontius Pilate, the Roman Governor of Judea, Pilate asked Jesus if He was a king.

"Jesus answered, 'You say that I am a king. In fact, the reason I was born and came into the world is to testify to the truth. Everyone on the side of truth listens to me'" (**John 18:37**). Jesus was born to bring forth the truth of God's word and plan of salvation for mankind.

Muhammad was used by the powers of evil to negate God's truth and deny God's plan of redemption and salvation through Jesus Christ.

"Make every effort to keep the unity of the Spirit through the bond of peace," Paul wrote to the church in Ephesus. "There is one body and one Spirit, just as you were called to one hope when you were called; one Lord, one faith, one baptism;" (**Ephesians 4:3-5**).

As hard as it is for Muslims and other non-Christians to accept this, the truth is that God, the Creator of the universe, the Judeo-Christian God, made only one way possible to reach Him and have fellowship with Him and that is through His One and Only Son in the flesh, Jesus Christ.

I am the way and the truth and the life. No one comes to the Father except through me.
Jesus Christ, John 14:6

In the Apostle John's first pastoral letter, he reminded the followers of Christ that, "Whoever has the Son has life; whoever does not have the Son of God does not have life" (**1 John 5:12**).

Paul, in his letter to Titus, offered a similar admonition. "To the pure, all things are pure, but to those who are corrupted and do not believe, nothing is pure. In fact, both their minds and consciences are corrupted. They claim to know God, but by their actions they deny him. They are detestable, disobedient and unfit for doing anything good" (**Titus 1:15-16**).

Lastly, in his letter to the church in Rome, Paul reminded the followers of Christ about the trap the Israelites fell into, which also applies to today. "They exchanged the truth about God for a lie, and worshiped and served created things rather than the Creator—who is forever praised. Amen" (**Romans 1:25**).

Chapter Conclusion

Apparently, if one is to use the Muslim holy book, the Qur'an, as a source text on the issue and relationship of Allah's love for mankind, it would seem that Allah neither seeks nor desires an intimate love relationship with his human creation. What love he does have is clearly conditional—*if you do such and such, then you might be worthy of my love.* If you are a Muslim you will never be assured of Allah's love. *If*, after your death, you make it to Paradise, then you can assume that Allah loves you. Of course, after you die it is too late to change your outcome with Allah.

Muhammad was forty years old and living in Mecca, Saudi Arabia when he first believed he had been visited by the angel Gabriel. Twelve years later, Muhammad and his followers fled to Medina, about 150 miles north of Mecca. It was from Medina that Muhammad and his forces started their reign of terror against neighboring tribes and communities. One only needs to read Muhammad's entries to the Qur'an during this period to get the picture of a bitter, hateful and vengeful man—the Apostle of Allah. Is it any wonder that Muhammad conceived of a god that had the same attributes as him?

The Jewish God, Yahweh or Jehovah, is overflowing with unconditional love. He loves His people, Israel—even if they sin. For God to include everyone into His family of love, He sent Jesus, His only begotten Son, to restore mankind in fellowship with God. God loves everyone and commands His followers to love everyone with the love of Christ.

This comparison between the two deities could hardly be more contradictory, as one tries to assess the character of God. The God of the Jews and Christians is loving and kind and desirous of an intimate, personal relationship with His children—all those whom He created. The god of the Muslims is unloving and vengeful and wants to remain distant to those he created. These two portrayals of God are incompatible and do not depict the same deity. God cannot both love His creation at the same time He seems disinterested. He cannot desire a close, personal relationship, yet want to remain at a distance. Nor can He claim those He created as His children and at the same time claim to be childless.

References.

1. *How many times does the word "Love" appear in the Qur'an?* Quora, December 2, 2017. Source: https://www.quora.com/How-many-times-does-the-word-Love-appear-in-the-Quran
2. Mahally, Farid. *A study of the word "love" in the Qur'an.* Source: https://answering-islam.org/Quran/Themes/love.htm
3. Ibid.
4. Caner, Ergun Mehmet and Emir Fethi Caner. *Unveiling Islam*, 2002. Kregel Publications, div. of Kregel. Inc., p.30.
5. Gabriel, Mark A. *Islam and Terrorism*, 2002. Published by FrontLine, a Strang Company, Lake Mary, Florida, p.5.

Chapter 9

A Personal vs. an Indifferent God

For there is one God and one mediator between God and mankind, the man Christ Jesus,

1 Timothy 2:5

The Christian and Jewish peoples of the earth have a unique and bonding relationship with their God like no other religion on earth. The Bible enforces and reinforces over and over that they are God's children—people that he dearly loves and for whom He demonstrates His compassion and forgiveness. It is clearly an intimate Father-child relationship.

Muhammad could not conceive of such a loving god that would take such a personal interest in him. Therefore, he taught his followers that their god was a god of detachment, one who remained aloof and separated from them. That concept of Allah remains as the core of Islam today.

In the first book of the Bible, in **Genesis 6:2**, Moses recorded the first reference of God's intimate relationship to His creation when he refers to mankind as "sons of God." This is a very important perception for the theology and belief system of both Jews and Christians. The Hebrew word for *son* used in this verse and throughout the Old Testament means one who is the *builder of the family name*. Those who are Christians and Jews are part of God's holy family. As builders of God's family on earth, Christians and Jews are to imitate their Father-God and His holiness in every way. This sense of belonging to God's family is alien to the Muslims. Allah has no family. He is a harsh and unyielding tyrant-master that takes pleasure in chastening those who attempt to follow his commands.

Moses strengthened this notion of God as Father when he encouraged the Jews during the Exodus from Egypt with these words: "You are the children of the Lord your God   " (**Deuteronomy 14:1**).

About 250 years later, the word of the Lord came to the prophet Nathan concerning King David and his descendants. The Lord told Nathan to reassure David that his kingdom would be established forever, starting with his son Solomon, and that "I will be his Father, and he shall be My son. . ." (**2 Samuel 7:14**, NKJV). God, through David, established an intimate fatherly relationship with His people that would be strengthened with the advent of Jesus, God's only begotten Son.

In the book of Jeremiah the prophet, God once again promised that He would be Israel's Father. "They will come with weeping; they will pray as I bring them back. I will lead them beside streams of water on a level path where they will not stumble, because I am Israel's father, and Ephraim is my firstborn son" (**Jeremiah 31:9**). Ephraim was one of the twelve tribes of Israel.

The God of the Christians and Jews yearns for this intimate, personal relationship with His human creation. King David understood this and wanted his son Solomon to know it and never forget it. David recited, "And you, my son Solomon, acknowledge the God of your father, and serve him with wholehearted devotion and with a willing mind, for the LORD searches every heart and understands every motive behind the thoughts. If you seek him, he will be found by you; but if you forsake him, he will reject you forever" (**1 Chronicles 28:9**).

One of the amazing things about Jehovah God is that He desires so much to commune with and "parent" His creation, that He even reveals Himself to those that do not know they are seeking Him. God disclosed to the prophet Isaiah, "I revealed myself to those who did not ask for me; I was found by those who did not seek me. To a nation that did not call on my name, I said, 'Here am I, here am I'" (**Isaiah 65:1**).

The LORD looks down from heaven on the sons of men to see if there are any who understand, any who seek God.
Psalm 14:2

From the testimonies of converted Muslims to Christianity, this is one of the most common ways that God, the only true God, reveals Himself to seekers of the truth. Often, when a Muslim is earnestly seeking the truth of God's existence, he or she will pray that Allah (or sometimes Jehovah God) will reveal himself or the truth of his existence to them. It is important to note that Allah *never* shows up in a vision, dream, revelation or appearance—but Jesus does, every time. That is, because God, through His Son Jesus, wants and desires that personal relationship. Allah cannot and will not reveal himself because he wants to stay detached from those he created, thus, clearly demonstrating once again that Allah is a false god— an evil spirit or likely Satan himself—who has no desire to adopt mankind into the family of God.

God Said: "This is My Son"

"This is how the birth of Jesus Christ came about: His mother Mary was pledged to be married to Joseph, but before they came together, she was found to be with child through the Holy Spirit" (**Matthew 1:18**).

An unidentified "angel of the Lord" appeared to Joseph in a dream and gave Joseph this assurance: "Joseph son of David, do not be afraid to take Mary home as your wife, because what is conceived in her is from the Holy Spirit. She will give birth to a son, and you are to give him the name Jesus [i.e. *the Lord saves*], because he will save his people from their sins" (**Matthew 1:20- 21**).

In the first chapter of Luke, the angel sent to Mary is identified as Gabriel.

> *In the sixth month, God sent the angel Gabriel to Nazareth, a town in Galilee, to a virgin pledged to be married to a man named Joseph, a descendant of David. The virgin's name was Mary. The angel went to her and said, 'Greetings, you who are highly favored! The Lord is with you.' Mary was greatly troubled at his words and wondered what kind of greeting this might be. But the angel said to her, 'Do not be afraid, Mary, you have found favor with God. You will be with child and give birth to a son, and you are to give him the name Jesus. He will be great and will be called the* **Son of the Most High***. The Lord God will give him the throne of his father David, and he will reign over the house of Jacob forever; his kingdom will never end'* (**Luke 1:26-33**, author's emphasis).

Gabriel, the same angel that purportedly visited Muhammad with the revelation of the Qur'an, revealed to Mary that her immaculately conceived child would be the *Son of the Most High* living God. He would also fulfill the prophecy of the ongoing reign of King David. Why would Gabriel, the angel of God, who revealed to Mary (whom Muslims revere) that she would give birth to the *Son of the Most High*, return in a vision to Muhammad that denied such a revelation over 600 years earlier? The clear answer: Gabriel did not visit Muhammad, nor did he reveal anything to Muhammad.

The Challenge for Muslims. The great challenge and struggle for the Muslim believer is who is telling the truth? Was it the Gabriel of Luke 1, who delivered the fulfilling prophecy of the Jewish Messiah, the Son of the living God, or the Gabriel of the Qur'an who refuted what he revealed to Mary?

The Qur'an also retells the story of Mary's virgin birth of Jesus (**Qur'an 19:15-34**). However, Muhammad, as Allah's messenger, as it was revealed to him by Gabriel, refers to Jesus' mother as Marium and identifies her as the sister of Aaron (and therefore Moses in **verses 27-28**) who lived nearly fifteen centuries earlier. This makes it look like Allah and his dispatched angel messenger were confused or forgetful as to who actually gave birth to God's promised Messiah. According to Muhammad and every Muslim believer since, Gabriel revealed that Jesus was not God's son. Actually, what is "revealed" is that Jesus is not Allah's son, which is correct, since Allah *is not* the God of the Jews and Christians.

Over 700 years before the birth of Christ and almost 1300 years before the birth of Muhammad, the prophet Isaiah prophesied: "The people walking in darkness have seen a great light; on those living in the land of the shadow of death a light has dawned. For to us a child is born, to us a son is given, and the government will be on his shoulders" (**Isaiah 9:2, 6a**).

Isaiah also prophesied that the Messiah would come from the lineage of Jesse, the father of David. This Messiah would be endowed with God's own Spirit—a Spirit of wisdom, understanding, counsel, power, knowledge and fear (reverence) of the Lord God Almighty. He will not judge or apply justice by what he sees or hears but by the heart of righteousness. He will smite the earth and its wicked inhabitants, not with the sword of vengeance, but with the word of God's truth. Righteousness and faithfulness will be his hallmark.

> *A shoot will come up from the stump of Jesse; from his roots a Branch will bear fruit. The Spirit of the LORD will rest on him – the Spirit of wisdom and of understanding, the Spirit of counsel and of power, the Spirit of knowledge and of the fear of the LORD—and he will delight in the fear of the LORD. He will not judge by what he sees with his eyes, or decide by what he hears with his ears; but with righteousness he will judge the needy, with justice he will give decisions for the poor of the earth. He will strike the earth with the rod of his mouth; with the breath of his lips he will slay the wicked. Righteousness will be his belt and faithfulness the sash around his waist* (**Isaiah 11:1-5**).

Muhammad not only did not fit the person in this prophecy, but he could not hold a candle to the one who was to fulfill it—Jesus Christ. Muhammad, of course, did not come from the ancestry of Jesse or King David. Even if he did, it is evident from his life that he was not bathed in the Spirit of Almighty God—the Spirit of wisdom, understanding, counsel, power, knowledge and reverence of the only true living God. His wisdom and understanding of God and His Holy Word was miniscule and often erroneous. His counsel was frequently nonsensical and/or barbaric. He could not demonstrate the power of Almighty God in his midst as all the prophets before him could. His knowledge of the history that went before him paled by comparison to the scholars of his day or any of the prophets he aspired to in the Bible. He revered not the God of the Bible but some pagan spirit that led him and all his followers astray from the true God of creation. And he did not convert people by the power of his words, but by the power of his sword.

Isaiah depicted the coming Messiah as a man of righteousness and peace. He would not even raise his voice in anger, nor so much as crush a tender reed. He would fulfill the covenant that God had made with the Jews and point the way to the truth for all non-believers, releasing them from the bondage of spiritual darkness.

Despite Islamic claims to the contrary, Muhammad did not and could not fulfill any such characteristics of God's anointed—apostle, prophet or otherwise. He was not a man of godly righteousness and peace; nor did he fulfill any covenant with the Jews or lead the unbelieving Gentiles in the way of truth. When Jesus preached He would frequently say, "Let them who have ears, hear." He did not bash those who refused his message into submission with a bloody scimitar, as did Muhammad.

> *"Here is my servant, whom I uphold, my chosen one in whom I delight; I will put my Spirit on him and he will bring justice to the nations. He will not shout or cry out, or raise his voice in the streets.*
>
> *A bruised reed he will not break, and a smoldering wick he will not snuff out. I faithfulness he will bring forth justice; he will not falter or be discouraged till he establishes justice on earth. In his law the islands will put their hope."*
>
> *This is what God the LORD says—he who created the heavens and stretched them out, who spread out the earth and all that comes out of it, who gives breath to its people, and life to those who walk on it:*
>
> *"I, the LORD, have called you in righteousness; I will take hold of your hand. I will keep you and will make you to be a covenant for the people and a light for the Gentiles, to open eyes that are blind, to free captives from prison and to release from the dungeon those who sit in darkness"* (**Isaiah 42:1-7**).

A Common Man. Once again, the prophet Isaiah, prophesied about the coming of the Jewish Messiah who would take away the sins of the world. Isaiah laid out the characteristics of this common man in **Isaiah 53:1-12**. Isiah begins his prophesy with: *Who has believed our message and to whom has the arm of the LORD been revealed?* Then he itemizes the character and mission of the Christ:

- He grew up before him like a tender shoot, and like a root out of dry ground.
- He had no beauty or majesty to attract us to him, nothing in his appearance that we should desire him.
- He was despised and rejected by mankind,
- a man of suffering, and familiar with pain.
- Like one from whom people hide their faces he was despised,

230

- and we held him in low esteem.
- Surely he took up our pain and bore our suffering,
- yet we considered him punished by God, stricken by him, and afflicted.
- But he was pierced for our transgressions,
- he was crushed for our iniquities;
- the punishment that brought us peace was on him,
- and by his wounds we are healed.
- We all, like sheep, have gone astray, each of us has turned to our own way;
- and the LORD has laid on him the iniquity of us all.
- He was oppressed and afflicted, yet he did not open his mouth;
- he was led like a lamb to the slaughter,
- and as a sheep before its shearers is silent, so he did not open his mouth.
- By oppression and judgment he was taken away.
- Yet who of his generation protested?
- For he was cut off from the land of the living;
- for the transgression of my people he was punished.
- He was assigned a grave with the wicked, and with the rich in his death, for sin,
- he will see his offspring and prolong his days,
- and the will of the LORD will prosper in his hand.
- After he has suffered, he will see the light of life and be satisfied;
- by his knowledge my righteous servant will justify many,
- and he will bear their iniquities.
- Therefore I will give him a portion among the great,
- and he will divide the spoils with the strong,
- because he poured out his life unto death, and was numbered with the transgressors.
- For he bore the sin of many, and made intercession for the transgressors.

What God Said about Jesus. The Gospels record three times when God spoke from heaven about the Father-Son relationship He had with Jesus. The first was when Jesus was baptized by John the Baptist in the River Jordan. "And a voice from heaven said, '**This is my Son, whom I love; with him I am well pleased**'" (**Matthew 3:17**; author's emphasis). Was God's confession of His Father-Son relationship with Jesus for Jesus' sake? No, Jesus already knew His place in God's heart. When God thundered from on high, *this is my son*, it was for the sake of John the Baptist and all those present.

231

The second time that it was recorded that God's voice burst forth from heaven was at the transfiguration of Jesus. Jesus took Peter, James and John up a mountain side with Him. While they were together, Jesus was *transfigured before them. His face shone like the sun, and his clothes became as white as the light.* To the astonishment of the three Apostles, Moses and Elijah appeared (**Matthew 17:1-3**).

> *While he was still speaking, a bright cloud covered them, and a voice from the cloud said, "This is my Son, whom I love; with him I am well pleased. Listen to him!"*

> *When the disciples heard this, they fell facedown to the ground, terrified. But Jesus came and touched them. "Get up," he said. "Don't be afraid." When they looked up, they saw no one except Jesus.* (**Matthew 17:5-8**; see also **Mark 9:7** and **Luke 9:35**).

The third time God spoke about His Son was right before Christ's crucifixion.

> *Jesus replied, "The hour has come for the Son of Man to be glorified. Very truly I tell you, unless a kernel of wheat falls to the ground and dies, it remains only a single seed. But if it dies, it produces many seeds. Anyone who loves their life will lose it, while anyone who hates their life in this world will keep it for eternal life. Whoever serves me must follow me; and where I am, my servant also will be. My Father will honor the one who serves me.*
> *"Now my soul is troubled, and what shall I say? 'Father, save me from this hour'? No, it was for this very reason I came to this hour. Father, glorify your name!"*
> *Then a voice came from heaven, "I have glorified it, and will glorify it again." The crowd that was there and heard it said it had thundered; others said an angel had spoken to him.*
> *Jesus said, "This voice was for your benefit, not mine*
> (**John 12:23-30**).

Jesus did not need to hear this confirmation from His Father in heaven. He knew who He was and His direct relationship to Father God. As Jesus said, God spoke for the benefit of those who were present with Him.

In Jesus' Own Words. In the Gospel of John, Jesus made it clear about His relationship to Almighty God.

Jesus declared, "For the one whom God has sent speaks the words of God, for God gives the Spirit without limit. The Father loves the Son and has placed everything in his hands. Whoever believes in the Son has eternal life, but whoever rejects the Son will not see life, for God's wrath remains on them" (**John 3:34-36**). Of course, non-believing skeptics might retort, "But anyone could make such a claim." True! However, Jesus backed up His claim with signs and wonders and by fulfilling hundreds of Old Testament prophecies, most of which were outside His control.

In **Matthew 11:27,** Jesus once again testified to His Sonship with God the Father. "All things have been committed to me by my Father. No one knows the Son except the Father, and no one knows the Father except the Son and those to whom the Son chooses to reveal him." In this verse, the Greek word for "know" means to be "intimately acquainted with." Jesus, as God's Son, was intimately acquainted with God as His Father. Through faith in Christ, believers can experience a similar unique relationship with God the Father. Muslims can have no such intimate relationship with their god, Allah.

Now this is eternal life: that they know you, the only true God, and Jesus Christ, whom you have sent.

Jesus Christ
John 17:3

Perhaps the most often quoted verse of the Bible comes from **John 3:16** where Jesus, in response to inquiries from the Pharisee, Nicodemus, told him, "For God so loved the world that he gave his **one and only Son**, that whoever believes in him shall not perish but have eternal life" (author's emphasis). The following two verses continue Jesus' proclamation. "For God did not send his Son into the world to condemn the world, but to save the world through him. Whoever believes in him is not condemned, but whoever does not believe stands condemned already because he has not believed in the name of God's one and only Son" (**John 3:17-18**).

Once again, Jesus clearly proclaimed Himself to be God's Son. His closest disciples believed it to be so and God Almighty, the Father of heaven and earth, confirmed it before witnesses that it was so to the fulfillment of prophecy.

In chapter 5 of the Gospel of John, Jesus provided further evidence of His Sonship to God. When Jesus healed a man on the Sabbath, the Jews sought to kill Him because He was "working" on the Sabbath and thus committing blasphemy.

> *If I testify about myself, my testimony is not true. There is another who testifies in my favor, and I know that his testimony about me is true.*
>
> *You have sent to John and he has testified to the truth. Not that I accept human testimony; but I mention it that you may be saved. John was a lamp that burned and gave light, and you chose for a time to enjoy his light.*
>
> *I have testimony weightier than that of John. For the works that the Father has given me to finish—the very works that I am doing—testify that the Father has sent me. And the Father who sent me has himself testified concerning me. You have never heard his voice nor seen his form, nor does his word dwell in you, for you do not believe the one he sent. You study the Scriptures diligently because you think that in them you have eternal life. These are the very Scriptures that testify about me, yet you refuse to come to me to have life.*
>
> *I do not accept glory from human beings, but I know you. I know that you do not have the love of God in your hearts. I have come in my Father's name, and you do not accept me; but if someone else comes in his own name, you will accept him. How can you believe since you accept glory from one another but do not seek the glory that comes from the only God?*
>
> *But do not think I will accuse you before the Father. Your accuser is Moses, on whom your hopes are set. If you believed Moses, you would believe me, for he wrote about me. But since you do not believe what he wrote, how are you going to believe what I say?"*(**John 5:31-47**).

Jesus made it clear, that not only did He have the authority from God, His Father, to do such works wherever and whenever needed, but that doing such good works were evidence that God the Father had sent Him. Since the Jews based their hopes on the words of Moses, Jesus admonished them for not believing Moses' prophecy about Him in **Deuteronomy 18:15, 18**.

After Jesus' miraculous feeding of the five thousand near the Sea of Galilee (**John 6:1-15**), Jesus later explained to His disciples what they had witnessed.

> *Jesus said to them, "Very truly I tell you, it is not Moses who has given you the bread from heaven* [the manna in the wilderness], *but it is **my Father** who gives you the true bread from heaven. For the bread of God is the bread that comes down from heaven and gives life to the world."*
>
> *"Sir," they said, "always give us this bread."*

> Then Jesus declared, "I am the bread of life. Whoever comes to me will never go hungry, and whoever believes in me will never be thirsty. But as I told you, you have seen me and still you do not believe. All those the Father gives me will come to me, and whoever comes to me I will never drive away. For I have come down from heaven not to do my will but to do the will of him who sent me. And this is the will of him who sent me, that I shall lose none of all those he has given me, but raise them up at the last day. For **my Father's will** is that **everyone who looks to the Son** and believes in him shall have eternal life, and I will raise them up at the last day" (**John 6:32-40**; author's emphasis).

When Jesus was healing people on the Sabbath, the Jewish leaders condemned Him. To which Jesus replied:

> Jesus gave them this answer: "I tell you the truth, **the Son can do nothing by himself**; he can do only what he sees his Father doing, because whatever the Father does the Son also does. For **the Father loves the Son** and shows him all he does. Yes, to your amazement he will show him even greater things than these. For just as the Father raises the dead and gives them life, even so **the Son gives life** to whom he is pleased to give it. Moreover, the Father judges no one, but has **entrusted all judgment to the Son**, that all may **honor the Son** just as they honor the Father. **He who does not honor the Son** does not honor the Father, who sent him.
> "I tell you the truth, whoever hears my word and believes him who sent me has eternal life and will not be condemned; he has crossed over from death to life. I tell you the truth, a time is coming and has now come when **the dead will hear the voice of the Son of God** and those who hear will live. For as the Father has life in himself, so **he has granted the Son to have life in himself**" (**John 5:19-26**; author's emphasis).

The fact that Muslims and others do not honor or accept Jesus Christ as the Son of God means that they do not honor the One and Only True God, the Father Almighty of Jesus Christ.

The Jewish leaders persisted in their accusations of Jesus' blasphemy for referring to Himself as the Son of God. They sought every opportunity to condemn Him and turn others against Him. During the Feast of Dedication, or Hanukkah, in Jerusalem, Jesus was once again confronted by the Jews who sought to stone Him on the spot.

Jesus answered them, "Is it not written in your Law, 'I have said you are gods'? [**Psalm 82:6**]. *If he called them 'gods,' to whom the word of God came—and the Scripture cannot be broken—what about the one whom the Father set apart as his very own and sent into the world? Why then do you accuse me of blasphemy because I said, 'I am God's Son'? Do not believe me unless I do what my Father does. But if I do it, even though you do not believe me, believe the miracles, that you may know and understand that the Father is in me, and I in the Father"* (**John 10:34-38**).

Even with His gruesome death pending, Jesus maintained His Sonship with God the Father. He refused to deny that heavenly connection even though it meant His assured horrific demise. Common sense would say: *Save yourself, refute this ridiculous claim of being the Son of God. No good can come of it but your painful death.* Jesus knew His origin and to whom He was about to return.

As Jesus and His disciples were on their way to Jerusalem during the Passover feast, He foretold of His coming death. "Now my heart is troubled, and what shall I say? 'Father, save me from this hour'? No, it was for this very reason I came to this hour. Father, glorify your name!' Then a voice came from heaven, 'I have glorified it, and will glorify it again.' The crowd that was there and heard it said it had thundered; others said an angel had spoken to him" (**John 12:27-29**). Although He knew what was ahead, Jesus refused to deny His Sonship with the Father God. Many Christians today, worldwide, under extreme persecution and even the threat of death, follow Jesus' example, refusing to deny their relationship to Jesus or deny that they are sons and daughters of the Most High God (see Chapters 11-13).

Again, in **John 16:33-17:3**, Jesus acknowledged His relationship to God. "I have told you these things," Jesus later told His disciples, "so that in me you may have peace. In this world you will have trouble. But take heart! I have overcome the world."

"After Jesus said this, he looked toward heaven and prayed: 'Father, the time has come. Glorify your Son, that your Son may glorify you. For you granted him authority over all people that he might give eternal life to all those you have given him. Now this is eternal life: that they may know you, the only true God, and Jesus Christ, whom you have sent.'"

Toward the end of his Gospel, the Apostle John made clear his objective when he wrote: "Jesus performed many other signs in the presence of his disciples, which are not recorded in this book. But these are written that you may believe that Jesus is the Messiah, the Son of God, and that by believing you may have life in his name" (**John 20:30-31**).

They Called Him Son of God. At the very beginning of his Gospel, the Apostle John made his belief and confession of faith in Jesus Christ crystal clear. "The Word [of God] became flesh," John confessed, "and made his dwelling among us. We have seen his glory, the glory of the one and only Son, who came from the Father, full of grace and truth" (**John 1:14**).

Three verses later, John continued, "For the law was given through Moses; grace and truth came through Jesus Christ. No one has ever seen God, but the one and only Son, who is himself God and is in closest relationship with the Father, has made him known" (**John 1:17-18**). Jesus' purpose was to represent God's grace and truth on earth. Although no one other than Jesus has ever seen God, Jesus made God known to all who would believe in Him and the One who sent Him.

Mark also began his Gospel with a similar acknowledgement about Jesus. "The beginning of the good news about Jesus the Messiah, the Son of God," (**Mark 1:1**).

After Jesus had calmed the storm on the Sea of Galilee as He and His disciples were sailing across, they came to the region of the Gergesenes on the eastern shore. Upon their arrival two demon-possessed men came charging out of the tombs. "'What do you want with us, Son of God?' they shouted. 'Have you come here to torture us before the appointed time?'" (**Matthew 8:29**; see also **Mark 5:7** and **Luke 8:28**). Even the demons knew who Jesus was and respected His authority.

Mark also reported that, "Whenever the impure spirits saw him, they fell down before him and cried out, 'You are the Son of God'" (**Mark 3:11**).

"Moreover," Luke wrote, "demons came out of many people, shouting, 'You are the Son of God!' But he rebuked them and would not allow them to speak, because they knew he was the Messiah" (**Luke 4:41**)

During another treacherous crossing of the Sea of Galilee the disciples were confronted with rough seas. As the rough seas continued during the night, the disciples saw Jesus coming toward them walking on the water (**Matthew 14:25-26**). Initially, they thought they were seeing a ghost, but Jesus then beckoned Peter to take a step of faith upon the water. Peter became afraid and began to sink, but Jesus reached out and saved him and the wind subsided (**Matthew 14:29-32**). "Then those who were in the boat worshiped him, saying, 'Truly you are the Son of God'" (**Matthew 14:33**).

On another occasion, when Jesus was ministering in the region of Caesarea Philippi, about 25 miles north of the Sea of Galilee, Jesus posed a question to the Apostles. "Who do people say the Son of Man is?" (**Matthew 16:13**). The Apostles suggested that people were saying that Jesus was John the Baptist or Elijah, Jeremiah or one of the other Old

Testament prophets who had returned. But Jesus wanted to know what His Apostles thought.

Simon Peter boldly responded, "You are the Messiah, the Son of the living God" (**Matthew 16:16**).

"Jesus replied, 'Blessed are you, Simon son of Jonah, for this was not revealed to you by flesh and blood, but by my Father in heaven'" (**Matthew 16:16-17**). Considering the environment of hostility in which Jesus was ministering, this was a very brazen statement by Peter.

Peter and the other apostles knew that for Jesus or them to claim that Jesus was God's Son, was blasphemy and punishable by death under Jewish law. But that did not deter them from such a belief and proclamation.

When Jesus called Nathanael to be an Apostle, He revealed to Nathanael that He already knew him and what he had been doing. "Then Nathanael declared, 'Rabbi, you are the Son of God; you are the king of Israel'" (**John 1:49**).

Before Jesus raised Lazarus from the dead in **John 11**, Jesus had a conversation with Martha, one of Lazarus' sisters. "Jesus said to her, 'I am the resurrection and the life. The one who believes in me will live, even though they die; and whoever lives by believing in me will never die. Do you believe this?'"

"'Yes, Lord,' she replied, 'I believe that you are the Messiah, the Son of God, who is to come into the world'" (**John 11:25-27**). Martha could have only known this by revelation knowledge from God and/or through witnessing the many miracles that Jesus performed.

"When the centurion and those with him who were guarding Jesus saw the earthquake and all that had happened, they were terrified, and exclaimed, "Surely he was the Son of God!" (**Matthew 27:54; Mark 15:39**). What had happened that made the centurion a believer in Jesus as the *Son of God*?

First, he likely witnessed Christ's last words as He cried out in agony, *Eli, Eli, lema sabachthani?* Translated, this means, "My God, my God, why have You forsaken Me?" (**Matthew 27:46; Mark 15:34**).

Second, during the sixth to the ninth hour (12 noon until 3:00 PM) leading up to Christ's death, complete darkness filled the land (**Matthew 27:45; Mark 15:33**).

Third, both Matthew and Mark recorded that at the very moment of Jesus' death, the veil of the Jewish temple in Jerusalem was torn in two from top to bottom as an earthquake occurred (**Matthew 27:51; Mark 15:38**). Additionally, Matthew reported that rocks split open and many graves were opened releasing dead saints and after Christ's resurrection these resurrected saints appeared to many in Jerusalem (**Matthew 27:51-53**).

The unknown author of the letter to the Hebrews often acknowledged that Jesus was the Son of God. "The Son is the radiance of God's glory and the exact representation of his being, sustaining all things by his powerful word. After he had provided purification for sins, he sat down at the right hand of the Majesty in heaven" (**Hebrews 1:3**).

Two verses later, the author wrote: "For to which of the angels did God ever say, 'You are my Son; today I have become your Father?' Or again, 'I will be his Father, and he will be my Son?' (**Hebrews 1:5**). The first quote was from **Psalm 2:7** and the second from **2 Samuel 7:14**.

"In the same way," the letter's author penned, "Christ did not take on himself the glory of becoming a high priest. But God said to him, 'You are my Son; today I have become your Father'" (**Hebrews 5:5**).

Paul Preached about Jesus as the Son of God. How did Saul, who became the Apostle Paul, know that Jesus was the Son of God? Unlike the original Apostles, Paul never knew Jesus in the flesh. The only way he could have known was through the revelation knowledge of the Holy Spirit. For him to preach so boldly in synagogues where he was in danger of being stoned to death for blasphemy, Saul had to be one hundred percent convinced that Jesus was indeed the Son of God.

Saul, as the Apostle Paul, would later write, that Jesus "through the Spirit of holiness was appointed the Son of God in power by his resurrection from the dead: Jesus Christ our Lord.   God, whom I serve in my spirit in preaching the gospel of his Son, is my witness how constantly I remember you" (**Romans 1:4, 9**).

"For if," Paul wrote, "while we were God's enemies, we were reconciled to him through the death of his Son, how much more, having been reconciled, shall we be saved through his life!" (**Romans 5:10**). Paul knew, without reservation, that the Jesus he preached was truly the Son of God. He never shied away from that declaration.

Further into his letter to the Christians in Rome, Paul makes it clear why it was so important for God to send His Son in the flesh. "For what the [Mosaic] law was powerless to do because it was weakened by the flesh, God did by sending his own Son in the likeness of sinful flesh to be a sin offering. And so he condemned sin in the flesh" (**Romans 8:3**). In order for mankind to have the option of being freed from sin, God had to send His sin offering in the form of a human being—fully human; yet divine as God's Son. The full benefit for those who believe, Paul reiterated, was that, "For those God foreknew he also predestined to be conformed to the image of his Son, that he might be the firstborn among many brothers and sisters" (**Romans 8:29**). Imagine that! Something Muslims and other non-Christians will never know: The glory and privilege of being a brother or sister to the Son of God. There can be no greater destiny, no greater satisfaction, no more blessed gift or reward than being a son or daughter of God and adopted into the household of God through His One and Only Son, Jesus Christ.

In his letter to the Galatians, Paul proclaimed: "But when the set time had fully come, God sent his Son, born of a woman, born under the law   Because you are his sons, God sent the Spirit of his Son into our hearts, the Spirit who calls out, *'Abba,* Father'" (**Galatians 4:4, 6**). *Abba* is an Aramaic word meaning "father" or in some circles, "daddy." Under Roman law at the time, those who were adopted into a Roman family had the same rights and privileges as biological children. Paul is letting the Christians in Rome know that they, through Jesus Christ, are adopted into the family of God and have the same rights and privileges as God's Son.

"The Son is the image of the invisible God, the firstborn over all creation," Paul told the church in Colosse, an ancient city in Asia Minor (**Colossians 1:15**). Christ's life on earth represented His Father's intent and purpose—to bring salvation to a lost world and to restore those who chose Jesus as Lord and Savior to their rightful place as sons and daughters of the King and heirs to His Kingdom.

The Doubters and Scoffers. In the Gospels of Matthew, Mark and Luke, Jesus tells a parable (an allegory) about wicked vineyard workers. The complete story follows.

> *Listen to another parable: There was a landowner who planted a vineyard. He put a wall around it, dug a winepress in it and built a watchtower. Then he rented the vineyard to some farmers and moved to another place. When the harvest time approached, he sent his servants to the tenants to collect his fruit.*
>
> *The tenants seized his servants; they beat one, killed another, and stoned a third. Then he sent other servants to them, more than the first time, and the tenants treated them the same way. Last of all, he sent his son to them. "They will respect my son," he said.*
>
> *But when the tenants saw the son, they said to each other, "This is the heir. Come, let's kill him and take his inheritance." So they took him and threw him out of the vineyard and killed him.*
>
> *Therefore, when the owner of the vineyard comes, what will he do to those tenants?*
>
> *"He will bring those wretches to a wretched end," they replied, "and he will rent the vineyard to other tenants, who will give him his share of the crop at harvest time."*
>
> *Jesus said to them, "Have you never read in the Scriptures: 'The stone the builders rejected has become the cornerstone; the Lord has done this, and it is marvelous in our*

eyes?'" [**Psalm 118:22-23**] (**Matthew 21:33-42**; also see **Mark 12:1-11** and **Luke 20:9-19**).

What point was Jesus trying to drive home to His disciples in this parable? First, we should identify the participants. The *landowner* Jesus referred to is God. The *vineyard* represents Israel whom God created. The *farmers* (in other Bible versions; *tenant farmers* or *vinedressers*) are the Jewish religious leaders. The *servants* are the prophets and priests of God whom God sent to the Israelites and who remained loyal to God. The *son* is Jesus, and the *other tenants* are the Gentiles or non-Jews. In this parable, Jesus is telling His followers God had sent His prophets and priests to inform the Jews about His Law and godly living, but they rejected it and those whom God sent. God then sent His One and Only Son with a message of hope, love and redemption, but the Jewish leaders rejected Jesus also, and turned Him over to Roman authorities to be crucified. In rejecting Jesus Christ as God's Son, they rejected the very cornerstone of God's plan of salvation for the Jews and all mankind.

This denunciation of Jesus as the Son of God continued right up to the moment Christ was lifted up on the cross. "You who are going to destroy the temple and build it in three days," the Jews mocked, "save yourself! Come down from the cross, if you are the Son of God!" (**Matthew 27:40**).

Another taunted, "He trusts in God. Let God rescue him now if he wants him, for he said, 'I am the Son of God'" (**Matthew 27:43**).

"The Jewish leaders insisted, 'We have a law, and according to that law he must die, because he claimed to be the Son of God'" (**John 19:7**). The Jewish leaders were more concerned about following *their* law than hearing and following God's words spoken by His Son.

About 40 years after Christ's crucifixion and resurrection, the writer to the Hebrews would pen: "How much more severely do you think someone deserves to be punished who has trampled the Son of God underfoot, who has treated as an unholy thing the blood of the covenant that sanctified them, and who has insulted the Spirit of grace?" (**Hebrews 10:29**).

When Jesus' teachings became too difficult for some of His followers to accept, many of them deserted Him. Jesus then asked the Twelve, His handpicked disciples, if they wanted to abandon Him also. "But Simon Peter answered Him, 'Lord, to whom shall we go? You have the words of eternal life. Also we have come to believe and know that You are the Christ, the Son of the living God'" (**John 6:68-69**, NKJV). Despite the wholesale defections from the less committed, Peter remained steadfast in His belief in who Jesus was and the validity of His words, despite denying knowing Christ right before His crucifixion.

The Purpose of God Revealing Himself in the Flesh. "Since the children have flesh and blood, he [Jesus] too shared in their humanity so that by his death he might break the power of him who holds the power of death—that is, the devil—and free those who all their lives were held in slavery by their fear of death. For surely it is not angels he helps, but Abraham's descendants. For this reason he had to be made like them, fully human in every way, in order that he might become a merciful and faithful high priest in service to God, and that he might make atonement for the sins of the people. Because he himself suffered when he was tempted, he is able to help those who are being tempted" (**Hebrews 2:14-18**).

God, in His infinite wisdom, sent His Son in the flesh like a normal human being so that He would experience life in the flesh just like all those He came to save from separation from God and eternal damnation. It was, and is, a perfect plan—one that could not have possibly been concocted by a human mind.

"Therefore," the author of Hebrews continued, "since we have a great high priest who has ascended into heaven, **Jesus the Son of God**, let us hold firmly to the faith we profess. For we do not have a high priest who is unable to empathize with our weaknesses, but we have one who has been tempted in every way, just as we are – yet he did not sin. Let us then approach God's throne of grace with confidence, so that we may receive mercy and find grace to help us in our time of need" (**Hebrews 4:14-16**). No one, not even Muslims who claim to have the true faith, have access to the throne of God. Allah is unapproachable. But believers in Jesus Christ as the Son of God have direct access to the throne of God, the Creator of all things, because of their undisputed relationship as a brother or sister in Christ and, therefore, a child of God.

The Apostle Paul, in quoting from both the prophets **Isaiah (25:8)** and **Hosea (13:14)**, wrote about the everlasting benefit of faith in Christ, "When the perishable has been clothed with the imperishable, and the mortal with immortality, then the saying that is written will come true: 'Death has been swallowed up in victory.' 'Where, O death, is your victory? Where, O death, is your sting?'" (**1 Corinthians 15:54-55**). For the believers in Jesus Christ as the Son of God, while the body dies and decays, the spirit within the believer has eternal life and, therefore, victory over death.

Paul, in his letter to his spiritual protégé, Timothy, explained it this way: "it has now been revealed through the appearing of our Savior, Christ Jesus, who has destroyed death and has brought life and immortality to light through the gospel" (**2 Timothy 1:10**). There is only one truth – and it is not in the Qur'an or any other *holy book* – by which a person can be saved unto eternal life and that is through the living Gospel of Jesus Christ.

For to which of the angels did God ever say, "You are my Son; today I have become your Father" [Psalm 2:7]?
Or again, "I will be his Father, and he will be my Son?"
[Psalm 89:26-27]
Hebrews 1:5

Once again, the writer to the Hebrews stated, "During the days of Jesus' life on earth, he offered up prayers and petitions with fervent cries and tears to the one who could save him from death, and he was heard because of his reverent submission. Son though he was, he learned obedience from what he suffered and, once made perfect, he became the source of eternal salvation for all who obey him" **(Hebrews 5:7-9)**. Through Jesus' obedience to His Father unto death on the cross, He was able to acquire the rarest gift of all for those who chose to follow Him – eternal life with His Father in Heaven.

Finally, the Apostle John wrote, "The one who does what is sinful is of the devil, because the devil has been sinning from the beginning. The reason the Son of God appeared was to destroy the devil's work" (1 John 3:8). The question every Muslim must ask himself or herself: *Did Muhammad destroy the devil's work?* **If he did not, why are you following him?**

We accept human testimony, but God's testimony is greater because it is the testimony of God, which he has given about his Son. Whoever believes in the Son of God accepts this testimony. Whoever does not believe God has made him out to be a liar, because they have not believed the testimony God has given about his Son. And this is the testimony: God has given us eternal life, and this life is in his Son. Whoever has the Son has life; whoever does not have the Son of God does not have life. I write these things to you who believe in the name of the Son of God so that you may know that you have eternal life.
1 John 5:9-13

The Final Summation. Just like the closing statements of a skilled attorney, the Apostle John lays out his case for all to hear and believe.

"If anyone acknowledges that Jesus is the Son of God, God lives in them and they in God" **(1 John 4:15)**.

"Everyone who believes that Jesus is the Christ is born of God, and everyone who loves the father loves his child as well" **(1 John 5:1)**.

"Who is it that overcomes the world? Only the one who believes that Jesus is the Son of God" (**1 John 5:5**).

No clearer three-point summation could be offered on why Jesus is the Christ, the Only begotten Son of God, and the rewards of following Him. For Muslims, there is no reward in following Allah—either in this world or the next.

In what might be considered his closing argument in his first letter, the Apostle John sums up the ministry and purpose of the coming of Jesus Christ, "We know also that the Son of God has come and has given us understanding, so that we may know him who is true. And we are in him who is true by being in his Son Jesus Christ. He is the true God and eternal life" (**1 John 5:20**). John, possibly in his 80s or even 90s at the time, and about 60 years after his close-knit life with Jesus, had a lot of time to reflect on the purpose of Jesus' short life and ministry. Yet, after all the time that had passed by, he was able to categorically state, "Anyone who runs ahead and does not continue in the teaching of Christ does not have God; whoever continues in the teaching has both the Father and the Son" (**2 John 1:9**).

The penalty for disbelieving in Jesus Christ as the Son of God is severe and eternal. "Whoever believes in the Son of God accepts this testimony. Whoever does not believe God has made him out to be a liar, because they have not believed the testimony God has given about his Son" (**1 John 5:10**). And, "Who is the liar? It is whoever denies that Jesus is the Christ. Such a person is the antichrist—denying the Father and the Son" (**1 John 2:22**).

Children of the Living God

The Book of Daniel in the Old Testament offers an interesting insight into the God of the Jews and Christians. Daniel had high favor with Belshazzar, King of Babylonia, but the king was murdered and 62-year old Darius the Mede took over the kingdom. In a plot against Daniel, the king's provincial rulers urged the king to issue a decree, that anyone who prayed to a god or man other than Darius would be thrown into the lion's den. Daniel, a devout Jew who worshipped the only true God, refused to obey. The king was distraught because he did not want to kill Daniel, but had to comply with his edict.

"The king said to Daniel, 'May your God, whom you serve continually, rescue you'" (**Daniel 6:16b**). Note that the king did not appeal to any pagan god for Daniel's deliverance, but rather to Daniel's God (who did have the absolute power to rescue Daniel).

The next morning, the king was anxious to see if Daniel's God had indeed saved him. "Daniel answered [the king's plea], 'O king, live forever! My God sent his angel, and he shut the mouths of the lions. They have not hurt me, because I was found innocent in his [God's] sight '''" (**Daniel 6:21-22**).

King Darius was overjoyed that Daniel's God had rescued him. "I issue a decree," he wrote to the peoples and nations of his Babylonian empire, "that in every part of my kingdom people must fear and reverence the God of Daniel. 'For he is the living God and he endures forever; his kingdom will not be destroyed, his dominion will never end (Daniel 6:26, author's emphasis).'" This was quite a proclamation for a gentile monarch. Darius did not formerly believe in a living, interactive personal God. When Daniel survived the certain death of the lion's den, Darius knew that Daniel's God was alive and personally cared about those who worshipped Him.

Jeremiah, who was a prophet during Daniel's captivity in Babylon, warned Israel not to stray and follow the gods and signs of their pagan neighbors. "But the LORD is the true God; he is **the living God**, the eternal King. When he is angry, the earth trembles; the nations cannot endure his wrath" (**Jeremiah 10:10**, author's emphasis).

The Apostle Paul would later reaffirm this call for Jews and Christians to follow the only true living God. "What agreement is there between the temple of God and idols [that are dead]? For we are the temple of **the living God**. As God has said: 'I will live with them and walk among them, and I will be their God, and they will be my people'" [**Ezekiel 37:27**] (**2 Corinthians 6:16**, author's emphasis).

Allah, the god of Muslims, has never walked among those who seek him or follow him. He is a disinterested god and not a living, interactive god in the affairs of mankind.

There is no god like the *living* God—the one and only personal God, who takes pleasure in having an intimate Father and son, or Father and daughter relationship with His creation.

Once again, the Apostle Paul reiterates the importance of this Father child relationship by quoting from the prophet **Hosea** (**1:10**): "I will call them 'my people' who are not my people; and I will call her 'my loved one' who is not my loved one," and, "It will happen that in the very place where it was said to them, 'You are not my people,' they will be called 'sons of the living God'" (**Romans 9:25-26**).

How does one procure such a cherished parental relationship with God? Paul spells it out in **Galatians 3:26-29**. "You are all sons of God through faith in Christ Jesus, for all of you who were baptized into Christ have clothed yourselves with Christ. There is neither Jew nor Greek, slave nor free, male nor female, for you are all one in Christ Jesus. If you belong to Christ, then you are Abraham's seed, and heirs according to the promise." This God of the Jews and Christians wants to have this personal relationship with *all* of His human creation, no matter what the origin of the individual. He clearly separates Himself from Allah, who wants no such personal relationship.

There is only one way to be assured of a personal Father-child relationship with the only living God, and that is through faith in Jesus Christ. "The [Holy] Spirit himself [within you] testifies with our spirit that we are God's children. *Now if we are children, then we are heirs*—heirs of God and co-heirs with Christ, if indeed we share in his sufferings in order that we may also share in his glory" (**Romans 8:16-17**; author's emphasis).

Paul clarifies how an experience with the living God through Christ is different than that of God's expression through the Law of Moses. "You show that you are a letter from Christ, the result of our ministry, written not with ink [of the Law] but with the Spirit of the living God, not on tablets of stone but on tablets of human hearts. . . . He has made us competent as ministers of a new covenant – not of the letter but of the Spirit; for the letter [of the Law] kills, but the Spirit gives life" (2 Corinthians 3:3, 6).

Jesus also made it clear about the type of relationship His followers were to expect and have with God. The only prayer He ever taught His disciples, He started by addressing God Almighty as "Our Father. . ." (**Matthew 6:9**).

For those who could not accept the living God as a spiritual father, "Jesus said to them, 'If God were your Father, you would love me, for I came from God and now am here. I have not come on my own; but he sent me'" (**John 8:42**). Those who do not, and cannot, accept Jesus as the Son of God will never be able to see or accept God as their heavenly Father. That is the conundrum and difficulty that all Muslims face and what keeps them in bondage to Allah, the unseen, non-revealing and impersonal god.

"In other words," the Apostle Paul noted, "it is not the natural children who are God's children, but it is the children of the promise who are regarded as Abraham's offspring" (**Romans 9:8**). Remember from Chapter 3, God never promised Ishmael and his descendants that He would be their God; nor did He claim that Ishmael was a child of the promise that God had made with Abraham.

Allah has no Children

God Created Mankind in His Image. What is **the importance of being a child of God?** According to the Apostle John, "He [Jesus Christ] came to His own [the Jews], and His own did not receive Him. But as many as received Him, to them **He gave the right** [authority] **to become children of God**, to those who believe in His name: who were born, not of blood, nor of the will of the flesh, nor of the will of man, but of God" (**John 1:11-13**; author's emphasis, NKJV). Through Christ, and Him only, Jesus' followers have been given the authority to be the true children of God. No wonder Muslims do not accept that they are Allah's or God's children. The only way anyone can be a child of God is through Christ.

As part of His priestly prayer for His followers, Jesus prayed, "Father, I want those you have given me to be with me where I am, and to see my glory, the glory you have given me because you loved me before the creation of the world.

"Righteous Father, though the world does not know you, I know you, and they know that you have sent me. I have made you known to them, and will continue to make you known in order that the love you have for me may be in them and that I myself may be in them" (**John 17:24-26**).

If you want to enjoy the glories of Heaven in the afterlife you must be a child of God through faith in Jesus Christ, the only One that God ever sent to earth to bring everlasting salvation to all those who would believe in Jesus Christ as Lord and Savior of their life.

> *Praise be to the God and Father of our Lord Jesus Christ, who has blessed us in the heavenly realms with every spiritual blessing in Christ. For he chose us in him before the creation of the world to be holy and blameless in his sight. In love he* [God] *predestined us for adoption to sonship* [as children] *through Jesus Christ, in accordance with his pleasure and will – to the praise of his glorious grace, which he has freely given us in the One he loves* (**Ephesians 1:3-6**).

Paul explained this unique relationship of God the Father with His children who accept Christ in another meaningful way. "Therefore, if anyone is in Christ, the new creation has come: The old has gone, the new is here!" (**2 Corinthians 5:17**). In a similar way, Paul, in his letter to the Ephesian church, wrote, ". . . put on the new self, created to be like God in true righteousness and holiness" (**Ephesians 4:24**). What a glorious opportunity and reality Christians have for intimate fellowship with their Father God, something the rest of the world can only fantasize about until they accept Jesus Christ as Lord and Savior of their lives.

Once again, to the Colossians, Paul proclaimed, ". . . put on the new self, which is being renewed in knowledge in the image of its Creator" (**Colossians 3:10**). For followers of Christ, as we grow in knowledge of Jesus and His call upon our life, and as we increase our understanding of God's word through preaching, teaching and Bible study, we gain a greater insight to our cherished and loving connection to God as our Father and our membership in the family of God.

> *In other words, it is not the children by physical descent who are God's children, but it is the children of the promise* [Jews and Christians] *who are regarded as Abraham's offspring.*
> **Romans 9:8**

"How great is the love the Father has lavished on us," the Apostle John penned, "that we should be called **children of God**! And that is what we are! The reason the world does not know us is that it did not know him [Jesus]. Dear friends, now we are **children of God**, and what we will be has not yet been made known. But we know that when Christ appears, we shall be like him, for we shall see him as he is" (**1 John 3:1-2**; author's emphasis). Wow! What a proclamation by the Apostle John. Believers in Christ have a distinct and unique relationship with their God that no one else in the world has and can only dream about. Non-Christians cannot understand this type of relationship, nor can they be a part of it unless they join the family of God through faith in Christ.

How does one know for sure that he or she is a child of God? Again, Paul wrote, "The Spirit himself testifies with our spirit that we are God's children" (Romans 8:16). Once a person accepts Jesus Christ as Lord and Savior, the Spirit of God enters that person and brings forth revelation knowledge and understanding. As Paul declared, God's Spirit bears witness with our spirit that we are God's children, His sons and daughters. Again, this is something that Allah denies for his followers, thus leaving them as spiritual orphans – an unclaimed people left to fend for themselves in a cruel and unjust world.

> *In this the children of God and the children of the devil are manifest: Whoever does not practice righteousness is not of God, nor is he who does not love his brother* [or sister in the Lord] (1 John 3:10, NKJV).

Allah is too High and Mighty to have Children. "And they [Jews and Christians] make the jinn [fallen angels or evil spirits] associates with Allah, while He created them, and they falsely attributed to Him sons and daughters without knowledge . . ." (**Qur'an 6:100**). Of course, the truth of the matter is that neither Jews nor Christians would ever claim that Allah was the father of Jesus or anyone else among their faithful, because Allah was not, and is not their God.

Since Allah has no children, he is the father to no one. In the Qur'an, the term "father" is only used in the context of a man's relationship to his children. It is never used to describe Allah's relationship to those who worship him. It is forbidden by the faithful

to demean Allah with such an earthly association. That Jesus would claim to be the Son of God was preposterous to Muhammad and continues to be unthinkable among Muslims today. Since Muslims draw up short of accusing Jesus of blasphemy, they assert that it was Jesus' apostles that falsely ascribed this *Son of God* association to Him. Allah cannot lower himself to have a son. If he can have no son, then he cannot have children.

"Allah, the god revealed in the Qur'an, is not a loving Father" (1). In fact, he is not a father image at all to Muslims. It is beneath Allah to be a father to anyone human. Muslims are therefore spiritual orphans—children of the Creator, but without a father.

Allah cannot have a son—or can he? The Qur'an provides a confusing picture of the birth of Jesus. On the one hand it states clearly that Allah *cannot* have a son. It is beneath him.

Allah has no sons: "Wonderful Originator of the heavens and the earth! How could He have a son when He has no consort, and He (Himself) created everything . . ." (**Qur'an 6:101**). So vehement is Allah's denial that he could have a son, that he threatens to annihilate the Christians for saying so. ". . . and the Christians say: The Messiah is the son of Allah; these are the words of their mouths; they imitate the saying of those who disbelieved before; may Allah destroy them; how they are turned away!" (**Qur'an 9:30**).

Numerous verses in the Qur'an staunchly proclaim that God [Allah] could never and would never have a son (**Qur'an 10:68; 18:4-5; 25:2; 19:35; 21:26; 37:151-152; 72:3; 112:3**) because "it is not worthy of the Beneficent God that He should take (to Himself) a son. There is no one in the heavens and the earth but will come to the Beneficent God as a servant" (**Qur'an 19:88-83**).

Now, if it was Gabriel that delivered to Muhammad the Qur'an as the Infallible word of Allah, how could he be so confused as to the relationship between Jesus and God Almighty? In the Qur'an, Gabriel insists (according to Muhammad) that God cannot and would not have a son. Yet, in the Bible, 600+ years before Gabriel "delivered" the Qur'an, Gabriel proclaimed that Mary's son, Jesus, would indeed be the promised Messiah, the Son of the one and only living God.

According to **Qur'an 39:4**, Allah can have a son if he wants to. "If Allah desire[s] to take a son to Himself, He will surely choose those He pleases from what He has created. Glory be to Him: He is Allah, the One, the Subduer (of all)."

Then there is this surah that states clearly that Allah can have a son if he wants to. "And mention Marium in the Book when she drew aside from her family to an eastern place; so she took a veil (to screen herself) from them; then We [Allah – and who else?] sent to her Our spirit [angel], and there appeared to her a well-made man.   He said: I am only a messenger of your Lord; That I will give you a pure [immaculately conceived] boy. She said: When shall I have a boy and no mortal has yet touched me, nor have I been unchaste? He said: Even so; your Lord [Allah] says: It is easy to Me: and that We may make him a sign to men and a mercy from Us; and it is a matter which has been decreed" (**Qur'an 19:16-17, 19-21**).

In **Qur'an 9:30**, Muhammad accuses both the Jews and Christians of blaspheming Allah by saying that he has a son and that they are worthy only of death for believing so. "And the Jews say: Uzair [Ezra] is the son of Allah; and the Christians say: The Messiah [Jesus] is the son of Allah; these are the words of their mouths; they imitate the saying of those who disbelieved before; may Allah destroy them; how they are turned away."

Notice that Muhammad is not content with people believing differently than him about God. If their perception of their god is not the same as his, then Allah is called upon to *destroy* them—not love them into his wellspring of faith.

On another point, regardless of Muhammad's assertion in this verse, there is no biblical record that the Jews believed that Ezra, a Babylonian exile, who was a scribe and teacher of the Law of Moses, was in any manner considered to be the Son of God (**Ezra 7:1-6**). This too, would have been blasphemy to the Jew.

Children are NOT a Blessing to Allah

In the eyes of Allah, children born to his human creation are not a blessing. In fact, children are but a temptation to draw one away from following Allah and his Apostle. "O you who believe! be not unfaithful to Allah and the Apostle, nor be unfaithful to your trusts while you know. And know that your property and your children are a temptation, and that Allah is He with Whom there is a mighty reward" (**Qur'an 8:27-28**).

By contrast, when the disciples of Jesus tried to stop the people from bringing their children before Jesus, Jesus rebuked His disciples. "Jesus said, 'Let the little children come to me, and do not hinder them, for the kingdom of God belongs to such as these'" (**Mark 10:14**). Jesus and the New Testament teach that children are a cherished treasure from God that He has entrusted to parents.

No such image is portrayed by Allah in the Qur'an. "And let not their [the unbeliever's] property and [the happiness which they may derive from] their children excite your admiration; Allah only wishes to chastise them with these in this world and (that) their souls may depart while they are unbelievers" (**Qur'an 9:85**).

While the God of the Bible calls believers to cherish their

children and bring them up in the way of the Lord (Proverbs 22:6), Allah sees them as an instrument of punishment for those that do not follow him.

Once again, in **Qur'an 18:46**, Allah gives the impression that children are unimportant to him. "Wealth and children are an adornment of the life of this world; and the ever-abiding [which endures forever are] the good works, are [far] better with your Lord in reward and better in expectation" [or source of hope]. It is good deeds that count with Allah and what brings one his reward, not the blessing of children.

The one who sins is the one who will die. The child will not share the guilt of the parent, nor will the parent share the guilt of the child. The righteousness of the righteous will be credited to them, and the wickedness of the wicked will be charged against them.
Ezekiel 18:20

Children, according to Allah, are also the source of much travail and wickedness. "O you who believe! surely from among your wives and your children there is an enemy to you; therefore beware of them; and if you pardon and forbear and forgive, then surely Allah is Forgiving, Merciful. Your possessions and your children are only a trial, and Allah it is with Whom is a great reward" (**Qur'an 64:14-15**).

It would appear that, not only does Allah not admit to having any children, but that he is jealous of them and that they are dangerous and have evil intent.

The Almighty Living God, however, adores children—children of His creation. "Yet to all who received him [Jesus]," the Apostle John confirmed, "to those who believed in his name, he gave the right to become children of God – children born not of natural descent, nor of human decision or a husband's will, but born of God" (**John 1:12-13**). Those who follow Christ, the Son of the Living God, have the indisputable right to become and to be called the *children of God.*

"For he [God] chose us in him [Christ] before the creation of the world," wrote the Apostle Paul, "to be holy and blameless in his sight. In love he [God] predestined us to be adopted as his sons through Jesus Christ, in accordance with his pleasure and will—to the praise of his glorious grace, which he has freely given us in the One he loves" (**Ephesians 1:4-6**).

Allah's Followers have No Purpose

There is no purpose to Allah's creation and life on earth other than self-serving satisfaction. Two verses in the Qur'an revealed to

Muhammad by Allah through Gabriel give the distinct impression that the purpose of Allah's devotees is to willy-nilly amble through life, engaging in self-pleasures and then they die when the impassionate Allah decides their life is over. When life is over, then will come Allah's judgment. However, he has given his followers neither the means by which to prepare for it, nor to be exempted from it by any other way than a tally of their good deeds outweighing their bad deeds.

Consider the saga of the wandering soul in **Qur'an 40:67-68**: "He it is Who created you from dust, [and] then from a small life-germ [sperm], [and] then from a clot, then He brings you forth as a child, [and] then [He ordains] that you may attain your maturity, [and] then that you may [grow to] be old—[though some of you (He causes to) die earlier]—and that you may reach an appointed term [of life], and that you may understand. He it is Who gives life and brings death, so when He decrees an affair [to be], He only says to it: Be, and it is."

Qur'an 57:20 offers another view of the aimless life. "Know that this world's life is only sport and play and gaiety [or a beautiful show] and boasting among yourselves, and vying in the multiplication of wealth and children . . . [and] then [in the end, just like a withered plant, your life] becomes dried up and broken down; and in the hereafter is a severe chastisement [or] forgiveness from Allah and [at] (His) pleasure; and this world's life is naught but [a] means of deception."

So, after a Muslim lives this apparent meaningless life on earth, he or she has to stand before Allah and receive his random judgment of one's life on earth based strictly on the scales of good outweighing evil. There is little freedom of choice because Allah will decide how your life should go and when it should end.

Christians, on the other hand, are given a clear picture of their purpose and mission while on earth and the rationale for their creation. The Bible states clearly that those whom God created are called to serve the Lord (**Deuteronomy 10:12-13**) and worship Him in joy and gladness (**Psalm 100:2**); to share God's love with others and do no harm (**Romans 13:9-10**); to be servants (**John 12:26**) and ambassadors for Christ (**2 Corinthians 5:20**) with a ministry of reconciliation (**2 Corinthians 5:18**). To live with Jesus as their example (**John 13:14-16; 1 Peter 2:21**); always doing that which is good (**1 Peter 3:13-17**); sharing the Gospel of good news with the world (**Matthew 28:19-20; Mark 13:10**).

Christians are called by God to make the world a better place—sharing, building, restoring, reconciling, forgiving, healing, nurturing, loving; demonstrating mercy and justice—and pointing the lost world to a redeeming, saving knowledge of Jesus Christ. Although Muslims are also called to draw unbelievers to their god, their methods are quite different and diverse (see the section on The Mission).

The God Who is There

Allah will not Hear Unless you Speak Arabic. One teaching of Islam is, Allah will not hear or understand a person unless one prays in Arabic. Despite the fact that over 80 percent of Muslims are not Arabs, and most of those do not speak or understand the Arabic language.

The main reason prayers are to be recited in Arabic and the Qur'an read in Arabic, appears to be because Muhammad said so, or Allah demands it, according to Iranian Masoud Mayahian and Ahmed H. Sheriff of al-Islam.org, the largest online Islamic digital library (2, 3).

The full explanation rendered by Masoud is that:

> *The main reason behind performing prayers only in Arabic after the fact that it is part of the prophet's (pbuh) sunnah and that in general, all forms of worship need to be dictated to us by Allah (swt) the way He wants them to be performed, is to avoid the alteration of the form of prayers throughout the different ages and to be protected from any potential change, and if every individual is to perform prayers in the language he/she speaks there would be a fairly great possibility of the alteration of the prayers by adding or omitting some words or even mixing it with superstition, there were also chances of these changes would leading to other changes in the fundamentals of the prayer and little by little the concept of praying would lose its importance and would be completely forgotten.*

At the bare minimum, Masoud asserted, every Muslim can learn the 20 Arabic words necessary for repetitive Islamic prayer.

Someone raised among Muslims who denies the obligatoriness of the prayer, zakat, fasting Ramadan, the pilgrimage, or the unlawfulness of wine or adultery, or denies something else upon which there is [Islamic] *scholarly consensus . . . and which is necessarily known as being of the religion . . . thereby becomes an unbeliever (kafir) and is executed for his unbelief . . .*

Reliance of the Traveller, f1.3

Sheriff admits, that while it would "seem logical that every Muslim should pray through his own mother language," so it would be possible to actually understand what he or she is saying to Allah, he quickly whisked that notion aside. He goes on to claim, as did Masoud, that it is only Arabic language that has the ability to correctly convey the serene beauty of communication with Allah. Only Arabic has the precise words that are acceptable to Allah.

"Moreover," Sheriff insisted, "it has been proved that no language, except Arabic, is capable of presenting such deep spiritual, moral and ethical expressions in such an eloquent manner. Therefore the choice of Arabic for Islamic prayers is not to be wondered upon."

Sheriff also contended, despite the fact that the Qur'an has been translated by Islamic scholars into multiple languages in order to evangelize non-Muslims, any translation other than Arabic is suspect and not the true word of Allah, but of humans.

> *Arabic in which the Holy Qur'an and traditions of the Prophet have been revealed has a special status and honour. This high status of Arabic is not due to its being the language of the Arabs; rather it is because of its being language of Qur'an chosen by Almighty God for conveying His last message and revelation.*
>
> *Muslims believe that the Holy Qur'an is the Word of God. As such, it is only befitting that the recitation of the word of God is done in the same form and language in which it was originally pronounced. Spiritually, a faithful Muslim finds himself ascending higher and higher with the support of the words of God as expressed in the original language which is Arabic (4).*

The God of the Christians and Jews, however, does not insist on one language or another for communication with Him. After all, He *is* the God that created them all (see the story of the Tower of Babel in **Genesis 11:1-9**).

Also, the regime of dos and don'ts of Islamic prayer are very strict and laborious. No deviation or exceptions are permitted; violations will bring severe chastisement or even death. Prayer time is obligatory and cannot be missed without extreme exceptions. Prayers must be at a certain time each day, in a certain manner, in proper clothing, with the proper position of hands and it is unlawful to interrupt your prayer once started. Prayers can only be said in certain approved locations and it is offensive to Allah for prayers to be said in a bathhouse, in the middle of a path, in a garbage dump, a slaughterhouse, a church, place that receives taxes, places likely contaminated with wine, or towards a tomb. Death is prescribed for a Muslim who neglects daily prayers (Source: *Reliance of the Traveller, A Classic Manual of Islamic Sacred Law*).

Christians, however, can pray in any language, anywhere, anytime, and God Almighty will hear. The original Bible—both Old and New Testaments—were in Hebrew, Aramaic and Greek. According to Wycliffe Global Alliance, of the over 7,000 world languages, there are portions of Bible scriptures translated into 3,350 of those languages as of October, 2018 (see http://www.wycliffe.net/statistics). The entire Bible is in 683 languages; the New Testament in 1,534 languages, and portions of scripture in another 1,133 tongues. The Good News for the followers of the One and Only True God is that HE does hear each and every prayer in every conceivable language and dialect.

The Christian faith teaches, with the support of its biblical scriptures, that Jehovah God, the Judeo-Christian God of the Old and New Testament, in the person of Jesus Christ and through the ministry and the indwelling presence of the Holy Spirit, changes a human life condition and experience from the inside, out. God chooses to change the heart and soul of man in order to achieve His intended inner and outer expression of one's faith in Him. "Whoever confesses that Jesus is the Son of God," the Apostle John taught, "God abides in him, and he in God" (**1 John 4:15,** NKJV).

Jesus on Repetitive Prayer. The Judeo-Christian God does not care in what language you talk to Him. All He cares about is that you stay in touch with Him in an intimate and personal way—to have a conversation with Him daily.

In **Matthew 6:7-8**, Jesus criticized those who sought to reach God with repetitive prayers in the synagogue, comparing them to "babbling like pagans." He then went on to provide His disciples with a sample prayer containing the essential elements of communication with God:

"This, then, is how you should pray:

Our Father in heaven, hallowed be your name,
your kingdom come, your will be done, on earth as it is in
heaven.
Give us today our daily bread.
And forgive us our debts, as we also have forgiven our
debtors.
And lead us not into temptation, but deliver us from the
evil one" (**Matthew 6:9-13**).

Some late Bible manuscripts add: *for yours is the kingdom and the power and the glory forever. Amen.*

Notice that Jesus started the prayer in a very personal and intimate way: *Our Father. . .* Whenever a Christian approaches God, that believer has the freedom and authority to come to God as "Father," as he or she prays in the name and power of Jesus Christ. In **Ephesians 5:20,** the Apostle Paul instructs Christ followers, "always giving thanks to God the Father for everything, in the name of our Lord Jesus Christ."

Changing from the Inside Out. Those who freely choose to follow Jesus Christ are given an abiding invitation to enter into an intimate personal relationship with God through faith in Jesus. Through Jesus, Christians know the character of their loving God. They know that God loves them so much that He wants to have an "abba" Father (or "Daddy") relationship with them (**Romans 8:15**). Muslims, on the other hand, are taught that Allah desires no such personal relationship with his human creation. Not only would Allah not leave his throne to dwell among people, but he would never sully his godhead with such a sinful alliance.

Islam, through the dictates of the Qur'an and the example of Muhammad, seeks to enforce changes upon the outer man, in order to bring about inner changes and peace. The history of the world and mankind is at our disposal to demonstrate that such religious enforcement of spiritual law from the outside-in, has never changed man's inner spirit; nor improved his relationship with his god nor with his neighbors.

". . . Allah guides whom He pleases to the right path" (**Qur'an 2:213**). There is no personal, intimate choice in following Allah. It is Allah that chooses whom he wants as his followers. In the Muslim world, there is no personal choice in accepting the tenets of faith of Islam. Yes, there are adult converts to the faith, but they are far and few between. Children born into Muslim families and adult non-believers, are coerced or persecuted into becoming Muslims at the threat of torture or death.

Christianity, on the other hand, as explained in the scriptures, is a personal relationship with Jesus Christ and a personal choice. A person chooses to become a Christian, a follower of Christ, because he or she makes an informed life-changing decision to accept Jesus' offer and plan of salvation; acknowledge Him as Lord and Savior and to follow the teachings of Jesus (see the Addendum at the end of the book, *A Sinner's Path to Salvation* for more details).

God Wants to Know You Personally. The central message of the Christian gospel is that: *God loves you and He wants to have a personal, intimate relationship with you.* This message is antithetical to the message of Islam and its prophet, Muhammad. Allah is distant and far away from the Muslim believer. He is unapproachable and uninterested in an intimate relationship with those who worship him. For the Muslim, it is inconceivable and blasphemous to think that Allah would demean himself and walk among his creation. In the Qur'an there are no recordings of Allah acting inter-personally with his creation through healing, deliverance, miracles, or other loving acts toward those he supposedly loves. Whereas, the Bible is full of such loving acts by the Almighty God and Father for the children He created.

Muslims are instructed to call upon Allah as the only true god, but he does not answer. "Surely those whom you call on besides Allah are in a state of subjugation like yourselves; therefore call on them, then let them answer you if you are truthful . . . And those whom you call upon besides Him [Allah] are not able to help you, nor can they help themselves" (**Qur'an 7:194, 197**). The irony here is, that calling upon Allah does not produce results, but calling upon the Christian God does, giving testimony to His existence.

Contrast Muhammad's preceding admonition with the reality of Elijah's confrontation with the prophets of Baal (**1 Kings 18**). All day long 450 prophets of Baal, the pagan god, sacrificed and cried out to him and pleaded with him to show himself through a miracle, but nothing happened. Elijah taunted them by saying that perhaps their god was asleep, deep in thought or away traveling. Then Elijah made his request of Jehovah God to reveal Himself and He miraculously did just that to prove that He was the only living God. To re-emphasize an earlier point, when Muslims cry out to Allah for truth and to reveal himself, he never does—instead Jesus has been known to reveal Himself in a dream or vision to those who are sincere in heart and seeking the truth.

Unlike Allah's selectivity in whom he will love, the God of the Bible wants all people to love Him because He loves all people. When the Apostle Peter was struggling with the thought of taking the Gospel of Jesus Christ to the Gentiles (the non-Jewish world), God gave him a vision. It took Peter a while to understand it, but he finally received God's truth and His heart for all mankind (see **Acts 10:9-23**).

The Apostle John stated how important it was for God to express His unreserved love through Christ. "In this the love of God was manifested toward us, that God has sent His only begotten Son into the world, that we might live through Him" (**1 John 4:9**, NKJV).

Jehovah God revealed himself in the person of Jesus Christ and in so doing invited all of mankind to enter into a personal relationship with Him through faith in Christ Jesus. Then, through the indwelling power of the Holy Spirit, God empowers Christians to live the godly, holy life by initiating life-changing spiritual and soulful change from within.

Remember, as a concise review of previous chapters, the essence of the salvation message of the Gospel is: Jesus died as a blood sacrifice for our sins—not only Christians, but for the whole world (John 3:16-17). Whoever calls upon the name of Jesus, confesses their sin and repents, and accepts Jesus' atoning work of the cross and confesses Him as Lord and Savior, will be saved.

Allah, on the other hand, offers no such opportunity for freedom from sin, nor a transformed life for his followers. Instead, Allah offers only bondage to sin and uncertain forgiveness. The only hope for the confessing Muslim of Allah's acceptance is to follow the letter of the law of good deeds and allegiance to Allah. This is what Jesus came to do—to set the Jews and all others free from the law. Jesus was not sent to do away with God's law, but to set free those bound by the law and its imprisonment. Christ-followers are still called to obey God's moral law. However, it is God's Holy Spirit that empowers the Christian to follow the moral law.

For the Muslim there is no room in the Islamic belief system for a personal relationship with Allah. One becomes a Muslim simply by confessing the *shahada*, that is the creed that, "There is no god but Allah, Muhammad is the messenger of Allah." That is the simple confession of faith for every Muslim. Once a Muslim, the faithful must adhere to the six doctrines of Islam: There is one god; angels (not the Holy Spirit) do the will of Allah; belief in the Torah, Gospel and the Qur'an; the prophets of Allah (Adam, Noah, Abraham, Moses, David, Jesus and Muhammad); Allah will judge all mankind, and there is a heaven and a hell for eternal life (5).

The Good News for the Muslim and all people, is that one can be restored to the One and Only true God through repentance and accepting the sacrifice for sin of Jesus Christ, and Him only.

"When Allah is discussed within the Islamic community," wrote the Caner brothers, "the absence of intimacy, atonement, and omni-benevolence becomes apparent. In all the terms and titles for Allah, one does not encounter terms of intimacy" (6).

For the Christian, however, intimacy with God is a foregone conclusion based on faith in Jesus Christ. The Apostle Paul illustrated it in this manner. "However, as it is written: 'No eye has seen, no ear has heard, no mind has conceived what God has prepared for those who love him' but God has revealed it to us by his Spirit. The Spirit searches all things, even the deep things of God. For who among men knows the thoughts of a man except the man's spirit within him? In the same way no one knows the thoughts of God except the Spirit of God. We have not received the spirit of the world but the Spirit who is from God, that we may understand what God has freely given us" (**1 Corinthians 2:9-12**).

Muslims have no idea what Allah requires of them other than that stated in the Qur'an. Christians, on the other hand, through the presence of the indwelling Holy Spirit, have a personal, near to their heart, access and insight into God's will for their life.

Historically, by Qur'anic edict, Muslims can only be transformed on the outside through obedience to Allah and good works. But even then, even the most faithful cannot be sure of Allah's full acceptance of them or their worthiness of Paradise. Christians, through the inner witness of the Holy Spirit and their acceptance of the salvation message and the saving work of Christ, have absolute assurance of God's presence in their life and eternal life with Him.

For the Christian, the message of the Gospel is that Jesus brought God down to man in the person of the Holy Spirit to dwell within man as a daily witness of God's loving presence with those who accept His saving grace through Christ. The message of the Qur'an and the prophet Muhammad, is that Allah is forever distant and detached from his creation and is too aloof and uninterested in a personal, loving relationship with humankind.

Jesus' promise to those who follow Him is simply this: "And surely I am with you always, to the very end of the age" (**Matthew 28:20**).

Jesus taught His followers, "I am the vine; you are the branches. If a man remains in me and I in him, he will bear much fruit; apart from me you can do nothing. If anyone does not remain in me, he is like a branch that is thrown away and withers; such branches are picked up, thrown into the fire and burned" (**John 15:5-6**).

But "Here is the profound weakness of [Islam] in which there is no genuine connection between God and human being," state the Caner brothers. "Allah guides people into the truth through his messenger Muhammad, but one should never anticipate speaking to Allah personally or relationally" (7).

"Surely my guardian is Allah," revealed Muhammad, "Who revealed the Book [Qur'an], and He befriends the good. And those whom you call upon besides Him are not able to help you, nor can they help themselves" (**Qur'an 7:196-197**). Muhammad insisted that there was no way to his god Allah except by Allah's choice. He rejected that Allah could have an intermediary such as Jesus or the Holy Spirit. Although he did not intend it to be interpreted this way, Muhammad was indeed correct, because Jesus and the Holy Spirit do not serve Allah, but only Jehovah God, the one and only true and living God.

God, through the prophet Jeremiah, said: "'Am I a God near at hand,' says the Lord, 'And not a God afar off'" (**Jeremiah 23:23**)? That simple but direct description of the God of the Jews and the Christians says volumes about the difference between the living God and the god of silence of the Muslims. God interacts with His creation; Allah does not.

Chapter Conclusion

Jews and Christians, in particular, are clearly set apart from Muslims in how each views their god and understands their relationship to him. For the Christian, God is a living, interacting presence in one's life—a divine presence that guides, comforts, loves, forgives, redeems and takes personal interest in their wellbeing and eternal destination. For the Muslim, Allah is a distant, impersonal and detached deity, according to the Qur'an and the teaching of Muhammad and really not that interested in the welfare and destiny of his human creation.

This is plainly illustrated by the relationship God establishes in the Bible with those He created, by continually referring to them as His children; a passionate Father-child connection—one that communicates passion and compassion for those He loves. Allah, however, is portrayed and worshipped as a detached, compassionless god who looks upon his creation as pawns to be dealt with as he sees fit, and without personal interaction.

While the God of the Christians established a means of personal communication through the indwelling Holy Spirit, Allah provides no such means of communication or means by which to understand his will and guidance. Muslims can pray and pray and never have any sense of Allah's direction for their life. Prayer for the Muslim is ritualistic, guided by an unending list of dos and don'ts that prescribe when and where to pray, what to wear, etc. Christians, however, give ready testimony to their prayers being answered and having the security of an inner peace that guides them and comforts them.

References

1. Gabriel, Mark A. *Islam and Terrorism*, 2002. Published by FrontLine, a Strang Company, p. 5.
2. Mayahian, Masoud. *As a Muslim, do you have to pray in Arabic? If yes, why? I know Christians all over the world pray in their own language, so why (if at all) do Muslims have to pray in Arabic? I'd think Allah understands everybody, no matter what language*, September 17, 2016. Source: https://www.quora.com/As-a-Muslim-do-you-have-to-pray-in-Arabic-If-yes-why-I-know-Christians-all-over-the-world-pray-in-their-own-language-so-why-if-at-all-do-Muslims-have-to-pray-in-Arabic-Id-think-Allah-understands-everybody-no-matter-what-language
3. Sheriff, Ahmed H. *Why Pray in Arabic*. Source: https://www.al-islam.org/ articles/why-pray-arabic-ahmed-h-sheriff
4. Ibid.
5. Caner, Ergun Mehmet and Emir Fethi Caner. *Unveiling Islam*, 2002. Kregel
Publications, div. of Kregel. Inc., p. 145.
6. Caner & Caner, p. 117.
7. Caner & Caner, p. 34.

Chapter 10

Preaching a Different Gospel

The Spirit clearly says that in later times some will abandon the faith and follow deceiving spirits and things taught by demons. Such teachings come through hypocritical liars, whose consciences have been seared as with a hot iron.
1 Timothy 4:1-2

I n his second letter to the church in Corinth, the Apostle Paul warned that there would be false teachers who would try to preach a different gospel than that of Jesus Christ crucified. "For such people are false apostles," he advised, "deceitful workers, masquerading as apostles of Christ. And no wonder, for Satan himself masquerades as an angel of light" (**2 Corinthians 11:13-14**).

Although Muhammad never claimed to be preaching on behalf of Christ, the gospel he did preach was the antithesis of the true Gospel that Jesus and His Apostles preached. Muhammad's "Gabriel" and Muhammad himself was such an *angel of light* that Paul warned about.

In the preceding chapter it was pointed out briefly that the Qur'an does not lay out any clear plan or purpose for Allah's creation—no means of reconciling sinful man with his god. That, of course, is no surprise, since Allah desires no personal relationship with his creation; no compassionate embrace for those from whom he demands absolute allegiance and adherence to his insurmountable and immeasurable laws. The Bible and the ministry of Jesus Christ, by clear contrast, present a precise plan for mankind to reconcile himself to the God of his creation. While Islam demands that its followers comply with the Islamic law of the Qur'an and Sunnah, the message of Christianity portrays a freedom from the curse of the Law via the New Covenant with God through faith in Jesus Christ and His saving work of the cross. Muhammad freed no one, but Jesus Christ frees all who will accept His redemptive sacrifice on the Cross of Calvary.

Christ redeemed us from the curse of the law by becoming a curse for us, for it is written: "Cursed is everyone who is hung on a pole" (**Galatians 3:13**; see also **Deuteronomy 21:23**).

For weak or waffling Christians who are confused or easily led astray, the Apostle Paul would likely repeat his admonition that he preached to the Galatians almost two thousand years ago: "I am astonished that you are so quickly deserting the one who called you to live in the grace of Christ and are turning to a different gospel—which is really no gospel at all. Evidently some people are throwing you into confusion and are trying to pervert the gospel of Christ. But even if we or an angel from heaven should preach a gospel other than the one we

261

preached to you, let them be under God's curse! As we have already said, so now I say again: If anybody is preaching to you a gospel other than what you accepted, let them be under God's curse!" (**Galatians 1:6-9**). Strong words from the one to whom Jesus appeared during Paul's journey to Damascus.

Moses was the first to warn God's people of preaching a different word of God or listening to a different word. "Do not add to what I command you," Moses warned, "and do not subtract from it, but keep the commands of the LORD your God that I give you" (**Deuteronomy 4:2**).

In his rebuke about following after false gods, Moses, once again, admonished the Israelites. "See that you do all I command you; do not add to it or take away from it" (**Deuteronomy 12:32**).

During His Sermon on the Mount Jesus fervently proclaimed, "For truly I tell you, until heaven and earth disappear, not the smallest letter, not the least stroke of a pen, will by any means disappear from the Law until everything is accomplished" (**Matthew 5:18**). Muhammad and Islamic scholars and religious leaders have
added back-breaking tons of "new" laws that burden Allah's followers— laws that do not bring people any closer to the One and Only True God, the Father of Jesus Christ.

"Do not add to his [God's] words, or he will rebuke you and prove you a liar," the wise King Solomon wrote (**Proverbs 30:6**).

Toward the end of his life, Solomon would reaffirm this maxim. "I know that everything God does will endure forever; nothing can be added to it and nothing taken from it. God does it so that people will fear him." (**Ecclesiastes 3:14**). With the coming of Jesus Christ, God fulfilled His plan for all mankind—an everlasting salvation through a better and everlasting covenant. Allah, through Muhammad, not only did not bring forth a new covenant, but he reversed the Gospel of Jesus Christ, pitching once again, God's human creation back into the pits of hell with no recourse for deliverance. That does not sound like a loving god, but rather the diabolical plan of Satan himself.

"And even if our gospel is veiled," Paul penned, "it is veiled to those who are perishing. The god of this age [Satan] has blinded the minds of unbelievers, so that they cannot see the light of the gospel that displays the glory of Christ, who is the image of God. For what we preach is not ourselves, but Jesus Christ as Lord, and ourselves as your servants for Jesus' sake. For God, who said, 'Let light shine out of darkness,' made his light shine in our hearts to give us the light of the knowledge of God's glory displayed in the face of Christ" (**2 Corinthians 4:3-6**).

The Apostle John also warned about false teachers and the anti-Christ. "I say this because many deceivers, who do not acknowledge Jesus Christ as coming in the flesh, have gone out into the world. Any such

262

person is the deceiver and the antichrist." Although Muhammad taught that Jesus was a prophet, he denied Jesus' deity and the true purpose for which God sent Him.

"Anyone who runs ahead," John continued, "and does not continue in the teaching of Christ does not have God; whoever continues in the teaching has both the Father and the Son. If anyone comes to you and does not bring this teaching, do not take them into your house or welcome them. Anyone who welcomes them shares in their wicked work" (**2 John 1:7, 9-11**).

The Nature of Sin is Obfuscated

"Enter through the narrow gate," Jesus preached. "For wide is the gate and broad is the road that leads to destruction, and many enter through it. But small is the gate and narrow the road that leads to life, and only a few find it" (**Matthew 7:13-14**).

Islamic law lists over 440 types of sin that a Muslim can commit to separate himself from the favor of Allah. Most are similar to that which Christians would consider sin—anger, cheating, greed, stealing, etc. However, some are strictly Islamic: a woman fasting without her husband's consent, zeal for a religion other than Islam, not accepting the truth when it conflicts with one's own "truth", loss of hope in Allah's mercy, neglecting to bless the Prophet, not performing a prescribed prayer and many, many more.

Reliance of the Traveller, w51.1

What the Bible Says About Sin. What is sin? Just about any dictionary defines sin as disobeying an acceptable law of God. Muslims would likely concur: That breaking a law of Allah would be sin. The biblical interpretation of sin is perhaps more concise. In the Bible, sin is seen as any thought or action that separates one from God—whether one believes in Him or not. What Islam portrays as sin is somewhat different than what God of the Bible considers sin.

Both the Bible and the Qur'an identify that Satan is a deceiver and the source of sin.

> *O men!* Muhammad revealed, *surely the promise of Allah is true, therefore let not the life of this world deceive you, and let not the arch-deceiver deceive you respecting Allah.*
> *Surely the Shaitan* [Satan] *is your enemy, so take him for an enemy; he only invites his party that they may be inmates*

of the burning fire.

(As for) those who disbelieve, they shall have a severe punishment, and (as for) those who believe and do good, they shall have forgiveness and a great reward (**Qur'an 35:5-7**).

In the New Testament of the Bible Satan is described as a deceiver, a thief, a liar and a murderer. "The thief [Satan] comes only to steal and kill and destroy;" Jesus proclaimed, "I have come that they may have life, and have it to the full" (**John 10:10**). The Apostle Peter reiterated this point of fact. "Be alert and of sober mind. Your enemy the devil prowls around like a roaring lion looking for someone to devour" (**1 Peter 5:8**).

All three synoptic gospels record Jesus' telling of the Parable of the Sower or Soils. In the parable Jesus explains about four types of people who hear God's word. In the first sowing of the word of God the "seed" fell by the wayside and the birds ate it. The second fell upon the rocks and did not take root. The third fell among the thorns and was choked out and the fourth fell upon fertile ground and took root (see **Matthew 13:1-9**; **Mark 4:1-9** and **Luke 8:9-15** for the full explanation of this parable).

"This is the meaning of the parable: The seed is the word of God," Jesus pointed out for the first sowing. "Those along the path are the ones who hear, and then the devil comes and takes away the word from their hearts, so that they may not believe and be saved. (**Luke 8:11-12**). God's word is true, not Allah's, and is essential for a godly life; a righteous life; one that glorifies God; provides everlasting salvation and eternal life with the Father.

Once again, when Jesus was confronting the hypocritical Pharisees, He decreed, "You belong to your father, the devil, and you want to carry out your father's desires. He was a murderer from the beginning, not holding to the truth, for there is no truth in him. When he lies, he speaks his native language, for **he is a liar and the father of lies**. (**John 8:44**).

The one who does what is sinful is of the devil, because the devil has been sinning from the beginning. The reason the Son of God appeared was to destroy the devil's work.

1 John 3:8

To do battle with the devil, Paul instructs Christ followers to, "be strong in the Lord and in his mighty power. Put on the full armor of God, so that you can take your stand against the devil's schemes" (**Ephesians 6:10-11**). And what is this "armor of God" of which Paul spoke? It is something that only the true followers of Jesus possess. Paul alerted Christians that, "our struggle is not against flesh and blood, but against the rulers, against the authorities, against the powers of this dark world and against the spiritual forces of evil in the heavenly realms" (**Ephesians 6:12**). Therefore, a Christian's weapons are spiritual ones: a waistband of God's truth; breastplate of righteousness; feet shod with the gospel of peace; shield of faith; helmet of salvation; sword of the Spirit (the word of God); praying always in the Spirit, and being watchful with perseverance (**Ephesians 6:14-18**).

GOD HATES SIN! Jehovah God hates evil doing, but Muhammad, the prophet of Allah, propagated evil doing at every opportunity. "You are not a God who takes pleasure in evil;" wrote the psalmist David, "with you the wicked cannot dwell. The arrogant cannot stand in your presence; you hate all who do wrong. You destroy those who tell lies; bloodthirsty and deceitful men the LORD abhors" (Psalm 5:4-6). God, through an unknown psalmist said: "I will set before my eyes no vile thing. The deeds of faithless men I hate; they will not cling to me" (Psalm 101:3).

The Apostle Paul proclaimed in his letter to the Christians in Rome, "for all have sinned and fall short of the glory of God," (**Romans 3:23**). Although the majority of Muslim believers would likely concur with that assessment, there is a line of thought, according to author John Gilchrist, known as the *Isma* **Doctrine** which proclaims that prophets, imams and certain other Islamic leaders are infallible and therefore sinless (1). That does not seem to be held by a majority of Muslims so it will not be explored here. However, it is presented in sections of the *Reliance of the Traveller.*

One thing is clear, however, Jehovah God of the Jews and Christians hates wrong doing, but Allah fosters it. "Since there is no such thing as forgiveness of sins in Islam," author Raza Safa wrote, "Muslims justify their sins. True conviction of sin does not exist in Islam" (2).

According to the Psalmist David, "But all sinners will be destroyed; there will be no future for the wicked. **(Psalm 37:38)**.

However, in another Psalm, David champions hope, "Restore to me the joy of your salvation and grant me a willing spirit, to sustain me. Then I will teach transgressors your ways, so that sinners will turn back to you." (**Psalm 51:12-13**). God would eventually provide sinners with a way back to Him through Jesus Christ.

Malachi, the last prophet to the Jews before Christ, chastised the faithless Jews some 400 years before the birth of Jesus. "You have wearied the LORD with your words. 'How have we wearied him?' you ask. By saying, 'All who do evil are good in the eyes of the LORD, and he is pleased with them' or 'Where is the God of justice?'" (**Malachi 2:17**).

In the New International Version (NIV) of the Bible there are

265

1,364 verses on the topic of sin; 44 verses about sinners and another 11 about iniquities. However, there is only one verse that mentions one sinless man, Jesus Christ.

By comparison, Muhammad was chief among sinners during his life on earth. God did not replace a sinless man and His word of truth with a sin-ladened man who fabricated "truth."

Instead, God had a plan, a faultless plan that He revealed to the prophet Isaiah over 1200 years before Muhammad was even a gleam in his mother's eyes. Isaiah is known as the Messianic prophet and in **Isaiah 59:1-2**, he prophesied, "Surely the arm of the LORD is not too short to save, nor his ear too dull to hear. But your iniquities have separated you from your God; your sins have hidden his face from you, so that he will not hear." God had and has a plan of salvation from sin for all mankind which he revealed in **Isaiah 61**.

> *The Spirit of the Sovereign LORD is on me, because the LORD has anointed me to proclaim good news to the poor.*
>
> *He has sent me to bind up the brokenhearted, to proclaim freedom for the captives and release from darkness for the prisoners, to proclaim the year of the LORD's favor and the day of vengeance of our God, to comfort all who mourn, and provide for those who grieve in Zion – to bestow on them a crown of beauty instead of ashes, the oil of joy instead of mourning, and a garment of praise instead of a spirit of despair.*
>
> *They will be called oaks of righteousness, a planting of the LORD for the display of his splendor* (**Isaiah 61:1-3**).

Jesus would later quote this prophesy in the synagogue in Nazareth as a testimony that He was sent by God to fulfill this word of God (see **Luke 4:16-21**).

In the Gospel of John, chapter 8, Jesus shared with the Jews the true nature of God's children. "If you abide in My word, you are My disciples indeed. And you shall know the truth, and the truth shall make you free" (**John 8:31-32**, NKJV). The Jews responded by saying that they were descendants of Abraham and had never been slaves to anyone, so how could Jesus set them free.

Despite their convenient lapse of Jewish history (the Jews were slaves in Egypt for 400 years), they responded, "Abraham is our father."

"'If you were Abraham's children,' said Jesus, 'then you would do what Abraham did. As it is, you are looking for a way to kill me, a man who has told you the truth that I heard from God. Abraham did not do such things. You are doing the works of your own father.'"

"'We are not illegitimate children,' they protested. 'The only Father we have is God himself.'" (**John 8:39-41**). Jesus, of course, was making a distinction between Abraham's biological descendants and God's spiritual descendants by faith. True children of Abraham follow Abraham's example of faith; illegitimate children follow the example of Satan. Although Jews can legitimately lay claim to being children of Abraham, Muslims cannot. However, ones' heritage does not provide any reassurance of salvation or an eternity in heaven.

"'Jesus said to them, 'If God were your Father, you would love me, for I have come here from God. I have not come on my own; God sent me. Why is my language not clear to you? Because you are unable to hear what I say. You belong to your father, the devil, and you want to carry out your father's desires. He was a murderer from the beginning, not holding to the truth, for there is no truth in him. When he lies, he speaks his native language, for he is a liar and the father of lies. Yet because I tell the truth, you do not believe me! Can any of you prove me guilty of sin? If I am telling the truth, why don't you believe me? Whoever belongs to God hears what God says. The reason you do not hear is that you do not belong to God'" (**John 8:42-47**). While Jesus was talking to the Jews, He could just as well have been exclaiming this to Muslims or anyone else who refuses to accept the truth of His word and the purpose of His coming to earth.

"Without Christ," Paul said, "we are slaves to sin" (see **Romans 7:13-25**).

> *What then? Shall we sin because we are not under the [Jewish or any other moral] law but under grace? By no means! Don't you know that when you offer yourselves to someone as obedient slaves, you are slaves of the one you obey – whether you are slaves to sin, which leads to death, or to obedience, which leads to righteousness? But thanks be to God that, though you used to be slaves to sin, you have come to obey from your heart the pattern of teaching that has now claimed your allegiance. You have been set free from sin and have become slaves to righteousness.*
>
> *I am using an example from everyday life because of your human limitations. Just as you used to offer yourselves as slaves to impurity and to ever-increasing wickedness, so now offer yourselves as slaves to righteousness leading to holiness. When you were slaves to sin, you were free from the control of righteousness. What benefit did you reap at that time from the things you are now ashamed of? Those things result in death! But now that you have been set free from sin and have become slaves of God, the benefit you reap leads to holiness, and the result is eternal life. For the wages of sin is death, but the*

gift of God is eternal life in Christ Jesus our Lord (**Roman 6:15-23**; author's emphasis).

What Islam Teaches. What about the source of sin? Both the Qur'an and the Bible recount the story of the *fall* of Adam and Eve (the Qur'an never uses her name). They both report that it was Satan's temptation that led to the departure from sinlessness. However, the Qur'an states that Adam and his wife repented of their sin in the Garden of Eden (**Qur'an 7:23**) and that Allah forgave them and set them on the right path (**Qur'an 2:37-38**). The Bible makes no such declaration of Adam and Eve repenting of their sin, nor of God forgiving them for their transgressions. To the contrary, Adam puts the blame on his wife for his sin and hides his guilt from God. Eve did likewise, but blamed Satan for her sin (**Genesis 3:8-13**). God then banishes them from the Garden and severely punishes them and all of their descendants (**Genesis 3:16-23**).

The Bible and Christian doctrine give credence to the concept that Adam introduced sin to mankind and was the source of *original sin*. The Qur'an makes no such acknowledgement. Muslims, however, do not believe that sin entered the world through Adam's disobedience. They believe Adam was the first prophet of Allah. They believe that man is basically created good until he sins. The Bible teaches, particularly through the New Testament, that man is born in sin and, if left to his own desires, will continue to sin and separate himself from God. Man's only hope for reconciliation with God is through the redemptive work of Christ on the cross.

According to the teaching of Islam there are "major" (*kabira*) and "minor" (*saghira*) sins. Supposedly there are 70 major sins—72 if you count the sin of committing a sin—and an unspecified number of minor sins that are displeasing to Allah and that have no specific punishment (see the Addendum at the end of this chapter). Islamic law lists over 440 sins in the *Reliance of the Traveller*. If a Muslim is fortunate enough to avoid the major sins (which is unlikely), his minor sins will be erased (see below). However, for the God of the Bible, sin is sin, there is no classification.

If you shun the great sins which you are forbidden, We will do away with your small sins and cause you to enter an honorable place of entering.
Qur'an 4: 31

The question arises, since the surah above comes from the chapter on Women or *al-Nisa* or *Nisa*, is the above instruction for women only or does it hold true for all of Allah's followers?

What the Qur'an does say, is that Allah commanded the angels and Satan (*Shaitan* or *Iblis*) to prostrate before Adam and worship him, but Satan refused. "And when We said to the angels: Make obeisance to Adam they did obeisance, but Iblis (did it not). He refused and was proud, and he was one of the unbelievers" (**Qur'an 2:34**). From a Judeo-Christian viewpoint and biblical teaching, for Jehovah God to command the angels or any other life form to worship anyone other than Him would be outright blasphemy.

"You shall not make for yourself an idol in the form of anything in heaven above or on the earth beneath or in the waters below," God spoke to Moses. "You shall not bow down to them or worship them; for I, the LORD your God, am a jealous God, punishing the children for the sin of the fathers to the third and fourth generation of those who hate me, but showing love to a thousand {generations} of those who love me and keep my commandments" (**Exodus 20:4-6**).

The Qur'an does state that Satan is the enemy of man (Qur'an 12:5, *et al*); that he misleads and deceives mankind (surah 4:117-121, *et al*) and makes sin attractive (Qur'an 6:43; 15:39). However, with respect to deception and sin, it would seem that Allah is put on the same footing with Satan. Allah, according to the Qur'an (surah 4:142), is a deceiver: "Behold, the hypocrites seek to deceive God—the while it is He who causes them to be deceived . . ." (3). It also pleases Allah for him to lead one into sin. "Whomsoever Allah causes to err [sin], there is no guide for him; and He leaves them alone in their inordinacy [overweening arrogance], blindly wandering on" (Qur'an 7:186).

There is no reasoning or justification for Allah's spontaneous and haphazard dealings with his creation. "And they who reject Our communications are deaf and dumb, in utter darkness; **whom Allah pleases He causes to err, and whom He pleases He puts on the right way**" (**Qur'an 6:39**; author's emphasis). It is Allah, not men and women, that chooses who will sin and who will not.

If Allah, deceives and leads whomever he chooses into sin, what hope does the Islamic believer have in reconciling himself or herself to their god? If Allah can lead anyone he chooses astray, perhaps he led Muhammad on the wrong path.

Furthermore, after Allah leads them into sin, he then tightens his breast and rejects them. "Therefore (for) whomsoever Allah intends that He would guide him aright, He expands his breast for Islam, and (for) whomsoever He intends that He should cause him to err, He makes his breast strait and narrow as though he were ascending upwards; thus does Allah lay uncleanness on those who do not believe" (**Qur'an 6:125**). After Allah rejects a person there is no way back to him, nor will he send anyone to guide them back on the right path. "Nay! Those who are unjust follow their low desires without any knowledge; so who can guide him whom Allah makes err? And they shall have no helpers" (**Qur'an 30:29**).

Allah Loves Sin—Not the Sinner. "Say: Nothing will afflict us save what Allah has ordained for us;" Muhammad revealed, "He is our Patron; and on Allah let the believers rely" (**Qur'an 9:51**).

Remember, Allah is in the sin business, not the forgiveness enterprise. ". . . Allah **makes whom He pleases err** and He guides whom He pleases   " (**Qur'an 14:4**, author's emphasis). How can any Muslim ever be sure that he is not being directed by Allah to do evil? But then, if he is doing evil, then it must be Allah's will. If forgiveness is to come, one might have to wait for it until Allah is good and ready to dispense it. "Except those who are patient and do good; they shall have forgiveness and a great reward" (**Qur'an 11:11**). But how long must one wait? Not a single Muslim could tell you, other than Allah's judgment will be certain at the end of their life. Once again, in **Qur'an 6:39**, Muhammad disclosed, "And they who reject Our commandments are deaf and dumb, in utter darkness; **whom Allah pleases He causes to err**, and whom He pleases He puts on the right way (author's emphasis)." So, the rationale would be, if one is sinning it must be Allah's will. It is his guidance and direction for one's life and cannot be resisted because it is by Allah's good pleasure.

The God of the Christians and Jews hates sin—all sin. He cannot be tempted to lead someone astray, nor does He cause anyone to sin. The Apostle James confirmed this: "When tempted, no one should say, 'God is tempting me.' For God cannot be tempted by evil, nor does he tempt anyone;" (James 1:13).

The Prophet . . . said:

"All of my Community shall be pardoned, save those who commit sins openly. Committing them openly includes a man who does something shameful at night, and when morning comes, Allah having hidden his act, he says, 'O So-and-so, last night I did such and such'; his Lord having concealed it for him at night, while in the morning he pulls away the cover with which Allah had concealed it for him."

Reliance of the Traveller, r35.1

Notice in the box above, that it is Allah who is hiding the person's sin and that it is the sinner who is condemned for confessing it to another. This is the complete opposite of what the Bible teaches. Both Jews and Christians are commanded to confess their sins—first to God and then to the one that they sinned against—and then to repent and seek God's forgiveness, as well as ask forgiveness from the one offended.

And he who comes up short in the scales of the Sacred Law is of the people of ruin, among whom there is also disparity of degree. If one sees someone who can fly through the air, walk on water, or inform one of the unseen, but who contravenes the Sacred Law by committing an unlawful act without an extenuating circumstance that legally excuses it, or who neglects an obligatory act without lawful reason, one may know that such a person is a devil Allah has placed there as a temptation to the ignorant. Nor is it farfetched that such a person should be one of the means by which Allah chooses to lead men astray, for the Antichrist will bring the dead to life and make the living die, all as a temptation and affliction to those who would be misled.

Reliance of the Traveller, w9.9

This quotation in the preceding box provides some interesting insight worth discussing. In the West, a common refrain by someone caught in the act of doing something wrong, i.e. sinning, is, "The devil made me do it." In Islam, however, according to this sacred script, a Muslim caught in the act of sinning can rightly claim that "Allah made me do it." Not only does Allah cause his followers to sin, but he uses others to tempt people to sin. It is almost like Allah gets a "kick" out of seeing people sin. After all, "Allah chooses to lead men astray."

The repetitive theme throughout the Qur'an is clear: It is Allah, along with the devil, who causes one to sin, and Allah is selective as to who will be a sinner.

"And if Allah please He would certainly make you a single nation, but He causes to err whom He pleases and guides whom He pleases; and most certainly you will be questioned as to what you did" (**Qur'an 16:93**). Qur'an 35:8 states the same thing, ". . . Now surely Allah makes err [sin] whom He pleases and guides aright whom He pleases . . ."

Despite the *Isma Doctrine* of the sinless Muhammad and prophets, even Muhammad believed he was a sinner. "O Allah! Forgive me my sins that I did in the past or will do in the future, and also the sins I did in secret or in public" (**Sahih al-Bukhari 9:93:482**). In the Qur'an (**Qur'an 47:19** and **48:2**) Allah revealed that Muhammad is among the community of sinners that need Allah's forgiveness.

"No evil befalls on the earth nor in your own souls, but it is in a book before We bring it into existence; surely that is easy to Allah" (**Qur'an 57:22**). Here it sounds like Allah has already predetermined whom he will have sin and that there is no recourse for the guilty party.

271

In Qur'an 32:13 Allah's purpose is made clear. It appears that his primary objective for his creation is to fill hell with them. "And if We had pleased We would certainly have given to every soul its guidance, but the word (which had gone forth) from Me was just: I will certainly fill hell with the jinn [spiritual beings] and men together."

Muslims believe humans are sinners because Allah willed it.
Pastor Shahram Hadian
Truth in Love Project founder
November 29, 2018

The Bible presents Adam and the nature of sin from an entirely different viewpoint. Adam was the prototype of the Christ to come. In **Genesis 1:26-27**, God makes it clear the nature of Adam and Eve's creation. "Then God said, 'Let us make man **in our image**, in our likeness, and let them rule over the fish of the sea and the birds of the air, over the livestock, over all the earth, and over all the creatures that move along the ground.' So God created man in his own image, **in the image of God** he created him; male and female he created them" (author's emphasis). God made man in His own image. Adam, God's first human creation, was also the son of God (**Luke 3:38**).

Through Adam, Sin and Death Entered the World. "For since death came through a man," the Apostle Paul wrote, "the resurrection of the dead comes also through a man. For as in Adam all die [in their sin], so in Christ all will be made alive [in the spirit]" (**1 Corinthians 15:21-22**). Jesus, also called the Son of God, was the second and last Adam. "So it is written:" Paul stated, "'The first man Adam became a living being' [**Genesis 2:7**]; the last Adam, a life-giving spirit" (**1 Corinthians 15:45**).

To the church in Rome, Paul explained this relationship of sin to Adam in this manner: "When Adam sinned, sin entered the world. Adam's sin brought death, so death spread to everyone, for everyone sinned. Yes, people sinned even before the law was given. But it was not counted as sin because there was not yet any law to break. Still, everyone died—from the time of Adam to the time of Moses—even those who did not disobey an explicit commandment of God, as Adam did. Now Adam is a symbol, a representation of Christ, who was yet to come" (**Romans 5:12-14**, NLT).

The Qur'an repeatedly gives the impression that almighty Allah can be persuaded to lead one into sin and therefore be tempted to do evil toward his creation. Not so with the Almighty God of the Jews and Christians.

Again, James, the brother of Jesus, reminds us, "When tempted, no one should say, 'God is tempting me.' **For God cannot be tempted by evil, nor does he tempt anyone**; but each one is tempted when, by his own evil desire, he is dragged away and enticed. Then, after desire has conceived, it gives birth to sin; and sin, when it is full-grown, gives birth to death" (**James 1:13-15**; author's emphasis).

Jesus' Sin Offering is Null & Void

The official Islamic teaching, as related in Chapter 2, is that Jesus did not die, but was taken to heaven in bodily form by Allah without dying on the cross and therefore was not resurrected. Jesus' death and resurrection is the centrality of the Christian faith that Muhammad and his satanic angel have been trying to destroy for over 1400 years.

For the wages of sin is death, but the gift of God is eternal life in Christ Jesus our Lord.
                                          Romans 6:23

For Allah followers, the blessing of God's sin offering through His Son Jesus Christ is null and void. They must now turn to the indecisive, non-redeeming god of the Qur'an—the one revealed to Muhammad in a satanic revelation. "Do they not know that whoever acts in opposition to Allah and His Apostle, he shall surely have the fire of hell to abide in it? That is a grievous abasement" (**Qur'an 9:63**). For a people in bondage to sin and sin afflicted upon them by their god, the revealing truth of Jesus Christ, the only sinless man in history, who sacrificed Himself on the cross for their sin and their sakes, should be welcomed news—but sadly, for the majority of Muslims, it is not, because of the domineering and controlling theology in which they are trapped.

Christ-followers are Dead to Sin. Those who willingly choose to follow Christ as their Lord and Savior are dead to sin. That does not mean that Christians do not sin. Christians are often accused of being hypocrites, but the truth is that Christians, except for the shed blood of Christ, are no different than anyone else. However, because of Christ, His crucifixion and resurrection, when a Christian does sin, he or she has Jesus Christ as an advocate before Father God.

In his first letter, the Apostle John made it clear that one of the greatest blessings Christ provided His followers was an opening to God. "My dear children, I write this to you so that you will not sin. But if anybody does sin, we have an advocate with the Father—Jesus Christ, the Righteous One. He is the atoning sacrifice for our sins, and not only for ours but also for the sins of the whole world" (**1 John 2:1-2**). No other faith offers this unique and blessed avenue to God's heart when one sins and seeks forgiveness.

> *For if we have been united together in the likeness of His death,* Paul wrote, *certainly we also shall be in the likeness of His resurrection, knowing this, that our old* [sinful] *man was crucified with Him, that the body of sin might be done away with, that* **we should no longer be slaves of sin.** *For he who has died has been freed from sin. Now if we died with Christ, we believe that we shall also live with Him, knowing that Christ, having been raised from the dead, dies no more. Death no longer has dominion over Him. For the death that He died,* **He died to sin once for all;** *but the life that He lives, He lives to God. Likewise you also,* **reckon yourselves to be dead indeed to sin,** *but alive to God in Christ Jesus our Lord.* (**Romans 6:5-11**; author's emphasis, NKJV).

Christian's—true Christ-followers—are dead to sin. The Good News for everyone, including all Muslims, is that Christ died for them too and through faith in Jesus and His sacrifice, they too can be set free from sin—even the sin imposed upon them by their god, Allah.

God made him who had no sin to be sin for us, so that in him we might become the righteousness of God.
2 Corinthians 5:21

To a world mired hopelessly in sin, the living God spoke these words through the prophet Isaiah: "Seek the LORD while he may be found; call on him while he is near. Let the wicked forsake his way and the evil man his thoughts. Let him turn to the LORD, and he will have mercy on him, and to our God, for he will freely pardon" (**Isaiah 55:6-7**).

God, the God of the Jews and Christians, and not Allah, desires to forgive sin. God, the infinite, living God, proved His great love for mankind in that, ". . . **While we were still sinners, Christ died for us.** Since we have now been justified by his blood, how much more shall we be saved from God's wrath through him!" (**Romans 5:8b-9**, author's emphasis).

For the Muslim there is No Sin Offering. Allah offers no means by which the Islamic believer can be reconciled with Allah and set free from his or her sin. It is a hopeless and unforgiving faith in a hopeless and unforgiving god, in a hopeless and unforgiving world. Christians, on the other hand, have a clear and secure hope in Jesus Christ.

"He was delivered over to death for our sins," preached and

wrote the Apostle Paul, "and was raised to life for our justification" (**Romans 4:25**).

In and of himself, man can never be justified and made right before God. It is only through the substitutionary death of Jesus Christ, the only Son of the living God, that man, placing his faith in the sacrificial work of Christ, can be set free from sin and the law of sin and death. While man could never have conceived of such a plan, God—the true God—did.

"For Christ died for sins once for all," the Apostle Peter preached in his first letter shortly before his own death, "the righteous for the unrighteous, to bring you to God. He was put to death in the body but made alive by the Spirit," (**1 Peter 3:18**).

Peter, like Paul, plainly understood the significance of Christ's substitutionary death in his place so that he and all those who put their faith in Jesus may be made right with God. Paul wrote this explanation to the Christians in Rome: "But the gift is not like the trespass. For if the many died by the trespass of the one man [Adam], how much more did God's grace and the gift that came by the grace of the one man, Jesus Christ, overflow to the many!" (**Romans 5:15**). Two verses later he clarified his spiritual point. "For if, by the trespass of the one man, death reigned through that one man, how much more will those who receive God's abundant provision of grace and of the gift of righteousness reign in life through the one man, Jesus Christ" (**Romans 5:17**).

This death on the cross for sin by proxy, while clearly part of God's simple plan for mankind, is hard for man to accept and a stumbling block for many, including Muslims. Mankind and all Muslims are determined to work out their own salvation. However, God's principle of personal salvation is so straightforward: "God made him who had no sin to be sin for us," Paul told the Corinthians, "so that in him we might become the righteousness of God" (**2 Corinthians 5:21**).

Righteousness before the only true God does not depend on the acts of men and women; it rests upon the saving grace of Jesus Christ and Him only. In this case, both Jews and Muslims share a common mindset and fate—neither can accept this easy road to salvation laid out by Jesus and His heavenly Father. "For just as through the disobedience of the one man [Adam] the many were made sinners, so also through the obedience of the one man [Jesus] the many will be made righteous" (**Romans 5:19**). Paul's analogy is simple: sin entered into the world through one man and it can leave through one man—Jesus Christ.

Part of the problem is that neither Jews nor Muslims can identify with an advocate, someone who could share in their pain and suffering and understand their need for a savior. "Therefore," wrote the unidentified author of the letter to the Hebrews, "since we have a great high priest who has gone through the heavens, Jesus the Son of God, let us hold firmly to

275

the faith we profess. For we do not have a high priest who is unable to sympathize with our weaknesses, but we have one who has been tempted in every way, just as we are—yet was without sin" (**Hebrews 4:14-15**).

Neither Jews nor Muslims can accept Jesus as the Son of God and therefore miss out on God's greatest blessing to the world of sinners. Sinful Muhammad could not fill this role of savior, nor any of the prophets or sages before him. Only Jesus Christ, the Son of God.

This [prayer] *is good, and pleases God our Savior, who wants all people to be saved and to come to a knowledge of the truth.*
1 Timothy 2:3-4

In chapter nine of the same letter, the writer brings to fruition the role of Jesus' sin offering. "But now he has appeared once for all at the end of the ages to do away with sin by the sacrifice of himself. Just as man is destined to die once, and after that to face judgment, so Christ was sacrificed once to take away the sins of many people; and he will appear a second time, not to bear sin, but to bring salvation to those who are waiting for him" (**Hebrews 9:26b-28**). Without this sacrifice for sin man has no recourse to reconcile himself to God. He is hopelessly lost in his own wretched despair with no escape from his propensity to sin.

Hundreds of years before Christ, God pleaded with the Israelites to return to Him. "I have swept away your offenses like a cloud, your sins like the morning mist. Return to me, for I have redeemed you" (**Isaiah 44:22**).

Around the same time frame, the prophet Micah revealed God's forgiving nature. "Who is a God like you, who pardons sin and forgives the transgression of the remnant of his inheritance? You do not stay angry forever but delight to show mercy. You will again have compassion on us; you will tread our sins underfoot and hurl all our iniquities into the depths of the sea" (**Micah 7:18-19**). It is clear that Allah is not only not a forgiving god—at least not until one is dead, and then it is too late. Forgiveness in the grave is useless and has no effect on the eternal life of man's spirit.

About a hundred years after Isaiah's and Micah's words, Jeremiah prophesied about God's coming plan. "'No longer will they teach their neighbor, or say to one another, *Know the LORD*, because they will all know me, from the least of them to the greatest,' declares the LORD. 'For I will forgive their wickedness and will remember their sins no more'" (**Jeremiah 31:34**). It is through the life and death of Jesus Christ that God implemented His plan of everlasting salvation and the release of His Holy Spirit, of whom Jesus said is "the Spirit of truth".

The world cannot accept him, because it neither sees him nor knows him. But you know him, for he lives with you and will be in you" (**John 14:17**).

Further, Jesus said, ". . . the Advocate, the Holy Spirit, whom the Father will send in my name, will teach you all things and will remind you of everything I have said to you" (**John 14:26**).

There is no Holy Spirit

Just like Jesus being the Son of God is essential to the Christian faith, so too is the Holy Spirit in the Triune Godhead. Muslims not only do not recognize the Trinity, but they are also confused about who is the Holy Spirit and His role or if He exists at all.

In the Christian faith, the Holy Spirit is what empowers the believer to live a godly life according to the teaching of Jesus Christ. In the Old Testament times God poured out His Holy Spirit on specific people for explicit tasks at designated times. In the New Testament, one of the promises of Jesus was that after His death and resurrection the Holy Spirit would be released to live within all believers.

"I have much more to say to you, more than you can now bear," Jesus shared with His disciples. "But when he, the **Spirit of truth**, comes, he will guide you into all the truth. He will not speak on his own; he will speak only what he hears, and he will tell you what is yet to come. **He will glorify me** because it is from me that he will receive what he will make known to you. All that belongs to the Father is mine. That is why I said the Spirit will receive from me what he will make known to you" (**John 16:12-15**; author's emphasis).

"But very truly I tell you, it is for your good that I am going away. Unless I go away, the Advocate will not come to you; but if I go, I will send him to you. When he comes, he will prove the world to be in the wrong about sin and righteousness and judgment: about sin, because people do not believe in me; about righteousness, because I am going to the Father, where you can see me no longer; and about judgment, because the prince of this world now stands condemned" (**John 16:7-11**). It is through the Holy Spirit that Jesus makes His spiritual presence available to all believers and true seekers of Him and God's truth.

"If you love me, keep my commands. And I will ask the Father, and he will give you another advocate to help you and be with you forever—the Spirit of truth. The world cannot accept him, because it neither sees him nor knows him. But you know him, for he lives with you and will be in you. I will not leave you as orphans; I will come to you. Before long, the world will not see me anymore, but you will see me. Because I live, you also

will live. On that day you will realize that I am in my Father, and you are in me, and I am in you. Whoever has my commands and keeps them is the one who loves me. The one who loves me will be loved by my Father, and I too will love them and show myself to them."

Then Judas (not Judas Iscariot) said, "But, Lord, why do you intend to show yourself to us and not to the world?"

Jesus replied, "Anyone who loves me will obey my teaching. My Father will love them, and we will come to them and make our home with them. Anyone who does not love me will not obey my teaching. These words you hear are not my own; they belong to the Father who sent me.

All this I have spoken while still with you. But the Advocate, the Holy Spirit, whom the Father will send in my name, will teach you all things and will remind you of everything I have said to you. Peace I leave with you; my peace I give you. I do not give to you as the world gives. Do not let your hearts be troubled and do not be afraid. (**John 14:15-27**).

When the Advocate comes, whom I will send to you from the Father— the Spirit of truth who goes out from the Father—he will testify about me.

John 15:26

<u>Important</u>. The Holy Spirit, the Third Person of the Trinity is essential for and in the life of a follower of Jesus Christ. Jesus explained it this way to Nicodemus, a Pharisee, who approached Jesus under the cover of darkness. It is not recorded that Nicodemus came to question Jesus, but only to present a statement of fact.

"Rabbi," Nicodemus said, "we know that you are a teacher who has come from God. For no one could perform the signs you are doing if God were not with him" (**John 3:2**).

The Bible gives the impression that Jesus ignored Nicodemus's statement and responded with, what seemed like a confusing answer to a question Nicodemus did not ask.

"Jesus replied, 'Very truly I tell you, no one can see the kingdom of God unless they are born again'" (**John 3:3**). Nicodemus' first thought must have been: *What? Where did that come from?*

However, Nicodemus did get caught up in Jesus' declaration and asked: "How can someone be born when they are old?" Nicodemus inquired. "Surely they cannot enter a second time into their mother's womb to be born!" (**John 3:4**).

"Jesus answered, 'Very truly I tell you, no one can enter the kingdom of God unless they are **born of water and the Spirit. Flesh gives birth to flesh, but the Spirit gives birth to spirit.** You should not be surprised at my saying, *You must be born again.* The wind blows wherever it pleases. You hear its sound, but you cannot tell where it comes from or where it is going. So it is with everyone born of the Spirit'" (**John 3:5-8**; author's emphasis).

There is no indication in this exchange that Nicodemus ever grasped what Jesus was saying. His last recorded statement illustrates his confusion. His last words were concise: "How can this be?" (**John 3:9**).

What Jesus was trying to convey to Nicodemus, as well as to all those who chose to follow Him, was that there are two aspects to a transformed life in Christ. The first is for the physical body—the one born of the flesh—that must reject sin, repent and seek and receive God's forgiveness. The second, is the spiritual man/woman that must be transformed from within by the power of the indwelling Holy Spirit of God (that was to be released upon Christ's resurrection). Jesus was also acknowledging that all people are born of the flesh, but it is the transforming power of the Holy Spirit, the second birth, that brings forth a transformed life in Christ.

Islam's View of the Holy Spirit. Remember, in Chapter 2, in the section on the Triune God, Muhammad replaced the Holy Spirit with Mary, the mother of Jesus as part of the Trinity. "And when Allah will say: O Isa son of Marium! Did you say to men, Take me and my mother for two gods besides Allah, he will say: Glory be to Thee, it did not befit me that I should say what I had no right to (say) . . ." (**Qur'an 5:116**).

"In Islam, the Holy Spirit is from Allah but is more like his breath," wrote Matt Slick, President and Founder of the Christian Apologetics and Research Ministry. "It is not self-aware. That is why Islam teaches that the Holy Spirit strengthened Jesus as well as others and that the Spirit of God was breathed into Adam and Mary. But Islam denies the Trinity and therefore says the Holy Spirit is a force, a presence" (4).

The Qur'an does acknowledge that the Holy Spirit was sent by Allah to strengthen Jesus (**Qur'an 2:87, 253, 5:110**) and that Allah breathed his spirit into Adam at creation (**Qur'an 15:28, 38:72**) and into Elizabeth, the mother of John the Baptist (**Qur'an 21:91**). However, this is similar to the Bible account of God breathing into the nostrils of Adam to give him life (**Genesis 2:7**) and not the same as God empowering a person with the indwelling of His Holy Spirit, the Third Person of the Trinity.

In the Qur'an, however, it is Jibreel (Gabriel) that brought revelation knowledge to Muhammad, not the Holy Spirit (whom is just a manifestation of Allah, i.e., his breath). "Say: Whoever is the enemy of Jibreel—for surely he revealed it [the Qur'an] to your heart by Allah's command, verifying that which is before it and guidance and good news for the believers (**Qur'an 2:97**). "In Islam, the Holy Spirit is Gabriel" (5).

> *The word 'spirit' is used in twenty places in the Qur'an, and in every case the Muslim believes that it is used of a 'subtle body' which has the capacity to penetrate coarse bodies. The angels and Jinn [evil spirits] are such subtle bodies, and to speak of Allah as a Spirit would, according to Muslim thought, imply that He is a created body. In the Islamic schema, the created "... angelic Holy Spirit is the angel Gabriel, the angel who announced the birth of Jesus to Mary (**Qur'an 3:40**) and brought the Qur'an to the prophet Muhammad"* (6).

Blaspheming the Holy Spirit. According to the New Testament of the Bible and the testimony of Jesus, the role of the Holy Spirit should not be taken lightly. "And so I tell you," Jesus exclaimed, "every kind of sin and slander can be forgiven, but blasphemy against the Spirit will not be forgiven. Anyone who speaks a word against the Son of Man will be forgiven, but anyone who speaks against the Holy Spirit will not be forgiven, either in this age or in the age to come" (**Matthew 12:31-32**). The same message attributed to Jesus is recorded in **Mark 3:28-29** and **Luke 12:10**. The passage in Mark adds this phrase: "they are guilty of an eternal sin."

This is an amazing spiritual lesson by Jesus. *Every kind of sin and slander can be forgiven, but blasphemy against the* [Holy] *Spirit will not be forgiven.* According to Jesus, a person can even speak against Him and be forgiven, but not the Holy Spirit—the person will *never* be forgiven. Why? And what is blasphemy against the Holy Spirit?

First, blasphemy is speaking against the Holy Spirit or denying His existence or refusing to accept the role and work of the Holy Spirit in one's life. Some of the most important roles of the Holy Spirit, remember, are to convict one of sin and to give testimony about Jesus. He is also responsible for setting up God's "temple" within the believer of Jesus Christ. If a person denies the role of the Holy Spirit then how can that person be convicted of sin, repent and receive God's forgiveness? Such a person would be condemned to eternal damnation—a very serious situation, indeed, and one that Christ and the Father in heaven wants all to avoid.

The Light of the Gospel vs. the Darkness of the Qur'an

"This is the verdict:" said Jesus, "Light has come into the world, but men loved darkness instead of light because their deeds were evil. Everyone who does evil hates the light, and will not come into the light for fear that his deeds will be exposed. But whoever lives by the truth comes into the light, so that it may be seen plainly that what he has done has been done through God" (**John 3:19-21**). Muslims are trapped in darkness. They are forbidden to read or even possess a Bible—the only source of God's truth which holds out a hope of salvation for them. Likewise, the Bible is banned in a wide majority of Muslim controlled countries. A Christian is prohibited from entering Mecca or its environs at any time for any reason. In other words, both truth and light—the light of God's word—are banned from the life of the Muslim. Muslim imams and their followers fear the truth and are blinded by the light of the Gospel. Darkness only gives way to more darkness. Even in America, the land of the free, Muslims fear being caught with a Bible, even though the Qur'an states that Muslims are to read and follow the teachings in the Torah and Gospel of Jesus (**Qur'an 5:68**) and that Allah sent Jesus with the truth (**Qur'an 2:87**).

Once again, in **John 8:12**, Jesus affirms that "I am the light of the world. Whoever follows me will never walk in darkness, but will have the light of life." The revelation of Allah in **Qur'an 5:15-16** would appear to confirm Jesus' words. "O followers of the Book [Bible]! Indeed Our Apostle has come to you making clear to you much of what you concealed of the Book and passing over much; indeed, there has come to you light and a clear Book from Allah; With it Allah guides him who will follow His pleasure into the ways of safety and brings them out of utter darkness into light by His will and guides them to the right path." Now, admittedly, this is a confusing verse. The first "Book" mentioned is clearly the Bible since the "followers of the Book" throughout the Qur'an are identified as Christians and Jews. But is the second use of the word "Book" the Qur'an or the Bible?

Historically and biblically, Jesus exemplified the revelation knowledge and light of Almighty God, not Allah or Muhammad. Wherever He went, multitudes, including Jewish religious leaders, marveled at His godly wisdom and enlightenment. The same cannot be said of Muhammad. For the most part, Jews, Christians and pagans of his era were not impressed or moved by Muhammad's words, life examples or tactics. While Muhammad claimed that the Bible (the *Taurat* or Torah and *Injeel* or Gospel) was revealed to Jews and Christians by Allah, it is apparent by his life, words and deeds that he believed little in what was revealed in the *Book* or Bible. In particular, the life and teachings of Jesus Christ, which Muhammad claimed to supersede, was in direct contradiction to what Muhammad taught and exemplified. Muhammad's warring nature quickly surfaced when the peoples of the Arabic peninsula rejected his preaching and espoused tenets of faith.

"The man who walks in the dark," Jesus said, "does not know where he is going. Put your trust in the light while you have it, so that you may become sons of light . . . I have come into the world as a light, so that no one who believes in me should stay in darkness" (**John 12:35b-36a, 46**). While God the Father sent Jesus to be *the light of the world*, it would appear—by the sole thunder of his deeds—that Muhammad was sent by Allah to usher in a new dominion of darkness. Whereas the message of Jesus brought freedom, the message of Muhammad returned to bondage all those who followed it.

Shortly before he was crucified upside down, the Apostle Peter wrote a letter to the persecuted Christians in the Roman provinces that now make up present-day Turkey. "But you are a chosen people," he reminded them, "a royal priesthood, a holy nation, a people belonging to God, that you may declare the praises of him who called you out of darkness into his wonderful light" (**1 Peter 2:9**). The lost, through the ministry of Christ's followers, were being called out of the darkness of oppression into the wondrous light of redemptive freedom. Contrast this independence with the slavery and subjugation that the message of Islam brought to the peoples of the Middle East, Northern Africa, Asia Minor and Southern Europe in its first one hundred years and continues to present to the world today.

"In him was life," the Apostle John wrote of Jesus, "and that life was the light of men. The light shines in the darkness, but the darkness has not understood (**John 1:4-5**). It is ironic, as this scripture points out, but the ones who actually live in spiritual darkness are the ones who have the most difficult time seeing the light of truth.

It is no great surprise, however, that Muslims have a hard time exiting their spiritual darkness in order to come into the light of spiritual truth. If they cannot accept the idea of a savior who can redeem them from their sins, how could they ever come to the light of God's forgiveness? "For he has rescued us from the dominion of darkness," Paul wrote from his prison cell in Rome, "and brought us into the kingdom of the Son he loves, in whom we have redemption, the forgiveness of sins" (**Colossians 1:13-14**). A person who cannot receive the reality of God's redemptive grace and forgiveness offered to them will not likely be set free from their spiritual and emotional bondage to darkness and evil.

Muslims are not alone in their life of darkness. All people live in sin and spiritual darkness according to Christ and His apostles until they acknowledge the free gift of salvation in Jesus Christ that God sent into the world over 2,000 years ago. "For you were once darkness," Paul again wrote from prison, "but now you are light in the Lord. Live as children of light (for the fruit of the light consists in all goodness, righteousness and truth) and find out what pleases the Lord. Have nothing to do with the fruitless deeds of darkness, but rather expose them" (**Ephesians 5:8-11**).

No Forgiveness and Reconciliation in Islam

In one of David's most popular Psalms, he penned, [God] "does not treat us as our sins deserve or repay us according to our iniquities" (**Psalm 103:10**). This is certainly true when one considers the true majesty of the God of all creation.

While Allah can forgive sin if he so pleases, he cannot redeem the sinner. Without a source or means of redemption, the only hope of salvation that a Muslim has available is that his inclination for sinning does not outweigh his accumulation of good deeds. But then, again, that may not be good enough to satisfy Allah. According to **surah 5:54**, Allah gives grace only *to whom he pleases.*

For a sinner—and all people are sinners—to live in sin without the hope of redemption and forgiveness only keeps them in bondage to sin. If there is no hope to be set free from sin, then why stop sinning? The shepherd-king, David, understood this; for he considered himself chief among the sinners.

> *Blessed is he whose transgressions are forgiven, whose sins are covered.*
> *Blessed is the man whose sin the LORD does not count against him and in whose spirit is no deceit.*
> *When I kept silent, my bones wasted away through my groaning all day long.*
> *For day and night your hand was heavy upon me; my strength was sapped as in the heat of summer. Selah*
> *Then I acknowledged my sin to you and did not cover up my iniquity. I said, "I will confess my transgressions to the LORD"—and you forgave the guilt of my sin. Selah* (**Psalm 32:1-5**)

David had an intimate, personal relationship with God long before Jesus, the redeemer, was revealed. He understood that his God could and would forgive him for his sins and that as long as he did not conceal them from the living God, God was just and would relieve him of the burden of his iniquities. His guilt that he carried for his sin was removed as long as he confessed his transgressions to the Lord. With the revelation and ministry of Christ, God made it clear that He would not condemn anyone for their sin as long as they confessed it and accepted the redeeming work of His Son. "Therefore, there is now no condemnation for those who are in Christ Jesus," the Apostle Paul taught, "because through Christ Jesus the law of the Spirit of life set me free from the law of sin and death. For what the law was powerless to do in that it was weakened by the sinful nature, God did by sending his own Son in the likeness of sinful man to be a sin offering. And so he condemned sin in sinful man, in order that the righteous requirements of the law might be fully met in us, who do not live according to the sinful nature but according to the Spirit" (**Romans 8:1-4**).

Jesus taught those who would listen how important it was to be set free from sin. It was essential to become an heir to the Kingdom of God. "To the Jews who had believed him, Jesus said, 'If you hold to my teaching, you are really my disciples. Then you will know the truth, and the truth will set you free.' . . . Jesus said, 'I tell you the truth, everyone who sins is a slave to sin. Now a slave has no permanent place in the family, but a son belongs to it forever. So if the Son sets you free, you will be free indeed'" (**John 8:31-32, 34-36**). Freedom from sin is vital to accepting one's sonship with the Father in heaven.

Where the Spirit of the Lord Jesus Christ is, there is Freedom from Sin. "But whenever anyone turns to the Lord, the veil is taken away," Paul wrote in his second letter to the church in Corinth. "Now the Lord is the Spirit, and where the Spirit of the Lord is, there is freedom. And we, who with unveiled faces all reflect the Lord's glory, are being transformed into his likeness with ever-increasing glory, which comes from the Lord, who is the Spirit" (**2 Corinthians 3:16-18**).

Key to this transformation that Paul talked about is the daily confession of sin, accepting God's forgiveness and receiving the redemptive work of the Cross. The Apostle John decreed it in this manner:

> *This is the message we have heard from him and declare to you: God is light; in him there is no darkness at all. If we claim to have fellowship with him yet walk in the darkness, we lie and do not live by the truth. But if we walk in the light, as he is in the light, we have fellowship with one another, and the blood of Jesus, his Son, purifies us from all sin.*
>
> *If we claim to be without sin, we deceive ourselves and the truth is not in us. If we confess our sins, he is faithful and just and will forgive us our sins and purify us from all unrighteousness. If we claim we have not sinned, we make him out to be a liar and his word has no place in our lives* (**1 John 1:5-10**).

Unlike the believers of the Islamic faith, it is not by any works of righteousness that deliver a Christian from sin. It is purely by the generous grace of God through faith in His Son, Jesus Christ. It is an act of faith, not works, which redeems one from sin. "Therefore," Paul wrote to the church in Rome, "since we have been justified through faith, we have peace with God through our Lord Jesus Christ, through whom we have gained access by faith into this grace in which we now stand. And we

rejoice in the hope of the glory of God" (**Romans 5:1-2**). In his letter to the Galatians, Paul emphasized the necessity and role of Christ's crucifixion to one's deliverance from sin and the sinful nature. "I have been crucified with Christ and I no longer live, but Christ lives in me. The
life I live in the body, I live by faith in the Son of God, who loved me and gave himself for me" (**Galatians 2:20**).

The Apostle Paul provides us with the reality of reconciliation with God in his letters to the Corinthians and the church in Rome. "All this is from God, who reconciled us to himself through Christ and gave us the ministry of reconciliation: that God was reconciling the world to himself in Christ, not counting people's sins against them. And he has committed to us the message of reconciliation" (**2 Corinthians 5:18-19**).

"For if, while we were God's enemies, we were reconciled to him through the death of his Son, how much more, having been reconciled, shall we be saved through his life! Not only is this so, but we also boast in God through our Lord Jesus Christ, through whom we have now received reconciliation" (**Romans 5:10-11**).

Sins Cannot be Remitted or Forgiven in Islam

According to former Muslim and author, Pastor Raza Safa, who converted to Christianity, ". . . not a single Muslim in the world can tell you boldly that his sins are forgiven and that he has eternal life" (7). When it comes to forgiveness, there are two great stumbling blocks for the Muslim. First, they cannot conceive of a compassionate, forgiving god that would redeem them from their sins here and now, rather than at the *judgment* after their death. Second, they cannot fathom and refuse to accept that a man, any man, could be sacrificed as a sin offering for anyone, much more for the good of all mankind.

Over 700 years before the birth of Jesus, Isaiah prophesied about the coming Messiah's mission. "But he was pierced for our transgressions, he was crushed for our iniquities; the punishment that brought us peace was upon him, and by his wounds we are healed" (**Isaiah 53:5**).

"The Lord is not slow in keeping his promise," the Apostle Peter wrote, "as some understand slowness. Instead he is patient with you, not wanting anyone to perish, but everyone to come to repentance" (**2 Peter 3:9**).

Muslims must Abstain from Sin. Muslims, like Christians and Jews, are to refrain from all sin and wickedness. However, when a Muslim sins, the only way back into Allah's grace is through repentance and good deeds. Repentance does not obliterate the sin or wipe it from the mind of Allah. The sin, though confessed and repented of, is still added to Allah's ledger of bad deeds. Also, it is not clear in the Qur'an or hadith

285

what actually constitutes sin other than blaspheming or defaming Allah or Muhammad. Whatever can be determined as sin must be overcome by whatever can be determined as an appropriate good deed.

The faithful Muslim never has absolute assurance that confession of sin will earn Allah's unconditional forgiveness for any offense. Christians, on the other hand, have a blood covenant with God through the sacrifice of Christ that guarantees them absolute forgiveness for any sin they commit.

To repeat a beautiful verse: "My dear children," the Apostle John proclaimed, "I write this to you so that you will not sin. But if anybody does sin, we have one who speaks to the Father in our defense—Jesus Christ, the Righteous One" (**1 John 2:1**). Christians may rest assured that when they commit a sin, if they confess it to God and seek forgiveness of both God and the one offended, they are made right with God because of Jesus' shed blood and His intercession before God on their behalf.

"And [there are] others [who] have confessed their faults, they have mingled a good deed and an evil one; [it] may [well] be [that] Allah will turn to them [and accept their repentance] (mercifully); surely Allah is Forgiving, Merciful" (**Qur'an 9:102**). Note that forgiveness for a Muslim's sins, even if confessed, is not a sure thing with Allah. He may forgive them or he may not—no one knows for certain.

For the Jew and Christian there is no doubt about God's forgiveness. "Praise the LORD, O my soul, and forget not all his benefits— who **forgives all your sins** and heals all your diseases, who **redeems your life from the pit** and crowns you with love and compassion" (**Psalm 103:2-4**, author's emphasis). In distinct contrast, Allah is selective in whom he may forgive. "And whatever affliction befalls you," Muhammad revealed in **Qur'an 42:30**, "it is on account of what your hands have wrought, and (yet) He pardons most (of your faults)."

In **Isaiah 43:25**, God, through the prophet Isaiah, makes it clear that His intentions are complete and absolute forgiveness for sin, to the extent that He will not even bring them to remembrance again. "I, even I, am he who blots out your transgressions, for my own sake, and remembers your sins no more."

David, the author of Psalm 103, made it clear that the true nature of his God and the God of the Jews and Christians was that of a compassionate and forgiving God that permanently removed the sins of those who transgressed against Him. "The LORD is compassionate and gracious," David wrote, "slow to anger, abounding in love. He will not always accuse, nor will he harbor his anger forever; he does not treat us as our sins deserve or repay us according to our iniquities. For as high as the heavens are above the earth, so great is his love for those who fear him; as far as the east is from the west, so far has he removed our transgressions from us" (**Psalm 103:8-12**). What a contrast to the god of the Muslims. Allah is an angry, vengeful god, who is indecisive about forgiveness and waits until after a believer's death to determine their degree of righteousness. Jehovah, the living God of the Judeo-Christian faiths is a compassionate, forgiving God who withholds His anger in exchange for unreserved love that removes sin forever from the repentant transgressor.

Allah is not a Forgiver and a Redeemer of Souls. Allah only offers a brief respite from his eventual retribution for one's sinfulness. "And if Allah had destroyed men for their iniquity," Muhammad revealed, "He would not leave on the earth a single creature, but He respites them [gives them a breather] till an appointed time; so when their doom will come they shall not be able to delay (it) an hour nor can they bring (it) on (before its time)" (**Qur'an 16:61**). Allah may offer temporary forgiveness on earth; however, no Muslim can be sure he or she has actually received it. The only thing they know for sure is that their deeds—good and bad—will be judged *after* their death when there is no hope of reconciliation.

It does appear that Allah offers to bargain on sin. "If you shun the **great sins** which you are forbidden, We will do away with your **small sins** and cause you to enter an honorable place of entering" (**Qur'an 4:31**, author's emphasis). As an alternate, does this mean if a Muslim commits a great sin, then his or her small ones will not be forgiven? And what is a great sin, and what is a small sin? Is the jihadist suicide bomber who murders innocent people committing a *great* sin? Not so, according to the Qur'an and the teaching of Muhammad. Instead, the jihadist murderer is awarded the highest honor by Allah—Paradise with 72 virgins (see the last section of this chapter). To God Almighty of the Jews and Christians, sin is sin. No sin is weighed greater than another, other than the sin of blasphemy against the Holy Spirit (**Matthew 12:31**).

Say to them, 'As surely as I live, declares the Sovereign Lord, I take no pleasure in the death of the wicked, but rather that they turn from their ways and live. Turn! Turn from your evil ways! Why will you die . . . ?'
Ezekiel 33:11

"But if a wicked person turns away from all the sins," Jehovah God spoke through the prophet Ezekiel, "they have committed and keeps all my decrees and does what is just and right, that person will surely live; they will not die" (**Ezekiel 18:21**).

The God of the Bible, the Judeo-Christian God and no other; the One who sent His only begotten Son, Jesus Christ into the world, desires that not one soul should be lost due to sin. God Almighty, not Allah, wants every human soul to experience everlasting salvation and life after death with Him.

"For I take no pleasure in the death of anyone, declares the

Sovereign Lord. Repent and live!" (**Ezekiel 18:32**).

The Apostle Peter made it clear that the Lord Jesus tarries in His return, in part, because He desires that none should perish in their sinfulness. "The Lord is not slow in keeping his promise [of His return], as some understand slowness. Instead he is patient with you, not wanting anyone to perish, but everyone to come to repentance" (**2 Peter 3:9**). The Lord Jesus, in His compassion for all mankind wants every soul to have the opportunity to receive Him as Lord and Savior by repenting and turning from their sin and receiving God's unchangeable forgiveness. Such a magnanimous offer you will not find anywhere in the Qur'an or other Muslim sacred writings. Allah is presented as a compassionless god who really does not care whether his followers go to hell or not.

"This is good [giving thanks to God and praying for those in authority], and pleases God our Savior," Paul wrote to Timothy, "who wants all people to be saved and to come to a knowledge of the truth. For there is one God and one mediator between God and mankind, the man Christ Jesus, who gave himself as a ransom for all people. This has now been witnessed to at the proper time" (**1 Tim 2:3-6**).

"What shall we say, then?" Paul asked rhetorically, "Shall we go on sinning so that grace may increase? By no means! We died to sin; how can we live in it any longer? Or don't you know that all of us who were baptized into Christ Jesus were baptized into his death? We were therefore buried with him through baptism into death in order that, just as Christ was raised from the dead through the glory of the Father, we too may live a new life" (**Romans 6:1-4**).

Jehovah God, speaking through the prophet Isaiah, once again promised that all transgressors would be delivered and set free from sin by the sacrificial death of His Son. "Therefore I will give him a portion among the great, and he will divide the spoils with the strong, because he poured out his life unto death, and was numbered with the transgressors. For he bore the sin of many, and made intercession for the transgressors" (**Isaiah 53:12**).

This forgiveness of sin, Jeremiah prophesied, would come through a personal knowledge of a personal God that would bear witness to one's own spirit, that indeed they had received God's forgiveness. "'No longer will a man teach his neighbor, or a man his brother, saying, *Know the LORD*, because they will all know me, from the least of them to the greatest,' declares the LORD. 'For I will forgive their wickedness and will remember their sins no more'" (**Jeremiah 31:34**).

Three disciples of Christ and authors of biblical epistles shared this redemptive truth with their fellow Christians. The Apostle Peter wrote, "He himself bore our sins in his body on the tree, so that we might die to sins and live for righteousness; by his wounds you have been healed. For you were like sheep going astray, but now you have returned to the Shepherd and Overseer of your souls" (**1 Peter 2:24-25**).

The Apostle Paul wrote to the church in Ephesus that, "In him we have redemption through his blood, the forgiveness of sins, in accordance with the riches of God's grace that he lavished on us with all wisdom and understanding" (**Ephesians 1:7-8**). The unknown author of the letter to the Hebrews penned, "How much more, then, will the blood of Christ, who through the eternal Spirit offered himself unblemished to God, cleanse our consciences from acts that lead to death, so that we may serve the living God!" (**Hebrews 9:14**). All three, as did the other Apostles and early disciples of Jesus, undoubtedly knew what it meant to be redeemed by the sacrifice of Jesus. They all lived under the Law of Moses and oppressive guilt, but now had been set free by a merciful and loving God.

The Apostle Paul, in his very thorough letter to the Christians in Rome, set forth the contrast between this new found freedom in Christ and the sinful nature of man.

> *Those who live according to the sinful nature have their minds set on what that nature desires; but those who live in accordance with the Spirit have their minds set on what the Spirit desires. The mind of sinful man is death, but the mind controlled by the Spirit is life and peace; the sinful mind is hostile to God. It does not submit to God's law, nor can it do so. Those controlled by the sinful nature cannot please God.*
>
> *You, however, are controlled not by the sinful nature but by the Spirit, if the Spirit of God lives in you. And if anyone does not have the Spirit of Christ, he does not belong to Christ. But if Christ is in you, your body is dead because of sin, yet your spirit is alive because of righteousness. And if the Spirit of him who raised Jesus from the dead is living in you, he who raised Christ from the dead will also give life to your mortal bodies through his Spirit, who lives in you* (**Romans 8:5-11**).

There is No Peace after Death. In 2010 a very interesting book was published, called, *Son of Hamas*, by Mosab Hassan Yousef. It is the autobiographical story of a son of a Hamas leader born in the Gaza Strip. Yousef started out as a teenage Hamas terrorist, but he became a very effective Israeli spy, saving many innocent lives from Hamas terrorist attacks.

Early in his story, Mosab recalls his father's Islamic view of death.

> *"This man is gone,"* [Mosab's father, Sheikh Hassan Yousef] *said as the dirt fell onto the dead man's face and neck*

and arms. "He left everything behind – his money, building, sons, daughters, and wife. This is the destiny of each of us."

He [Mosab's father] *urged us to repent and stop sinning. And then he said something I had never heard from my father: "This man's soul will soon return to him and two terrible angels named Munkar and Nakir* [The Denied and The Denier] *will come out of the sky to examine him. They will grab his body and shake him, asking, 'Who is your God?' If he answers incorrectly, they will beat him with a big hammer and send him down into the earth for seventy years. Allah, we ask you to give us the right answers when our time comes!*

". . . And if his answers are not satisfactory, the weight of the dirt above him will crush his ribs. Worms will slowly devour his flesh. He will be tormented by a snake with ninety-nine heads and a scorpion the size of a camel's neck until the resurrection of the dead, when his suffering may earn Allah's forgiveness" (8).

Munkar and Nakir are the names of Muslim angels who test the faith of the dead when they are in the grave. This story matches what is presented in the *Reliance of the Traveller.*

"The Trial of the Grave." *The first of these matters is the questioning of Munkar and Nakir, two tremendous, awe-inspiring personages* [angels of the grave]*who sit a servant upright in his grave, body and soul, and ask him about the unity of Allah and the messengerhood of the Prophet . . . saying, "Who is your Lord, what is your religion, and who is your prophet?" It is they who try people in the grave, their questioning being the first ordeal after death. It is also obligatory to believe in the torment of the grave, that it is a fact, is just, and affects both body and soul, in the way Allah wills* (**ROT, v2.2**).

The Prophet . . . passed by two graves and said: "These two are being tormented, and not for anything excessive: one of them did not free himself from traces of urine, while the other was a talebearer" (**ROT, p31.2(1)**).

In the *Reliance of the Traveller*, it also says that reading the Qur'an for the dead will actually benefit the dead as well as the one who reads it to the dead.

As for reciting the Koran for the deceased, whether at his grave or far from it, scholars disagree as to whether the reward for it reaches him. The scholarly majority hold that it does reach him, and this is the truth, especially if the reciter afterwards donates the reward of what he has read to the deceased. In such a case the reciter also receives the reward for his recital without this diminishing anything from the reward of the deceased (**ROT, w35.1**).

Praying to or for the dead or reading scripture to the dead is not taught in the Bible, nor will it do the dead person any good. The Bible makes it clear, that once a person is dead, there is the judgement and nothing or no one can benefit the dead person. In **Deuteronomy 18:11**, God forbids people to try and communicate with the dead. God spoke through Moses that to do so is akin to witchcraft and sorcery.

"Just as people are destined to die once, and after that to face judgment," (**Hebrews 9:27**). After one dies there is no communication, no opportunity to reverse one's life after death fate, no repentance, no redemption. The living can pray for the dead all they want, it will do no good for the deceased.

"For there is one God and one mediator between God and mankind," Paul wrote Timothy, "the man Christ Jesus," (**1 Timothy 2:5**). No amount of prayer or intercession for the deceased will change his or her status in the grave. Their only chance at redemption was while he or she was alive.

God's Grace Does Not Exist for the Muslim

The Law of Moses handed down to the Jews by Yahweh, the God of the Jews, like any religious law, was a series of you *shall* and *shall not* do as God commands. The Law was impossible to keep, for all men were sinful and weak. "Clearly **no one is justified before God by the law**," Paul wrote to the church in Galatia, "because, 'The righteous will live by faith'" [**Habakkuk 2:4**] (**Galatians 3:11**, author's emphasis). To the Christians in Rome, Paul offered this observation: "The law was added so that the trespass might increase. But where sin increased, grace increased all the more, so that, just as sin reigned in death, so also grace might reign through righteousness to bring eternal life through Jesus Christ our Lord" (**Romans 5:20-21**).

Say: I am only a mortal like you; it is revealed to me that your god is one God, therefore whoever hopes to meet his Lord, he should do good deeds, and not join any one in the service of his Lord.
Qur'an 18:110

By contrast, **the law of good and evil reigns supreme in Islamic teaching**. Only good works can offset evil deeds and not the saving grace of Allah. "And (as for) those who believe and do good deeds, these are the dwellers of the garden; in it they shall abide" (**Qur'an 2:82**). Once again, in the same surah, Muhammad reveals the benefits of good deeds. "And spend in the way of Allah and cast not yourselves to perdition with your own hands, and do good (to others); surely Allah loves the doers of good" (**Qur'an 2:195**).

Islamic teaching reverses God's word in the New Testament on *grace* and reinstitutes the *Law of Works*. In Islam, one can only satisfy Allah by doing what he demands.

According to the Bible, however, sinful man can never do enough good deeds to offset his sinfulness. God knew that from the very beginning of time. God sought a man that would answer His call to righteousness. "The people of the land practice extortion and commit robbery;" God spoke through the prophet Ezekiel, "they oppress the poor and needy and mistreat the alien, denying them justice. I looked for a man among them who would build up the wall and stand before me in the gap on behalf of the land so I would not have to destroy it, but I found none" (**Ezekiel 22:29-30**). God wanted an intercessor; someone to stand in the gap and take on the burden of sin of mankind, but none was blameless enough to answer the call. About one hundred years earlier, the prophet Isaiah revealed what would be God's ultimate solution for man's redemption. "He saw that there was no one, he was appalled that there was no one to intervene; so his own arm worked salvation for him, and his own righteousness sustained him. He put on righteousness as his breastplate, and the helmet of salvation on his head; he put on the garments of vengeance and wrapped himself in zeal as in a cloak" (**Isaiah 59:16-17**). In order to redeem man from his own sinful destruction, God would extend His *own arm* in the person of His Son to bring about salvation for His children.

God's eventual solution for mankind's sinful separation from Him was to bring about redemption and reconciliation by His own hand. Once again, through the prophet Isaiah, God revealed His loving intent. "But now, this is what the LORD says—he who created you, O Jacob, he who formed you, O Israel: 'Fear not, for I have redeemed you; I have summoned you by name; you are mine. When you pass through the waters, I will be with you; and when you pass through the rivers, they will not sweep over you. When you walk through the fire, you will not be burned; the flames will not set you ablaze. For I am the LORD, your God, the Holy One of Israel, your Savior'" (**Isaiah 43:1-3a**). A few verses later in the same chapter, God revealed that no one else would be able to bring about this deliverance; this redemptive reconciliation of His creation with Him. "'I, even I, am the LORD, and **apart from me there is no savior**. I have revealed and saved and proclaimed—I, and **not some foreign god** among you. You are my witnesses,' declares the LORD, 'that I am God. Yes, and from ancient days I am he. No one can deliver out of my hand. When I act, who can reverse it'" (**Isaiah 43:11-13**, author's emphasis)?

For the Old Testament Jew, there was only one hope for removing the curse of the law (as illustrated in **Deuteronomy 28**), and that was to offer an animal sacrifice—to shed the blood of a warm-blooded animal. However, it was the high priest that had to make the sacrifice; the sinner could not come before God and do it. God's plan all along was to set the stage to end the blood sacrifice of the law once and for all with the shed blood of the Lamb of God, His only begotten Son, Jesus Christ. "When you were dead in your sins and in the uncircumcision of your sinful nature," the Apostle Paul proclaimed to the church in the Greek city of Colossae, one hundred miles west of Ephesus, "God made you alive with Christ. He forgave us all our sins, having **canceled the written code** [the law], with its regulations, that was against us and that stood opposed to us; he took it away, nailing it to the cross" (**Colossians 2:13-14**, author's emphasis).

To the Galatians, Paul declared, "Christ redeemed us from the **curse of the law** by becoming a curse for us, for it is written: 'Cursed is everyone who is hung on a tree'" [**Deuteronomy 21:23**] (**Galatians 3:13**, author's emphasis). Christ did not do away with the Law of Moses; He only put to death the curse for not keeping the law. "Do not think that I have come to abolish the Law or the Prophets;" Jesus told His listeners, "I have not come to abolish them but to fulfill them. I tell you the truth, until heaven and earth disappear, not the smallest letter, not the least stroke of a pen, will by any means disappear from the Law until everything is accomplished" (**Matthew 5:17-18**).

In many of his letters to the churches in Asia Minor, Paul hammered home the point that, because of Christ's sacrifice, those who would accept it by faith were no longer under the curse of the law. There was no amount of good works that could redeem a person from sin and the law of consequences. "For when we were controlled by the sinful nature," Paul wrote, "the sinful passions aroused by the law were at work in our bodies, so that we bore fruit for death. But now, by dying to what once bound us, we have been released from the law so that we serve in the new way of the Spirit, and not in the old way of the written code" (**Romans 7:5-6**). No longer would it suffice for the blood of goats and bulls to be shed for a sin sacrifice. God, through Christ, had made a new and everlasting covenant with mankind through the shed blood of His Son. "But the ministry Jesus has received is as superior to theirs as the covenant of which he is mediator is superior to the old one, and it is founded on better promises" (**Hebrews 8:6**).

This new covenant concept was not an easy one for the Jew to accept. Even Paul, a devout Jew, struggled with it from time to time. "We know that the law is spiritual;" he confessed, "but I am unspiritual, sold as a slave to sin. I do not understand what I do. For what I want to do I do not do, but what I hate I do. And if I do what I do not want to do, I agree that the law is good. As it is, it is no longer I myself who do it, but it is sin living in me. I know that nothing good lives in me, that is, in my sinful nature. For I have the desire to do what is good, but I cannot carry it out. For what I do is not the good I want to do; no, the evil I do not want to do—this I keep on doing" (**Romans 7:14-19**).

Despite his pitiful struggle, Paul understood God's redemptive plan and each time he fell captive to sin he would turn to the saving work of his Lord and Savior, Jesus Christ. "So I find this law at work:" Paul admitted to the young Christians in Rome, "When I want to do good, evil is right there with me. For in my inner being I delight in God's law; but I see another law at work in the members of my body, waging war against the law of my mind and making me a prisoner of the law of sin at work within my members. What a wretched man I am! Who will rescue me from this body of death? Thanks be to God—through Jesus Christ our Lord!" (**Romans 7:21-25a**).

For the Muslim faithful there is no deliverance, no respite from the law of Allah and his judgment. Only good works offer any hope of reconciliation with Allah. The law reigns supreme for Muslims. Failure to keep the law can only be offset by good deeds. "Allah originates the creation, then reproduces it, then to Him you shall be brought back. And at the time when the hour shall come the guilty shall be in despair. And they shall not have any intercessors from among their gods, and they shall be deniers of their associate-gods" (**Qur'an 30:11-13**). There is no mediator for the sinful Muslim; none that can plead his case before Allah and no assurance of ever being reconciled with Allah in this life or the next.

Muslims, as do Jews and Christians, claim to be descendants of Abraham. If God, through the revelations of Jesus and His Apostles, revealed that redemption from sin can only be obtained by grace through faith in Christ's death and resurrection, then why would He take it back through a new revelation through Muhammad, declaring that salvation or redemption from personal sin can only be achieved through man's own efforts at good works by keeping an impossible law?

"Therefore," Paul continued, "since we have been justified through faith, we have peace with God through our Lord Jesus Christ, through whom we have gained access by faith into this grace in which we now stand. And we rejoice in the hope of the glory of God" (**Romans 5:1-2**).

"The sting of death is sin," wrote the Apostle Paul, "and the power of sin is the law. But thanks be to God! He gives us the victory through our Lord Jesus Christ" (**1 Corinthians 15:56-57**). Without the sweet sacrifice of Christ that brought redemption and reconciliation with God, Christians would be no better off than those that follow the dictates of Islam. "So I say," penned Paul in his letter to the church in Galatia, "live by the Spirit, and you will not gratify the desires of the sinful nature. For the sinful nature desires what is contrary to the Spirit, and the Spirit what is contrary to the sinful nature. They are in conflict with each other, so that you do not do what you want. But if you are led by the Spirit, you are not under law" (**Galatians 5:16-18**).

The Apostle Paul spent much of his effort in his sixteen-chapter letter to the Christians in Rome thoroughly explaining the nature of the law and sin, and how believers in the saving work of Christ were set free from the law of sin and death. "The mind of sinful man is death, but the mind controlled by the Spirit is life and peace; the sinful mind is hostile to God. It does not submit to God's law, nor can it do so. Those controlled by the sinful nature cannot please God" (**Romans 8:6-8**).

Paul further revealed, that keeping the law did not make one righteous before God. "Now we know that whatever the law says," he articulated, "it says to those who are under the law, so that every mouth may be silenced and the whole world held accountable to God. Therefore no one will be declared righteous in his sight by observing the law; rather, through the law we become conscious of sin. But now a righteousness from God, apart from law, has been made known, to which the Law and the Prophets testify. This righteousness from God comes through faith in Jesus Christ to all who believe. There is no difference, for all have sinned and fall short of the glory of God, and are justified freely by his grace through the redemption that came by Christ Jesus" (**Romans 3:19-24**).

A few verses later, Paul proclaimed, "For we maintain that a man is justified by faith apart from observing the law. . . Do we, then, nullify the law by this faith? Not at all! Rather, we uphold the law" (**Romans 3:28, 31**). It is no longer the law that dictates the actions of the Christian; it is the Spirit of God living within each believer. "For sin shall not be your master," Paul wrote three chapters later, "because **you are not under law**, but under grace" (**Romans 6:14**, author's emphasis).

Muhammad Reversed God's Plan of Salvation

In the book of the prophet Ezekiel, three times God says through the prophet, that He takes no pleasure in seeing the wicked perish (**Ezekiel 18:23, 32, 33:11**; the last two verses cited earlier in this chapter).

Shortly after Pentecost (the outpouring of the Holy Spirit on Jesus' disciples), Peter started preaching the simplicity of the Gospel and what Christ had accomplished by His death on the cross and resurrection from the dead. "Repent and be baptized," he proclaimed to the crowd in Jerusalem, "every one of you, in the name of Jesus Christ for the forgiveness of your sins. And you will receive the gift of the Holy Spirit" (**Acts 2:38**). It is as simple *and* as difficult as that: repent and be baptized. To repent means to turn from sin and to accept Christ's redemptive work of the cross and becoming the righteousness of God through Jesus. Not an easy task for sin-ladened man or woman. But remember, Jesus promised His followers that he would send a Helper, a Comforter, the Holy Spirit, to strengthen and guide each one that choses to follow Christ. Allah offers no such help or comfort. Muslims are on their own to figure out life and how to abstain from sin.

A little later, Peter once again proclaimed, "Repent, then, and turn to God, so that your sins may be wiped out, that times of refreshing may come from the Lord" (**Acts 3:19**).

By distinct contrast, and in complete reversal of what Christ had accomplished and what His Apostles preached throughout Judea and Asia Minor and beyond, Allah, through Muhammad preached a gospel not of redemption and forgiveness, but of condemnation and salvation through works—works which are never satisfactory to Allah.

Salvation Comes from Confession of Faith, Not by Works. Allah offers no plan of redemption or salvation; no freedom of choice in what one chooses to believe. The Muslim lives in a constant state of anxiety, never knowing that his deeds will be good enough before Allah to assure him of everlasting life in heaven. Muslims live strictly by the law, the Qur'anic law as Allah revealed to Muhammad one verse at a time, and often at times when it benefited Muhammad and his objectives.

"In Islam," the Caner brothers revealed in their book, *Unveiling Islam*, "it is hoped that salvation is earned through one's good works. . . .

"There is no security for the believer of Islam (9)."

Not one Muslim who has died or who now lives knows his fate after death. "So no soul knows what is hidden [after death] for them of that which will refresh the eyes; a reward for what they did. Is he then who is a believer like him who is a transgressor? They are not equal" (**Qur'an 32:17-18**).

These two verses must be confusing to a Muslim. If a believer in Allah is not like a transgressor, then all Muslim believers must be sinless and all sinners are non-Muslim. However, even the most spiritually uninformed know that all men are sinners through and through. No one is perfect and without sin—no one except Jesus Christ the Son of God. Yet, Muhammad promises his followers in verses 19 and 20 that those who do (unspecified) good will abide in paradise, while those who do (unspecified) evil will abide in hell. Despite his unqualified proclamation, not even Allah's Apostle knew where he would spend eternity. Upon the death of a faithful Muslim, 'Uthman bin Maz'un, the one who nursed 'Uthman during his declining days, asked the Prophet what 'Uthman's post death future might be.

"But who else is worthy of [honor] (if not 'Uthman)?"

To which Muhammad replied, "As to him, by Allah, death has overtaken him, and I hope the best for him. By Allah, though I am the Apostle of Allah, yet I do not know what Allah will do to me" [after I die] (**hadith 5:58:266**). **Muhammad had no clue and no hope of eternity, even though he was Allah's chosen Apostle—the one who was to deliver Allah's final message to all mankind; a message not of salvation, but of hopelessness.**

"If you ask a Muslim what will happen to him when he dies," Pastor Reza Safa wrote, "he will answer, 'Only God knows!'

"Muslims do not have assurance of salvation . . . the word *salvation* is unknown to them (10)."

Muhammad never sacrificed his life for anyone. As a result, Muslims live in their sin until the day they die, hoping that when they appear before Allah in the hereafter, their good deeds will outweigh their bad ones and tip the scale in their favor. If their good deeds measure up to be insufficient, well then, it's just too late and their soul will burn in the eternal fires of hell.

By comparison, all those who call upon the name of Jesus Christ, in heartfelt sincerity, are assured of their salvation. "Although he was a son, he learned obedience from what he suffered and, once made perfect, he became the source of eternal salvation for all who obey him" (**Hebrews 5:8-9**).

"Salvation [to rescue; deliver; bring to safety]," the Apostle Peter boldly preached before the Sanhedrin in Jerusalem, "is found in no one else [other than Jesus Christ], for there is no other name under heaven given to men by which we must be saved" (**Acts 4:12**).

Sadly, for the Muslim believer in Allah, there is no salvation and no reconciliation with him. "And We have made every man's actions to cling to his neck," Allah revealed to Muhammad, "and We will bring forth to him on the resurrection day a book which he will find wide open: Read your book; your own self is sufficient as a reckoner against you this day. Whoever goes aright, for his own soul does he go aright; and whoever goes astray, to its detriment only does he go astray; nor can the bearer of a burden bear the burden of another, nor do We chastise until We raise an apostle" (**Qur'an 17:13-15**). Every bad deed and every good deed that a Muslim performs during his or her life will go with them to the grave. Allah will then review them from his book on the day of resurrection and weigh the good against the bad. There is no grace; no forgiveness. Every believer in Allah will stand spiritually naked before Allah waiting upon his judgment. There will be no intercessor; no mediator before Allah on behalf of the faithful. Only their works will be judged.

"Why is it so important that Muslims do what Allah wants?" wrote author and former Muslim, Dr. Mark Gabriel. "It's because Islam is a religion of works. Entrance to Paradise (heaven) must be earned. The sad part is that Muslims can never have assurance of salvation (11)."

Once a bad deed is done there is no going back to redeem it, nor is there anyone who will intercede before Allah for them. ". . . are there for us then any intercessors so that they should intercede on our behalf?" Muhammad asked in **Qur'an 7:53**. "Or could we be sent back so that we should do (deeds) other than those which we did? Indeed they have lost their souls, and that which they forged has gone away from them." Once a Muslim dies there is no hope for them. Nor is there any hope for them while they are alive.

Even Muhammad was uncertain about his future after death. "Say: I am not the first of the apostles, and I do not know what will be done with me or with you [by Allah]: I do not follow anything but that which is revealed to me, and I am nothing but a plain warner" (**Qur'an 46:9**).

"Surely," Muhammad revealed, "they who believe and do good deeds and keep up prayer and pay the poor-rate they shall have their reward from their Lord, and they shall have no fear, nor shall they grieve" (**Qur'an 2:277**). While the Qur'an talks about Allah's mercy toward believers, it says very little about Allah's grace (cf. **Qur'an 3:31**).

To receive Allah's love and mercy, a believer must follow the law—the law of good deeds, charity and prayer. Although Christians are called to the same godly ideals, it is in response to their salvation at the hands of a loving, forgiving God, not a performance, in order to gain God's favor. Those who come to God through Christ know that their sins are too great; that they are too weak to retain God's favor without the shed blood of Christ covering their sins and their sinfulness.

Without Christ, no one has the authority or the mediation to approach God for forgiveness and reconciliation.

Islam provides for no such approach to Allah. While Christ is presented in the Bible as God's sinless Son, the Qur'an presents Allah's "messenger," Muhammad, as a murderous, sin-laden human being with many imperfections. He was so imperfect that he tried to commit suicide several times and sought to kill his followers. Something Jesus never did; never considered and never would. Jesus loves God, His Father, He loves life and He loves everyone—even those who sought to kill and did kill Him.

The essence of the New Testament is that God so loved the world that He sent His only Son to redeem it; to save it from its own sinful destruction. In a dream God revealed to Joseph that his betrothed, Mary, was with child. "She will give birth to a son, and you are to give him the name Jesus, because he will save his people from their sins" (**Matthew 1:21**). Muhammad, on the other hand, was sent by Allah to destroy his followers.

"And the measuring out on that day [of judgment] will be just;" Muhammad proclaimed in **Qur'an 7:8-9**, "then as for him whose measure (of good deeds) is heavy [exceeding his bad deeds], those are they who shall be successful [in entering paradise]; and as for him whose measure (of good deeds) is light, those are they who have made their souls suffer loss because they disbelieved in Our communications."

Jesus came to destroy the works of the devil, Muhammad, to implement them. "Dear children," the Apostle John wrote, "do not let anyone lead you astray. He who does what is right is righteous, just as [Jesus] is righteous. He who does what is sinful is of the devil, because the devil has been sinning from the beginning. The reason the Son of God appeared was to destroy the devil's work. No one who is born of God will continue to sin, because God's seed remains in him; he cannot go on sinning, because he has been born of God. This is how we know who the children of God are and who the children of the devil are: Anyone who does not do what is right is not a child of God; nor is anyone who does not love his brother" (**1 John 3:7-10**).

No one can earn or work toward God's salvation. "For it is by grace you have been saved, through faith—and this not from yourselves, it is the gift of God—not by works, so that no one can boast" (**Ephesians 2:8-9**). To be saved, means to be justified by the grace of God through faith in Jesus Christ—to be declared innocent and accepted by God—with the guaranteed results of eternal life. "Therefore," Paul affirmed, "since we have been justified through faith, we have peace with God through our Lord Jesus Christ, through whom we have gained access by faith into this grace in which we now stand. And we rejoice in the hope of the glory of God" (**Romans 5:1-2**).

God's plan of salvation is rather simple and available to anyone—Muslim, Jew, Hindu, Buddhist, or atheist—anyone who would call upon the name of Christ. "That if you confess with your mouth, 'Jesus is Lord,' and believe in your heart that God raised him from the dead," the Apostle Paul proclaimed, "you will be saved. For it is with your heart that you believe and are justified, and it is with your mouth that you confess and are saved . . .for, 'Everyone who calls upon the name of the Lord will be saved" (**Romans 10:9-10, 13**).

Oppression Replaces Freedom of Choice in Islam

Jesus made it abundantly clear what His life on earth was all about. "To the Jews who had believed him, Jesus said, 'If you hold to my teaching, you are really my disciples. Then you will know the truth, and the truth will set you free'" (**John 8:31-32**). Again, He said, "So if the Son sets you free, you will be free indeed" (**John 8:36**).

Many years after Christ's death, the Apostle Paul picked up on Jesus' teaching of freedom. "You have been set free from sin and have become slaves to righteousness" (**Romans 6:18**). Again, Paul wrote to the Roman church, "because through Christ Jesus the law of the Spirit who gives life has set you free from the law of sin and death" (**Romans 8:2**).

To the church in Corinth, Paul wrote a similar reminder. "Now the Lord is the Spirit, and where the Spirit of the Lord is, there is freedom" (**2 Corinthians 3:17**). And to the Galatian church, Paul proclaimed, "It is for freedom that Christ has set us free. Stand firm, then, and do not let yourselves be burdened again by a yoke of slavery" (**Galatians 5:1**). The slavery Paul was talking about was man's slavery to sin. While physical slavery is confining and sometimes painful, it is spiritual and emotional imprisonment that wears on the hearts and souls of men and women, and keeps mankind living under oppression and tyranny. The precepts of Islam present neither the philosophy nor reality of spiritual or physical freedom.

Life of true spiritual and emotional freedom can only be appropriated by faith in Jesus Christ. There is no other road to this freedom except through a personal relationship with Christ that brings one into an intimate relationship with the living God of the Jews and Christians. No other religion offers such an opportunity—such a release from bondage.

True freedom is unique to Judeo-Christian theology. It does not exist in the Islamic faith. ". . . to earn this religious freedom Muslims believe they must deprive religious freedom to others," wrote the Caner brothers in their book, *Unveiling Islam* (12).

When Jesus returned to His hometown of Nazareth early in His ministry, he opened the scroll of the prophet **Isaiah (61:1)** and read these words that described His coming as the promised Messiah. "The Spirit of the Sovereign LORD is on me, because the LORD has anointed me to preach good news to the poor. He has sent me to bind up the brokenhearted, to proclaim **freedom** for the captives and release from darkness for the prisoners" (**Luke 4:18**, author emphasis). Since time began, man has been in bondage to sin and separated from God.

The Jews sacrificed animals in an effort to free them from their sins. Muslims labor at what they perceive to be "good works" to overshadow their sinful nature. Christians freely receive forgiveness for their sins and are set free from the bondage of sin and spiritual death by the grace of God and the sacrifice of Christ on the cross. Paul preached in his letter to the new Christians in Rome, "For we know, that our old self was **crucified with him** so that the body of sin might be done away with, that we should no longer be slaves to sin – because anyone who has died has been freed from sin" (**Romans 6:6-7**, author's emphasis).

The Apostle Peter insisted, "Live as free men, but do not use your freedom as a cover-up for evil; live as servants of God" (**1 Peter 2:16**). True Christianity is a religion of freedom—not freedom to gratify personal wants and desires, but freedom to serve Almighty God and those whom He loves. Islam, as revealed by Muhammad and taught by Islamic clerics, is a religion of oppression that seeks to take away the freedom of individuals, cultures, societies and countries, and forcefully make them submit to the perceived law of Allah. There is no freedom of choice; no exercise of free will permitted. Apostle Peter warned about false prophets that would seek to enslave what God had set free. "They promise them freedom," Peter wrote, "while they themselves are slaves of depravity—for a man is a slave to whatever has mastered him" (**2 Peter 2:19**).

The final goal of freedom in Christ for the Christian is not just to be separated from sin, but to secure a place in heaven with God. "But now that you have been set free from sin and have become slaves to God, the benefit you reap leads to holiness, and the result is eternal life. For the wages of sin is death, but the gift of God is eternal life in Christ Jesus our Lord" (**Romans 6:22-23**). Paul, an apostle of Jesus Christ, who before his reproach by Christ and his conversion, was a frequent persecutor and murderer of Christians. He had considered himself to be a leader among sinners, yet was set free from his sinful nature and eternal damnation through the redemptive work of Christ.

Heaven is a Perverted Place for Muslims

In Islam, Everyone Goes to Hell First. Every one of Allah's followers goes to hell first. In **Qur'an 19:67-72**, Allah, through Muhammad states: "Again We do certainly know best those who deserve most to be burned therein. And there is not one of you but shall come to it, this is an unavoidable decree of your Lord. And We will deliver those who guarded (against evil), and We will leave the unjust therein on their knees." So, despite Allah's plea to make sure the believer's good deeds exceed his bad deeds, in the end it makes no difference to Allah; he's going to send everyone to hell anyway.

If every Muslim knew this verse, which most likely they do not, it should scare the "hell" out of them and cause them to come running to the freedom and security of Christ.

It is obligatory to hold that true believers in the oneness of Allah . . . will be taken out of hell after having paid for their sins, through the generosity of Allah Mighty and Majestic. No one who is a true monotheist will abide in the fire forever.
Reliance of the Traveller, v2.7

Remember, Muhammad, the Apostle of Allah, the revealer of truth, was not sure of his fate after death. "Say: I am not the first of the apostles, and I do not know what will be done with me or with you. " (**Qur'an 46:9**).

A good maxim to adhere to is: *If the leader you are following does not know where he is going, it would be a good idea not to follow him.*

Houris **(Virgins) and Rivers of Wine in Paradise**. For the Muslim faithful who are successful in passing through Allah's judgment of fire, they are awarded paradise, a place of personal, hedonistic pleasures: young virgin women and boys; sex; rivers of wine to drink from, without getting drunk; servants and complete aggrandizement of personal indulgence, along with fine clothes.

Paradise, however, apparently is just for men. Women (virgin women) are only mentioned with respect to meeting the sexual and other needs of Allah's chosen men. "And convey good news to those who believe and do good deeds, that they shall have gardens in which rivers flow; whenever they shall be given a portion of the fruit thereof, they shall say: This is what was given to us before; and they shall be given the like of it, and they shall have **pure mates** in them, and in them, they shall abide" (**Qur'an 2:25**, author's emphasis).

> *Surely those who guard (against evil) shall be in gardens and bliss, rejoicing because of what their Lord gave them, and their Lord saved them from the punishment of the burning fire. Eat and drink pleasantly for what you did, reclining on thrones set in lines, and We will unite them to large-eyed beautiful ones* [houris].
> *And (as for) those who believe and their offspring follow them in faith, We will not diminish to them aught of their work; every man is responsible for what he shall have wrought. And We will aid them with fruit and flesh such as they desire. They shall pass therein from one to another a cup wherein there shall be nothing vain nor any sin. And round them shall go boys of theirs as if they were hidden pearls* (**Qur'an 52:17-24**).

Apparently, the concept of Heaven portrayed here is one that meets one's fleshly desires—the sin that one was to avoid on earth, one is now free to indulge in, in paradise. "Surely those who guard (against evil) are in a secure place. In gardens and springs; They shall wear of fine and thick silk, (sitting) face to face; Thus (shall it be), and We will wed them with Houris pure, beautiful ones. They shall call therein for every fruit in security; They shall not taste therein death except the first death, and He will save them from the punishment of hell" (**Qur'an 44:51-56**). **Qur'an 55:54-59, 55:70-77** and **78:31-34** repeats Muhammad's promise to his followers, which appealed to their earthly lusts.

Apparently, for the Muslim man who reaches paradise, anything goes. All the lust and sin that was forbidden to him on earth will now be freely available to him. The central theme of paradise for the Muslim male who is fortunate enough to enter it, is the overwhelming availability of *houris*—young, voluptuous virgins with full breasts and large dark eyes. "And you shall not be rewarded except (for) what you did. Save the servants of Allah, the purified ones. For them is a known sustenance, fruits, and they shall be highly honored, in gardens of pleasure, on thrones, facing each other. A bowl shall be made to go round them from water running out of springs, white, delicious to those who drink. There shall be no trouble in it, nor shall they be exhausted therewith. And with them shall be those [houris] who restrain the eyes, having beautiful eyes; as if they were eggs carefully protected" (**Qur'an 37:39-49**).

The Muslim men of paradise are free to engage the houris whenever they feel like it. They are pure, and no man or jinni has ever had sex with them. "In them shall be those [maidens] who restrained their eyes; before them neither man nor jinni [invisible beings] have touched them" (**Qur'an 55:56**). The houris are there in paradise for one reason: to serve the needs of the Muslim man. "Then We have made them virgins, loving, equals in age, for the sake of the companions of the right hand" (**Qur'an 56:36-38**).

Jesus said that there will be no marriage in heaven, but that everyone "will be like the angels in heaven" (**Matthew 22:30**). Jesus, in responding to the Sadducees (the Jewish religious leaders who did not fully accept the doctrine of the resurrection of the dead) on the issue of marriage in heaven, stated: "But those who are considered worthy of taking part in that age and in the resurrection from the dead will neither marry nor be given in marriage, and they will no longer die; for they are like the angels. They are God's children, since they are children of the resurrection" (**Luke 20:35-36**).

Heaven for the Jihadist. There is one sure way, according to the teaching of Muhammad, for the Muslim to reach paradise. The jihadist or holy warrior has special favor with Allah. To kill Allah's enemies—all non-Muslims—is the only guaranteed way to paradise. "The Prophet said . . . 'Paradise has one-hundred grades which Allah has reserved for the Mujahidin [holy warriors] who fight in His Cause" (**hadith 4:52:48**, narrated by Abu Huraira).

Abdullah Al Araby, writer for the Islam Review, confirmed that, "The only assurance a Muslim has of going to Paradise is through fighting for the cause of spreading Islam (Jihad), and being martyred in the process

(13)." The Caner brothers also concur: "Eternal security is further based on a Muslim's hatred toward enemies of Allah (14)."

Both the Qur'an and the hadith also agree that it is the jihadist, the one who murders for the *cause of Allah*, and not the doer of good deeds, who will be awarded paradise without Allah passing judgment. "Therefore let those [who] fight in the way of Allah, who sell this world's life for the hereafter; and whoever fights in the way of Allah, [whether] he be slain or be he victorious, We shall grant him a mighty reward" (**Qur'an 4:74**).

"The Prophet said, 'Nobody who dies and finds good from Allah (in the Hereafter) would wish to come back to this world even if he were given the whole world and whatever is in it, except the martyr who, on seeing the superiority of martyrdom, would like to come back to the world and get killed again (in Allah's Cause).' Narrated Anas: The Prophet said, 'A single endeavor (of fighting) in Allah's Cause in the afternoon or in the forenoon is better than all the world and whatever is in it'" (**hadith 4:52:53**, narrated by Anas bin Malik).

Not only are jihadists, including the suicide bombers of the world, granted a free pass to paradise, but according to a number of Islamic sources, including one cited by the Caner brothers, jihadists enter a palace in paradise where there are "seventy couches made of gold and emerald on which lay virgins, untouched by man prepared for their bridegrooms" (15). An obscure source that claims to be from Muhammad, and that is repeatedly cited by jihadist leaders to encourage the martyrdom of their followers, is that they will receive 72 virgins upon entering paradise.

The ones who are assured an abode in hell are not the murderous mujahidin, but those who reject Allah. "And (as to) those who disbelieve in and reject My communications, they are the inmates of the fire, in it they shall abide" (**Qur'an 2:39; 5:10; 9:63**).

"Now a man came up to Jesus and asked, 'Teacher, what good thing must I do to get eternal life?'

"'Why do you ask me about what is good?' Jesus replied. 'There is only One who is good. If you want to enter life, obey the commandments.'

"'Which ones?' the man inquired.

"Jesus replied, 'Do not murder, do not commit adultery, do not steal, do not give false testimony, honor your father and mother, and love your neighbor as yourself'" (**Matthew 19:16-19**). Muslims have had a long history of not loving their neighbors or being at peace with those nearby. To the contrary, they have had a long, sorted and bloody history of murder, adultery, rape, thievery, deception, lies and hatred for their neighbors. This is certainly not a résumé that would get one into the heaven of Jehovah God.

Chapter Conclusion

One of the core beliefs of the Christian is that he/she has been redeemed from his/her sin by the shed blood of Christ, and has been made righteous in the eyes of God, his/her heavenly Father. This redemption from sin and reconciliation with God is alien to the Muslim believer. Allah does not want to redeem his creation, nor can he redeem it. He is not interested in reconciliation between himself and those who follow him.

No Muslim is assured of going to Heaven. To the contrary, Islamic teaching is that everyone goes to hell first and it is by Allah's discretion whether or not a Muslim has passed the test of having completed enough good deeds to offset his or her sinfulness. In Christianity, no number of good deeds can offset one's sinfulness. That is why mankind needed a savior that was fulfilled through the coming of Jesus Christ, not by Muhammad, who reversed all that Christ stood for and accomplished.

The Christian faith, through Christ's work of redemption, offers hope—the only source of hope—to all mankind to be made right with Almighty God. Islam offers no hope, only hopelessness and despair. There is no assurance for the Muslim believer, who is taught to live by Allah's law, that he or she could ever please Allah enough or do enough good deeds to warrant his favor at the time of judgment after death. The Christian, however, is taught that it is by faith—faith in Christ—not deeds, that one is saved from everlasting fire and promised eternal life with the heavenly Father.

References.

1. Gilchrist, John. *Muhammad and the Religion of Islam*, 1986. Jesus to the Muslims, p. 273.
2. Safa, Reza F. *Inside Islam: Exposing and Reaching the World of Islam*, 1996 Charisma House, p. 81.
3. *Qur'an*, Muhammad Asad translation. Isamicity.com. Source: http://www.islamicity.com.
4. Slick, Matt. *Islam by topic: Holy Spirit.* Source: https://carm.org/topic-islam-holy-spirit
5. *The Holy Spirit in Islam and Christianity.* Islam for Christians, October 16, 2016. Source: http://www.islamforchristians.com/holy-spirit-islam-christianity/
6. Langford, Michael. *Islam's Errant Versions of the Holy Spirit.* Intercede, Vol. XXXVI, No. 1, January/February, 2019.
7. Safa, p. 81.
8. Yousef, Mosab Hassan. *Son of Hamas*, 2010, Tyndale Momentum, p. 17.

9. Caner, Ergun Mehmet and Emir Fethi Caner. *Unveiling Islam*, 2002. Kregel Publications, div. of Kregel. Inc., p. 31.
10. Safa, p. 80.
11. Gabriel, Mark A. *Islam and Terrorism*, 2002. Published by FrontLine, a Strang Company, p. 27.
12. Caner and Caner, p.35.
13. Al Araby, Abdullah, *Nothing in Common.* IslamReview.com. http://www.islamreview.com/ articles/nothingincommon.shtml. Accessed November 11, 2006.
14. Caner and Caner, p. 35.
15. Caner and Caner, p. 193.

Chapter 11

A Sacrificial Life vs. Islamic Martyrdom

For it is better, if it is God's will, to suffer for doing good than for doing evil.

1 Peter 3:17

There is a great disparity in understanding between Christianity and Islam and their respective followers in what constitutes living a sacrificial life according to Biblical and Qur'anic dictates. In the Gospel of John Jesus set the standard for His followers in that He laid down His life for others. "I am the good shepherd," Jesus said. "The good shepherd lays down his life for the sheep" (**John 10:11**). Later, Jesus would tell His disciples, "Greater love has no one than this: to lay down one's life for one's friends" (**John 15:13**).

In the Apostle John's first letter, written from Ephesus between 85-90 A.D., he reminded Christ followers of Jesus' sacrifice and the example it set. "This is how we know what love is: Jesus Christ laid down his life for us. And we ought to lay down our lives for our brothers and sisters" (**1 John 3:16**).

In His Sermon on the Mount, Jesus taught, "Blessed are those who are persecuted because of righteousness . . ." (**Matthew 5:10**) and "Blessed are you when people insult you, persecute you and falsely say all kinds of evil against you because of me" (**Matthew 5:11**). However, despite such promised persecution, Jesus advised His followers to let their light shine among non-believers so they would see His followers' good deeds and give glory to God (**Matthew 5:16**).

Jesus understood that His teaching was revolutionary and the consequences His followers would encounter following His example. "If the world hates you, keep in mind that it hated me first. If you belonged to the world, it would love you as its own. As it is, you do not belong to the world, but I have chosen you out of the world. That is why the world hates you" (**John 15:18-19**).

"I have told you these things, so that in me you may have peace. In this world you will have trouble [tribulation, NKJV]. But take heart! I have overcome the world." (**John 16:33**).

Similar teachings and admonitions cannot be found in Islam or preached by Muhammad. Muslims do believe that they are the persecuted ones. However, their call is not to demonstrate love and peace, but to retaliate and inflict harm. They are called to love one another, but not to make even friends with non-believers.

Instead of fighting for Him (as Muhammad constantly commanded his followers), Jesus required His disciples to answer a higher calling of personal sacrifice. "Then Jesus said to his disciples, 'Whoever wants to be my disciple must deny themselves and take up their cross and follow me'" (**Matthew 16:24**; also **Mark 8:34**; **Luke 9:23**).

"But whoever disowns [renounces] me before others," Jesus warned, "I will disown before my Father in heaven" (**Matthew 10:33**). Christians are never to renounce their faith in Christ. Every year for two millennia thousands of Christians have freely chosen persecution and death rather than deny Christ. As you learned in Chapter 7, Muslims are permitted to lie if their lie serves a higher good. While they are forbidden to lie *about* Allah they can deny him if they believe that their life is threatened.

Paul, in his letter to his Greek convert to Christ, Titus, wrote, "They [Cretans] claim to know God, but by their actions they deny him. They are detestable, disobedient and unfit for doing anything good" (**Titus 1:16**). Paul, as did Jesus, had little tolerance for those who were liars and deceivers; especially those who would deny God.

A Sacrificial Life. Jesus Christ willingly shed His own blood so that all those who called upon His name would be delivered from their sins and live. Muhammad shed the blood of others so that he and his followers could live in luxury as robber barons.

Since the beginning of mankind, God's established law required the shedding of blood to atone for man's sin against God. However, God forbid the shedding of innocent human blood to accomplish that purpose. God commanded, "**Whoever sheds human blood**, by humans shall **their blood be shed**; for in the image of God has God made mankind" (**Genesis 9:6**; author's emphasis). In the Old Testament, before the advent of Christ, God required the shedding of animal's blood as a sacrifice for sins. However, that sacrifice could only be carried out by the Jewish High Priest. God did not intend that imperfect sacrifice to continue forever.

The sacrifice of blood to end all sacrifice for sin could only be accomplish through the shed blood of a man, but not any man, only the Son of God, Jesus Christ. In his letter to the Roman Christians, Paul wrote, "God presented Christ as **a sacrifice of atonement**, through **the shedding of his blood**—to be received by faith. He did this to demonstrate his righteousness, because in his forbearance he had left the sins committed beforehand unpunished" (**Romans 3:25**; author's emphasis).

In his letter to the church in Colosse, Paul wrote, "For God was pleased to have all his fullness dwell in him, and through him to reconcile to himself all things, whether things on earth or things in heaven, by making peace through his blood, shed on the cross" (**Colossians 1:19-20**).

The writer to the Hebrews put it this way: "In fact, the law requires that nearly **everything be cleansed with blood**, and **without the shedding of blood there is no forgiveness**" (**Hebrews 9:22**; author's emphasis). Jewish law, as established by Jehovah God, required the shedding of blood for the atonement of sin. There could be no other way; no other sacrifice. Repetitive sacrifice of animal blood or that of innocent humans was imperfect and was not acceptable. God did not accept the shedding of innocent blood by Muhammad, nor will He accept the shedding of innocent blood by Muslims or anyone else today. There is only one sacrifice that God Almighty ever accepted and that was the shed blood of His Son, Jesus Christ.

The Apostle Peter penned, "For you know that it was not with perishable things such as silver or gold that you were redeemed from the empty way of life handed down to you from your ancestors, but with the precious blood of Christ, a lamb without blemish or defect" (**1 Peter 1:18-19**). Throughout history, man has attempted to redeem himself through a variety of means. But God made it clear that He has and will only accept one atoning sacrifice for sin. There is no other recourse for mankind to receive God's everlasting forgiveness and eternal life with Him than to accept Jesus' atoning sacrifice of the cross and His resurrected life.

"He is the atoning sacrifice for our sins, and not only for ours but also for the sins of the whole world," the Apostle John proclaimed (**1 John 2:2**).

John continued in his first letter, "This is love: not that we loved God, but that he loved us and sent his Son as an atoning sacrifice for our sins" (**1 John 4:10**).

The Only Mediator Between God and Man. The consequence of Christ's sacrifice is that He became the *only* mediator between God and man. No one can approach God except through Jesus Christ. That is the unabashed truth of the Christian faith and the unchangeable word of God. Paul, in his first letter to his protégé, Timothy, wrote, "For there is one God and one mediator between God and mankind, the man Christ Jesus," (**1 Timothy 2:5**). There is and can only be one mediator between God and man and that is the perfect and sinless Son of God. It cannot and was not Muhammad, or any other human being. Muhammad did not and could not serve as the arbitrator between God and man. He was a sin-laden man who was the annihilator in the name of his god; not a mediator.

"But in fact the ministry Jesus has received is as superior to theirs [the Jewish High Priests] as the covenant of which he is **mediator** is superior to the old one, since the new covenant is established on better promises" (**Hebrews 8:6**). Jesus, as God's final and perfect mediator, accomplished all that God ever intended. Jesus was God's final solution for the atonement of man's transgressions. God did not and would not send a sin-burdened, imperfect Muhammad or anyone else to undo what Christ had so willingly accomplished as the fulfillment of God's perfect plan of everlasting salvation.

"For this reason [of a perfect sacrifice] Christ is the mediator of a new covenant, that those who are called may receive the promised eternal inheritance—now that he has died as a ransom to set them free from the sins committed under the first covenant" (**Hebrews 9:15**).

Persecution and Martyrdom

"Christians & Jewish martyrs say; 'I will die for what I believe.' A Muslim martyr says; 'you will die for what I believe (1).'" The underlying principle and foundation of Christianity is love: God's love for His human creation; Jesus' expression of God's love by His sacrifice on the cross for all mankind and His commandment to all His followers to love everyone—fellow believers, non-believers and even enemies. Muslims, however, are taught and called by the teachings of the Qur'an and Islam's revered prophet, Muhammad, to hate all those who oppose Islam—not only to hate, but to kill and annihilate *all* infidels and secure the world for Allah.

This latter religious dogma and mindset is difficult for the Western mind, and particularly those bathed in the teachings of Christ, to comprehend and absorb. However, it is this dramatic and fundamental difference that is essential for the non-Muslim world to grasp if it is to come to grips with and neutralize this rapidly expanding ideology that threatens the free world and all that it cherishes.

While hate and murder are not alien to Western culture and history, it is hard for most to fathom that one's religion calls for them to hate someone or kill them just for the sake of doing so, or because they do not believe the way you do. But that is the relentless and unparalleled dictate of Islam and its religious leaders, whether housed in Iran, England or the United States. It is the common thread that holds the religion together—hate in the name and *cause of Allah*.

One thing Islam and Christianity do have in common is persecution. However, the commonality is in the word and concept only, not in how it is played out in one's faith. Christ's ministry and teaching in the New Testament call for Christians to sacrifice their life for another.

Jesus was the shining example of such sacrifice for His disciples. "The reason my Father loves me," He told them, "is that I lay down my life—only to take it up again. No one takes it from me, but I lay it down of my own accord. I have authority to lay it down and authority to take it up again. This command I received from my Father" (**John 10:17-18**). While Jesus' ultimate sacrifice was in obedience to God, it was also His personal choice. He *did not* have to go to the cross, but He did in obedience to His Father in heaven and out of love for all mankind. Muhammad did not lay down his life, his life was taken from him by sickness.

This call for Christians to sacrifice demonstrated in many forms.

Christians are called to sacrifice their money, property, time and talents in service to others or in meeting the needs of those less fortunate. But Christians are also called, like Jesus, to make the ultimate sacrifice, if necessary, for the cause of their faith. Although, in developed and free societies it is hard to comprehend the need for such sacrifice in today's world, the truth is, Christians all over the world give their lives daily at the hands of others who persecute them and kill them just because they are peace-loving Christians. Christians are also called to take their faith to the definitive test. When faced with persecution or even death, they are not to deny their faith or their Lord and Savior, Jesus Christ.

In December, 2014, Reverend Franklin Graham was interviewed by Ruth Gledhill of *Christian Today* in London. Among other comments, Graham stated that Islam has "not been hijacked by radicals" and that it is "a religion of war" that has not changed in over 1400 years (2). In observing the atrocities that are being committed by the Islamic State, the Taliban and Boko Haram, Graham noted, "This is Islam. It has not been hijacked by radicals. This is the faith, this is the religion. It is what it is. It speaks for itself." Of course, Graham has been routinely criticized for his outspoken views on Islam, even though he speaks the truth.

Graham is not an Islamophobic or Muslim hater as the media try to portray him. To the contrary. "I think it is very important" Graham affirmed, "that we do all that we can to try to share God's love with Muslims because they have no hope outside of dying in Jihad. I want them to know, you do not have to die for God. God died for us. He sent His Son to die for us."

The universalism of Islam, in its all-embracing creed,
is imposed on the believers as a continuous process of warfare,
psychological and political, if not strictly military...
The Jihad, accordingly, may be stated as a doctrine of a
permanent state of war, not continuous fighting.
Majid Khadduri
War and Peace in the Law of Islam, © 1955, p.64

Muslims are also called to sacrifice, but from a quite different perspective and for a much different purpose. While they are called to be charitable within their own circles, they are not required to sacrifice their goods or resources for the sake of helping non-Muslims. If they are persecuted or threatened with death, the teaching and example of Muhammad gives them permission, if it will spare their life, to deny Allah. They are not called to lay down their life for someone else. But the jihadists—which can be any Muslim who takes the teaching of Muhammad seriously—are called to sacrifice their lives, not to save others—but to take the lives of others.

"Jihad is at the core of the 'religion of peace,'" Amil Imani wrote in September, 2018. "Jihad occupies most of Islam's theology and concerns. Jihad is addressed in 9% of the Mecca Quran; 24% of the Median [sic] Quran; and in 67% of the Sira. True to form, Muslims claim that the emphasis on jihad is about the individual battling his own faults and flaws, the so-called 'greater jihad,' and not that of battling others, the 'lesser jihad.'

"As a matter of fact," Imani continued, "only 2% of the jihad of the Hadith refers to the greater jihad, while the other 98% is about the lesser jihad, or the jihad of the sword" (3).

The World of the Jihadist

The Two Jihads. There are two jihads or jihadist practices in Islam. They are referred to as the *lesser* or lower jihad and the *greater* or higher jihad. The lesser jihad is warfare against infidels or non-believers. The greater jihad refers to a Muslim's spiritual war against his inner self. The one the West *hears* about all the time from Muslim leaders is the greater jihad. It sounds so noble and pious and inoffensive toward non-Muslims.

However, it is the lesser jihad—the war against non-Muslims—that people in the West *experience* on a daily basis.

"Jihad" means to war against non-Muslims, and is etymologically derived from the word "mujahada," signifying warfare to establish the religion. And it is the lesser jihad. As for the greater jihad, it is spiritual warfare against the lower self, which is why the Prophet . . . said as he was returning from jihad, "We have returned from the lesser to the greater jihad."

Reliance of the Traveller, o9.0

---

164 Jihad Verses in the Qur'an. What is *jihad*? If you listen to and believe the westernized version put forth by Muslims and their leaders, *jihad* is just a search for inner peace by a Muslim. However, that is not what the Qur'an teaches and Muhammad taught. From those two sources, *jihad* is a clear commandment from Allah to pursue, persecute and kill all non-Muslims or even unfaithful Muslims. Yoel Natan of Answering-Islam has compiled 164 jihad-related verses in the Qur'an. Only 5 verses were revealed in Mecca when Muhammad was trying to win over converts from the Jewish, Christian and pagan populations. The other 159 were revealed in Medina after Muhammad sought revenge on those who ran him and his band of followers out of Mecca (Source:

https://answeringislam.org/Quran/Themes/jihad_passages.html).

The scriptural basis for [the lesser] *jihad, prior to scholarly consensus . . is such Koranic verses as:*
  (1) *"Fighting is prescribed for you" (Koran 2:216);*
  (2) *"Slay them wherever you find them" (Koran 4:89);*
  (3) *"Fight the idolators utterly" (Koran 9:36);*

"I [Muhammad] *have been commanded* [by Allah] *to fight people until they testify that there is no god but Allah and that Muhammad is the Messenger of Allah, and perform the prayer* [of faith, the shahada]*, and pay zakat* [almsgiving]*. If they say it, they have saved their blood and possessions from me, except for the rights of Islam over them. And their final reckoning is with Allah;"* . . .

"To go forth in the morning or evening to fight in the path of Allah is better than the whole world and everything in it."
                    Reliance of the Traveller, o9.0(1)(2)(3)

According to Islamic law, as expressed in the ROT quotes above, the lesser jihad, the warfare against non-Muslims, is not an option, it is mandatory for every able-bodied Muslim—male and female. Most Muslims will deny this, but in doing so, will be applying another battleground tactic, *taqiya* or lying, as disclosed in Chapter 7. Notice too, that this jihad battle is unending, it continues as long as there are infidels who refuse to bend a knee to Allah and submit to Muslim rule. Muhammad stated that there is nothing better in the whole world than fighting for the cause of Allah. A Muslim's whole existence and blessing depends on his or her willingness to fight infidels for the sake of Allah.

In the *Reliance of the Traveller* there is a whole section on "The Obligatory Character of [the lesser] Jihad."

- *Jihad is a communal obligation. When enough people perform it to successfully accomplish it, it is no longer obligatory upon others. . . .*
- *If none of those concerned perform jihad, and it does not happen at all, then everyone who is aware that it is obligatory is guilty of sin. . .*
- *As for subsequent times, there are two possible states in respect to non-Muslims. The first is when they are in their own country, in which case jihad* [see o9.8 to follow] *is a communal*

313

obligation . . . The second state is when non-Muslims invade a
Muslim country or near to one, in which case jihad is personally
*obligatory . . . (**ROT, o9.1**).*

It cannot be any clearer. Whether in a Muslim country or for
Muslims residing in a non-Muslim country, jihad—the warfare jihad—is
obligatory for every able-bodied Muslim, whenever the call to do so goes
forth.

In fact, according to Muhammad in **Qur'an 4:95**, those who are
able (age of puberty and up) and do not participate, are considered to be
inferior Muslims whom Allah will not reward.

> *The holders back* [from jihad] *from among the believers,*
> *not having any injury, and those who strive hard in Allah's way*
> *with their property and their persons are not equal* [to the
> jihadists]; *Allah has made the strivers* [jihadists] *with their*
> *property and their persons to excel the holders back a (high)*
> *degree, and to each (class) Allah has promised good; and Allah*
> *shall grant to the strivers above the holders back a mighty reward.*

Also in the *Reliance of the Traveller*, there is a section on "The
Objectives of Jihad."

> *The caliph* [the successor to the Prophethood of
> Muhammad] *makes war upon Jews, Christians, and Zoroastrians*
> *(N: provided he has first invited them to enter Islam in faith and*
> *practice, and if they will not, then invited them to enter the social*
> *order of Islam by paying the non-Muslim poll tax (jizya) . . . (and*
> *the war continues) until they become Muslim or else pay the non-*
> *Muslim poll tax . . .* (**ROT, o9.8**).

The poll tax or *jizya* is essentially extortion money demanded from
non-Muslims living in a Muslim-controlled territory or country. It is
assessed for the privilege of remaining alive under Muslim control. In part,
this ongoing jihad is based on **Qur'an 9:29** where Muhammad proclaimed:
"Fight those who do not believe in Allah, nor in the latter day, nor do they
prohibit what Allah and His Apostle have prohibited, nor follow the religion
of truth, out of those who have been given the Book, until they pay the tax
in acknowledgment of superiority and they are in a state of subjection."

Nothing could be clearer about what is in store for Western society
if it does not wake up to the realities of true Islam and those millions who
adhere to it faithfully.

Military Jihad is What Motivates Muslims. The incidents of modern day jihad across the globe are so numerous it would be impossible to report them all here. As an example, however, Islam was birthed in jihad and grew by jihad. During Muhammad's life alone, he personally led 27 battles but only participated in 9 (4). In the first ten years after Muhammad's death, Muslims went on a rampage throughout Arabia, Iraq, Syria, Egypt and Northern Africa and even reaching into Asia Minor and southern Europe. Over 40 battles of attempted and successful conquest were waged as the Islamic hoards pillaged and slaughtered all those who refused to bend a knee to their god.

"We are not fighting terrorism," Amil Imani declared in a piece he wrote in December, 2018. "We are engaging in an ideological battle between freedom, conservatism, democracy, individual rights, capitalism, 'Christian' ethics [versus] Islamic jihad, communism-socialism, theocracy, and tyranny" (5).

Trying to take Jihad from the Quran and the Sunnah is [like] trying to take sweetness out of honey.
New York "Mufti" Muhammad Ibn Muneer
December 5, 2018 (6)

Muhammad ibn Muneer (cited in the prior box) was born in Philadelphia and is an American homegrown jihadist with 10,000 YouTube subscribers. In his December 5 presentation, which was transcribed by MEMRI (Middle East Media Research Institute), Muneer asserted that the lesser jihad (warfare) far exceeded the higher jihad (self-examination). According to Muneer, while the higher jihad is commendable, it pales in comparison to the lower jihad—fighting in the cause of Allah.

The transcription penned this summary of Muneer's lesson on jihad: ". . . one should not confuse any of them [those who die for any other reason than fighting for Allah] with the martyr who was killed in battle, who holds the highest status of martyrdom. He warned the audience not to treat lesser forms of Jihad, such as seeking knowledge and giving da'wa [Islamic proselytizing], as if they are equal to fighting for the sake of Allah" (7).

"Violence is at the very core of Islam," Imani contends. "Violence is institutionalized in the Muslim's holy book, the Quran, in many verses:" **8:39** [*And fight with them until there is no more persecution and religion should be only for Allah* . . .]; **8:65** [*O Prophet! Urge the believers to war* . . .]; **9:5** [*. . . slay the idolators wherever you find them, and take them captives and besiege them and lie in wait* . . .]. There are many more verses in the Qur'an that could be cited and have

315

been previously. There is, of course, in the Bible many incidents of incitement to violence by God's people. The stark difference, however, is that those who read the Bible today see those citations as historic and for followers of God to understand the lesson therein and not as a command to do the same. For Muslims, the Qur'an and Muhammad's words are not just historic but injunctions for living today—every word.

". . . the Quran commands the believer repeatedly," Imani continued in his assessment "—to make jihad on even the people of the book, Jews and Christians, are specifically targeted. Islam essentially invented the idea that Christians, Jews, and pagans are abomination and offensive to Allah" (8).

Once again, Imani wrote, "True Muslim believers therefore become the enforcers, hit men and mercenaries for their god, in order to establish a global Caliphate for their parasitic clergy. Their targets are artificially constructed adversaries.

"Muslim believers hence are instructed to fear the 'great Satan' [the United States], and are told that if they do not live up to Allah's calls to Jihad, they themselves are offensive to Allah and to their families.

"A true Muslim does not and cannot believe in freedom of choice. In the religion of Islam—Submission—everything is up to Allah, as clearly and repeatedly stipulated in the Quran" (9).

On November 22, 2018, as Americans were celebrating Thanksgiving, an American Roman Catholic priest, Mario Alexis Portella, was being interviewed by the Italian newspaper, *La Verità*. In the interview, he is quoted as saying, "I have seen the massacres in Iraq and I say: having a dialogue with Islam is impossible" (10).

"The violence," the priest confessed, "is to be found in the pages of the Quran. There is no single authority who speaks for them, this facilitates the extremists.

"Only one has to look at the original Islamic texts that speak the truth; those texts however are ignored by scholars and activists who maintain that they are being misinterpreted by those who terrorism and the Islamization of the world. It is simply not true.

"Christianity, however, is based on the peace and love of God, while Islam justifies killing and war in its sacred texts. This makes it difficult individualize a constructive path with Muslims. It is more of a political problem than a religious one," Portella concluded.

Nearly three weeks after the Portella interview, as if to prove his point, the Syrian Observatory for Human Rights reported that Islamic State terrorists had massacred nearly 700 prisoners in eastern Syria in just a two month period. The prisoners, largely civilian, were among the 1,350 soldiers and civilians being held by the Islamic State fighters near the Iraqi border (11).

The Alternate Christian Response

First, Love the Brethren. During His brief ministry on earth, Jesus taught His followers many things. One teaching, however, seems to stand out among all others. Right before Jesus told Peter that he would deny knowing Jesus, Jesus gave His disciples what He considered His most important command after that of loving God. "A new command I give you: Love one another," Jesus instructed. "As I have loved you, so you must love one another. By this all men will know that you are my disciples, if you love one another" (**John 13:34-35**).

In a world of so much hate—then, now and in the future— Jesus knew that there would be one thing that would set His followers apart from all others: How they share His love with each other. It was not that they were to love each other exclusively, but rather, out of this love they would be able to love others and thus distinguish themselves among all the peoples of the earth. He later reaffirmed this commandment. "As the Father has loved me, so have I loved you. Now remain in my love   My command is this: Love each other as I have loved you" (John 15:9, 12).

In the Qur'an and the teachings of Muhammad, the concept of unconditional love is only vaguely implied and does not extend beyond fellow believers in Allah.   Not even Allah offers his adherents unconditional love. Allah only loves the doers of good (**Qur'an 2:195**), those that trust him (**Qur'an 3:159**) and fight for him (**Qur'an 61:4**). However, as you read in Chapter 8, he does not love sinners (**Qur'an 3:57**).

Except for the command to love Allah, the theology of love is glaringly absent from the Qur'an. In fact, there are more verses in the Qur'an that tell believers what or who Allah *does not* love then there are stating what Allah *does* love. Followers of Islam are called to love Allah before he will love them (**Qur'an 3:31, 5:54**). Whereas, the theme throughout the Bible is that God loved us, His creation, before we loved Him. Once again, this verse of scripture bears repeating: *For God so loved the world that he gave his one and only Son, that whoever believes in him shall not perish but have eternal life. For God did not send his Son into the world to condemn the world, but to save the world through him* (**John 3:16-17**). Jehovah God's love is unconditional and extended toward those who do not love or acknowledge Him. Allah's love comes to the believer only after a Muslim expresses love toward Allah; and Allah's love is *only* for the believer, no one else.

"No one has ever seen God;" the Apostle John admitted, "but if we love one another, God lives in us and his love is made complete in us" (**1 John 4:12**). While God is invisible, He expresses His love for His children by how those that believe in Him love one another. This is the most common way that people see the love of God in their lives, is through the love shared with them by other believers.

"If anyone says, 'I love God,' yet hates his brother," John continued, "he is a liar. For anyone who does not love his brother, whom he has seen, cannot love God, whom he has not seen. And he has given us this command: Whoever loves God must also love his brother" (**1 John 4:20-21**).

Second, Love the Unbeliever. Not only is the overall concept of love fleeting in the Qur'an, but in no uncertain terms it surely does not extend to non-believers—either by Allah or any of his followers. All those who are not Muslim are seen as adversaries and enemies of Allah and Islam (see Chapter 13). "Allah's Apostle said, 'I have been ordered to fight with the people till they say, 'None has the right to be worshipped but Allah,' and whoever says, 'None has the right to be worshipped but Allah,' his life and property will be saved by me except for Islamic law, and his accounts will be with Allah, (either to punish him or to forgive him)'" (**hadith 4:196**). Unlike Christianity, there is no concept within Islam to love the unbeliever into the fold of believers.

Even in the Old Testament, the word of God to the Jews was to love people and not seek to do them harm. "Do not seek revenge or bear a grudge against one of your people, but love your neighbor as yourself. I am the LORD" (**Leviticus 19:18**). Even foreigners (who were non-believers) were to be treated with love. "The alien living with you must be treated as one of your native-born. Love him as yourself, for you were aliens in Egypt. I am the LORD your God" (**Leviticus 19:34**). Again, in **Deuteronomy 10:19**, Moses instructed the Jews ". . . to love those who are aliens, for you yourselves were aliens in Egypt."

When a rich man asked Jesus what he must do to inherit eternal life, Jesus was succinct. "Jesus replied, ''Do not murder, do not commit adultery, do not steal, do not give false testimony, honor your father and mother,' and 'love your neighbor as yourself'" (**Matthew 19:18-19**). While the term *neighbor* meant someone close by, it did not necessarily mean someone who was a fellow believing Jew or Christian. A similar command was not and could not be given by Muhammad to his followers because Muhammad practiced the opposite of what Jesus taught and required of His disciples.

When a Pharisee, who was an expert in the Law of Moses, inquired of Jesus, "Teacher, which is the greatest commandment in the Law?" Jesus gave him a reply similar to that of the rich man.

Jesus answered: "'Love the Lord your God with all your heart and with all your soul and with all your mind.' This is the first and greatest commandment. And the second is like it: 'Love your neighbor as yourself.' All the Law and the Prophets hang on these two commandments" (**Matthew 22:36-40**).

The Apostle Paul, taking his example from Jesus and Proverbs, advanced Jesus' teaching even further. "On the contrary: 'If your enemy is hungry, feed him; if he is thirsty, give him something to drink. In doing this, you will heap burning coals on his head' [**Proverbs 25:21-22**]. Do not be overcome by evil, but overcome evil with good" (**Romans 12:20-21**).

Paul further instructed the Roman Christians to, "Let no debt remain outstanding, except the continuing debt to love one another, for he who loves his fellowman has fulfilled the law. The commandments, 'Do not commit adultery,' 'Do not murder,' 'Do not steal,' 'Do not covet,' and whatever other commandment there may be, are summed up in this one rule: 'Love your neighbor as yourself.' Love does no harm to its neighbor. Therefore love is the fulfillment of the law" (**Romans 13:8-10**).

Not long after Paul founded the church in Galatia, a small group of Jewish Christians tried to convince the new faithful that they needed to follow certain aspects of Jewish law in order to be fully followers of Christ. Paul vehemently rejected such notions and wrote a stern letter to the members of the young church. "You, my brothers, were called to be free," he affirmed. "But do not use your freedom to indulge the sinful nature; rather, serve one another in love. The entire law is summed up in a single command: 'Love your neighbor as yourself.' If you keep on biting and devouring each other, watch out or you will be destroyed by each other" (**Galatians 5:13-15**). In this last sentence, Paul pointed out the result and consequence of failing to love one another—whether fellow believers or unbelieving neighbors.

Third, Love Your Enemy. Where Christianity and Islam really separate on the issue of love is with respect to the treatment of real or perceived enemies. Christ taught His disciples to love their enemies, no matter who they were. Muhammad, however, led murderous raids and commanded his followers to kill non-believers wherever they could be found (**Qur'an 2:191, 193**, et al). Among treasured Islamic scriptures there are whole *books* comprising hundreds of verses inciting the faithful to fight and kill non-believers for the cause of Allah. Islam is not a peaceful religion!

On December 18, 2005, *The Australian* quoted from the fiery 60-page script of one of Islam's leaders, Sheikh Mukhlas of Indonesia.

"You who still have a shred of faith in your hearts, have you forgotten that to kill infidels and the enemies of Islam is a deed that has a reward above no other. . .

"Aren't you aware that the model for us all, the Prophet Mohammed and the four rightful caliphs, undertook to murder infidels as one of their primary activities, and that the Prophet waged jihad operations 77 times in the first 10 years as head of the Muslim community in Medina?" (12).

The rantings of a madman? Perhaps, for these are the words of Sheikh Mukhlas of Indonesia, the one responsible for the Bali bombing of 2002. He might be deemed an Islamic madman had he not truthfully cited the Prophet of Islam, Muhammad, as his inspiration and example. For Muhammad was indeed all that Mukhlas proclaimed: a murderer of infidels and a frequent wager of war against those who refused to accept Islam. So what has changed in Islam's approach to the non-believer over fifteen centuries? Nothing!

"You shall not murder" is Jehovah God's commandment to His followers in the Old Testament (**Exodus 20:13**). The Qur'an, on the other hand, *commands* the faithful to "kill" and "slaughter" ALL non-believers, i.e., ALL non-Muslims, including Muslims deemed to be unfaithful adherents to Islam. Jesus expanded on this Old Testament commandment by teaching His followers that, "You have heard that it was said to the people long ago, 'Do not murder, and anyone who murders will be subject to judgment.' But I tell you that anyone who is angry with his brother will be subject to judgment (**Matthew 5:21-22a**). Here, Jesus associates anger with murder. It is the precursor to the act of killing. Hatred of Jews, Christians and non-Muslims, in general, reigns supreme among many Muslims. All an imam or other Muslim leader has to do to whip the Muslim faithful into a hate-filled frenzy is to call upon them to kill the Jews and Christians for the cause of Allah.

Jesus not only commanded His disciples to love their enemies but to also to pray for those who persecuted them. "You have heard that it was said, 'Love your neighbor and hate your enemy.' But I tell you: Love your enemies and pray for those who persecute you, that you may be sons of your Father in heaven. He causes his sun to rise on the evil and the good, and sends rain on the righteous and the unrighteous. If you love those who love you, what reward will you get? Are not even the tax collectors doing that?" (**Matthew 5:43-46**).

Jesus wanted His followers to stand out in a world of hate and sin. Telling someone to love their enemy was an unheard of and seemingly ridiculous request considering the environment in which He and his followers lived. To command one to love his enemies was bad enough, but to pray for them also seemed a step too far. But that was Jesus' example that was His godly uniqueness that no one could match before Him, during His era or in the future. Neither Muhammad, nor anyone in history, could hold a candle to Jesus, His teaching, or His mission.

A Christian martyr, on the other hand, is one who dies at the hands of another while refusing to deny his or her faith in Christ or in the protection of the innocent. A Christian who deliberately takes another's life without just cause is a murderer. On the other hand, an adherent to the Islamic faith and its prophet Muhammad, is declared a martyr if he is slain in the course of slaying "the enemies" of Allah. Allah, according to Muhammad and the Qur'an, rejoices in this type of martyrdom. While the martyr following the way of Christ takes no life but willingly lays down his own for the sake of Christ, the Muslim martyr achieves his lofty goal by killing others, including innocent people.

Muhammad rejoiced and delighted in seeing his enemies tortured, beheaded and enslaved. It was Allah's will for the unbelievers, he would claim. Jesus would and does rejoice and take delight in one enemy soul repenting and coming to eternal glory with Him and the Father. Jesus called upon God and His followers to bless His enemies and pray for those who persecute His followers. Muhammad cursed and called upon Allah to curse his enemies and commit them to hell.

Paul, in expressing this new philosophy of Jesus said, "Very rarely will anyone die for a righteous man, though for a good man someone might possibly dare to die" (**Romans 5:7**). His point was that Jesus, a sinless and righteous man, not only chose to die for those that might be considered good, but also for those who were vile sinners through and through. Again, such a concept is not to be found or espoused in the Qur'an or anywhere else in Islamic belief or teaching. According to Islam, the unrepentant sinner or non-believer is worthy of nothing less than *severe chastisement* or death.

Even the wise King Solomon saw the folly of killing just for the sake of killing.

> *My son, if sinners entice you, do not give in to them. If they say, "Come along with us; let's lie in wait for someone's blood, let's waylay some harmless soul; let's swallow them alive, like the grave, and whole, like those who go down to the pit; we will get all sorts of valuable things and fill our houses with plunder; throw in your lot with us, and we will share a common purse" – my son, do not go along with them, do not set foot on their paths; for their feet rush into sin, they are swift to shed blood* (**Proverbs 1:10-16**).

Sacrificial murder—that is sacrificing one's life while taking the lives of others (combatants or non-combatants)—is the only assured way that a Muslim has of getting to heaven or Paradise. "Christ's 'Martyrdom' on the cross," wrote author James Arlandson, "means that Christians do not have to die in a holy war to be guaranteed heaven (13)." As televised images and reports from the Middle East and elsewhere in the Muslim world reveal, certain Muslims have no reservations about sacrificing their own children or the children of others in the so-called *cause of Allah* (14).

However, the Apostle Paul taught that the followers of Jesus should see themselves as *living sacrifices* for the cause of Christ—not as martyrs who kill others, but as saints called to sacrifice all for the sake of others. "Therefore, I urge you, brothers, in view of God's mercy, to offer your bodies as living sacrifices, holy and pleasing to God – this is your spiritual act of worship. Do not conform any longer to the pattern of this world, but be transformed by the renewing of your mind" (**Romans 12:1-2a**).

The question must be asked by any serious seeker of spiritual truth: Has the once forgiving, loving God as revealed by and through Jesus Christ—who died an agonizing death on the cross for the atonement of the sins of all mankind—changed His mind a scant 600 years after Christ's death? Was it all for nothing and now revenge, murder and mayhem are the only ways to convince the world that He loved them and wanted a relationship with Him?

The Apostle Peter reaffirmed Jesus' teaching, that the way to God's heart was to be loving and compassionate, even to one's enemies. "Finally, all of you, live in harmony with one another;" Peter preached, "be sympathetic, love as brothers, be compassionate and humble. Do not repay evil with evil or insult with insult, but with blessing, because to this you were called so that you may inherit a blessing" (**1 Peter 3:8-9**).

Prophet of Change. Jesus was the last and only true prophet of change. As the Son of God, He completely and truthfully revealed the passion, character and heart of God to the human race. Muhammad had no special link or claim to insight with God. Jesus' revelation of God, His Father, was consistent, loving and built upon the message and prophesies of the Old Testament. The message that Muhammad brought to mankind was inconsistent, diabolical, hateful, murderous and self-serving of his power hungry, depraved and domineering mentality.

Muhammad financed his armies and raids on his neighbors by sacking the towns and plundering his "enemy." He also collected revenue through the tax assessed upon non-believers and taking mostly women and children into captivity and selling them as slaves. As noted previously, during his lifetime as Allah's Apostle/Prophet, Muhammad led 27 raids or battles against those who refused to submit to him and sent his armies out on 47 more without him (15).

The God of the Bible did not decide that his Son had failed in his mission in drawing people to Himself through the salvation message. God did not change His mind and decide it would be better to coerce people into His kingdom through oppression and murder.

"When your Lord revealed to the Angels: I am with you, therefore make firm those who believe. I will cast terror into the hearts of those who disbelieve," Allah revealed to Muhammad. "Therefore strike off their heads and strike off every fingertip of them. This is because they acted adversely to Allah and His Apostle; and whoever acts adversely to Allah and His Apostle—then surely Allah is severe in requiting (evil)"

322

(**Qur'an 8:12,13**). This is certainly not the image of the loving, compassionate and forgiving Jehovah God of the Jews and Christians. "They ask you about the windfalls," Allah instructed Muhammad. "Say: The windfalls are for Allah and the Apostle. So be careful of (your duty to) Allah and set aright matters of your difference, and obey Allah and His Apostle if you are believers" (**Qur'an 8:1**). Whatever plunder there was, 20% went to Allah and Muhammad, his kin, the needy and orphans, and the remaining 80% could be divided among his raiders (**Qur'an 8:41**).

"Mohammedanism has produced an enslaved personality. 'Its Koran demands intellectual slavery;'" preached the popular missionary Methodist bishop, Charles Galloway, in the chapel of Emery College in Georgia in 1898, "'its harem requires domestic slavery; its state implies and enforces both religious and a civil slavery.' The Koran puts a premium upon war, offering the highest rewards to those who slay the greatest number of infidels. Mohammed's cardinal principle, the end justifies the means, consecrated every sort of persecution and violence . . . The citizen is the slave of the [Islamic] state; he has no rights to be respected. Mohammedanism is an absolute despotism, the most gigantic engine of intolerance and persecution the world ever saw. . . In every land swept by this heartless despotism it has left a tale and trail of blood'" (16).

Jesus brought forth a world-changing attitude toward others with a very simple principle: ". . . love your neighbor as yourself" (**Matthew 19:19**). If one is loving others as he is loving himself, how can he then hate or murder someone? "You have heard that it was said," Jesus preached during the Sermon on the Mount, "'Eye for eye, and tooth for tooth.' [**Exodus 21:24; Leviticus 24:20; Deuteronomy 19:21**] But I tell you, Do not resist an evil person. If someone strikes you on the right cheek, turn him the other also" (**Matthew 5:38-39**). Again, a few verses later He repeated the concept. "You have heard that it was said, 'Love your neighbor and hate your enemy.' But I tell you: Love your enemies and pray for those who persecute you, that you may be sons of your Father in heaven. He causes his sun to rise on the evil and the good, and sends rain on the righteous and the unrighteous. If you love those who love you, what reward will you get? Are not even the tax collectors doing that?" (**Matthew 5:43-46**).

This model of kind and benevolent treatment of one's enemies was an unheard of proposal during the time of Jesus (or any time prior) and continues to be to this day. It is hard enough loving those close to you without being called to love those who are out to do you harm. But that is what made Jesus the unique and radical change merchant. He presented the inconceivable as plausible and with God's help it was possible to accomplish. Muhammad brought forth

nothing new under the sun. He preached hate which was the accepted norm for his time and for all the history that went before him.

"But I tell you who hear me:" Jesus said once again, "Love your enemies, do good to those who hate you, bless those who curse you, pray for those who mistreat you . . . If you love those who love you, what credit is that to you? Even 'sinners' love those who love them . . . But love your enemies, do good to them, and lend to them without expecting to get anything back. Then your reward will be great, and you will be sons of the Most High, because he is kind to the ungrateful and wicked" (**Luke 6:27-28, 32-33, 35**).

The Apostle Paul, who before his conversion to Christianity was its primary persecutor as the Pharisee, Saul of Tarsus, embraced this teaching of Jesus. "Bless those who persecute you;" he wrote to the Roman Christians, "bless and do not curse. Rejoice with those who rejoice; mourn with those who mourn. Live in harmony with one another. Do not be proud, but be willing to associate with people of low position. Do not be conceited.

"Do not repay anyone evil for evil. Be careful to do what is right in the eyes of everyone. If it is possible, as far as it depends on you, live at peace with everyone. Do not take revenge, my friends, but leave room for God's wrath, for it is written: 'It is mine to avenge; I will repay,' says the Lord" (**Romans 12:14-19**).

For those who did not and will not follow His teaching on love, Jesus had some stern words of rebuke.

> *Jesus said to them, "If God were your Father, you would love me, for I came from God and now am here. I have not come on my own; but he sent me. Why is my language not clear to you? Because you are unable to hear what I say. You belong to your father, the devil, and you want to carry out your father's desire. He was a murderer from the beginning, not holding to the truth, for there is no truth in him. When he lies, he speaks his native language, for he is a liar and the father of lies. Yet because I tell the truth, you do not believe me! Can any of you prove me guilty of sin? If I am telling the truth, why don't you believe me? He who belongs to God hears what God says. The reason you do not hear is that you do not belong to God"* (**John 8:42-47**).

Chapter Conclusion

Throughout human history there has been only one way to appease God for one's sins and that was through a blood sacrifice. In Jewish history, God called for the sacrifice of animal blood to atone for man's sin. With the coming of Jesus Christ, God's Son, God introduced one last, all-encompassing sacrifice for sin, the shed blood of His Son. Jesus' willingness to be obedient to the Father accomplished what no other sacrifice before could accomplish—the final and lasting sacrifice of human blood as an everlasting atonement for man's sin against God. Muhammad, on the other hand, did not shed his blood for anyone, he only shed the blood of others for self-glorification.

There is a clear and concise difference in how Christians and Muslims are to treat those who do not believe as they do. In both circles, the faithful are to be charitable with their brethren in the faith. But that is where the similarity stops. Christ called His followers to give to those who were the enemies of His disciples—to love them and pray for them—even as they were being persecuted by them.

Muslims, however, are not called to such a gracious extension of love and charity. To the contrary, they are called to persecute and kill all those who refuse to see life their way and follow Allah. In each case, the adherents of Christianity and Islam are light and dark examples of their respective religions. They are images in the flesh of the unseen God and Allah. Although there are historical examples of violence in both the Bible and Qur'an, the God of the Bible, through the revelation knowledge of Jesus Christ, does not call for violence against non-believers, nor do Judeo-Christian leaders of today call for violence citing the dictates of biblical scripture. However, Islamic scholars and leaders of today continue to call for violence against non-Muslims, citing the examples and teachings of Muhammad in the Qur'an and elsewhere.

References.

1. Keohane, Steve. *Muhammad: Terrorist or Prophet?* BibleProbe.com, 200402007. IIttp://bibleprobe.com/muhammad.htm. Accessed April 1, 2007.

2. Chapman, Michael W. *Rev. Franklin Graham: Islam 'Is a Religion of War.* CNSNews, December 10, 2014. Source: https://www.cnsnews.com/blog/ michael-w-chapman/rev-franklin-graham-islam-religion-war (accessed January 2, 2019).

3. Imani, Amil. *The Nature and Development of Jihad.* Geller Report, September 18, 2018. Source: https://gellerreport.com/2018/09/nature-development-jihad.html/

4. Spencer, Robert. *The History of Jihad, from Muhammad to ISIS.* Bombardier Books, An Imprint of Post Hill Press, 2018, pp. 45-46.

5. Imani, Amil. *Jihad: Islam's Engine.* Geller Report, December 26, 2018. Source: https://gellerreport.com/2018/12/jihad-islam-engine.html/

6. *NY Cleric Ibn Muneer: Islam Without Jihad is Like Honey Without the Sweetness; Don't Apologize for Speaking the Truth about Jihad, Jews, and Christians.* MEMRI, December 5, 2018. Source:

https://www.memri.org/ tv/ny-mufti-ibn-muneer-martyrdom-battlefield-highest-jihad-apologize-jews-christians/transcript

7. Ibid.
8. Imani, Amil. *Jihad: Islam's Engine.*
9. Ibid.
10. Geller, Pamela. *Catholic priest: "Islam is not a religion of peace. Dialogue is useless unless the Quran changes."* Geller Report, December 1, 2018. Source: https://gellerreport.com/2018/12/ florence-islam-quran.html/
11. *ISIS kills 700 prisoners in Syria: Watchdog.* New York Post, December 19, 2018. Source: https://nypost.com/2018/12/19/isis-kills-700-prisoners-in-syria-watchdog
12. *The Australian*, December 18, 2005. Accessed February 1, 2007 (Posted on: http://www.jihadwatch.org/archives/2005/12/009459.html).
13. Arlandson, James M. *Does Islam Improve on Christianity?* Answering-Islam.org. Http://answering-islam.org.uk/Authors/Arlandson/fruit_inspection.htm. Accessed November 2, 2005.
14. Winston, Emanuel A., July 17, 2001. *Abomination: The Sacrificing of Children.* Http://www.tzemach.org/fyi/docs/Winston/july17-01.htm. Accessed March 12, 2003.
15. Keohane.
16. Galloway, Bishop Charles B. *Christianity and the American Commonwealth,*
1898, p. 26-27. Reprinted in 2005 by American Vision, Inc.

Chapter 12

Proselytizing

The fruit of the righteous is a tree of life, and he who wins souls is wise.
Proverbs 11:30

Christians, out of the joy and peace of knowing Jesus, want to share their faith with others—to bring them into the saving knowledge of Jesus Christ, their Lord and Savior. According to the Qur'an and the traditions of Islam, Muslims are called to share their religion by subduing and conquering those who do not believe as they, and thus rule the world. Christians, by stark contrast, are called as followers of Jesus to save the world by leading each person one by one, to salvation from their evil intentions—not by coercion or persecution, but by a gentle persuasion and revealing of what they believe to be the truth about God.

The tradition and history of Islam is a bloody one, rife with continuous harassment, persecution, subjugation and killing of non-believers or infidels. Christianity, of course, is not absolved of dark periods in its history—the Crusades, the Reformation, the Inquisition, colonization and slavery to name a few. However, the tenets of faith of Christianity and the teaching of Jesus do not support such historical aberrations from the truth of the Gospels. On the other hand, the violent activities of the Muslim faithful are fully supported by Islamic teaching that has not changed since the inception of Islam nearly fourteen hundred years ago.

Proselytize Through Love and Service

No Compulsion in Religion. In **Qur'an 2:256**, Muhammad proclaimed that *there is no compulsion in religion* or *no coercion in matters of faith* (1). The implication and understanding is that there is to be no forcing of one to believe one way or the other. Yet, the Qur'an and hadith are full of Muhammad's proclamations to harass, persecute and kill ALL those who refused to accept Islam as their belief and Allah as their God or Muhammad as their prophet. For example, in the very same surah, Muhammad readily contradicts himself (and thus, the word of Allah) in **verse 193** when he advocates, "Fight with them [the unbelievers] until there is no persecution, and religion should be only for Allah..."

He it is Who sent His Apostle with the guidance and the true religion that He may make it prevail over all the religions; and Allah is enough for a witness (Qur'an 48:28).

327

Islamic scholars, religious leaders and the estimated 1.5 billion adherents are not content for Islam just to be one of the world's religions. They want Islam to dominate and be the *only* religion and Islamic shari'a (Islamic law) to be the only law of the land.

"It is useful to remind people," wrote Hugh Fitzgerald of Jihad Watch, "that over the past 1400 years many, perhaps most, of those who converted to Islam did so not because they were convinced of the truth of Islam, but in order to stay alive and avoid the humiliating status of dhimmi [Islam's subjugated people]. The Hindus of India perhaps were responsible for more converts to Islam than any other people, simply because there were so many more of them to begin with. Most of the 520 million Muslims in the subcontinent today—172 million in India, 195 million in Pakistan, 153 million in Bangladesh—are descendants of Hindus (to a lesser extent, Buddhists, Sikhs, and Jains) who converted to Islam long ago to escape the humiliating status of dhimmi" (2).

Although this verse has been cited before, **Qur'an 9:5** commands faithful Muslims to "Fight and slay the Pagans wherever you find them, and seize them, beleaguer them, and lie in wait for them in every stratagem (of war); but if they repent, and establish regular prayers and practice regular charity, then open the way for them: for Allah is Oft-forgiving, Most Merciful." Further, **Qur'an 4:89** states, "Those who reject Islam must be killed. If they turn back (from Islam), take (hold of) them and kill them wherever you find them . . ." This does not sound like a merciful god with a merciful approach to evangelism. *Accept what I believe or I will kill you,* appears to be the evangelical cry of Islam.

Satan wants to disseminate his plans and ideas among humans and entice them to follow him radically. If Satan also gives these human beings social, political or religious status, they will become vessels for him to use against the church and the plan of God.
Pastor Reza F. Safa, *Inside Islam*, 1996, p. 15

Furthermore, where the teaching of Christianity is to befriend others, including non-believers, the teaching of Muhammad prohibits faithful Muslims from even making friends with Christians or Jews (**Qur'an 5:51**). In **Qur'an 47:4**, Muhammad even advocates extreme hostility and cruelty toward infidels. "So, when you meet those who disbelieve, smite (their) necks till when you have killed and wounded many of them, then bind a bond firmly (on them)", that is take them as captives. It needs to be pointed out once again, that this *is not* an isolated teaching in the Qur'an or hadith, but rather the rule of Islamic law. It is a harsh, merciless, and unforgiving religion and a Muslim believer that says differently is either deceived or is practicing deception.

To *win souls,* **as is the common phraseology in Christian circles, has nothing to do with coercion, intimidation or persecution. Christianity is a personal religion requiring a personal decision without the heavy-handedness of another "guiding" the way. Christians are to freely share the gospel of Jesus Christ and then let the Holy Spirit convict the person of the truth of what was shared. Most Christians that share their faith are "seed planters"—sowing their faith and letting God do the salvation work.**

Since there is no plan of salvation—rescuing souls from the pit of hell—within Islamic theology, there is no plan to calmly, lovingly and patiently share one's faith as a testimony to an unbeliever. It is, despite Muhammad's proclamation, a faith by compulsion. A faith that coerces and brow beats one into believing a lie—a lie that draws people away from the true saving message of Jesus Christ.

Jesus made it very clear on how His message was to be disseminated. The unsaved were to be reached and converted by the Gospel being preached: "As you go, preach this message: 'The kingdom of heaven is near.' Heal the sick, raise the dead, cleanse those who have leprosy, drive out demons. Freely you have received, freely give" (**Matthew 10:7-8**). Nowhere in the Qur'an does it tell Muslims to *preach* the Islamic message to the unbeliever. Not only were the disciples of Jesus to preach the message of salvation, but they were to imitate Jesus through acts of healing and deliverance. Muhammad never healed anyone, nor could he command his followers to follow such a compassionate example.

"And this gospel of the kingdom will be preached in the whole world as a testimony to all nations," Jesus told His disciples, "and then the end will come" (**Matthew 24:14**). The Apostle Mark recorded in his gospel, "Then the disciples went out and preached everywhere, and the Lord worked with them and confirmed his word by the signs that accompanied it" (**Mark 16:20**). The "signs" Mark was referring to were the miracles of healing and deliverance performed through the disciples as they exercised their faith. No such documentation has ever been forthcoming for those that follow the teachings of Muhammad.

This preaching of the Gospel by the disciples of Jesus was, once again, a fulfillment of Old Testament prophecy. "Their voice goes out into all the earth, their words to the ends of the world. In the heavens he has pitched a tent for the sun" (**Psalm 19:4**). However, the disciples could not fully preach the Gospel until Christ's crucifixion and resurrection had been accomplished. "He told them, 'This is what is written: The Christ will suffer and rise from the dead on the third day, and repentance and forgiveness of sins will be preached in his name to all nations, beginning at Jerusalem'" (**Luke 24:46-47**). Even the Apostles, Jesus' closest travel companions, did not fully understand the purpose of Jesus' mission until after he died and was resurrected and appeared to them once again.

In his letter to the Colossians (Greek gentiles), Paul illustrated his full comprehension of this gospel.

"We always thank God, the Father of our Lord Jesus Christ, when we pray for you, because we have heard of your faith in Christ Jesus and of the love you have for all the saints—the faith and love that spring from the hope that is stored up for you in heaven and that you have already heard about in the word of truth, the gospel that has come to you. All over the world this gospel is bearing fruit and growing, just as it has been doing among you since the day you heard it and understood God's grace in all its truth" (**Colossians 1:3-6**). Later in the same chapter, he continued. "Once you were alienated from God and were enemies in your minds because of your evil behavior. But now he has reconciled you by Christ's physical body through death to present you holy in his sight, without blemish and free from accusation—if you continue in your faith, established and firm, not moved from the hope held out in the gospel. This is the gospel that you heard and that has been proclaimed to every creature under heaven, and of which I, Paul, have become a servant" (**Colossians 1:21-23**).

The "Great Commission"

After His resurrection and before He ascended into heaven, Jesus conveyed to His disciples what has become to be known in the Christian world as the "Great Commission" – the command to make disciples throughout the world. "Then Jesus came to them and said, 'All authority in heaven and on earth has been given to me. Therefore go and make disciples of all nations, baptizing them in the name of the Father and of the Son and of the Holy Spirit, and teaching them to obey everything I have commanded you. And surely I am with you always, to the very end of the age'" (**Matthew 28:18-20**). This was not a radical call to war or oppression of the masses, but a call to share the *good news* of salvation and God's redemptive love.

By contrast, you might recall from earlier chapters that, as Muhammad lay dying, he commanded his followers to purge the Arabian Peninsula of non-believers. Also, at the end of his life, as Muhammad was reflecting on his "career" he was quoted as saying: "I have been sent with the shortest expressions bearing the widest meanings, and I have been made victorious with terror. . . ." (**hadith 4:52:220**). Jesus, of course, never harbored such claims of aggression toward anyone or any country or people.

"You are the **salt of the earth**," Jesus instructed His followers during the Sermon on the Mount. "But if the salt loses its saltiness, how can it be made salty again? It is no longer good for anything, except to be thrown out and trampled by men. You are the **light of the world**. A city on a hill cannot be hidden. Neither do people light a lamp and put it under a bowl. Instead they put it on its stand, and it gives light to everyone in the house. In the same way, let your light shine before men, that they may see your good deeds and praise your Father in heaven" (**Matthew 5:13-16**, author's emphasis).

Jesus wanted His disciples to be set apart from all others as a pure example of God's love for His creation. During the time of Jesus and throughout history, salt has been a necessary ingredient and commodity for the nations and peoples of the world. Jesus wanted His disciples to be the "necessary ingredient" from which others would draw the life of God. He wanted them to be a light in the midst of a dark world of sin so that all people would be drawn to Him and His heavenly Father.

The disciples of Jesus then and now are to be shining examples of a compassionate, forgiving God who wants everyone to share eternal life with Him. By now you have discovered that the same cannot be ascribed to Allah, his Apostle or his followers.

Through the Christian's personal relationship with their saving God and the joy of their salvation, they have the desire to see others share in the same discovery. As the Apostle Paul wrote to the Philippians, "For it is God who works in you to will and to act according to his good purpose. Do everything without complaining or arguing, so that you may become blameless and pure, children of God without fault in a crooked and depraved generation, in which you shine like stars in the universe as you **hold out the word of life** – in order that I may boast on the day of Christ that I did not run or labor for nothing" (**Philippians 2:13-16**, author's emphasis).

It is through the internal working of the Holy Spirit within the Christian that they are motivated to share God's grace and mercy. Muslims have no such internal witness of their unseen god and therefore are not motivated from within but from the controlling, oppressive environment in which they live and are brainwashed from birth to death. It is impossible to share life out of the darkness of one's soul. Muhammad could not do it, nor have any of his followers since. "Do not repay anyone evil for evil," admonished Paul. "Be careful to do what is right in the eyes of everybody. If it is possible, as far as it depends on you, live at peace with everyone. Do not take revenge, my friends, but leave room for God's wrath, for it is written: 'It is mine to avenge; I will repay,' says the Lord. On the contrary: 'If your enemy is hungry, feed him; if he is thirsty, give him something to drink. In doing this, you will heap burning coals on his head.' Do not be overcome by evil, but overcome evil with good" (**Romans 12:17-21**). Apostle Paul, in keeping with the message of Christ, reminded the Christians in Rome, who were under extreme persecution from the Romans, to *live at peace with everyone* no matter what the cost. Not only to live at peace, but to extend the grace and mercy of God to their enemies. This was also impossible for Muhammad to do and for his followers. If one does not follow a god of compassion, mercy and forgiveness, it is not likely that you are going to be able to demonstrate anything different.

Too often Christians believe that is up to them to win over a soul by their great, bombastic knowledge of biblical truths. The reality is that most Christ followers are called to be seed planters, sowing wherever there is fertile soil of interest. We are not called to confront in an unloving manner, although God's truth of the Gospel, is by nature, confrontational, dividing truth from error; good from evil. This is especially true when attempting to share the truth of the Gospel with a Muslim. It must be done in love as an ambassador of Christ and with the mindset that you may be only the seed planter unless God reveals otherwise through His Holy Spirit.

The Apostle Paul, through his letter to the church in Ephesus, wrote a word of wisdom that is a good reminder for anyone desiring to be a good witness. He cautioned that all Christ followers must "reach unity in the faith and in the knowledge of the Son of God and become mature, attaining to the whole measure of the fullness of Christ. **Then** we will no longer be infants, tossed back and forth by the waves, and blown here and there by every wind of teaching and by the cunning and craftiness of people in their deceitful scheming. Instead, **speaking the truth in love**, we will grow to become in every respect the mature body of him who is the head, that is, Christ. (**Ephesians 4:13-15**; author's emphasis).

While knowledge of the truth concerning Islam is helpful to discern and understand a Muslim's beliefs and mindset, it should not be used to ridicule or demean their faith, understanding the depth of bondage under which they have lived in an oppressive society.

"Cain's spirit," wrote former devout Muslim, Reza Safa, "is the kind of spirit that Satan uses to come against the righteous man. This kind of religious spirit is an open door for demonic influence. This religious spirit is hateful, vengeful, murderous and bloodthirsty. It is resentful, unforgiving and does not know mercy" (3).

Cain, a son of Adam and Eve, was banished from Eden to live in the Land of Nod (**Genesis 4:16**) which was east of Eden. "You will be a restless wanderer on the earth," God told Cain (**Genesis 4:12b**). Many biblical scholars place the Land of Nod (Hebrew for wandering or vagrancy) in the Middle East, perhaps in Iran. If so, it should not be a great surprise that the murderous spirit of Cain still survives to this day in the Middle East. Remember also, from Chapter 3, the curse of Ishmael from whom Arab Muslims claim their parentage. God told Abraham and Sarah that Ishmael would "be a wild donkey of a man; his hand will be against everyone and everyone's hand against him, and he will live in hostility toward all his brothers" (**Genesis 16:12**).

Such hostility is brought forth by Muhammad in many Qur'anic verses such as the following.

> *O you who believe! Do not take My enemy and your enemy for friends: would you offer them love while they deny what has come to you of the truth, driving out the Apostle and yourselves because you believe in Allah, your Lord? If you go forth struggling hard in My path and seeking My pleasure, would you manifest love to them? And I know what you conceal and what you manifest; and whoever of you does this, he indeed has gone astray from the straight path* (**Qur'an 60:1**).

The God of the Jews and Christians, however, calls upon those who believe in Him to live at peace with one another. "Finally, all of you, live in harmony with one another; be sympathetic, love as brothers, be compassionate and humble," the Apostle Peter reminded the Christians throughout the Roman provinces. "Do not repay evil with evil or insult with insult, but with blessing, because to this you were called so that you may inherit a blessing. For, 'Whoever would love life and see good days must keep his tongue from evil and his lips from deceitful speech. He must turn from evil and do good; he must seek peace and pursue it. For the eyes of the Lord are on the righteous and his ears are attentive to their prayer, but the face of the Lord is against those who do evil'" (**1 Peter 3:8-12**). Christians are called unequivocally to do good at every opportunity; to *seek peace and pursue it* – to be peacemakers in a world at war with itself.

A few verses later, Peter again called the new Christians to pursue goodness regardless of the outcome. "Who is going to harm you if you are eager to do good? But even if you should suffer for what is right, you are blessed. 'Do not fear what they fear; do not be frightened.' But in your hearts set apart Christ as Lord. Always be prepared to give an answer to everyone who asks you to give the reason for the hope that you have. But do this with gentleness and respect, keeping a clear conscience, so that those who speak maliciously against your good behavior in Christ may be ashamed of their slander. It is better, if it is God's will, to suffer for doing good than for doing evil" (**1 Peter 3:13-17**). Christians are called to do good deeds for others and to speak in love. Compare that to the hostile acts and words of hate that are coming forth from the Muslim regions of the world.

The Apostle Paul, like his Savior, Jesus, put it into agrarian terms that his hearers would understand. "Do not be deceived: God cannot be mocked. A man reaps what he sows. The one who sows to please his sinful nature, from that nature will reap destruction; the one who sows to please the Spirit, from the Spirit will reap eternal life. Let us not become weary in doing good, for at the proper time we will reap a harvest if we do not give up. Therefore, as we have opportunity, let us do good to all people, especially to those who belong to the family of believers" (**Galatians 6:7-10**).

It is a simple analogy: one can only harvest what one plants. Planting wheat seed will not yield a harvest of melons. Sowing hate will not produce love. Sowing acts of mercy and love, while they may not always produce a reciprocating response, will never yield hate unless it is in the darkened and deceived mind and spirit of the recipient. Eventually, love wins out and when it is sowed continuously, it *will* yield a crop of similar genome.

> *Then we will no longer be infants, tossed back and forth by the waves, and blown here and there by every wind of teaching and by the cunning and craftiness of people in their deceitful scheming. Instead, speaking the truth in love, we will grow to become in every respect the mature body of him who is the head, that is, Christ* (**Ephesians 4:14-15**).

Muhammad's Method

After settling in Medina, the remainder of the seventh century became a bloody one as the Muslims sought to spread their new found influence and conquest outside the Arabian Peninsula. Although Muhammad had planned and/or led numerous raids against his enemies while in Mecca, beginning in 624 A.D., Muslim violence in the name of Allah escalated. During the remainder of that century, Muslim faithful marched in no less than one hundred battles, raids and conquests. Muslim influence and domination quickly spread throughout the Arab world of the Middle East, as well as North Africa, the Mediterranean and parts of south central Asia. Pagans, Jews and Christians were systematically exiled from their homeland, converted or murdered (4, 5).

There are numerous examples in Islamic sacred texts that specify how Muslims are to convert non-believers to Islam. None of them include attracting the infidel to Islam by the demonstration of one's righteousness or charity; nor does it include preaching words of Good News that contain a message of Allah's hope, mercy, forgiveness and unfailing love. However, what they do contain is the directive to bring unbelievers into the fold through persecution, oppression, and by torture and death if necessary. An example is the hadith below of Sahih Muslim that is credited to Muhammad's instruction.

It has been reported from Sulaiman b. Buraid through his father that when the Messenger of Allah (may peace be upon him) appointed anyone as leader of an army or detachment he would especially exhort him to fear Allah and to be good to the Muslims who were with him. He would say: **Fight in the name of Allah and in the way of Allah. Fight against those who disbelieve in Allah.** *Make a holy war, do not embezzle the spoils; do not break your pledge; and do not mutilate (the dead) bodies; do not kill the children.* **When you meet your enemies who are polytheists, invite them to three courses of action.** *If they respond to any one of these, you also accept it and withhold yourself from doing them any harm.* **Invite them to (accept) Islam; if they respond to you, accept it from them and desist from fighting against them.** *Then invite them to migrate from their lands to the land of Muhairs and inform them that, if they do so, they shall have all the privileges and obligations of the Muhajirs. If they refuse to migrate, tell them that they will have the status of Bedouin Muslims and will be subjected to the Commands of Allah like other Muslims, but they will not get any share from the spoils of war or Fai' except when they actually fight with the Muslims (against the disbelievers).* **If they refuse to accept Islam, demand from them the Jizya.** *If they agree to pay, accept it from them and hold off your hands.* **If they refuse to pay the tax, seek Allah's help and fight them.** *When you lay siege to a fort and the besieged appeal to you for protection in the name of Allah and His Prophet, do not accord to them the guarantee of Allah and His Prophet, but accord to them your own guarantee and the guarantee of your companions for it is a lesser sin that the security given by you or your companions be disregarded than that the security granted in the name of Allah and His Prophet be violated When you besiege a fort and the besieged want you to let them out in accordance with Allah's Command, do not let them come out in accordance with His Command, but do so at your (own) command, for you do not know whether or not you will be able to carry out Allah's behest with regard to them* [(6); author's emphasis].

The opponents of Islam during Muhammad's day, throughout fourteen centuries of history and now, have only three choices when confronted by Muslim jihadists: Embrace Islam; pay the Islamic *jizya* (poll tax) and live as subjugated citizens within the Muslim protectorate or die.

The brutality of the Muslim advance is well illustrated in The Battle of the Trench in 627 against the Jewish Banu Qurayzah tribe of

335

Medina. After their conquest and surrender, Muhammad left their fate up to one of his warriors. The warrior suggested that all the Jewish men should be beheaded and their wives and children taken captive. This sounded fair to Muhammad and he had all 800-900 Jewish men systematically so dispatched, with himself actively participating in the beheadings (7).

Such vicious treatment of the captives of war effectively wiped out all Jewish resistance in the area. Such treatment of the captives of war was largely practiced then, as it is now, by the Islamic world. It is firmly supported by Allah's revelation to Muhammad.

> *When you sought aid from your Lord, so He answered you: I will assist you with a thousand of the angels following one another. . .   When your Lord revealed to the angels: I am with you, therefore make firm those who believe. I will cast terror into the hearts of those who disbelieve. Therefore strike off their heads and strike off every fingertip of them.*
>
> *This is because they acted adversely to Allah and His Apostle; and whoever acts adversely to Allah and His Apostle— then surely Allah is severe in requiting (evil)* (**Qur'an 8:9, 12-13**).

Fighting is ordained for Muslims by Allah and his Apostle as the primary method of spreading the "message" of Islam.

"Fighting is enjoined on you," Muhammad revealed from Allah, "and it is an object of dislike to you; and it may be that you dislike a thing while it is good for you, and it may be that you love a thing while it is evil for you, and Allah knows, while you do not know" (**Qur'an 2:216**). That is, fighting the enemies of Allah—which are ALL non-believers—is required or commanded for all Muslims by Allah and his Apostle. Of course, when one is victorious there is booty to be procured from the vanquished, and the faithful wanted to know how it should be distributed. Not unexpectedly, Muhammad shared this self-serving revelation from his god. "They ask you about the windfalls [of battle]. Say: The windfalls are for Allah and the Apostle. So be careful of (your duty to) Allah and set aright matters of your difference, and obey Allah and His Apostle if you are believers" (**Qur'an 8:1**).

Naturally, one of the surest ways to rally the faithful into battle is to abase, dehumanize and demonize your non-believing foe. Muhammad was quite adept at securing Allah's revelation and approval when it came to suppressing his enemies. "Surely the vilest [most hated] of animals in Allah's sight are those who disbelieve [infidels], then they would not believe" (**Qur'an 8:55**). In addition to referring to Jews as pigs and apes

(**Qur'an 2:65**, **5:60** and **7:166**), non-believers as a whole are dehumanized in the sight of Islam's god and its prophet.

"Surely those who disbelieve from among the followers of the Book [the Jews] and the polytheists [the Christians] shall be in the fire of hell, abiding therein; they are the worst of men" (**Qur'an 98:6**). Islam demonizes all non-believers, thus fostering the justification for mistreatment, deprivation and murder. For the true follower of Islam, such persecution of the non-believer is only advancing their already determined destiny of hell and, therefore, not only justified, but the carrying out of Allah's judgment. "O Prophet! Urge the believers to war;" Allah commanded Muhammad, "if there are twenty patient ones of you they shall overcome two hundred, and if there are a hundred of you they shall overcome a thousand of those who disbelieve, because they are a people who do not understand" (**Qur'an 8:65**).

Two years after Muhammad and his military junta fled to Medina in 622, Muhammad mapped out a very aggressive plan of oppression and military conquest of his neighbors. While Muhammad and his followers were in Mecca, he was somewhat more conciliatory toward Jews and other non-believers in the hope they would convert to his theology. However, after being run out of Mecca, Muhammad developed a much more hostile approach toward conversion—convert or die.

In 624 Muhammad orchestrated his first major battle against the Quraysh Jews of Mecca in the Battle of Badr. It gave him the opportunity to take out his vengeance on the tribe that rejected him. He was ruthless, ordering the beheading of those who survived the carnage (8, 9). In the same year, emboldened by his victory over the Quraysh, Muhammad led a campaign of terror against the Bani Qainuqa (aka Bani Qaynuqa) Jews of Medina, expelling any survivors from their homeland (10, 11). Such raids became the primary way in which Muhammad financed the expansion of Islam and kept his warriors happy with plundering the vanquished.

The following year, the Quraysh who had fled to fight another day, were bent on revenge and had amassed around 3,000 warriors. In the ensuing Battle of Uhud (a mountain near Mecca) the Quraysh were successful in defeating Muhammad's forces, but Muhammad would not accept defeat and once again he would carry out his revenge upon the Quraysh (12). With his vengeance against the Jews running high, Muhammad also exiled the Jewish Banu Nadir tribe from Medina (13).

Three years after the massacre of the Banu Qurayzah, Muhammad, with 10,000 Muslim warriors, conquered Mecca. He ordered the slaughter of all who resisted. The Ka'bah (or Ka'aba), the site of idol worship in Mecca, was established as the center of Islam (14). A year later, the remaining Arabic tribes, fearing Muhammad's wrath, accepted Islam. Now Muhammad could turn his attention to his war against Christians.

The death of Muhammad in 632 did not halt the Muslim advance. The bloody post mortem campaigns began a reign of terror that brought the conquest of the Middle East and beyond. Abu Bakr, Muhammad's faithful friend, was elected the first Caliph (Islamic leader). Under his direction and the caliphs that would follow him, the brutal expansion of Islam continued throughout the rest of the seventh century with the conquests of Bahrain, Oman, Yemen, Iraq, Damascus, Syria, Jerusalem, Egypt, Persia and bold invasions into Western Russia, Asia Minor, North Africa, the Island of Cyprus, Sicily and the siege of Constantinople in 677 (15). The battles were mostly land grabbing offenses to expand the reaches of Islam. There was no mercy given. Accept Islam or die.

The first one hundred years of Islam's attacks and conquering raids throughout the Middle East and beyond would set the stage for centuries of bloody conquests to follow. The 8th Century would see Islam expanding its empire with attacks on the Berbers of North Africa, the conquest of Spain, invasion of Constantinople, the Battle of Tours in France, and a century of battles and revolts throughout the Islamic region. By the end of the 11th century the Muslim vanguard had conquered the holy city of Jerusalem, the Middle East and the Mediterranean countries. In an effort to regain this formerly controlled Christian territory, the first of the Crusades was launched in 1095.

The pattern of Islamic barbarity continues into the modern era and the 21st century. According to Steve Keohane, from 1970-2000, "there were 43,721 terrorist attacks worldwide; 113,425 people were killed. Over 82,126 injured. Over 90% of these barbaric acts were committed by Muslims" (16).

Chapter Conclusion

It is clear that the two dominating religions of the world—Islam and Christianity—have very divergent ideas on how to win converts to their religious beliefs. Christians are called to share Christ out of their personal experience and passion for their Lord and Savior. Muslims are called to advance the cause of Islam by any means necessary, including violence, oppression, subjugation and murder.

While the call to peaceful evangelism is made clear through the teaching of Christ and the instruction of the New Testament, it is also very clear that the Qur'an and the teaching of its prophet commands Islam to be spread by violence, not peace, and not an inner witness from a compassionate, merciful god.

Those that Islam seeks to win over to the cause of Allah are given three options: Submit to Islam, pay the poll tax and live as secondary citizens under Islam, or fight to the death. Since the birth of

Christianity, its message has been one of personal choice. Christians are not to coerce or force any person to accept Christ, but to only share the Gospel and let the Holy Spirit of God convict and convince a person to accept and receive salvation from Jesus Christ.

References.

1. *Qur'an*, Muhammad Asad translation. Isamicity.com. Http://www.islamicity.com. Quransearch. Accessed August 10, 2007.
2. Fitzgerald, Hugh. *"No Compulsion in Religion?" What About the Mass Conversion of Hindus?* Geller Report, April 11, 2018. Source: https://gellerreport.com/2018/04/mass-conversion-hindus.html/
3. Safa, Reza F. *Inside Islam: Exposing and Reaching the World of Islam*, 1996. Charisma House, p. 16.
4. *Islamic History (Chronology).* Http://www.barkati.net/English/chronology.htm. Accessed January 30, 2007.
5. Spencer, Robert. *The Truth About Muhammad, Founder of the World's Most Intolerant Religion*, 2006. Regnery Publishing, Inc., chapters 6-8.
6. Sahih Muslim Book 019, Hadith Number 4294.
7. Spencer, pp. 129-130.
8. *Islamic History.*
9. Spencer, pp. 103-106.
10. *Islamic History*
11. Spencer, pp. 111-112.
12. Spencer, pp. 117-119.
13. *Islamic History.*
14. Spencer, pp. 146, 149.
15. *Islamic History.*
16. Keohane, Steve *Muhammad: Terrorist or Prophet?* BibleProbe.com, 200402007. Http://bibleprobe.com/muhammad.htm. Accessed April 1, 2007.

Chapter 13

Treatment of Non-believers

You have heard that it was said, "Love your neighbor and hate your enemy." But I tell you, love your enemies and pray for those who persecute you, that you may be children of your Father in heaven. He causes his sun to rise on the evil and the good, and sends rain on the righteous and the unrighteous. . .

Matthew 5: 43-48

The biblical scripture above which cites the admonition of Christ, is scoffed at by Muslims and others as an impossibility and a sign of weakness. Indeed, among those of the Christian faith there is much disagreement about adhering to Jesus' words about how to treat one's enemies. Among Christians and Christian denominations there are those who are pacifists or conscientious objectors who refuse to take up arms against another. They believe they are following the directive of Jesus on how to deal with enemies or those who hate them, persecute them, or seek to kill them. Others of the Christian faith believe equally as strong, that self-defense is the biblical imperative and that there is such a thing as a "just war" or call to arms.

While the Qur'an seems obsessed with Allah's retribution toward the "infidels" or "unbelievers," the Bible mentions God's vengeance against those who do not believe rather sparingly. In the Old Testament, non-Jews are mostly referred to as the "uncircumcised." In the New Testament, the term, "Gentile" replaces the reference to a non-Jew. Rather than retribution, the God of the Bible first seeks to bring the lost into His kingdom through acts of love and mercy and the testimony of His Son, Jesus Christ.

While the Apostle Paul warned the Corinthians not to be "yoked together with unbelievers," he was not advocating that the Corinthians disassociate themselves from the non-believers around them or to cause them any harm (**2 Corinthians 6:14a**). Instead, he was calling upon them to guard their new faith from the temptations of the Greek pagans they were living among and not fall once again into the bondage of spiritual darkness. "For what do righteousness and wickedness have in common? Or what fellowship can light have with darkness?" (**verse 14b**)

To the Ephesians, Paul wrote, "Let no one deceive you with empty words, for because of such things God's wrath comes on those who are disobedient. Therefore, do not be partners with them. For you were once darkness, but now you are light in the Lord. Live as children of light (for the fruit of the light consists in all goodness, righteousness and truth) and find out what pleases the Lord. Have nothing to do with the fruitless deeds of darkness, but rather expose them" (**Ephesians 5:6-11**).

Christians were not and are not called to oppress those who do not believe as they believe, but instead, they are to shine the light of the Gospel in the midst of spiritual darkness and expose non-believers to the truth of the Gospel of Jesus Christ by how they walk and talk. The rule that Jesus taught His disciples in the art of relating to others was, "Be merciful, just as your Father is merciful" (**Luke 6:36**).

The principle laid down by Jesus was to show mercy and extend God's love to all people, whether they were fellow Christians or not. God is love, and it was He that first loved His creation. Those that choose to follow Him through faith in Jesus Christ, in turn, have His love to share with others, including non-believers. The Apostle John wrote it down this way.

> *Dear friends, let us love one another, for love comes from God. Everyone who loves has been born of God and knows God. Whoever does not love does not know God, because God is love. This is how God showed his love among us: He sent his one and only Son into the world that we might live through him. This is love: not that we loved God, but that he loved us and sent his Son as an atoning sacrifice for our sins. . . .*
>
> *If anyone acknowledges that Jesus is the Son of God, God lives in him and he in God. And so we know and rely on the love God has for us.*
>
> *God is love. Whoever lives in love lives in God, and God in him* (**1 John 4:7-10, 15-16**).

Muslims, however, are not sure that their god, Allah, loves them, and therefore have no wellspring of inner love to share with others. Since their god offers no personal relationship, no father-child identity, no plan of forgiveness and redemption, there is no sense of Allah's caring embrace.

When the well is empty there can be no satisfying the thirsty soul—whether it be your own or someone else's.

Hatred of the Jews and Unbelievers

Ever since the Jews of Arabia refused to accept Muhammad as a prophet of their God, the followers of Islam have been repeatedly conditioned, that is, brainwashed, into a livid hatred of them and Christians, by association. Much of the hatred that is generated and fomented by Islamic scholars and imams is founded on absolute fabrications that have no basis in fact or history.

341

Take, for example, an essay written by Muhammad Al-Munajjid (1). The author claims to draw his information from the Jewish Talmud to justify, "Why do we hate the Jews? We hate them for the sake of our Lord, we hate them for the sake of Allaah because they slandered Allaah and they killed and slandered His Prophets." The Talmud, first of all, is the written record of Jewish oral law and its subsequent discussions and expounding by rabbinic leaders. There are two versions: the Palestinian (compiled sometime during the 4th century) and the Babylonian (compiled around 500 A.D.). While the Talmud helped refine or resolve certain legal issues of the Torah, it did not supersede that which was handed down through Moses.

In the end, the Muslim, both externally and internally, must passionately hate those who stand against the expansion of Allah's cause.

Ergun Mehmet Caner and Emir Fethi Caner
Unveiling Islam, 2002, p. 36

Among the outlandish things that Al-Munajjid claims are in the Talmud:

- *The sperm of a non-Jew is like the sperm of an animal.*
- *Every Jew has to do his utmost to prevent all other nations from having any possessions on earth. . . .*
- *If God had not created the Jews, there would be no blessing on earth.*
- *The souls of the Jews are dear to God . . . all other souls . . . are devilish souls. . .*
- *The Jew is not at fault if he attacks the honour of a non-Jewish woman . . . the non-Jewish woman is considered to be an animal.*
- *The Jews have the right to rape non-Jewish women.*
- *Fornication with a non-Jew, whether male or female is not punishable, because they (non-Jews) are the descendants of animals.*
- *That God is not infallible. . . .*
- *. . . that the rabbis have authority over God. . . .*
- *. . . that God consults the rabbis on earth when there is a problem for which He cannot find a solution in heaven.*
- *. . . that the teaching of the rabbis cannot be undone or changed, even by the command of God.*

In the highly acclaimed and award winning documentary, *Obsession: Radical Islam's War Against the West*, a segment shows a Muslim production for Arab television promoting the common belief among Arab Muslims that Jewish pastries for the Jewish religious holiday of Purim are made with the blood of sacrificed young Christian boys (2). This was confirmed by no less than the Saudi Arabian government in 2002 (3).

To the non-Muslim West, all this hyperbole and fallacy might be laughable if not for the realization that Muslims worldwide gobble this misinformation up as the truth without their own due diligence, thus giving their already mistrust of the Jews further justification for their hatred of them.

"O Prophet!" Allah revealed to Muhammad, "Strive hard against the unbelievers and the hypocrites and be unyielding to them; and their abode is hell, and evil is the destination" (**Qur'an 9:73**). This commandment of Allah is quite a contrast to the commandments of Jesus for His followers to love the non-believer and reach out to them by sharing the Gospel of good news.

"Fight those who do not believe in Allah, nor in the latter day, nor do they prohibit what Allah and His Apostle have prohibited, nor follow the religion of truth, out of those who have given the Book, until they pay the tax in acknowledgment of superiority and they are in a state of submission" (**Qur'an 9:29**).

This Qur'anic verse commands that Muslims must fight against four groups of people: those who do not believe in Allah; those who do not believe in the last day; those who do what Allah and Muhammad prohibit; and those who do not submit to Islam as the true religion.

"Those who believe fight in the way of Allah, and those who disbelieve fight in the way of the Shaitan [Satan]. Fight therefore against the friends of the Shaitan; surely the strategy of the Shaitan is weak" (**Qur'an 4:76**). NOTE: In the Islamic world, it is the Jews and Christians that are portrayed as devils or agents of Satan and the United States, in particular, as "The Great Satan."

In Islamic teaching there is no room for parity with the West or the non-Muslim, no compromise, no mercy, no conciliation.

"Whoever is the enemy of Allah and His angels and His apostles and Jibreel [Gabriel] and Meekaeel [Michael], so surely Allah is the enemy of the unbelievers" (**Qur'an 2:98**). *All* non-believers are enemies of Allah, and whoever is an enemy of Allah is an enemy of Islam, and whoever is an enemy of Islam is an enemy of every Muslim. Therefore, it only makes sense to the Muslim faithful that Allah would call upon them to kill the unbelievers (**Qur'an 9:5**). No such open-ended command exists in the Bible for any of God's people to indiscriminately kill their enemies

343

or those who do not believe as they do.

The Qur'an calls upon all Muslims not to befriend Jews and Christians (**Qur'an 5:51**). It further tells the Muslim faithful that the Jews are cursed because of their unbelief (**Qur'an 5:78**). Thus, this gives even further rationalization for Muslims to hate Jews and Christians by association since they follow the Jewish Messiah and support the validity of the Jewish existence. **Proverbs 3:29-30**, written by King Solomon, reprimands the followers of Jehovah God to "not plot harm against your neighbor, who lives trustfully near you. Do not accuse a man for no reason—when he has done you no harm." Jews have attempted to live at peace with their Muslim neighbors in the Middle East for centuries and in Israel for the last seventy years, but to no avail (recall Chapter 3). Just like the Muslims of Muhammad's era, the Muslims, for eons have persecuted the Jews in their midst and then point the finger at the Jews claiming they were the aggressor.

The Rise of 21ˢᵗ Century Anti-Semitism. The Muslim psychology of hating the Jew is supported by their holy book. "Abasement [degradation or humiliation] is made to cleave to [the unbelievers] wherever they are found, except under a covenant with Allah and a covenant with men, and they have become deserving of wrath from Allah, and humiliation is made to cleave to them; this is because they disbelieved in the communications of Allah and slew the prophets unjustly; this is because they disobeyed and exceeded the limits" (**Qur'an 3:112**). Anything is justified when it comes to the treatment of Jews and other non-believers. The goal is to demean and persecute the unbeliever until only Muslims exist.

Although this directive from Allah was over 1,400 ago, it is still upheld by many modern day Muslims and their clergy. With the 21ˢᵗ century influx of Muslim refugees into European Union countries, the specter of anti-Semitism has once again raised its ugly head. Such anti-Jew sentiment has not been seen in Europe since the days of Nazi Germany, almost 80 years ago.

Not only has Jew hatred been on the rise throughout Europe, but Europe's tolerance for it also seems to be rising. For example, in September, 2018 a review panel for the United Kingdom's Teaching Regulation Agency, exonerated Harpeet Singh, head of mathematics at Sandye Place Academy in Bedfordshire, England for anti-Semitic remarks on his Facebook page. Two of Singh's posts were considered "offensive and racist" but not "anti-Semitic."

In one post, Singh wrote: "Every sane human is anti-Semitic. Because you bastards have made Zionism synonymous with the mistreatment of Palestinians. Billions are anti-Semitic and proud of it." In another he posted: "Of course we hate Jews. Israel is the most evil regime on the planet. Supported by Jews from within, and from around the world" (4). While the panel declared Singh not anti-Semitic, they determined that he was unfit to teach until at least 2021.

Anti-Semitism has also risen sharply on the North American continent. In Canada, the number of hate crimes against Jews skyrocketed 60 percent (actually 62.9%) in 2017 from the previous year. Shimo Koffler, CEO for the Centre for Israel and Jewish Affairs stated, "History demonstrates that those who target Jews and other minorities pose a threat to society as a whole. All Canadians should be vigilant in standing against hate"(5).

Such a rise in Jew hatred in Canada should be no surprise since the Canadian government frequently panders to radical Islamists and provides them with a platform to preach their hatred of Jews. In the fall of 2018, Toronto, Canada hosted an Islamic conference that featured such well-known inflammatory Jew haters as Nazir Ahmed, a former member of the British House of Lords; Ustadh Abdelrahman Murphy, a Muslim activist; Imam Siraj Wahhaj, an unindicted co-conspirator in the 1993 bombing of the World Trade Center in New York; Boonaa Mohammed from Toronto who still claims that the "evil Zionists" were responsible for the September 11, 2001 Islamist attack on America, and the United States' own anti-Semite, Linda Sarsour (6).

In the fall of 2018, the Federal Bureau of Investigation (FBI) released its annual report on hate crimes for 2017 (7). Of the 7,175 documented hate crimes, 1,679 were determined to be religious in nature. Of this number, 58.1 percent were deemed as anti-Jewish and 18.7 percent were anti-Islam. Compared to the 6,121 hate crimes reported for 2016, the total number of hate crimes rose 17 percent, as did the anti-Jewish hate crimes (8). Hate crimes against Muslims dropped significantly from 24.5 percent of religious victims in 2016 to 18.7 percent in 2017.

What the Qur'an and Islamic Law Teach. The Qur'an commands that the followers of Allah must continue to fight against the infidels until there is only one religion, and that is Islam.

"And fight with them [the unbelievers] until there is no more persecution and religion should be only for Allah; but if they desist, then surely Allah sees what they do" (**Qur'an 8:39**).

According to Muhammad and Islamic law, there are only three options for non-believers: they can convert to Islam; they can remain as Jews or Christians but pay an annual non-believer tax or *jizya*; or they can die for their unwillingness to submit to the heavy hand of Islam.

While Islam forbids its followers to pay or charge interest, it is okay to extort money from infidels or suppress them with usury to gain the upper hand. The God of the Jews and Christians forbids such tactics. "In you are people who accept bribes to shed blood; you take interest and make a profit from the poor. You extort unjust gain from your neighbors.

345

And you have forgotten me, declares the Sovereign LORD" (**Ezekiel 22:12**).

In the *Reliance of the Traveller*, the book of Islamic Law, there is a clear picture of how Muslims are to view Jews (and Christians).

- *By Him in whose hand is the soul of Muhammad, any person of this Community, any Jew, or any Christian who hears me and dies without believing in what I have been sent with will be an inhabitant of hell* (*ROT*, w4.3).

- On the payment or indemnity for the loss of life or injury: *The indemnity for the death or injury of a woman is one-half the indemnity paid for a* [Muslim] *man. The indemnity paid for a Jew or Christian is one-third of the indemnity paid for a Muslim* [man](*ROT*, o4.9).

- Jews are extremists because they accuse Mary of fornication and Christians are extremists because they refer to Jesus as God (*ROT*, p75:23).

- *The caliph makes war upon Jews, Christians, and Zoroastrians provided he has first invited them to enter Islam in faith and practice . . .* (*ROT*, o9.8).

- Judaism and Christianity are *remnant cults* that are unacceptable to Allah and Muslims (*ROT*, w4.1(2)).

There are many more injunctions in Islamic law that could be presented, but the reader should get the picture: any belief other than Islam is unacceptable and those following such beliefs warrant Allah's wrath.

Praising the Killer of an Infidel

Islamic Rules of Retaliation and Reward. Within Islamic culture and law there is a certain prescribed forgiveness for murder that carries no punishment. It comes straight from the teachings of Muhammad and is recorded in the hadith.

"The legal regulations of Diya (Blood-money) and the (ransom for) releasing of the captives, and the judgment that no Muslim should be killed in Qisas (equality in punishment) for killing a Kafir (disbeliever)" (**hadith 9:83:50**). *Qisas* is the retaliatory *eye for an eye* justice system within Islam. While killing a Kafir is acceptable under any circumstance, the killing of a fellow Muslim is not. "Allah's Apostle said, 'The blood of a Muslim who confesses that none has the right to be worshipped but Allah and that I am His Apostle, cannot be shed except in three cases: In Qisas for murder, a married person who commits illegal sexual intercourse and the one who reverts from Islam (apostate) and leaves the Muslims'" (**hadith 9:83:17**).

In the *Reliance of the Traveller* (*A Classic Manual of Islamic Sacred Law*), there is a lengthy section (o1.1 – o3.13) on retaliatory killing—when it is permitted and when it is not. Suffice it to say, that it is illegal according to Islamic law for a Muslim to retaliate and kill another Muslim who has killed a non-Muslim [(o1.2(2)], or killed a Jew or Christian [(o1.2(3)], or a father or mother who has killed their offspring (i.e., honor killing) [(o1.2(4)]. In other words, it is not permissible for a Muslim to kill another Muslim who has killed a non-Muslim, a Jew or Christian or their own children. This is all permitted under Islamic law without punishment.

This concept of justice, alone, should raise serious concerns in Western societies. How can a person who believes in such convoluted justice follow the constitutional law of Western countries; how can they be judges or members of law enforcement; how can they serve as state and federal lawmakers with an adherence to the antithesis of Western jurisprudence?

Islam seems to have a disproportionate share of people committing horrific acts, while quoting the Qur'an or their holy prophet as the justification. For example, on March 3, 2006, Mohammed Taheri-azar., an Iranian national and graduate of the University of North Carolina, drove his rented Jeep Cherokee into a crowd of nine students in an attempt to kill them all. Was he angry with them? Had they abused or otherwise mistreated him? Did he even know them? The answer is "no" to all three questions. His reasoning was quite basic from his viewpoint. "Allah gives permission in the Quran," he wrote in a letter to the ABC television affiliate in Durham, North Carolina, "for the followers of Allah to attack those who have raged war against them, with the expectation of eternal paradise in case of martyrdom and/or living one's life in obedience of all of Allah's commandments found throughout the Quran's 114 chapters" (9). He was quick to add that, "I did not act out of hatred for Americans, but out of love for Allah instead."

According to Muhammad and the Qur'an, unbelievers (infidels or *kafir*), are considered an *open enemy* of Allah, Muhammad, Muslims and Islam (**Qur'an 4:101**) and worthy only of *disgraceful chastisement* (humiliation and suffering) from Allah to be carried out by Allah's faithful (**Qur'an 4:102**).

Palestinian Terrorist Rewards. For Islamic jihadists that cannot wait for their reward in paradise, the Palestinian Authority (PA), headed by President Mahmoud Abbas, has a financial reward for them and their families that is funded by foreign monies.

In 2017 alone, according to then Israeli Defense Minister, Avigdor Liberman, Abbas and the PA paid out a whopping $347 million in benefits to Palestinian terrorists and/or their families. To qualify for this "pay-for-slay" program, as it is euphemistically called, one must meet certain standards.

- PA terrorists who only get a 3-5 year sentence for their terroristic deed, receive $580/month, which is equivalent to a normal Palestinian income.
- Terrorists who are to be imprisoned for 20 years or more (likely for murder of Israeli citizens) are rewarded with payments of over $2,900/month for the rest of their lives.
- Arab terrorists with Israeli citizenship get a $145/month bonus.
- Terrorists with wives and/or children receive even more.
- For the one who is sentenced to life in prison for murder, he or she gets much more.
- A terrorist in prison for 30 years or more receives $3,360/month.

According to the disclosure, on average, the PA pays out an estimated $276 million per year to Palestinian terrorists and their families, thus assuring that the onslaught of Palestinian attacks and terror against Israel and its citizens will continue. In just a four year period (2014-2017), the PA paid terrorists $1.12 billion. Where does all this money come from to promote ongoing terror attacks? In part, from Israel's own tax payments to the PA (which its politicians are attempting to cease). However, the majority of financial resources comes from outside foreign aid, including the United States, which is supposed to go toward improving the lives of the Palestinian people (10).

Israel and the United States Take Action. Finally, in early 2019, the Israeli government implemented an approved law from 2018 and withheld $138 million in tax revenue due the PA. The amount was based on the PA's released budget for terrorist payouts in 2018 (11).

In 2018, the United States Congress also took action against the Palestinian Authority and its propensity for rewarding terrorists. In December, 2017, the U.S. House passed the Taylor Force Act (H.R. 1164) and the U.S. Senate overwhelmingly passed it on March 23, 2018. The Act was named after Taylor Force from Lubbock, Texas, a retired military veteran, who was murdered by a PA terrorist in Israel on March 8, 2016. The purpose of the Act was to "prohibit certain FY2018-FY2023 economic support assistance that directly benefits the Palestinian Authority. . . ." The Act's thrust is to withhold such funds until the PA takes steps to cease the violence against American and Israeli citizens; stops the "pay-for-slay" reward system for terrorists; terminates all current reward programs; and the PA publicly denounces all acts of violence and is investigating such.

Also in 2018, the U.S. Congress passed the Anti-Terrorism Clarification Act of 2018 (S.2946), or ATCA. This Act permits U.S. citizens, who are victims of terrorist attacks, to seek and "obtain compensatory and punitive damages" through lawsuits filed in a U.S. district court against "those who commit, aid, or abet terrorist activity." Such suits can also be brought against U.S. designated terrorist groups, such as the PA and the Palestinian embedded Hamas terrorist organization.

As a result of the ATCA, the PA released a statement saying, as of February 1, 2019 (the day the Act took effect), they do not want to receive any more financial aid from the United States (12). PA cabinet leader, Rami Hamdallah, sent a letter to the U.S. State Department requesting all U.S. aid end on January 31 "to avoid any lawsuits against the PA leadership under the Anti-Terrorism Clarification Act   "

Hamdallah stated, "We do not want to receive any money if it will cause us to appear before the courts."

According to the Secretary General of the PLO Executive Committee, Saeb Erekat, the Palestinians will lose $844 million in U.S. aid.

The President Trump administration also decided to stop funding the UN agency for "Palestinian refugees" (UNRWA), at an estimated $350 million/year.

No One Leaves Islam

"Leaving Islam is the ugliest form of unbelief (kufr) and the worst" (*Reliance of the Traveller*, o8.0). According to Islamic sacred law (shari'a) there are 20 "Acts that entail leaving Islam" (*ROT*, o8.7(1)-(20). They include:

1. *To prostrate to an idol. . . .*
2. *To intend to commit unbelief. . . .*
3. *To speak words that imply unbelief. . . .*
4. *To revile Allah or His messenger. . . .*
5. *To deny the existence of Allah. . . .*
6. *To be sarcastic about Allah's name. . . .*
7. *To deny any verse of the Koran. . . .*
8. *To mockingly say, "I don't know what faith is;"*
9. *To reply to someone who says, "There is no power or strength save through Allah:" Your saying "There's no power or strength, etc. won't save you from hunger;"*
10. *For a tyrant....... to reply "I act without the decree of Allah;"*

11. *To say that a Muslim is an unbeliever. . . .*
12. *Refusing to teach someone the Shahada. . . .*
13. *To describe a Muslim or someone who wants to become a Muslim in terms of unbelief. . . .*
14. *To deny the obligatory character of something which is by the consensus of Muslims is part of Islam. .*
15. *To hold that any of Allah's messengers or prophets are liars. . . .*
16. *To revile the religion of Islam. . . .*
17. *To believe that things in themselves or by their own nature have any causal influence independent of the will of Allah;*
18. *To deny the existence of angels or jinn, or the heavens;*
19. *To be sarcastic about any ruling of the Sacred Law;*
20. *Or to deny that Allah intended the Prophet's message . . . to be the religion followed by the entire world.*

Numbers 14 and 20 are noteworthy for non-Muslims. No Muslim wants to be labelled an apostate. In number 14, if a Muslim denies the "obligatory character" of an Islamic law directive that is held to be true by "the consensus of Muslims" as essential to Islam, then they will be declared an apostate. **One of those obligations declared to be essential to Islam is waging jihad or war against all non-believers.** Remember, both the "lesser" (war) and the "greater" (self-reflection) jihad are obligatory for every male Muslim. When the call for the lesser jihad is declared, every Muslim must heed the call or be marked as an infidel worthy of death.

Apostasy as a Criminal Offense. In 2014, the Global Legal Research Center released their survey of *Laws Criminalizing Apostasy in Selected Jurisdictions* of 23 Muslim countries (13). Countries highlighted that treat apostasy as an offense punishable by execution are: Afghanistan, Brunei, Mauritania, Qatar, Saudi Arabia, Sudan, the United Arab Emirates, and Yemen. Some countries, the report noted, also use their apostasy laws to convict someone for crimes other than for leaving the faith. "For example, in Mauritania, Saudi Arabia, Jordan, and Yemen, individuals were charged with apostasy for their writings or comments made on social media."

In a few countries, such as Afghanistan, Brunei, Sudan and Yemen, a person convicted of apostasy can have their sentence overturned if they agree to renounce their new faith and return to Islam. In most Islamic countries, the survey noted, apostasy and its criminalization is a part of the country's penal code. However, in Saudi Arabia, where there is only shari'a law, it is the religious law that dictates the outcome.

In many Islamic countries, however, law or no law, far too often it is the local citizenry that determines the consequences for apostasy, and justice is swift before authorities are able to intervene or are unwilling to risk their lives before an angry mob.

. . . it is obligatory for the caliph (or his representative) to ask him [the apostate] *to repent and return to Islam. If he does, it is accepted from him, but if he refuses, he is immediately killed.* Reliance of the Traveller, o8.2

There is no indemnity for killing an apostate (or any expiration, since it is killing someone who deserves to die). Reliance of the Traveller, o8.4

In a 2008 apostasy trial in Egypt, the judge ruled against a man who converted to Christianity and wanted that reflected on his Egyptian identification card. A reasonable request. However, the judge ruled that the man's conversion violated Egyptian law. In doing so, the judge cited Article II of the Egyptian constitution that made Islamic law the "source" of all Egyptian secular law. The judge also concluded, since Islam is the "final" and "most complete" religion, its followers already experience freedom of religion, and to reject it for an inferior religion like Judaism or Christianity, is unacceptable (14).

Does Allah Play a Role in Apostasy? One of many conflicts in Islam is that Allah leads people into unbelief (**Qur'an 4:88**), then he commands that those that disbelieve must be killed (**Qur'an 4:89**).

"What is the matter with you, then," Muhammad exclaimed, "that you have become two parties about the hypocrites, while Allah has made them return (to unbelief) for what they have earned? Do you wish to guide him whom Allah causes to err? And whomsoever Allah causes to err, you shall by no means find a way for him.

"They desire that you should disbelieve as they have disbelieved, so that you might be (all) alike; therefore take not from among them friends until they fly [flee] (their homes) in Allah's way; but if they turn back [to enmity], then seize them and kill them wherever you find them, and take not from among them a friend or a helper" (**Qur'an 4:88-89**).

Another Qur'anic verse (cited previously), that Muslims like to quote, to ignorant infidels, in order to portray Islam as an all-accepting religion, is **Qur'an 2:256**, which states: "There is no compulsion in religion. . ."

Now, here is another Islamic puzzle. Earlier, in the same surah, Muhammad, relaying Allah's message, proclaims, "And fight with them [the unbeliever] until there is no persecution, and religion should be only for Allah, but if they desist, then there should be no hostility except against the oppressors" (**Qur'an 2:193**).

351

Of course, there is no true mystery here once a person understands the true character of Allah and Islam. The true and clear message of Islam—despite the vehement protestations of Muslims everywhere—is that a non-Muslim or *kafir* can believe what he or she wants, but you will be persecuted for your belief; made to convert to Islam or die.

In black and white contrast, Jesus taught His disciples that if one believer left the fold and became spiritually lost, they were to go after him and rescue him and bring him back into the kingdom of God—but not by force.

"What do you think?" Jesus asked His disciples. "If a man owns a hundred sheep, and one of them wanders away, will he not leave the ninety-nine on the hills and go to look for the one that wandered off? And if he finds it, I tell you the truth, he is happier about that one sheep than about the ninety-nine that did not wander off. In the same way your Father in heaven is not willing that any of these little ones should be lost" (**Matthew 18:12-14**). Instead of going after someone who has left the faith in an effort to kill them, Jesus recommended that those who leave should be won back with care and compassion.

There are many examples in the hadith on how Muslims are to deal with apostates. Here is one such instruction.

"Narrated 'Ikrima: Some Zanadiqa (atheists) were brought to 'Ali and he burnt them. The news of this event, reached Ibn 'Abbas who said, 'If I had been in his place, I would not have burnt them, as Allah's Apostle forbade it, saying, *Do not punish anybody with Allah's punishment (fire)*. I would have killed them according to the statement of Allah's Apostle, *Whoever changed his Islamic religion, then kill him*'" (**hadith 9:84:57**).

The following verse 58 also recorded the killing of a Jew who had converted to Islam and then converted back to Judaism, saying, "This is the judgment of Allah and His Apostle."

A few verses later, the fate of an apostate is once again reaffirmed. ". . . No doubt I heard Allah's Apostle saying, 'During the last days there will appear some young foolish people who will say the best words but their faith will not go beyond their throats (i.e. they will have no faith) and will go out from (leave) their religion as an arrow goes out of the game. So, where-ever you find them, kill them, for whoever kills them shall have reward on the Day of Resurrection'" (**hadith 9:84:64**).

In the preceding hadith, not only is the Muslim to kill the apostate, but he will receive a special reward on the Day of Resurrection.

"Surely," Muhammad reaffirmed, "those who disbelieve and die while they are disbelievers, these it is on whom is the curse of Allah and the angels and men all" (**Qur'an 2:161**).

According to Silas, a frequent contributor to the web site, Answering-Islam, "Muslims living in the Mideast have no problem with the concept of putting apostates to death. But to Muslims living in the West it is an embarrassing Islamic edict   A close examination of the Quran, Hadith, and Sirat [Sirah or written stories of Muhammad] will show that indeed, the punishment for leaving Islam, either under an Islamic government, or not, was execution" (15).

There are thousands of modern day martyrs who have been killed because they turned away from Islam and embraced Christianity. In Somalia, a country that is nearly 100 percent Sunni Muslim, Ali Mustaf Maka'il, a 22-year old college student, was shot in the back and killed on September 7, 2006, shortly after he converted to Christianity. He had harmed no one (16).

In today's world, however, the killing of apostates is not limited to Muslim countries. In Australia, for instance, a Muslim medical doctor stabbed his wife to death because their 17-year old daughter became a Christian (17). Why did he kill his wife and not his daughter? It is because, in the Muslim household, it is the wife who is responsible for the guidance and welfare of the daughters. These are only two of the thousands of "honor killings" that occur throughout the Muslim world every year in order to take revenge on a Muslim or their family when they choose to leave Islam.

"O Prophet! Strive hard against the unbelievers [deniers of the truth] and the hypocrites [those who pretend religious devotion to Allah] and be unyielding to them;" Allah revealed to Muhammad, "and [if they do not repent] their abode is hell, and evil is the destination. They [the hypocrites] swear by Allah that they did not speak [anything wrong], and certainly they did speak [denying the truth], the word of unbelief, and disbelieved after their [surrender to] Islam, and they had determined upon what they have not been able to effect, and they did not find fault [with the Faith] except because Allah and His Apostle enriched them out of His grace; therefore if they repent, it will be good for them; and if they turn back, Allah will chastise them with a painful chastisement [great suffering] in this world and the hereafter, and they shall not have in the land any guardian or a helper [to give them comfort]" (**Qur'an 9:73, 74**).

Remember, in **hadith 9:83:17** previously cited in this chapter, that Muhammad, in the name of Allah, granted that a Muslim or Muslims may take the life of one who has murdered someone, committed adultery or has left the faith. "He who disbelieves in Allah after having believed," Muhammad declared, "not he who is compelled while his heart is at rest on account of faith, but he who opens (his) breast to disbelief – on these is the wrath of Allah, and they shall have a grievous chastisement (**Qur'an 16:106**)." Here, a crafty distinction is presented. A Muslim can deny his faith without being an apostate if he feels compelled to do so before his enemy, while at the same time in his heart he confesses Allah. However, a Muslim who truly turns from Allah is to be killed.

Chapter Conclusion

There are, clearly, two divergent methods of dealing with infidels or unbelievers, and apostates or those that leave the faith of Islam or Christianity. In Islam, infidels and apostates cannot be tolerated and must be eliminated for the sake of Allah. The Qur'an and the teachings of Muhammad are quite clear on this issue. There are no modifications or exceptions – infidels and apostates are to be killed if they refuse to convert or re-convert to Islam. Non-believers, not apostates, can escape the death penalty (on occasion) if they submit to paying the oppressive poll tax or *jizya*.

Christians, however, are called to reach out to the unbeliever, not persecute them. If a Christian leaves the faith, he or she is free to do so, but Jesus advised His disciples to make an effort to rescue the lost one who has strayed from the faith, and rejoice with the Father in heaven at the return of one of His children.

Although the God of the Bible identifies the Jews as His chosen people, Allah, the god of the Qur'an repeatedly calls upon his followers to persecute the Jews and to seek them out and kill them. Such Jew hatred has given rise once again to a wave of worldwide anti-Semitism not seen since the days of Hitler.

Islam is all about oppressing people, both Muslims and non-Muslims. Christianity is all about setting the captives free to experience the loving, merciful true God of all creation. While slavery in the Christian world was finally put to rest over 150 years ago, slavery in parts of the Muslim world still exist. Sexual slavery and child exploitation in particular are rampant throughout many Islamic societies. In Western societies the killing of the innocent (except in matters of abortion) is a punishable offense, in Islam it is often a celebrated reality.

References.

1. Al-Munajjid, Muhammad. *The True Nature of the Enmity Between the Muslims and the Jews*. Source: http://www.alminbar.com/khutbaheng/9022.htm (accessed December 3, 2006).
2. *Obsession: Radical Islam's War Against the West* (Documentary). Trinity Home Entertainment, 2007.
3. *Saudi Government Daily: Jews Use Teenagers' Blood for 'Purim' Pastries*. The Middle East Media Research Institute, *Special Dispatch Series – No. 354*, March 13, 2002. Source: https://www.memri.org/reports/saudi-government-daily-jews-use-teenagers-blood-purim-pastries (accessed May 23, 2007).

4. *UK teacher who wrote 'of course we hate Jews' found not anti-Semitic.* The Times of Israel, September 5, 2018. Source: https://www. timesofisrael.com/uk-teacher-who-wrote-of-course-we-hate-jews-found-not-anti-semitic/

5. *Antisemitism rises in Canada, Jews remain most targeted minority group.* Jerusalem Post, December 2, 2018. Source: https://www.jpost. com/Diaspora/ Antisemitism-rises-in-Canada-Jews-remain-most-targeted-minority-group-573302

6. Koren, Daniel and Ran Ukashi. *SIGN OUR PETITION: Demand Islamic Group Remove Hateful Speakers from Toronto Conference.* B'nai Brith Canada, September 26, 2018. Source: https://www. bnaibrith.ca/sign_our_petition_demand_islamic_group_remove_hateful _speakers_from_toronto_conference

7. *Uniform Crime Report, Hate Crime Statistics 2017.* U.S. Department of Justice, Fall, 2018. Source: https://ucr.fbi.gov/hate-crime/2017/topic-pages/incidents-and-offenses.pdf

8. *2016 Hate Cries Statistics.* U.S. Department of Justice. Source: https://ucr.fbi.gov/hate-crime/2016/topic-pages/victims

9. *Muslim: I Attacked 'Out of Love for Allah.'* WorldNetDaily.com, March 15, 2006. Source: http://www.worldnetdaily.com/news/article.asp? ARTICLE_ID=49276 (accessed March 16, 2006).

10. Danan, Deborah. *Palestinian Authority Paid Terrorists and Their Families Nearly $350 Million in 2017.* Breitbart, January 10, 2018. Source: http://www.breitbart.com/jerusalem/2018/01/10/ palestinian-authority-forked-out-close-to-350-million-in-terrorist-salaries-in-2017/

11. *Terror stipends cost Palestinians $138m in withheld tax revenues.* World Israel News, February 17, 2019. Source: https://worldisraelnews.com/terror-stipends-cost-palestinians-138m-in-withheld-tax-revenues/?utm

12. Halevi, Dalit. *'We don't want the US money.'* Arutz Sheva 7, January 1, 2019. Source: http://www.israelnationalnews.com/News/News. aspx/258443

13. Goitom, Hanibal. *Laws Criminalizing Apostasy in Selected Jurisdictions.* Global Legal Research Center, The Law Library of Congress, May, 2014. Source: https://www.loc.gov/law/help/ apostasy/index.php (accessed November 9, 2018).

14. *'No one leaves Islam,' judge rules.* WorldNetDaily, February 1, 2008. Source: http://www.worldnetdaily.com/index.php?pageId=45832

15. Silas, *The Punishment for Apostasy from Islam.* Source: http://answering-islam.org. uk/Silas/apostasy.htm. Accessed February 7, 2007.

16. Ireland, Michael. *Convert from Islam to Christianity Killed.* WorldNetDaily, September 16, 2006. Source: http://www.worldnetdaily.com/news/ article.asp?ARTICLE_ID= 52004 (accessed September 16, 2006).

17. *Muslim Stabs Wife When Daughter Becomes Christian.* WorldNetDaily, October 14, 2006. Source: http://www.worldnetdaily.com/news/ article.asp?ARTICLE_ID= 52437 (accessed October 14, 2006).

Chapter 14

Islam in America

For God has not given us a spirit of fear, but of power and of love and of a sound mind.
2 Timothy 1:7 (NKJV)

*W*hile Muslims work 24/7 for their cause, i.e., to infiltrate our schools, our law enforcement agencies, our healthcare system, and run for an office with the help of our Democrats, who provide them with the necessary tools, regrettably, only a fraction of Americans understands [sic] the real threat. Most Americans are completely asleep, wrote Amil Imani in September 2018 (1).

Ten years earlier, on September 25, 2008, Geert Wilders, a Dutch politician and founder of the Netherlands' Party of Freedom, gave a speech in New York City at the invitation of the Hudson Institute, a politically conservative think tank headquartered in Washington, DC. Wilders is an outspoken critic of Islam and the Islamization of Europe, and often maligned as an Islamophobe. However, his observations and concerns about Europe and America are worth heeding.

Toward the beginning of his speech, he had this warning:

> *I come to America with a mission. All is not well in the old world. There is a tremendous danger looming, and it is very difficult to be optimistic. We might be in the final stages of the Islamization of Europe. This not only is a clear and present danger to the future of Europe itself, it is a threat to America and the sheer survival of the West. The danger I see looming is the scenario of America as the last man standing. The United States as the last bastion of Western civilization, facing an Islamic Europe. In a generation or two, the US will ask itself: who lost Europe? Patriots from around Europe risk their lives every day to prevent precisely this scenario form becoming a reality (2).*

The Islamic ideology and its Muslim adherents have very effectively infiltrated just about every aspect of American life, as it has throughout much of Europe—culture, government and politics, military, education, law enforcement, religious thought, the media, and constitutional law. Nothing has been left untouched or without influence. Wilders' warning has been fleshed out in real terms throughout Western civilization.

Ominous Signs? Getting an accurate measurement of the number of mosques in the United States is as difficult as an accurate tally on America's Muslim population. In 2000, there were an estimated 1,209

356

mosques in the United States. By 2010, the number had grown to 2,106, for a 74 percent increase (3).

In 2018, the United States of America Mosque Directory (http://www.mosquemasjids.com) listed 2,182 mosques. States with over 100 mosques included California (246), Florida (121), Illinois (112), New Jersey (109), New York (258) and Texas (168). However, this website, the author noticed, did not list all the mosques in the U.S. In a brief review, in cities and towns where it is known that mosques exist, the website did not list them. In 2015, on a website that no longer exists, it was reported that there were 3,186 mosques in the U.S. The only thing that is reasonably certain, wherever there is a Muslim population, there is likely a mosque nearby.

While large mosques in urban areas are easily identified, mosques in smaller communities may be in former residences or commercial buildings and overlooked. Large metro areas, like New York City with 192 mosques and Chicago with 90 mosques, represent the largest number of mosques. However, in 2000, suburban mosques only represented 16 percent of the total mosques in the U.S., but by 2010, they represented 28 percent. In 2010, 76 percent of the mosques did not exist in 1980 (4).

At the same time that the Muslim population and Islamic influence is growing in the United States, there are numerous signs that the Christian community is waning. In March, 2016, Pew Research Center released a report on, *10 demographic trends that are shaping the U.S. and the world* (5). Among the findings was the noted decline in those who identified with a Christian expression of faith, from 2007 to 2014.

Changing religious affiliation:	2007	2014
Evangelical	26.3%	25.4%
Catholic	23.9%	20.8%
Mainline Protestant	18.1%	14.7%
Unaffiliated	16.1%	22.8%
Non-Christian faiths	4.7%	5.9%

While adherence to Christian expressions is declining, those who are unaffiliated or adhere to non-Christian beliefs are increasing. In addition, the report disclosed that the world population is anticipated to shift in favor of Muslims from 2010 to 2050. In 2010, the world Christian population was estimated at 2.17 billion or 31.4 percent of the total world population. In the same year, the Muslim population was estimated to be 1.6 billion or 23.2 percent. However, in 2050, while the Christian population in the world is expected to grow by 34.6 percent to 2.92 billion, it will still only be 31.4 percent of the total population. During the same period, the Muslim population is expected to grow by 72.5 percent to 2.76 billion or 29.7 percent of the total world population.

As an indication of this decline of Christianity in America, it has been estimated that between 2006 and 2012, 30,000 church congregations closed their doors. However, this is not the complete picture. During the same period, there was an explosion in growth of non-denominational churches, from 79,000 in 2006 to 84,000 in 2012. From 1990 to 2008, the number of Christians worshipping at non-denominational churches grew from 194,000 to 8 million (6). From 2006 to 2012, non-Christian places of worship doubled, from 13,000 to 26,000.

Be sure you know the condition of your flocks, give careful attention to your herds;
Proverbs 27:23

In April, 2016, the Barna Group published a survey in which was reported a "silent migration" from the Christian church. They estimated that 3,500 people leave the church every day. In 2015, it was predicted that 1.2 million would leave the church and 10,000 churches would close for good. The main reason people leave, Barna noted, was that worshippers no longer felt connected to their church—a trend that has been going on for several decades. The real worrisome statistic—80 percent of 14-33 year olds said that church was no longer important to them.

"Millennials don't look for a church facility that caters to the whims of pop culture. They want a community that calls them to deeper meaning," reported Barna Group researcher, Clint Jenkin (7).

Muslims in America. In 2017 and 2018, Pew Research Center released two polls that provide some interesting insights into America's Muslim population. The 2017 poll took the pulse on how non-Muslim Americans viewed Muslims. On the issue of whether the Islamic religion is more likely than others to incite violence among its followers, 70 percent of Republicans said, yes, in 2016 (up from 33% in 2002). Among Democrats, only 26 percent said, yes (up from 22% in 2002). Those who are politically independent, went from 26 percent in 2002 to 39 percent in 2016.

In the same poll, on the issue of Islam conflicting with democracy, 44 percent agreed that it did, while 46 percent said it did not. Those who agreed that there was a conflict were lowest among those age 18-29, college graduates (38% each), and Democrats (30%). For those who believed there was a conflict, it was highest among those aged 50-64 (52%), high school educated (49%) and Republicans (65%). The 2017 Pew poll also showed that the older one is, the more likely to believe that

Islam encourages violence: age 18-29 (27%), 30-49 (41%), 50-64 (45%) and 65+ (50%) (8).

In the 2018 survey, Pew asked Muslims, both American born and immigrant, about their experience in America. Of the Muslims surveyed, 42 percent were born in America. The survey results illustrated that there may not be as many "hard core" Muslims in America as one might believe. Among both U.S. born and immigrant Muslims, only 65 percent said their religion was important to them. Additional poll results are below (9).

% of U.S. Muslims:	U.S. Born/Immigrant
Religion important	65/65%
Pray 5x/day	39/44
Fast during Ramadan	79/80
Attend mosque weekly	40/45
Eat halal food	50/47
Wear head covering	46/40
Satisfied with life in America	17/38
Difficult to be Muslim in America	62/40
Americans are friendly	30/73

Overall, the results would appear to indicate that many Muslims in America are nominal or cultural Muslims and not strict adherents to their faith. This observation, on the surface, would appear to bode well for those desiring to engage Muslims in a conversation about the saving grace of Jesus Christ.

The Rise of Anti-Semitism in America

In just the first two months of 2017, there were 95 anti-Semitic attacks or threats against Jewish community centers and day schools, reported Seth Frantzman, writing for *The Algemeiner*. During the Obama administration there were a reported 84 anti-Semitic incidents per month (10). That would be over one thousand in a year. According to FBI data cited, from 2009 to 2015, there were over 7,000 anti-Jew incidents, but no arrests were made. Under Obama, the number of anti-Semitic assaults almost doubled. Despite the thousands of anti-Semitic incidents during that seven year period, the media was mostly silent, noted Frantzman.

Any attacks, whether anti-Semitic or anti-Muslim, are unacceptable in a country that honors free speech and freedom of religion. Offenses against Jews, Muslims or anyone else because of religious beliefs must be duly and equally reported and offenders equally charged and prosecuted.

A review of FBI data on hate crimes for 2016 and 2017, indicated that anti-Muslim hate crimes dropped by 11 percent, but anti-Semitic hate crimes dramatically increased 37 percent from FY2016 to FY2017 (11, 12). From FY2016 through FY2017, religious hate crime against Muslims dropped from 24.5 percent of the total to 18.7 percent. However, hate crimes against Jews increased from 54.4 percent to 58.7 percent of the total religious-based hate crimes. Total number of victims of all types of hate crime rose 11.5 percent, from 7,615 victims in FY2016 to 8,493 in FY 2017.

In New York City, where over one million of America's estimated 5.3 million Jews live, the NYC Police Department reported a significant increase in anti-Semitic hate crimes in 2018. The NYPD logged 183 anti-Semitic crimes in 2018, a jump of 22 percent from 2017 and an increase of 38.6 percent from 2016 (13).

The rise of anti-Semitism should be a surprise when one considers the massive amounts of money that finds its way into America's universities from Muslim countries (more on this to follow). The kingdom-nation of Qatar, for instance, a known sponsor of Islamic terror (notably, Hamas and ISIS), spends millions buying up Western real estate, including Hollywood's Miramax Studios. Not without purpose, the Al Thani dynasty, also invests heavily in America's K-12 educational system (14).

In Newton, Massachusetts, for example, parents of high school students have complained for six years about the anti-Semitic curriculum being used by the school's teachers. Although the Newton Superintendent of Schools promised to purge the offensive materials, nothing has happened. Teachers typically attend a five-day summer training course on, "the dynamics of the Middle East," sponsored by a company called Primary Source. It turns out that the company is supported by four foundations, including the Qatar Foundation International, which is an "investment" outreach of Qatar's ruling Al Thani family. Since 2009, the AL Thani's have given over $30 million to American K-12 schools, as well as an unknown amount to teacher training companies like Primary Source (15).

Despite the fact that the materials used by Primary Source are heavily infused with Islamic, anti-Jew bias, no such disclosure or disclaimer is provided on the materials. More on how Islam is being presented in America's schools and universities will be presented in, *Teaching Islam in America's Schools & Universities*, later in this chapter.

The National Director of the Anti-Defamation League (ADL), Jonathan Greenblatt, told The Jerusalem Post in an October, 2018 interview, that he was greatly concerned that anti-Semitism was becoming "normalized" in the United States. He cited ADL statistics of a 34 percent increase in anti-Semitic incidents from 2016 to 2017, with a 57 percent jump in 2017 over the previous year—the greatest single-year increase since ADL started tracking anti-Semitic events in 1979 (16).

Islamophobia—Islam's Diversionary Tactic

Islamophobia—the New "Racism." At the prestigious Georgetown University, the oldest Catholic and Jesuit college/university in America, founded in 1789, there is a full-fledged offering on Islamophobia. The University, where it costs over $71,000 per year in tuition, room & board and other expenses (2017/18 school year) is well known for its Social Sciences and Multi/Interdisciplinary Studies.

It offers an extensive course for unsuspecting students on "Islamophobia is Racism." Islam, of course, is not a race but, nevertheless, the course introduction makes it clear that anti-Islam sentiments are equal to the anti-Black horrors of America's past. Muslims have never thought of Islam as a race, until American apologists convinced them of it. The key to the course's slant is in its Preface.

> *This syllabus **reframes** "Islamophobia" as "anti-Muslim **racism**" to more accurately reflect the intersection of race and religion   a focus on anti-Muslim racism is connected to an analysis of history and forms of dominance—from white supremacy, slavery and settler colonialism, to multiculturalism and security logics of war and imperialism—that produce various forms of racial exclusion as well as incorporation into racist structures* (17; author's emphasis).

Reframing: A psychological technique used to change the direction of the discussion on a topic to suit the presenter's way of looking at things.

Obviously, there is no attempt to present alternate viewpoints, but rather to assign blame for Islam's deficiencies to racism, white supremacy, slavery, colonialism, multiculturalism, war and imperialism—not surprisingly, the same rhetoric and excuses that Islamists have been using for centuries to explain away their barbaric behavior and conquests—and the same excuses former President Obama used during his Middle East presentations abroad throughout his presidency.

More on the subject of Islam in America's educational system will be presented in, *Teaching Islam in America's Schools & Universities*, later in this chapter.

In September 2017, the left-leaning Haas Institute, on the campus of the University of California, Berkeley, released a report on what was termed the "anti-Sharia movement" in the United States. In order to illustrate the premise of an anti-Muslim wave across the country, Haas documented the 216 anti-Sharia laws introduced into state legislatures from 2000 to 2016. They tried to tie the genuine concern, of state citizens, of using Muslim shari'a law to settle issues outside the U.S. Constitution to "rising anti-Muslim sentiment, discrimination, securitization and acts of violence against Muslims and those perceived to be Muslim. . . ." Of the 216 bills presented, only 20 were enacted in various states. The majority of the bills (177) had more to do with preventing foreign laws from superseding U.S. law and not strictly shari'a.

Despite that realization, Haas reported, "As a result of these organized Islamophobia efforts, the anti-Sharia legislation movement has been established, and continues to expand, by an unfounded fear of 'creeping Sharia,' proliferated by fabrications, lies, and intentionally misconstrued information surrounding Muslims in the United States" (18).

The terms of "Islamophobia" and "Islamophobe" started cropping up in the latter part of the 20th century and were readily adopted by the political left, Islamic apologists and Muslims, as a way to shut down any criticism or reasonable debate about Islam. In essence, the cry of "Islamophobia" has become the most valuable weapon of both Muslims and non-Muslims, in their defense of Islam without having to address any of the legitimate concerns of citizens in the West.

Britain's Sara Khan, who created the Commission for Countering Extremism, told the British Daily Mail on September 16, 2018, [Islamists] "and their sympathisers weaponise [sic] Islamophobia in an attempt to shut down legitimate debate about Islamic extremism while undermining the general struggle against anti-Muslim hatred" (19). Khan noted that the same groups knowingly and purposely "use and abuse" civil and human rights laws of the West to further their Islamic agenda. Any time you can demean, demonize or accuse your adversary of "racism," of "Islamophobia," or being an "Islamophobe" or "anti-Muslim," you can clamp down on any opposition to your own hateful rhetoric and actions. That is the primary weapon of Islam worldwide, including within the United Nations, where UN member Muslim countries have been trying to stifle any debate about Islam for decades. From a Western mindset, if one cannot handle debate and criticism about one's ideology and beliefs, then there must be something wrong about the ideology that you do not want fully exposed.

On September 9, 2016, two days before the 15th anniversary of America's September 11 Islamists' attack, Public Radio International (PRI.org) published a decidedly misleading article, *Islamophobia is on the rise in the US. But so is Islam.* The data used in the article does not support the claim of the title. The chart used by PRI shows a spike in anti-Muslim incidents, right after 9/11, to just under 500, but anti-Muslim incidents dropped to around 150 the next year. Between 2003 and 2013, the number of anti-Muslim incidents in the U.S. fluctuated between approximately 100-150 per year, with 2014 (the last year the PRI chart illustrated) at about 150 such events (20).

The FY2017 FBI statistics on Hate Crimes reported 314 anti-Muslim incidents, which were significantly below the 975 reported anti-Semitic incidents (21).

Hate Speech in U.S. Mosques

America Forewarned. In 2005, the Center for Religious Freedom of Freedom House in Washington, DC, published an 89-page investigative report, *Saudi Publications on Hate Ideology Invade American Mosques* (22).

Among the findings was this conclusion: "Not only does the government of Saudi Arabia not have a right—under the First Amendment or any other legal document—to spread hate ideology within U.S. borders, it is committing a human rights violation by doing so."

In addition, the Center for Religious Freedom found these egregious offenses against the safety and security of American citizens:

- *Various Saudi government publications . . . assert that it is a religious obligation for Muslims to hate Christians and Jews and warn against imitating, befriending, or helping them in any way, or taking part in their festivities and celebrations;*
- *The documents promote contempt for the United States because it is ruled by legislated civil law rather than by totalitarian Wahhabi-style Islamic law. They condemn democracy as un-Islamic;*
- *The documents stress that when Muslims are in the lands of the unbelievers, they must behave as if on a mission behind enemy lines. Either they are there to acquire new knowledge and make money to be later employed in the jihad against the infidels, or they are there to proselytize the infidels until at least some convert to Islam.*
- *One insidious aspect of the Saudi propaganda examined is its aim to replace traditional and moderate interpretations of Islam with extremist Wahhabism, the officially-established religion of Saudi Arabia. . . . other Muslims . . . are condemned as infidels.*
- *Sufi and Shiite Muslims are viciously condemned;*
- *For a Muslim who fails to uphold the Saudi Wahhabi sect's sexual mores . . . "it would be lawful for Muslims to spill his blood and to take his money;"*

- *. . . those who convert out of Islam, the Saudi Ministry of Islamic Affairs explicitly asserts, they "should be killed;"*
- *Saudi textbooks and other publications in the collection, propagate a Nazi-like hatred for Jews, treat the forged Protocols of the Elders of Zion as historical fact, and avow that the Muslim's duty is to eliminate the state of Israel;*
- *Regarding women, the Saudi publications instruct that they should be veiled, segregated from men and barred from certain employment and roles.*

James Woolsey, Jr., former head of the CIA (Central Intelligence Agency) and chairman of the board at Freedom House, commented on the Saudi publications discovered: [Such publications that] "advocate an ideology of hatred have no place in a nation founded on religious freedom and toleration."

The report also concluded that the Saudi government publications indicate a "totalitarian ideology of hatred that can incite to violence." Of the publications acquired, 90 percent were in Arabic and were translated by two independent translators.

Partly as a result of this report and other revelations from around the world of the nefarious activities of the Saudis, Rep. Dave Brat (R-VA-7) sponsored and introduced H.R. 5824 on July 14, 2016, under the title, "Religious FIRE Act" (FIRE = Freedom International Reciprocity Enhancement). On August 11, 2016, the bill was referred to the "Subcommittee on Crime, Terrorism, Homeland Security, and Investigations" and has not resurfaced since. The purpose of the bill:

> *This bill prohibits a foreign national of a country that limits the free exercise of religion in that country from making any expenditure in the United States promoting a religion.*
> *An asset consisting of such an expenditure or the proceeds of such an expenditure is subject to U.S. forfeiture.*

In 2016, when the bill was introduced, Bob Goodlatte (R-VA-6) was chairman of the Subcommittee, and in 2019, Jerrold Nadler (D-NY-10) took over as chairman. It is not likely that the Religious FIRE Act will see the light of day in the near future.

"Muslims are infatuated with building as many mosques as possible and the Saudis are just as happy to finance them all," wrote Amil Imani in December, 2018. Muslims love to build mosques where churches are or used to be, as a symbol of their victory over the (often clueless) infidels. ". . . as long as there are Muslims who believe that the entire world rightfully belongs to them and all non-Muslims are usurper infidels, they will do everything they can to claim the planet for Allah and cleanse it of unbelievers," Imani claimed (23).

In April, 2016, Ralph Peters, retired U.S. Army Lt. Col. and former Fox News strategic analyst, wrote a lengthy piece for the *New York Post* on the dangers of the Saudi Arabian government's unfettered and undeterred establishment of its hateful brand of Wahhabi Islam throughout America.

"Iran is our external enemy of the moment. Saudi Arabia is our enduring internal enemy, already within our borders and permitted to poison American Muslims with its Wahhabi cult," wrote Peters.

"Iran humiliates our sailors, but the Saudis are the spiritual jailers of hundreds of millions of Muslims, committed to intolerance, barbarity and preventing Muslims from joining the modern world. And we help," he continued. Peters went on to cite, that an estimated 80 percent of American mosques are built or partially funded by the Saudis. (This author has not been able to verify the source of that statistic, although it is often cited by others).

The Saudi goal is clear, Peters noted, they do not want Muslims assimilating into American or Western culture, but rather to adhere to their brand of violent, jihad-producing Islam.

"The Saudis build Muslims mosques and madrassas but not hospitals and universities," Peters wrote.

Peters also took the opportunity to slam the stupidity of the U.S. government and its leaders. "The basic fact our policy-makers need to grasp about the Saudis is that they couldn't care less about the welfare of flesh-and-blood Muslims (they refuse to take in Syrian refugees but demand Europe do so). What the Saudis care about is Islam in the abstract. Countless Muslims can suffer to keep the faith pure. . . .

"But our real problem is here and now, in the United States. Consider how idiotic we've been, allowing Saudis to fund hate mosques and madrassas, to provide Jew-baiting texts and to do their best to bully American Muslims into conformity with their misogynistic, 500-lashes worldview. Our leaders and legislators have betrayed our fellow citizens who happen to be Muslim, making it more difficult for them to integrate fully into our society" (24).

U.S. Mosques—Seeds of Terror. Probably every week throughout America, imams or Islamic scholars preach Islamic sermons of hate and violence, only the general public knows nothing about it. If it was not for the Middle East Media Research Institute (MEMRI) in Washington, DC, no one might know. MEMRI makes it their job to capture the recorded sermons and diatribes and translate the Arabic or Farsi into English, in an effort to disclose what is really being preached among America's Muslims.

Paul Sperry, a former Hoover Institute media fellow and author of the bestselling book, *Infiltration: How Muslim Spies and Subversives*

Have Penetrated Washington (2005), penned in January 2018, "Muslim clerics are threatening the lives of Jews from the pulpits of American mosques, and they are doing it with virtual impunity, say former US law-enforcement officials who worry that the rhetoric could lead to violent attacks."

In the last six months of 2017, he noted, "at least five prominent US imams have been caught on tape preaching violence against Jews in sermons at mosques across America." Despite such hate speech, Muslim preachers are rarely, if ever, arrested, charged and prosecuted. If Christians were caught preaching such hate against Muslims, they would be arrested and prosecuted to the fullest extent of the law.

Some of the incidents Sperry listed:

- Houston imam, Raed Saleh Al-Rousan, who advocated for Muslims to "fight the Jews." His lecture was translated by MEMRI.
- On the same day that Al-Rousan preached,, Imam Abdullah Khadra, of Raleigh, NC, cited the Jew-killing hadith, claiming that Muhammad "gave us the glad tidings that we will fight those Jews until the rocks and the trees will speak: 'Oh Muslim, this is a Jew behind me.'" The sermon was again translated by MEMRI.
- In December, 2017, Sheikh Ramadan Elsabagh, Garland, Texas, posted his hateful anti-Jew prayer on Facebook: "Oh Allah, destroy the Zionists and their allies." His proclamation was translated by Investigative Project on Terrorism.
- In New Jersey, December 8, 2017, Imam Aymen Elkasaby, called his fellow Muslims to "martyrdom" in order to take revenge on the "apes and pigs" (Jews). Elkasaby then went on and prayed for Allah to annihilate the Jews.
- In July, 2017, Imam Ammar Shahin, of the Davis Islamic Center in Northern California, railed against the filthy Jews and called for their extermination.

"Terror experts," Sperry wrote, "say such hateful rhetoric is more common in US mosques than generally understood, and they blame the Obama administration's gutting of mosque surveillance programs for the growing belligerence. The NYPD [New York Police Department] also ended its surveillance program in 2014 following complaints by Muslim groups" (25).

Mid-2011, the *Perspectives on Terrorism* journal of the Terrorism Research Initiative and the Center for Terrorism and Security Studies, published a survey of 100 U.S. mosques to see how closely they adhered to shari'a, particularly as it advocated violence against non-believers. The results showed that 51 percent of the mosques had publications that "severely" promoted violence; 30 percent "moderately" called for violence, and only 19 percent had no publications on violence. Shari'a-compliant mosques were more likely to harbor publications on violence against infidels. However, in 84.5 percent of the mosques, "the imam recommended studying violence-positive texts." Also, 58 percent of the mosques had guest imams known to preach violent jihad.

> *The debate over the connection between Islam and its legal doctrine and system known as Sharia on the one hand and terrorism committed in the name of Islam on the other rages on among counter terrorism professionals, academics, policy experts, theologians, and politicians. Much of this debate centers on the evidence that the perpetrators of violence in the name of Islam source the moral, theological, and legal motivations and justifications for their actions in Sharia. Much of the opposition to this focus on Sharia centers on the argument that Sharia is and has been historically malleable and exploited for good and bad causes* (26).

In July, 2015, Paul Sperry reported that the North America Islamic Trust (NAIT) in Oak Brook, Illinois, held the title to 300-plus mosques in the United States and financed 500-plus Islamic centers in America (27).

America's Home Grown Islamic Terrorists

***An Explanatory Memorandum* of the Muslim Brotherhood.** Discovering the Muslim Brotherhood's *An Explanatory Memorandum*— the Muslim Brotherhood's plan to infiltrate and overtake America—can only be the result of God's intervention. On a hot, sultry day, in August, 2004, a vigilant Maryland Transportation Authority police officer noticed a woman videotaping the support beams of the Chesapeake Bay Bridge near a parked SUV. She stood out because of her traditional Islamic garments. The officer wisely decided to make a traffic stop and discovered that the woman's husband at the wheel was Ismail Selim Elbarasse of Annandale, Virginia. Mr. Elbarasse was detained for an "outstanding material witness warrant" for a case involving the Hamas terrorist group. A former board member of the Islamic Association for Palestine and a Hamas activist, Mr. Elbarasse was definitely a person of interest.

Shortly after this incident, the Washington, DC office of the FBI decided to raid Elbarasse's residence and discovered a hidden sub-basement that contained the archives of the Muslim Brotherhood of North America and the *Memorandum* (28). Some of the pertinent aspects of the

Memorandum are presented in the following excerpts. A complete copy of *An Explanatory Memorandum* is in the full *Compendium* version of this work.

> *One: The Memorandum is derived from:*
> *1 - The general strategic goal of the Group in America which was approved by the Shura Council and the Organizational Conference for the year* [1987] *is "Enablement of Islam in North America, meaning: establishing an effective and a stable Islamic Movement led by the Muslim Brotherhood which adopts Muslims' causes domestically and globally, and which works to expand the observant Muslim base, aims at unifying and directing Muslims' efforts, presents Islam as a civilization alternative, and supports the global Islamic State wherever it is."*
>
> *Two: An Introduction to the Explanatory Memorandum:*
> *"elements" of the general strategic goal . . .*
> *[l- Establishing an effective and stable Islamic Movement led by the Muslim Brotherhood.*
> *2- Adopting Muslims' causes domestically and globally.*
> *3- Expanding the observant Muslim base.*
> *4- Unifying and directing Muslims' efforts.*
> *5- Presenting Islam as a civilization alternative*
> *6- Supporting the establishment of the global Islamic State wherever it is].*
>
> *Three: The Concept of Settlement:*
> *Settlement: "That Islam and its Movement become a part of the homeland it lives in."*
> *Establishment: "That Islam turns into firmly-rooted organizations on whose bases civilization, structure and testimony are built."*
> *Stability: "That Islam is stable in the land on which its people move."*
> *Enablement: "That Islam is enabled within the souls, minds and the lives of the people of the country in which it moves."*
> *Rooting: "That Islam is resident and not a passing thing, or rooted "entrenched" in the soil of the spot where it moves and not a strange plant to it."*
>
> *Four: The Process of Settlement:*
> *- In order for Islam and its Movement to become "a part of the homeland" in which it lives, "stable" in its land, "rooted" in the spirits and minds of its people, "enabled" in the live of its society and has firmly-established "organizations" on which the Islamic structure is built and with which the testimony of civilization is achieved, the Movement must plan and struggle to obtain "the*

keys" and the tools of this process in carry out this grand mission as a *"Civilization Jihadist"* responsibility which lies on the shoulders of Muslims and - on top of them - the Muslim Brotherhood in this country [author's emphasis].

3- Understanding the historical stages in which the Islamic Ikhwani [Brotherhood] activism went in this country:

A- The stage of searching for self and determining the identity.

B- The stage of inner build-up and tightening the organization.

C- The stage of mosques and the Islamic centers.

D- The stage of building the Islamic organizations - the first phase.

E- The stage of building the Islamic schools - the first phase.

F- The stage of thinking about the overt Islamic Movement - the first phase.

G- The stage of openness to the other Islamic movements and attempting to reach a formula for dealing with them - the first phase.

H- The stage of reviving and establishing the Islamic organizations - the second phase. We believe that the Group is embarking on this stage in its second phase as it has to open the door and enter as it did the first time.

4- Understanding the role of the Muslim Brother in North America:

The process of settlement is a *"Civilization-Jihadist Process"* with all the word means. The Ikhwan must understand that their work in America is a kind of grand Jihad in eliminating and **destroying the Western civilization from within and "sabotaging" its miserable house** by their hands and the hands of the believers so that it is eliminated and God's religion is made victorious over all other religions. Without this level of understanding, we are not up to this challenge and have not prepared ourselves for Jihad yet. *It Is a Muslim's destiny to perform Jihad* and work wherever he is and wherever he lands until the final hour comes, and there is no escape from that destiny except for those who chose to slack. But, would the slackers and the Mujahedeen [Islamic guerilla fighters] *[Islamic guerilla fighters]* be equal [author emphasis].

8- Absorbing Muslims and winning them with all of their factions and colors in America and Canada for the settlement project, and making it their cause, future and the basis of their Islamic life in this part of the world:

. . . *"Take from people ... the best they have,"* their best specializations, experiences, arts, energies and abilities. By people here we mean those within or without the ranks of

*individuals and organizations. **The policy of "taking" should be with what achieves the strategic goal and the settlement process*** [author's emphasis].
10- Growing and developing our resources and capabilities, our financial and human resources with what suits the magnitude of the grand mission:
If we examined the human and the financial resources the Ikhwan alone own in this country, we and others would feel proud and glorious. And if we add to them the resources of our friends and allies, those who circle in our orbit and those waiting on our banner, we would realize that we are able to open the door to settlement and walk through it seeking to make Almighty God's word the highest.

DHS: *We are a nation under attack.* U.S. Marine, Gen. John Kelly, as President Trump's Secretary of the Department of Homeland Security, delivered a speech on the status of America's security to the George Washington University Center for Cyber and Homeland Security on April 18, 2017. After his opening remarks and accolades to the many men and women in the military and law enforcement who strive every day to keep Americans safe, Secy. Kelly got the audience's attention with this blunt proclamation:

> *But make no mistake—we are a nation under attack.*
> *We are under attack from criminals who think their greed justifies raping young girls at knifepoint, dealing poison to our youth, or killing just for fun.*
> *We are under attack from people who hate us, hate our freedoms, hate our laws, hate our values, hate the way we simply live our lives.*
> *We are under attack from failed states, cyber-terrorists, vicious smugglers, and sadistic radicals.*
> *And we are under attack every single day. The threats are relentless.*

Secy. Kelly's remarks were, indeed, sobering and will likely remain so for some time. One of his grave concerns was America's complacency and lack of vigilance. "For a brief moment," he remarked, "after the attacks of 9/11, our nation shook off its complacency, and realized our American values had a mortal enemy called radical Islam. But as the years have passed we've grown complacent protected by the effectiveness of our worldwide intelligence collection, and the heroics of all those in uniform including our military, local law enforcement, and the men and women of DHS.

"The threat to our nation and our American way of life has not diminished. In fact, the threat has metastasized and decentralized, and the risk is as threatening today as it was that September morning almost 16 years ago.

"As I speak these words the FBI has open terrorism investigations in all 50 states, and since 2013, there have been 37 ISIS-linked plots to attack our country."

Then, Secy. Kelly lowered the *boom*. "This is all bad news, but it gets much worse." His great concern was, as the Islamic caliphate of ISIS collapsed in Iraq and Syria, as it did by the end of March, 2019, the surviving Islamic terrorists would flee to fight another day elsewhere. ". . . the expectation is that many of these 'holy warriors' will survive departing for their home countries to wreak murderous havoc in Europe, Asia, the Maghreb [Northwest Africa region of Arab nations], the Caribbean and the United States."

On America's Homefront, the Secretary expressed concern as well. "Over the past few years, we've seen an unprecedented spike in homegrown terrorism. In the past 12 months alone, there have been 36 homegrown terrorist cases in 18 states" (29).

In March, 2018, the new FBI Director, Christopher Wray, announced that the FBI had 3,000-plus open terror investigations throughout the 50 states. This included suspected ISIS terroristic threats, homegrown terrorist suspects and domestic terrorism cases. Director Wray also noted that a top priority for the FBI was foreign espionage—principally by the Chinese—a threat he believed was considerably underestimated (30).

Uncontrolled Immigration—the Gateway to Islamic Terror

Islam's Northern and Southern Door. In January, 2019, the House Homeland Security Committee Majority Staff Report on, *Stopping Terrorist Travel Through Illicit Pathways to the Homeland*, was released. In the report, the concern was raised about the growing threat of Islamic terrorists in Latin America, especially that of Hezbollah (31).

Who is Hezbollah? The name stands for the "Party of God" and first emerged in Lebanon in 1982. While not officially a part of the expansive Muslim Brotherhood terrorist network, Hezbollah, a Shi'ite terrorist organization with deep ties to Iran, has gained significant power and presence in Lebanon. The history of the group includes kidnappings and car bombing, principally against Israelis and Westerners.

In this century, Hezbollah has increased its political and social standing in Lebanon and turned the once Christian nation into a Muslim-controlled country on Israel's northern border. As of Lebanon's May 6, 2018 election, Hezbollah now controls the politics and direction of Lebanon.

According to the Report, Hezbollah has had a known presence in Latin America since the early 1990s. For Arab terrorists, Latin America offers an exceptional route into America. Most Arabs can easily pass for Latinos due to skin tone, and once they master the Spanish language, may easily pass as Latino, thus opening up their prospects of getting into the U.S., either legally or illegally.

"The Lebanon-based FTO [Foreign Terrorist Organization] is especially active in the Tri-Border Area (TBA) of Brazil, Paraguay, and Argentina, which is also home to significant Shia Islam and Lebanese diaspora communities," the Report revealed. Hezbollah uses illicit businesses and smuggling to raise significant cash for its terrorist operations in Argentina and elsewhere in Latin America. They focus on money laundering and the narcotics trade. The Department of Homeland Security (DHS) has made it a priority to track and identify Special Interest Aliens (SIAs) in Latin America, as well as in the Middle East and other countries. In 2018, a DHS Committee delegation to Panama was told by Panamanian officials, that "tens of thousands of SIAs have entered Panama since 2014." Columbian officials also told the Committee staff that hundreds of SIAs have entered their country every year for the past few years. ". . . nearly all the SIA migrants were headed to the United States and originated from the Middle East, Asia, and Africa—including Syria, Pakistan, Afghanistan, Somalia, Bangladesh, India, Eritrea, and many others. Additionally, encounters with these special interest individuals resulted in the seizure of tens of thousands of fraudulent documents—including passports and visas—that facilitated travel from their countries of origin through the Americas."

On America's border with Mexico, DHS Border Patrol Agents regularly apprehend SIAs. As of September, 2018, for instance, agents had caught 630 Bangladeshi nationals during FY2018 trying to sneak into the United States near the Laredo, Texas crossing. This was a 300 percent jump from FY2017 arrests of SIAs in that area. Laredo is a favorite target of SIAs and other illegals due to 170 miles of river and no protective barriers. America's vast northern border with Canada is also ripe for undetected SIA crossings, the Report noted.

The Report included a testimonial quote from Rear Admiral Brian Hendrickson from his appearance before the House Foreign Affairs Committee on May 23, 2018.

The region is also home to networks that specialize in smuggling illegal immigrants from places like Afghanistan, Pakistan, Yemen, Syria, and Iraq, all places where terrorist organizations like al-Shabab, ISIS, al-Qaeda and their affiliates operate. Now migrant smuggling is not uncommon. What makes these networks different is the type of people who enlist their services to attempt to enter the U.S. homeland undetected. Some of these people have ties to terrorism and some have intentions to conduct attacks in the homeland.

Uncontrolled and Unvetted Immigration Threatens National Security. During the years of the Obama presidency, America received a record number of Muslim refugees. During FY2013 to FY 2016, a four year period, a record number of Muslim refugees entered the U.S., far more per year than the previous eleven years. In FY2016, of the 85,000 refugees that were allowed to immigrate to the U.S., 46 percent were Muslims. Two Muslim countries, Syria and Somalia, both harboring Islamic terrorists, represented over half of the 38,901 Muslim refugees admitted in FY2016. Other Muslim refugees came from Afghanistan, Iraq, Myanmar and other countries. Since FY2002 through FY2016, a 15 year period, Pew Research Center concluded that the U.S. has received 399,677 Christian refugees and 279,339 Muslim refugees. Those two groups represented 46 percent and 32 percent, respectively, of the total number of all refugees admitted during that period (32).

According to FY2019 data from the U.S. Customs and Border Protection Agency, in January, 2019, 47,893 immigrants were apprehended trying to enter the U.S. illegally. This was down only slightly from the 51,857 arrests in November, 2018 and 50,749 in December. In FY2018, CBPA agents apprehended 396,579 people along the Southwest Border of the United States. No one knows for sure how many thousands escaped being caught. Of those trying to enter the U.S. in FY2018, 124,511 or 31.4 percent were deemed inadmissible for various reasons.

Between FY2014 and FY2019, 2.5 million people were apprehended trying to cross the U.S.-Mexico border, over half a million people per year. That does not count the people that enter legally, or those that enter illegally, but are not caught (33).

In May, 2018, FBI Director Christopher Wray, told the Senate Appropriations subcommittee on Commerce, Justice, Science, and Related Agencies, that the FBI was surveilling several hundred homegrown terror suspects, not including domestic extremist groups.

Sen. Susan Collins (R-ME) asked how the FBI was dealing with the growing cyber threat, where terrorists are getting their motivation and training over the Internet.

Wray responded, "We have about 1,000 investigations into exactly the kind of people you're describing, covering all 50 states as I'm sitting here right now. And that's not even counting, you know, the al-

Qaeda investigations, the traditional ISIS investigations, the domestic terrorism investigations, but just the group you're talking about.

"And what makes it so hard," he continued, "is that there are not many dots to connect with some of these people. They pick soft targets, they use easy to use weapons, you know, IEDs, cars, knives, guns. And they can make decisions on the spur of the moment. We're trying to get better at looking for red flags, as to when people who are getting radicalized sort of make that switch into potentially mobilizing" (34).

Sen. Diane Feinstein (D-CA), a Jew, expressed concern about the rise in hate crimes against Muslims. "Given this tremendous increase, what is the FBI doing to increase its investigative resources related to hate crimes?" she wanted to know. As pointed out previously, since 2002, hate crimes against Muslims have remained relatively stable according to FBI hate crime statistics. However, anti-Semitic attacks have skyrocketed.

Again, revisiting former DHS Secretary, Gen. John Kelly's remarks at George Washington University's Center for Cyber and Homeland Security, Kelly argued for greater control and security of the nation's borders.

> *There is no better argument for secure borders than TCOs* [Transnational Criminal Organizations]. *And since the first week of President Trump's administration, we have been actively securing our borders and enforcing our immigration laws. Not only is this our right as a sovereign nation—it is our responsibility to ensure the safety of the American public.*
>
> *People who illegally cross our borders do not respect the laws of our nation. We want to get the law breakers off our streets, and out of the country, for the good of our communities.*
>
> *But being serious about our borders and our laws is not just good for the American people—it will also save lives. In FY 2016, CBP* [Customs and Border Protection] *saved nearly 4,000 near-death individuals who found themselves lost in the desert trying to cross our border* (35).

In the *House Homeland Security Committee Majority Staff Report, 2018-2019*, previously cited, the Committee expressed concern about the dispersal of Islamic terrorists with the collapse of the Islamic State caliphate.

> *While ISIS has lost at least 90 percent of the physical territory it previously captured, the terrorist group has not been fully defeated and remains committed to inspiring attacks against the United States and the West. The protracted civil war in Syria, the impending removal of U.S. troops in Syria, and ongoing*

instability in Iraq continue to provide the conditions for ISIS and other terror groups to persist and thrive online.

Additionally, the spillover effects from the near elimination of the physical caliphate have changed the nature of the threat. This includes a foreign fighter diaspora—consisting of individuals who have either returned home, often undetected by law enforcement, or who have gone to or are in search of the next jihadi theatre (e.g. Africa)—which poses a heightened threat around the globe and to the Homeland.

Russia had the largest number of citizens travel to Syria and Iraq to become foreign fighters, with an estimated 3,417, including 400 who have returned, followed by Saudi Arabia with roughly 3,244, of which 760 have returned, then Jordan with approximately 3,000, of which 250 have returned, Tunisia followed with 2,926, of which 800 have returned, France with 1,910, of which 271 have returned, and lastly, the United States had more than 250 foreign fighters attempt to join ISIS, with less than 129 foreign fighters actually joining the fight, of which 7 have returned (36).

The Consequences of Uncontrolled & Undocumented Immigration. In September, 2018, the Immigration Reform Law Institute (IRLI), the legal affiliate of the Federation for American Immigration Reform (FAIR), released a report stating that during the Obama years, a potential 39 million Americans had their Social Security numbers stolen by illegal immigrants (37). Under the Freedom of Information Act (FOIA), IRLI sued the Social Security Administration, "seeking records related to its Obama-era decision to halt sending 'no-match' letters to employers. The long-held practice of sending the letters had been used to prevent fraud through the use of stolen Social Security number (SSN) data by illegal aliens and other criminals. A 'no-match' letter informed employers and employees, usually in response to an employee W-2 wage report, that the name or SSN reported by the employer did not match a name or SSN combination reflected in SSA's records."

The Social Security files obtained by IRLI indicated that from 2012 to 2016, there were 39 million instances "where names and Social Security numbers on W-2 tax forms did not match the corresponding Social Security records. Additionally, over $409 billion was added to the Earnings Suspense File (ESF), which holds uncredited wages that can't be correctly matched to SSA's database. From 1937 to 2005, $519 billion was reported to be sitting in the ESF. In tax year 2016, that number rose to over $1.5 trillion."

Interestingly, President Obama scraped the decades-old exercise of "no-match" letters only eight days before the implementation of his DACA (Deferred Action for Childhood Arrivals) amnesty for illegal immigrants.

On March 6, 2017, Catherine Herridge, Chief Intelligence correspondent for Fox News, reported that a DHS official said that of the FBI's 1,000 domestic terrorism investigations, 300 involved refugees admitted into the U.S. She said, that this was "the first official concrete linkage between the refugee program and terrorism."

Then Attorney General, Jeff Sessions, remarked, "Like every nation, the United States has a right to control who enters our country and to keep out those who would do us harm" (38).

In late September, 2016, Breitbart Texas received leaked FBI documents that disclosed that there were 7,712 "terrorist encounters" throughout the United States in just one year (July 20, 2015 to July 20, 2016). The events were highest in California (879), New York (827), Texas (585), Florida (569), District of Columbia (415), Michigan (414) and Illinois (411). The data obtained was from the FBI-administered "Terrorist Screening Center." Among the information was a pie chart that broke down the encounters with known or suspected Islamic terrorists. There were 89 encounters with Sunni Muslims, 56 with Shi'a Muslims and 70 with "Other International Terrorist Groups or Affiliates." Every one of the 50 states was impacted by such encounters (39).

One of the biggest trouble spots in the United States for Muslim refugees has been Minneapolis, Minnesota, home to the largest Somali population in the country. While most Somali are trying to live a peaceful life, there has been an element of their youth that has been getting drawn into international Islamic terrorism.

In a twelve year span, more Somali young men and boys in Minneapolis have joined, or attempted to join, an Islamic terrorist group abroad, than in any other part of the U.S. FBI records reveal that 45 Somali males from that city had joined either al-Shabab (the Somali terrorist group) or ISIS in Iraq and Syria. In 2018, another dozen Somali were arrested, as they attempted to leave the U.S. to join ISIS. "Then," a federal official told Fox News, "as ISIS came back, we saw a whole bunch of people no longer headed for Somalia. They were headed for Iraq and Syria. That really caught us off-guard, we didn't see that coming. It didn't make sense to us. We understood why kids were going back to Somalia, but going to Syria was another we issue" (40).

Since 2007, it is known by the FBI that 23 Somali men have made it to Somalia to join al-Shabab, where some of them have been killed or turned into suicide bombers, fighting against Ethiopia or the weak Somali government.

Robin Simcox, an expert on terrorism and national security for The Heritage Foundation, commented. "For over a decade, Islamist terror groups have been able to recruit from Minnesota. This is, in part, because Minnesota has a large Muslim population compared to other parts of the U.S. However, it is also because there have been small segments of the Somali community there that have struggled to integrate into the U.S. Al-Shabaab and ISIS have exploited this— upon religious, political cultural and identity issues to offer a compelling alternative to Western democracy" (41).

In August, 2018, Homeland Security officials and U.S. politicians were stunned when two Iranians were arrested in California and charged with spying on Jewish and Israeli facilities. Rep. Peter Roskam (R-IL-6) believed that, "This is the tip of the iceberg." He believed that the terrorist-sponsoring Iranian Islamic government has many clandestine operations in the United States. "This is not a surprise and this is a result of the Iran regime getting financial support from the Obama administration in the Iran deal," he suggested.

Roskam's suspicions are joined by other politicians and terrorism experts that have warned about Iran establishing "sleeper cells" throughout the U.S. Within the U.S., these agents are operating without detection and could be laying the foundation for a major homeland attack. Of the two Iranians that were caught, one had dual citizenship (U.S. and Iran) and the other was an Iranian citizen living in California.

One U.S. official told *The Washington Free Beacon*, that he agreed with Rep. Roskam's assessment, and that Iran has had a "vast espionage and information operations in the United States" for some time, operating with impunity.

Sen. Marco Rubio (R-FL), stated, "I am deeply alarmed by the Justice Department's new indictment against alleged Iranian agents. Iran's regime has sponsored terrorist attacks against Americans abroad and our allies, and may now be seeking to target American citizens, as well as Jewish or Israeli facilities, on U.S. soil."

Rep. Roskam added: "The takeaway is we can take the Iranians at face value. They were declarative during the Iran negotiations: They were not willing to make any commitments as it relates to their state sponsorship of terror. It's clear they haven't. This can't be a surprise to anyone. It is entirely consistent with what they've been communicating. The surprise is, the idea, anyone thought they were slowing down or giving up their aggressive disposition" (42).

Islam in American Government

Islam and the U.S. Constitution are not Compatible. The First Amendment of the United States of America Constitution reads:

Congress shall make no law respecting an establishment of religion, or prohibiting the free exercise thereof; or abridging the freedom of speech, or of the press; or the right of the people peaceably to assemble, and to petition the Government for a redress of grievances.

America was the first nation in the history of the world to have such an extensive and all-inclusive "Bill of Rights." Islam neither acknowledges nor believes in any of the freedoms presented in this treasured law of America.

In Islamic countries, it is the government that dictates the religion for its citizens. There is no freedom of choice for an individual to decide whether or not to worship Islam's god. All must worship Allah or face severe persecution and consequences. Islamic governments, the mullahs and imams respect no religion other than Islam. In many Muslim countries, if one is allowed to remain a Jew or Christian, you must pay a "poll tax" that allows you to be a second class citizen. However, you cannot express your faith openly or share it with others. You are a prisoner of the confines of Islam. If your father is a Muslim, the moment you are born, you are a Muslim also. If you decide to leave Islam later in life, you risk abandonment by your family, at least, or death.

Freedom of speech does not exist in Islam. It is Islam's religious leaders and scholars that determine what one can say, especially if it pertains to Islam or its prophet, Muhammad. If one says anything critical or judgmental about Islam or Muhammad, one can go to prison or be executed. You are not allowed to question the ideology or its leaders. Their word is of Allah and infallible.

In Islamic countries, Islam is the Law. Islam functions as the Executive, Legislative and Judicial branches of government and dictates what every citizen is to believe and do. No freedom of thought or discussion is permitted.

Islam also does not observe freedom of the press. All official media must comply with Islamic teaching and not deviate in their presentations. Media releases are often fabricated to order to present the official positions of the Islamic government and to toe the line of Islamic propaganda.

The right to peacefully assemble or petition the government with grievances does not exist in Muslim countries. They are dictatorships. While there have been frequent citizen protests in places like Egypt and Iran, they are met with brutal force and death to silence any opposition to Islamic dictatorial rule.

Islam also dictates what women must wear, how they must behave, what she can do in public and basically suppress a woman's life so that it is not her own, but only that which is dictated by her male superior.

Bottom line: Islam is oppressive, dictatorial and entraps men and women in a veil of bondage with no escape without severe consequences. It is the very antithesis of what America's Founders envisioned and implemented by the wisdom of God Almighty.

Aiding and Abetting the Enemy. In *An Explanatory Memorandum* previously presented, one of the primary goals of Islamists in America is to establish a *Civilization-Jihadist Process* where the Muslim faithful carry out a *grand Jihad in eliminating and **destroying the Western civilization from within and "sabotaging" its miserable house***. That Civilizational Jihad is well underway and getting well established throughout the United States. It is being aided, either deliberately or unknowingly by members of the U.S. government, politicians, businesses, the judicial courts, Jews and Christians and the ignorant American public, in general.

David Horowitz, founder and president of the Freedom Center, put together a list of the Muslim groups and organizations that are well entrenched in American life. At last count he listed 217, many of them present on the campuses of some of America's leading colleges and universities (43). His listing, however, falls far short of the total number of Islamic groups and organizations known to exist in America. The list does not include all the CAIR state chapters around the country, nor the hundreds of Muslim Student Association (MSA) chapters on America's university campuses. Nor does it include the thousands of mosques in the U.S. that essentially function as strategic military planning board rooms.

According to U.S. Aid, in FY2017, of the 50 Muslim majority countries, 49 received U.S. foreign aid (44). The total foreign aid budget for that fiscal year was $50.1 billion. Of that amount, Muslim countries received $21.398 billion, or 42.7 percent. About 140 countries receive U.S. foreign aid each year, 35 percent of them are Muslim. Afghanistan, due to the war effort there, received the largest amount, $5.7 billion. However, in 2009 and 2013, the Palestinians in Gaza and the West Bank received $1 billion each year.

A fact sheet from the Bureau of Near East Affairs, reveals that since the 1979 Egypt-Israel Treaty of Peace, the United States has given Egypt over $40 billion in military aid and another $30 billion in economic assistance (45). This aid was freely given, despite the realization that Egypt is still a Muslim country that persecutes and kills Christians and destroys their churches.

A Faucet is Turned Off. Since 1994, the United States has given over $5 billion to the Palestinians, plus an additional $6+ billion through the United Nations Relief and Works Agency (UNRWA). However, in 2018, under President Donald Trump, the aide to the Palestinians was significantly cut. First, the U.S. repurposed $231.532 million of FY2017 monies that were intended for assistance in Gaza and the West Bank. Then, the U.S. cut its humanitarian contributions to UNRWA, from $359.3 million in FY2017 to $65 million for FY2018 (46).

The Washington Post reported that, up until the cut in funds, the U.S. was providing monies for 30 percent of UNRWA's annual budget—a disproportionate share for a UN member state. In a written statement the U.S. State Department said, it "will no longer commit further funding to this irredeemably flawed operation" (47).

The Muslim Brotherhood at Work. In *An Explanatory Memorandum*, the Muslim Brotherhood laid out a very strategic plan of action to overtake America. They are well on their way to accomplishing their goal, thanks to the complicity of American officials and others. The Gatestone Institute, in April, 2013 put together a 19-page summary on the Muslim Brotherhood and just how well they have implemented their plan (48). It will not be reviewed here, but the reader is encouraged to link on to the reference cited.

Allah is our objective. The Prophet is our leader. The Qur'an is our law. Jihad is our way. Dying in the way of Allah is our highest aspiration.
Motto of the Muslim Brotherhood

Key Muslim Brotherhood organizations that are well established in America include: Benevolence International Fund, Council for American-Islamic Relations (CAIR), Islamic Circle of North America (ICNA), Islamic Society of North America (ISNA), Muslim American Society, Muslim World League, Muslim Youth of North America, North American Islamic Trust (NAIT), The Fiqh [shari'a jurisprudence] Council of North America, and The Muslim Student Association (MSA).

CAIR and the MSA are the most vociferous and belligerent representations. CAIR is a powerful, intimidating arm of the Muslim Brotherhood that has very effectively pushed its way into just about every aspect of American life. Headquartered in Washington, DC, it has at least 26 state offices around the country, including Alabama, Arizona, California (3 locations), Connecticut, Florida, Georgia, Illinois, Kansas, Michigan, Minnesota, Missouri, New Jersey, New York, Ohio (3 locations), Oklahoma, Pennsylvania (2 locations), Texas (3 locations) and Washington. Essentially, CAIR aggressively intimidates and forces local and state governments, schools, businesses and the general public to comply with the Islamic view of life or be sued for discrimination under a variety of America's civil rights laws.

All Muslims are above the law and above all non-Muslims who have no rights in affairs with Muslims.
Mustafa Carroll, CAIR Director, Texas

Muslims Running for Office in Record Numbers. In the 2018 mid-term election cycle, a record number—90—Muslims ran for state or federal offices in America. That was a substantial increase over the dozen or so that ran in 2016. The majority of the Muslim candidates belong to the Democratic Party (49). House representative, Andre Carson (D-IN), a Muslim, could hardly contain his excitement with the election of fellow Muslims, Ilhan Omar (D-MN) and Rashida Tlaib (D-MI). "In 2030 we may have about 30, 35 Muslims in Congress," Carson proclaimed.

"Then we're talking about Madame Chair Rashida. We're talking about Madame Chair Ilhan," he added. "Hell, we could be saying Speaker of the House Ilhan, Speaker of the House Rashida, Senator Rashida, Governor Ilhan, President Fatima, Vice President Aziza" (50).

New representatives, Omar and Tlaib, did not disappoint Carson and other democrats, as they quickly gained the reputation as the Democrats' new firebrands, spouting forth one anti-Semitic, anti-Christian or anti-Trump remark after another. In their first three months in office, hardly a day went by without some offensive, anti-American statement.

Shortly after her swearing in as Michigan's new congresswoman, Rep. Tlaib was quick to offend sensitive ears with her expletive laced tirade on, "We're gonna impeach the mother****r" [President Trump] (51). Not very professional; not very American, but it did get cheers and hoots from her Democratic faithful. Tlaib is a vociferous Palestinian-American born in Detroit. She is university educated and an attorney, so, for some, it was a shock to hear such gutter language from an elected lawmaker.

Rep. Omar, a Somali refugee, who immigrated to the U.S. and Minnesota at a young age, made even more noise with offensive, often anti-Semitic, anti-American or anti-Christian tweets or statements, in her first three months in office. She has shown little respect or decorum in her daily duties as the newly elected first Somali in the U.S. Congress. She once tweeted (in 2012) that, "Israel has hypnotized the world, may Allah awaken the people and help them see the evil doings of Israel. #Gaza #Palestine #Israel" (52).

Islam in America's Churches

And what accord has Christ with Belial? Or what part has a believer with an unbeliever?
2 Corinthians 6:15

"A Common Word" and Interfaith Dialogue. On October 13, 2007, an initial group of 138 Muslim scholars, Muslim religious leaders and Muslim organization leaders from around the world penned an open letter, *A Common Word between Us and You* (ACW), to leaders of Christianity worldwide (53). It was a veiled attempt to establish that there is common ground among Muslims, Christians and Jews, including the worship of the one and same god. The fact that some of the signatories represented known U.S.-based terror sponsoring groups was not comforting. The premise for the letter was a citation from the Qur'an:

> *Say: O People of the Scripture! Come to a common word between us and you: that we shall worship none but God, and that we shall ascribe no partner unto Him, and that none of us shall take others for lords beside God. And if they turn away, then say: Bear witness that we are they who have surrendered (unto Him)* (**Aal 'Imran 3:64**).

The substance and appeal of the lengthy letter is that we all (Muslims, Christians and Jews) have the same heritage, worship the same god and desire peace in the world. "The future of the world depends on peace between Muslims and Christians", the Muslim letter begins. "The basis for this peace and understanding already exists," it continues. "It is part of the very foundational principles of both faiths: love of the One God, and love of the neighbour. These principles are found over and over again in the sacred texts of Islam and Christianity. The Unity of God, the necessity of love for Him, and the necessity of love of the neighbour is thus the common ground between Islam and Christianity."

The Letter from the Muslims is built on three premises. 1. That Muslims and Christians worship the same God. 2. That both faiths have a common love of their neighbors. 3. That Muslims and Christians have a common foundation. All of which, to the discerning Christian, is false. Christians do not worship the same god as Muslims. Muslims are not taught to love their non-Muslim neighbors, as Christians are commanded. Muslims and Christians do not have a "common word" or "common faith" as a basis of coming together.

The letter submits that Allah is a god of love and that he wants nothing more than justice and freedom of religion for all. The first section of the ACW letter is subtitled, *Love of God.* It presumes, of course, that Christians worship Allah, the god of Islam, which Muslims portray as the same God of Christians. The authors offer up this problem for Christians: "The central creed of Islam consists of the two testimonies of faith or *Shahadahs* [Muslim prayer of faith], which state that: *There is no god but God, Muhammad is the messenger of God.* These Two Testimonies are the *sine qua non* [indispensable condition] of Islam. He or she who testifies to them is a Muslim; he or she who denies them is not a Muslim." That is the *bottom line* that supersedes all the Muslim rhetoric: If you are not a Muslim, you are an infidel that is worthy of persecution and death. Forget all the proclamations that Islam offers *freedom of religion* or that it is a *religion of peace*. Those and many more claims are the deceptive lies of Satan.

Missing from all the Qur'anic texts cited on "love" are the realities that Christians, Jews and all non-Muslims, according to Allah in the Qur'an, are deemed enemies of Islam and are worthy only of Allah's wrath, as well as that of his followers.

The authors of the ACW correctly state, ***Love of God as the First and Greatest Commandment in the Bible.*** They then dutifully cite Moses' commandment to love God in **Deuteronomy 6:4-5** and **Matthew 22:34-40** where Jesus states that the "Greatest Commandment" was to love God and the second was to love your neighbor. No such second commandment exists in Islam.

The second section is titled, *Love of the Neighbour.* Again, the authors cite Qur'anic verses to misleadingly justify their premise. Absent are the Qur'an verses that command Muslims not to be friends with Christians (**Qur'an 3:28, 118; 5:51, 80,** et al) or how to deceive infidels.

The third section, *Come to a Common Word Between Us and You,* postulates, "Whilst Islam and Christianity are obviously different religions—and whilst there is no minimizing some of their formal differences—it is clear that the *Two Greatest Commandments* are an area of common ground and a link between the Qur'an, the Torah and the New Testament." Once again, there are more than just *formal differences* between Islam and Christianity and there is no *common ground and a link between the Qur'an, the Torah and the New Testament.* Islam is fundamentally opposed to Christianity and Judaism and the teachings of the Torah and the Bible. If Muslims truly believed there was common ground, they would permit themselves to read the Bible. However, it is forbidden to them on the false and unproven premise that the Bible was corrupted by Jews and Christians.

An estimated one-third of the Muslim signatories have Muslim Brotherhood connections.

You can read more of *A Common Word between Us and You* at this website: http://www.acommonword.com/the-acw-document/.

The "Christian" Response. Despite the glaring falsehoods and deceptions of the ACW, on November 18, 2007, a full page ad was published in the New York Times, with the heading: *Loving God and Neighbor Together: A Christian Response to A Common Word Between Us and You* (54). It was authored by scholars at the Yale (University) Center for Faith & Culture and was initially signed by 300 Christian leaders from around the world. The letter agreed with the Muslim letter premise of having a common goal with Muslims of loving God and loving one's neighbor and implied that Muslims and Christians worship the same God. Many well-known Christian leaders (pastors, priests, Christian college, university and seminary leaders and heads of Christian organizations and denominations) signed on to the letter, thus agreeing with its content.

The letter started out by affirming Islam as an Abrahamic faith and then in the second paragraph stated,

> . . . we want to begin by acknowledging that in the past (e.g. in the Crusades) and in the present (e.g. in excesses of the "war on terror") many Christians have been guilty of sinning against our Muslim neighbors. Before we "shake your hand" in responding to your letter, we ask forgiveness of the All-Merciful One [Allah] and of the Muslim community around the world.

The crusades were the response from Pope Urban II and the kings of Europe to recover southern Europe from decades of insurgency by murderous Muslims from Africa and the Middle East and recover the Holy Land from Islamic domination. That the signatories would plead for Allah's forgiveness is a travesty of the Christian faith. Although the Crusades turned out to be horrific in the purging of Islam from Europe, it was necessitated by the barbarous invasion of merciless Muslim hoards over the previous centuries. Did the Muslims, in the ACW, offer an apology for their predecessors invading Europe again and again, murdering hundreds of thousands throughout much of Europe? Not then, not ever. The "war on terror" was, of necessity, brought on by Islamic invasion and a horrific attack on America's homeland. However, ACW did not put forth a plea for forgiveness—not then, not ever.

Throughout the letter it is stressed or implied that God and Allah are one and the same. The signatories accept the Muslim premise and lie, that Muslims are commanded to love their neighbor just like Christians. However, there is no such command in Islam. While Muslims are called to love each other (but fail to do so), there is no such requirement in the Qur'an to love non-Muslims.

Under the subheading, *Love of God*, the creators of the letter state: "We find it equally heartening that the God whom we should love above all things is described as being Love. In the Muslim tradition, God, 'the Lord of the worlds,' is 'The Infinitely Good and All-Merciful.'" In other words, our God is your god. How blasphemous and disrespectful to the One and Only true God as revealed by Jesus Christ.

Under the subtitle, *Love of Neighbor*, the authors of the letter offer this observation: "We find deep affinities with our own Christian faith when 'A Common Word Between Us and You' insists that love is the pinnacle of our duties toward our neighbors. 'None of you has faith until you love for your neighbor what you love for yourself,' the Prophet Muhammad said." As Christians, what Muhammad, a false prophet, said, is meaningless and we should not be giving any credence to it or him, no matter how much we want to appease Muslims.

The next paragraph starts with, "We applaud when you state that "justice and freedom of religion are a crucial part" of the love of neighbor." While it may be politically correct to acknowledge Islam's self-proclaimed "justice and freedom of religion," the reality throughout the present world and the history of Islam, is that neither have existed nor do exist. Remember, the Qur'an, Islamic law and other Islamic sacred texts proclaim that in the world only Islam can exist and that all Muslims are to strive daily to do their part in conquering the world for Islam.

In signing off, the Christian authors end with this paragraph:

> "Let this common ground" – the dual common ground of love of God and of neighbor – "be the basis of all future interfaith dialogue between us," your courageous letter urges. Indeed, in the generosity with which the letter is written you embody what you call for. We most heartily agree. Abandoning all "hatred and strife," we must engage in interfaith dialogue as those who seek each other's good, for the one God unceasingly seeks our good. Indeed, together with you we believe that we need to move beyond "a polite ecumenical dialogue between selected religious leaders" and work diligently together to reshape relations between our communities and our nations so that they genuinely reflect our common love for God and for one another.

Muslims are not interested in "interfaith dialogue." All they want is opportunities to deceive the gullible Christian *dhimmis* (those deceived by Muslims and living under Muslim rule). They want to get into our churches and proclaim their lies as truth. They will not allow Christians in their mosques to preach the Gospel of truth. There is no common ground; there is no *interfaith dialogue*. Muslims are only interested in such one-way dialogue as long as it meets their objective of establishing the *ummah* (Muslim community in America).

The Christian response letter is brief, only three and a half pages, but it is followed by 37 ½ pages of endorsees. Many church denominations are represented, including, Roman Catholic, Lutheran and Evangelical Lutheran, Episcopal, Presbyterian, United Methodist, Mennonite, Church of the Brethren, Anglican, United Church of Christ, Congregational, Reformed Church of America, Vineyard and many others.

385

It also included representatives from numerous universities, Christian Colleges and Universities and Christian Seminaries. Some of note are: Catholic Theological Union, University of Pennsylvania, Yale University and Yale Divinity School, Fuller Theological Seminary, Princeton Theological Seminary, DePaul University, Hartford Seminary, Union Theological Seminary, Concordia University (St. Paul, MN), Goshen College, Harvard Divinity School, Bethel University and Bethel Seminary (San Diego), Wheaton College, University of Chicago, Lutheran School of Theology, Gonzaga University and many, many more.

Some Christian organizations of note signing on were, Evangelicals for Middle East Understanding, World Evangelical Alliance, Youth with a Mission, Sojourners, The Navigators, National Association of Evangelicals, Mennonite Central Committee and others.

You can read the entire letter of Christian response, as well as see the initial 350 signatories, at: https://faith.yale.edu/common-word/common-word-christian-response.

Do Judeo-Christian Faiths Have Any Common Ground With Islam? There is not, nor can there ever be, any "common ground" between Islam and the Judeo-Christian faiths.

For Christian leaders and Christians to accept common ground or a *common word* with Muslims,

- they must accept that Muhammad was a prophet of God Almighty;
- that Jesus was not part of God's plan for mankind;
- that there is no salvation through Jesus Christ;
- that Allah is just another name for the One and Only True God of the Bible;
- that God, through Muhammad, reversed His plan of Salvation through Jesus Christ;
- that Jesus is not Lord and Savior, or the Son of God;
- that God's love is conditional (because Allah's love is);
- that God hates the sinner, but loves the sin;
- that it is God that causes one to sin;
- that God desires to send all people to hell, because Allah does;
- believe the lie that Muslims are commanded to "love their neighbors" (it does not exist in the Qur'an or teachings of Muhammad);
- that Jesus was not crucified or raised from the dead in the resurrection;
- that we achieve God's favor through our works and not by faith;
- that there is no assurance of salvation;
- that heaven is a place of personal gratification and perversion;

386

- that the Holy Spirit does not exist or play a role in the life of a Christian;
- and many other Biblical truths would have to be rejected.

Jesus said that in the End Times ". . . false christs and false prophets will rise and show great signs and wonders to deceive, if possible, even the elect" (**Matthew 24:24**). The Apostle Paul, in his second letter to the church of the Thessalonians, wrote, "and with all unrighteous deception among those who perish, because they did not receive the love of the truth, that they might be saved. And for this reason God will send them strong delusion, that they should believe the lie, that they all may be condemned who did not believe the truth but had pleasure in unrighteousness" (**2 Thessalonians 2:10-12**). Many leaders in the Christian church as well as in Christian colleges, universities and seminaries are being deceived by the evil one. In their desire to see harmony between Christians, Jews and Muslims, they are casting aside foundational principles and teachings of the Gospel of Jesus Christ. Although Jesus called His followers to love all people, He did not call them to cast aside wisdom, understanding and discernment of the devil's tactics, nor to make an alliance with evil.

Paul also wrote to his protégé, Timothy, warning him about *deceiving spirits* in the End Times. "Now the Spirit expressly says that in latter times some will depart from the faith, giving heed to deceiving spirits and doctrines of demons, speaking lies in hypocrisy, having their own conscience seared with a hot iron" (**1 Timothy 4:1-2**). Unfortunately, too many Christian leaders, in an effort to be more in line with the world and to be politically correct, are abandoning the teachings and doctrines of the Christian faith and are succumbing to *deceiving spirits* and the *doctrines of demons.*

In an attempt to bring peace between Muslims and the Judeo-Christian world, there is a desperate move to acquiesce to the satanic faith of Islam. This will not bear forth good fruit, but only more deception and weakening of the Christian faith.

"Do not be deceived," the Apostle Paul wrote, "God is not mocked; for whatever a man sows, that he will also reap" (Galatians 6:7).

"A Common Word" Outbreak. One of the outcomes of the *Common Word* was for churches to hold an "Interfaith Sunday," June 26, 2011. Muslims, Jews and Christians were invited into churches around the country. Some churches covered up crosses, crucifixes and baptisteries, or anything else that might offend Muslims—never mind offending Christ. Qur'ans replaced Bibles in the pews and the Qur'an was given equal place with the Bible and the Torah on the altar.

At The Cathedral Church of Saint Peter and Saint Paul— commonly known as the Washington National Cathedral—and home of the Episcopal Church, on Interfaith Sunday, in place of the baptismal fountain in the center aisle, were candle-lit stands for the Bible, Torah and Qur'an.

There was no communion, but, instead there were readings from the books of the "three Abrahamic faiths." The service was ordered to promote "religious tolerance."

"Imam Mohamed Magid," it was reported, "the president of the Islamic Society of North America, chanted a passage from the Koran about the value of diversity."

Rev. Dr. C. Welton Gaddy, then president of the Interfaith Alliance, stated emphatically, "No one verse or one passage in any book of scripture should be allowed to hijack or hold hostage the central truth, the overarching as well as pervasive moral mandate, which emerges from the full sweep of truth in those books of scripture," he said. "Cherry picking isolated texts . . . allows mean-spirited people to turn the scripture of our religions into weapons" (55).

On that Interfaith Sunday (or weekend), not one mosque offered to open its doors for a similar show of "common ground."

Another apparent result of the "Common Word" is the development of *Faith Shared: Uniting in Prayer and Understanding—A Project of Interfaith Alliance and Human Rights First* (http://www.faithshared.org/). How can Christians and Muslims pray together when they are praying to different gods? Again, this noble endeavor presumes falsely that Christians and Muslims are Abrahamic faiths that worship the same God.

The Lutheran ELCA Church appears to be trying a different strategy, that of shutting down dissent. In some communities where conservative, evangelical Christians have been trying to educate the communities to the realities and challenges of Islam, the local ELCA church or churches have posted newspaper display ads. The ads typically headline in big bold letters, "FAITH OVER FEAR." After citing **1 John 4:18** (perfect love casts out fear), the ad states: *Some in our communities have misconceptions about our Muslim neighbors. This has led to false rumors and unfounded fear.* The ad then says what the undersigned Lutheran churches believe.

Teaching Islam in America's Schools & Universities

He alone, who owns the youth, gains the future.
Adolf Hitler

Islamic research institutes funded by the royal family have crept into such prestigious American institutions of higher learning as American University in Washington, D.C., Duke University, Howard University,

John Hopkins University, Georgetown University, Syracuse University and many other institutions of higher learning. To demonstrate their infinite capacity for compassion toward the U.S. after the September 11, 2001 attacks, the Saudis shortly thereafter pledged one billion U.S. dollars—not for the victims of the attacks, but—to evangelize American college campuses and prisons in order to gain more terrorist converts to their radical brand of Wahhabi Islam. Establishment of such institutes and mosques is much more wide spread across Europe where Islam is rapidly gaining a solid foothold.

The degree and ease with which Islam has crept into America's primary and secondary school systems in the early 21st century is scary and mind-blowing. It has been facilitated by ignorant and clueless staff, administrators, school boards, boards of trustees and mostly ignored by parents and communities. The rapid surge has been largely funded and implemented by the Arab kingdoms of Saudi Arabia and Qatar, which possess two of the most radical forms of Islam.

The ruling family of Qatar, Al Thani, has invested billions of their petro dollars around the world to further their political and theological agendas. In addition to supporting terrorist groups like ISIS and Hamas, they have invested in Hollywood's Miramax studios and have poured millions into American K-12 education in an effort to control what is taught about Islam in America's classrooms (56).

The Al Thani Qatar Foundation sponsors teacher training outfits like Primary Source in New England which provides summer training courses for teachers on such topics as "the dynamics of the Middle East." For years, parents of Newton High School in Massachusetts have complained to Newton Superintendent of Schools that the Islamic curriculum their children were being taught was bigoted, false and anti-Semitic. However, their petitions have fallen on deaf ears. The Qatar Foundation is a longtime supporter of the Muslim Brotherhood and known Islamic hate preachers.

In Britain, the reality of Islam's influence in the schools has gotten so bad, that counter-extremism expert, Kamal Hanif, believes that British primary schools need to return to teaching about "democracy, the rule of law and tolerance to counter the potentially poisonous views of family members." A number of schools have been caught forcing Islamic practices on students. Since 2014, British schools have been mandated to teach British values as a way to counter Islamic extremism. "Groups," Hanif commented, "increasingly and cynically use human rights to promote Islamic ideology" (57).

In America, it is also imperative that schools return to teaching America's Founding principles and documents that set America aside as a unique, God-inspired nation. Also, it is important to instruct students on

389

the rule of law in a diversified society and, yet, not relinquish one's core beliefs under the pressure of others.

Islam in America's Primary Schools. The National Teacher Training Institute, created in 1989 as an outreach of New York's *thirteenWNET* public television, produces teacher training and lesson videos for America's public schools. In 2005, with funding from the U.S. Department of Education, it produced the video series, *Access Islam* and offers ten lesson plans for upper elementary and middle school students, starting in grades 4-8. All the glories and niceties of Islam that impressionable youth need to know are provided. The ten Lesson Plans include: Lesson 1, *Religion and the First Amendment*; Lesson 2, *The Five Pillars of Islam*; Lesson 3, *Salat: Prayer in Muslim Life*; Lesson 4, *Ramadan Observance*; Lesson 5, *Qur'an: Sacred Scripture of Islam*; Lesson 6, *The Hajj: Journey to Mecca*; Lesson 7, *Scholarship and Learning in Islam*; Lesson 8, *Islam in America*; Lesson 9, *Women in Islam*; Lesson 10, *Art in the Muslim World* (58). No corresponding lesson plan on the NTTI site on Christianity or Judaism could be found by this author.

William J. Bennetta (now deceased), the sole creator and president of The Textbook League, made it his mission in life to review textbooks being used in America's schools. His reviews and criticisms were much appreciated and respected. In 2003, he took upon himself to review the *Arab World Studies Notebook.* He summarized his review in an e-mail letter of October 8, 2003, to a Stuart Elliot in Wichita, Kansas, who had enquired of his findings.

> *Writing an analysis of a patently fraudulent publication is the most demanding task of all, for this reason: Although one can see immediately that the publication is a hoax, one still must give an extraordinary amount of time to studying it and to demonstrating its deceitfulness in some detail.*
>
> *. . . the "Notebook" is published jointly by the Middle East Policy Council and by "AWAIR: Arab World And Islamic Resources and School Services."*
>
> *On page v of the "Notebook," in the section titled "Introduction," Audrey Shabbas writes: "Believing firmly that teachers are the vanguard of change in any society, AWAIR has taken as its mandate, to impact the very resources chosen and used by teachers as well as the training and sensitizing of teachers themselves." The articles in the body of the "Notebook" soon make clear what Shabbas's phrase "training and sensitizing" means. It means subjecting teachers to heavy bombardment with religious and political propaganda.*

The Notebook is a vehicle for disseminating disinformation, including a multitude of false, distorted or utterly absurd claims that are presented as historical facts. I infer that the "Notebook" has three principal purposes: inducing teachers to embrace Islamic religious beliefs; inducing teachers to embrace political views that are favored by the MEPC and AWAIR; and impelling teachers to disseminate those religious beliefs and political views in schools.

On page 11 of the "Notebook," an item labeled as a lesson plan tells that "Jesus is an important figure" in Islam. On page 13, in another lesson plan, a list of quotations from the Koran includes three statements that mention Jesus. And on page 16, a third lesson plan says (with little regard for syntax) that Islam "Recognize Jesus in their religion" (59).

On September 24, 2010, the Texas State Board of Education met to resolve the issue of the ever spreading insertion of Islam within the state's educational system. The Board took its role seriously because state education departments across the country often look to Texas for guidance on the purchase of educational books for their schools. On that day, the following "Resolutions" were "resolved" (60).

WHEREAS pro-Islamic/anti-Christian bias has tainted some past Texas Social Studies textbooks, such as:

• In one instance, devoting 120 student text lines to Christian beliefs, practices, and holy writings but 248 (more than twice as many) to those of Islam; and dwelling for 27 student text lines on Crusaders' massacre of Muslims at Jerusalem in 1099 yet censoring Muslims' massacres of Christians there in 1244 and at Antioch in 1268, implying that Christian brutality and Muslim loss of life are significant but Islamic cruelty and Christian deaths are not (see documentation in Appendix I-A);

• In another instance, allotting 82 student text lines to Christian beliefs, practices, and holy writings but 159 (almost twice as many) to those of Islam; describing Crusaders' massacres of European Jews yet ignoring the Muslim Tamerlane's massacre of perhaps 90,000 co-religionists at Baghdad in 1401, and of perhaps 100,000 Indian POWs at Delhi in 1398; thrice charging medieval Christians with sexism; and saying the Church "laid the foundations for anti-Semitism" (see documentation in Appendix I-B);

• In a third instance, spending 139 student text lines on Christian beliefs, practices, and holy writings but 176 on those of Islam; claiming Islam "brought untold wealth to thousands and

a better life to millions," while "because of [Europeans' Christian] religious zeal ... many peoples died and many civilizations were destroyed;" and contrasting "the Muslim concern for cleanliness" with Swedes in Russia who were "the filthiest of God's creatures" (see documentation in Appendix I-C); and,

WHEREAS *pro-Islamic/anti-Christian half-truths, selective disinformation, and false editorial stereotypes still roil some Social Studies textbooks nationwide, evidenced by:*

• Patterns of pejoratives towards Christians and superlatives toward Muslims, calling Crusaders aggressors, "violent attackers," or "invaders" while euphemizing Muslim conquest of Christian lands as "migrations" by "empire builders" (see documentation in Appendix II);

• Politically-correct whitewashes of Islamic culture and stigmas on Christian civilization, indicting Christianity for the same practices (e.g., sexism, slavery, persecution of out-groups) that they treat non-judgmentally, minimize, sugarcoat, or censor in Islam (see documentation in Appendix II);

• Sanitized definitions of "jihad" that exclude religious intolerance or military aggression against non-Muslims—even though Islamic sources often include these among proper meanings of the term—which undergirds worldwide Muslim terrorism (see documentation in Appendix II);

The Muslim agenda in America cannot be any clearer, yet there are those in politics, education and the Church that bend over backwards to accommodate the Muslim plan for America and America's children.

In June, 2008, Gilbert T. Sewall, writing a report, *Islam in the Classroom: What the Textbooks tell us,* for the American Textbook Council (ATC) in New York, expressed his serious concerns.

• Many political and religious groups try to use the textbook process to their advantage, but the deficiencies in Islam-related lessons are uniquely disturbing. History textbooks present an incomplete and confected view of Islam that misrepresents its foundations and challenges to international security. • Misinformation about Islam is more pronounced in junior high school textbooks than high school textbooks. • Outright textbook errors about Islam are not the main problem. The more serious failure is the presence of disputed definitions and claims that are presented as established facts. • Deficiencies about Islam in textbooks copyrighted before 2001 persist and in some cases have grown worse. Instead of making corrections or adjusting contested facts, publishers and editors defend

misinformation and content evasions against the record. Biases persist. Silences are profound and intentional. • *Islamic activists use multiculturalism and ready-made American political movements, especially those on campus, to advance and justify the makeover of Islam-related textbook content.* • *Particular fault rests with the publishing corporations, boards of directors, and executives who decide what editorial policies their companies will pursue.*

    Publishers have developed new world and U.S. history textbooks at three different grade levels. Errors about Islam that occurred in older textbooks have not been corrected but reiterated. Publishers have learned of contested facts and have had the time to correct imbalances. But instead of making changes, they have sustained errors or, in deliberate acts of self-censorship, have removed controversial material.

    Having made a valuable point about state-sponsored terrorism, Glencoe's Modern Times broadens the subject, switching to a new section entitled "Islamic Militants: A Clash of Cultures." "Terrorist acts became more frequent in the later twentieth century," the text begins, abandoning the stated subject from the start. "Acts of terror have become a regular aspect of modern society around the globe." Then the book continues:

    Terrorism has been practiced since ancient times. In the modern period, one example occurred in Russia in the late 1800s, when radical reformers bombed trains or assassinated officials to fight the czar's repression. The causes of recent world terrorism are complex. Some analysts say this terrorism is rooted in the clash of modern and Islamic cultures. They argue that because many states in the former Ottoman Empire did not modernize along Western lines, Muslims have not accommodated their religious beliefs to the modern world. Other analysts note that the Christians and Muslims have viewed each other with hostility since at least the time of the Crusades. Others suggest that poverty and ignorance lie at the root of the problem—extremists find it easy to stir up resentment against wealthy Western societies. Finally, some say terrorism would be rare if the Israeli-Palestinian conflict could be solved (61).

    In *History Alive! The Medieval World and Beyond*, the report noted that the "textbook [was] long on chapters filled with adulatory lessons on Islam."

    In *World History: Medieval and Early Modern Times*, there is this erroneous implication that people converted to Islam because they were "attracted by Islam's message of equality and hope for salvation."

Islam, as you will remember provides no such thing as equality or hope of salvation.

The ATC report concluded, in part, "None of this is accidental. Islamic organizations, willing to [provide] misinformation, are active in curriculum politics. These activists are eager to expunge any critical thought about Islam from textbook and all public discourse. They are succeeding, assisted by partisan scholars and associations. . . It is alarming that so many individuals with the power to shape the curriculum are willfully blind to or openly sympathetic to these efforts."

The incidents of Islam in America's schools are vast and blatant. Far too many to report here. However, they include such offences as students being required to dress like Muslims, recite the *shahada*, the Muslim prayer of faith, learn certain Muslim doctrines; sit through Islamic proselytizing videos; read slanderous and false texts about Christians and Jews, while absorbing false glorifications of Islam.

In 2015, at Spring Hill Middle School in Spring Hill, Tennessee, students were forced to write, "There is no god but Allah; Muhammad is his prophet" (62). Although any vestige of Christianity has long been purged from America's public schools, Islam has been given a free pass to indoctrinate America's youth—and most parents, the Church and communities sit idly by.

"Textbook errors," according to *The Federalist*, are so common that several independent organizations review textbooks full-time. The Florida-based Citizens for National Security has issued the most comprehensive reviews about how textbooks treat Islam, and Chairman William Saxton says he fields about six related inquiries per day.

"CFNS reports chronicle sins of omission and commission—such as saying "war broke out" between Palestinians and Israelis although one side was the aggressor, glossing over historical realities such as "Muslims holding slaves and proselytizing by the sword, and inaccuracies such as stating Jesus was a Palestinian when Palestine did not exist during his recorded earthly life.

"One of CFNS's YouTube videos points out that the high school history textbook used in the Boston bombers' public school, Cambridge Latin School, makes straightforward religious claims about Islam no textbook would mimic in a description of any other religion: 'Muhammad's teachings, which are the revealed word of God...' An unbiased textbook would say something like "Muslims believe Muhammad's teachings are the revealed word of God" (63).

Controlling University Thought. In the past few years, as reported by Foreign Schools Gift and Contracts Report (https://studentaid.ed.gov/sa/about/data-center/school/foreign-gifts), from January 1, 2012 to June 30, 2018 a large number of American universities received hundreds of millions in donations and "contract" monies from Muslim countries—

mostly Arab countries and mainly Saudi Arabia and Qatar. While the largest portion of the monies received is designated as "contracts," presumably for tuition and fees for foreign Muslim students, there was also millions designated as "gifts" and research.

For instance, the University of Arkansas, in a four year period, from June 30, 2013 to June 30, 2017, took in $49.648 million from just three Muslim countries, Iraq, Kurdistan and Saudi Arabia. Over $40 million came from the Republic of Iraq, Higher Committee. Johns Hopkins University, in Baltimore, Maryland, from January 30, 2012 to June 1, 2018, received almost $64 million from over 20 Muslim countries—all of it designated as "monetary gifts." George Mason University, in Fairfax, Virginia received $64.875 million noted as "contracts" from January 23, 2012 to July 31, 2017. The great majority came from the Royal Embassy of Saudi Arabia.

The Associated Press, in analyzing the data, determined that at least $354 million went to 37 American institutions of higher learning from the Saudi Arabia alone—government or its controlled institutions—since 2011. Most of the money was for Saudi students attending various schools (64). Another $114 million was not accounted for as a result of some schools not disclosing the specific source of Saudi Arabian funding. This included $40 million to Johns Hopkins University and $28 million to Harvard University.

As reported in The Daily Caller on October 31, 2018, during the period of 2011-2016, Georgetown University (a Jesuit school) received almost $400 million from 18 foreign countries. However, 86.3 percent or $344-plus million came from five Muslim countries, of which Qatar was the largest contributor with $332.8 million (65).

In another attempt to control the campus narrative on Islam, the Muslim Students Association of the United States and Canada (MSA) or MSA National was established by members of the Muslim Brotherhood in 1963 on the campus of the University of Illinois. The MSA is essentially a sect of the radical Wahhabi brand of Islam of Saudi Arabia and is heavily supported by the Saudis. As of 2018 there were an estimated 600 U.S. campus chapters of MSA.

In the opinion of Alex Alexiev, of the Center for Security Policy, "The Saudis over the years set up a number of large front organizations, such as the Al Haramain Foundation, the Muslim World League, the World Assembly of Muslim Youth, and a great number of Islamic 'charities.'

"MSA National was the precursor of ISNA [the Islamic Society of North America], ICNA [the Islamic Circle of North America], MAYA [the Muslim Arab Youth Association], IMA [the Islamic Medical Association of North America], AMSS [the Association of Muslim Social Scientists], AMSE [the Association of Muslim Scientists and Engineers],

MYNA [Muslim Youth of North America], Islamic Book Service, and the North American Islamic Trust.

"The majority of Muslim Student Associations at U.S. colleges are dominated by Islamist and anti-American agendas, as are most of the numerous Islamic centers and schools financed by the Saudis. Intolerance and outright rejection of American values and democratic ideals are often taught also in the growing number of Deobandi schools that are frequently subsidized by the Saudis" (66).

Islamophobia—for University Credit. In a publication called, *Higher Education Today*, one of the two authors who was a "higher education administrator," shared a distasteful experience she had with the parent of a prospective student. She classified it as an "Islamophobic" incident. She and her co-author went on to write:

> *Muslim Americans and international Muslim students on campuses around the country experience blatant Islamophobia and microaggressions in many forms. Research shows microaggressions include stares in public, feelings of alienation and assumptions of religious homogeneity. Unfortunately, such experiences are often a reflection of the negative attitudes toward Muslims held by a significant portion of society* (67).

No doubt her experience was distasteful, inappropriate and hurtful, but in no way did it represent "a significant portion of society." Accusations of *Islamophobia* has become the new catch phrase for everything distasteful or assumed to be negative about Muslims. It has become what *anti-Semitism* has been for the Jews. There are, indeed, way too many people, who are small-minded and hateful, that take out their frustrations on others they perceive to be offended by, but that is the exception in America, not the rule. America and Americans are still among the most accepting, generous and compassionate people, often going the second and third mile to be kind or help someone in need.

In going to, what would appear to be the extreme on the issue of Islamophobia, prestigious Georgetown University has established a whole curriculum around the subject. It is, of course, supported with a generous donation of $20 million from the Saudi royal family to the school's Prince Alwaleed Bin Talal Center for Muslim-Christian Understanding (CMCU), which houses the "Bridge Initiative" and the "research project" on "the problem of Islamophobia" (68).

It is surprising, that among higher academics, no one seems to have discovered that Islam *is not* a race. Islam is an ideology made up of people from many ethnic and racial backgrounds. Some of the "key terms" listed in the Syllabus that are presumably catch words or offensive, include: Anti-Muslim Racism, Capitalism, Colonialism, Countering Violent Extremism, Empire, Gender Violence, Gender, Homonationalism, Islamophobia, Patriot Act and a host of other words or phrases. The Syllabus is too lengthy to review here, but the reader is encouraged to visit the website linked to this reference (69).

I will close with this absurdity. Todd Starnes, of Fox News, reported in March, 2018, that to sneeze in the library of Simmons College in Boston, and someone says, "God bless you" it could be considered an "Islamophobic microaggression" (70).

Chapter Conclusion

Since the first colonists, America has always been a country of immigrants. Of the estimated 243 countries (192 sovereign nations) in the world, America is the only nation that likely has representation from virtually all of them. The United States has become the least homogenous country in the world. Millions of non-Americans seek to come to America every year—to visit or to seek residency. Millions more try to get into the U.S.A. illegally. America is the biggest "melting pot" of nationalities and ethnicities the world has ever known. In the midst of this great cultural diversity, American citizens have always been a welcoming citizenry, willing to absorb an ever-increasingly diverse population. For most of the first four centuries of the nation's existence, those arriving on America's shores were eager to participate in the American dream and adopt, as well as, embrace American culture, laws, education, language and even the country's predominant religion of Christianity.

This enthusiasm for America has dramatically changed in the last few decades as a new and much less adapting group of immigrants have sought the freedom, safety and security of America. Although Muslims from various countries have lived quiet, respectable lives in the country almost since the country's founding, the new wave of Muslims have no intention of assimilating or adjusting to American culture and laws or anything else deemed to be American. Islam in America and the world now represents America's greatest challenge to constitutional, cultural and religious survival since the Civil War. The new brand of Islamic immigrants are intent on transforming America into their image of Islamic dominance. If America fails to clearly recognize this assault on its sovereignty, laws and culture, and effectively confront it and quell its advance, it will no longer be the "Land of the Free and the Home of the Brave." It will become just another Islamic oppressive hellhole in the world—the former bastion of freedom and security that everyone once sought for personal safety and prosperity.

References.

1. Imani, Amil. *Muslims Focus on the Goal.* Geller Report, September 27, 2018. Source: https://gellerreport.com/2018/09/muslims-focus-goal.html/

2. *America as the Last Man Standing.* The Centre for Counterintelligence and Security Studies, Alexandria, VA. Original posting on the CI Centre website, but no longer available.

3. *How Many Mosques Are There in the United States?* Reference. Source: https://www.reference. com/world-view/many-mosques-united-states-8b4fc81d9af1eb60 (accessed March 24, 2019).

4. Ibid.

5. Cohn, D'Vera and Andrea Caumont. *10 demographic trends that are shaping the U.S. and the world.* Pew Research, March 31, 2016. Source: http://www.pewresearch.org/fact-tank/ 2016/03/31/10-demographic-trends-that-are-shaping-the-u-s-and-the-world/ (accessed August 30,2018)

6. Randall, Rebecca. *How Many Churches Does America Have? More Than Expected.* Christianity Today, September 14, 2017. Source: https://www.christianitytoday.com/news/2017/september/ how-many-churches-in-america-us-nones-nondenominational.html (accessed March 24, 2019).

7. *By the Numbers: Growth & Decline of the Church.* Barna Group, April 9, 2015. Source: http://nationalblackroberegiment.com/ shocking-statistics-church-decline/ (accessed March 24, 2019).

8. *Muslims in America: Immigrants and those born in U.S. see life differently in many ways.* Pew Research Center, April 17, 2018. Source: http://www.pewforum.org/essay/muslims-in-america-immigrants-and-those-born-in-u-s-see-life-differently-in-many-ways/

9. Schoffstall, Joe. *Soros Bankrolled Unverified 'Hate Crime' Database Used by Major Media Outlets.* The Washington Free Beacon, March 27, 2019. Source: https://freebeacon.com/issues/soros-bankrolls-unverified-hate-crime-database-used-by-major-media-outlets/

10. Frantzman, Seth. *Why Were the 7,000 Antisemitic Incidents Under Obama Largely Ignored?* The Algemeiner, March 1, 2017. Source: https://www.algemeiner.com/2017/03/01/why-were-the-7000-antisemitic-incidents-under-obama-largely-ignored/ (accessed November 2, 2018).

11. *Uniform Crime Report, Hate Crime Statistics, 2016.* U.S. Department of Justice, Federal Bureau of Investigation, Fall, 2017.

12. *Uniform Crime Report, Hate Crime Statistics, 2017.* U.S. Department of Justice, Federal Bureau of Investigation, Fall, 2018.

13. Kerstein, Benjamin. *New York City Police Data Reveals Spike in Antisemitic Hate Crimes in 2018.* The Algemeiner, December 27, 2018. Source: https://www.algemeiner.com/2018/11/14/ fbi-us-antisemitic-hate-crimes-spiked-37-percent-in-2017/

14. Feoktistov, Ilya. *How Foreign Terrorist Funders Get U.S. Public Schools to Teach Anti-Jew Propaganda.* The Federalist, October 3, 2018. Source: https://thefederalist.com/ 2018/10/03/foreign-terrorist-funders-get-u-s-public-schools-teach-anti-jew-propaganda/
15. Ibid.
16. Wilner, Michael. *ADL head warns: U.S. at risk of 'normalizing' antisemitism.* The Jerusalem Post, October 29, 2018. Source: https://www.jpost.com/Diaspora/Antisemitism/ADL-head-warns-US-at-risk-of-normalizing-antisemitism-570568
17. *Islamophobia is Racism.* Georgetown University. Source: https://islamophobiaisracism. wordpress.com/ (accessed December 1, 2018)
18. *Islamophobia.* Haas Institute, UC Berkeley, September 8, 2017. Source: https://haasinstitute. berkeley.edu/global-justice/islamophobia/legalizing-othering (accessed Sept. 28, 2018)
19. Murphy-Bates, Sebastian. *Extremist groups are 'weaponising' Islamophobia and using human rights to promote ideology, says counter-terror campaigner.* Daily Mail Online, September 16, 2018. Source: https://www.dailymail.co.uk/news/article-6173281/Extremist-groups-weaponising-Islamophobia-using-human-rights-promote-ideology.html
20. Habib, Samra. *Islamophobia is on the rise in the US. But so is Islam.* PRI's The World, September 9, 2016. Source: https://www.pri.org/stories/2016-09-09/muslims-america-are-keeping-and-growing-faith-even-though-haters-tell-them-not (accessed February 5, 2019).
21. *Uniform Crime Report, Hate Crime Statistics, 2017.*
22. *Saudi Publications on Hate Ideology Invade American Mosques.* Center for Religious Freedom, Freedom House, 2005.
23. Imani, Amil. *The Mosque: House of Worship or House of Terrorism.* Gellar Report, December 20, 2018. Source: https://gellerreport.com/2018/12/ mosque-worship-terrorism.html/
24. Peters, Ralph. *How Saudi Arabia dangerously undermines the United States.* New York Post, April 16, 2016. Source: https://nypost.com/2016/04/16/how-saudi-arabia-undermines-the-united-states/ (accessed March 30, 2019).
25. Sperry, Paul. *Radical imams are spewing anti-Semitism in the US with impunity.* New York Post, January 27, 2018. Source: https://nypost.com/2018/01/27/radical-imams-are-spewing-anti-semitism-in-the-us-with-impunity/
26. Kedar, Dr. Mordechai and David Yerushalmi, Esq. *Sharia Adherence Mosque Survey: Correlations between Sharia Adherence and Violent Dogma in U.S. Mosques. Perspectives on Terrorism* journal, 2011. Source: http://www.terrorismanalysts.com/pt/index.php/pot/article/view/sharia-adherence-mosque-survey/html
27. Sperry, Paul. *Authorities ignore US mosques at center of Islamic terrorist attacks.* New York Post, July 26, 2015. Source: https://nypost.com/ 2015/07/26/the-us-mosque-link-between-islamic-attacks-that-authorities-are-ignoring/

28. Rich, Eric and Jerry Markon. *Va. Man Tied to Hamas Held as Witness.* Washington Post, August 25, 2004. Source: http://www.washingtonpost.com/wp-dyn/articles/A28476-2004Aug24_2.html (accessed March 28, 2019).

29. Kelly, Gen. John. *Home and Away: DHS and the Threats to America, Remarks delivered by Secretary Kelly at George Washington University Center for Cyber and Homeland Security.* Department of Homeland Security, April 18, 2017. Source: https://www.dhs.gov/news/2017/04/18/home-and-away-dhs-and-threats-america

30. Hinneberg, Cheryl. *FBI has 3,000+ active terrorism investigations in US, director says.* American Military News, March 22, 2018. Source: https://americanmilitarynews.com/ 2018/03/fbi-has-3000-active-terrorism-investigations-across-us-director-says/ (accessed Sept. 28, 2018).

31. *Stopping Terrorist Travel Through Illicit Pathways to the Homeland.* House Homeland Security Committee Majority Staff Report, 2018-2019.

32. Connor, Phillip. *U.S. admits record number of Muslim refugees in 2016.* Pew Research Center, October 5, 2016. Source: http://www.pewresearch.org/fact-tank/2016/10/05/u-s-admits-record-number-of-muslim-refugees-in-2016/ (accessed August 30, 2018)

33. *Southwest Border Migration FY 2019.* U.S. Customs and Border Protection. Source: https://www.cbp.gov/newsroom/stats/sw-border-migration

34. Johnson, Bridget. *FBI Director: 1,000 Homegrown Terror Investigations Active, Not Counting 'Traditional' ISIS, al-Qaeda Suspects.* PJ Media, May 17, 2018. Source: https://pjmedia.com/homeland-security/fbi-director-1000-homegrown-terror-investigations-active-not-counting-traditional-isis-al-qaeda-suspects/

35. Kelly, Gen. John.

36. *Stopping Terrorist Travel Through Illicit Pathways to the Homeland.*

37. *39 MILLION: IRLI Investigation Reveals Massive Identity Fraud by Illegal Aliens.* Immigration Reform Law Institute, September 11, 2018. Source: http://www.irli.org/single-post/ 2018/09/11/39-MILLION-IRLI-Investigation-Reveals-Massive-Identity-Fraud-by-Illegal-Aliens

38. Herridge, Catherine. *300 refugees subjects of FBI terror investigations, U.S. officials say.* Fox News, March 6, 2017. Source: http://www.foxnews.com/ us/2017/03/06/300-refugees-subjects-fbi-terror-investigations-u-s-officials-say (accessed September 28, 2018).

39. Darby, Brandon. *Leaked FBI Data Reveal 7,700 Terrorist Encounters in USA in One Year; Border States Most Targeted.* Breitbart, September 26, 2016. Source: https://www.breitbart.com/border/2016/09/26/leaked-fbi-data-reveal-7700-terrorist-encounters-usa-one-year-border-states-targeted/amp/? (accessed January 11, 2019).

40. McKay, Hollie. *How Minneapolis' Somali community became the terrorist recruitment capital of the US.* Fox News, February 16, 2019. Source: https://www.foxnews.com/us/how-rep-ilhan-omars-minnesota-

district-became-the-terrorist-recruitment-capital-of-the-us-officials-highly-concerned

41. Ibid.
42. Kredo, Adam. *Arrest of Iranian Spies in U.S. Just 'Tip of the Iceberg,' Lawmaker Warns.* The Washington Free Beacon, August 29, 2018. Source: https://freebeacon.com/national-security/arrest-iranian-spies-u-s-just-tip-iceberg-lawmaker-warns/
43. Horowitz, David. *Islamist Groups.* DiscovertheNetworks.org. Source: http://archive.discoverthenetworks.org/guideDesc.asp?catId=8&type=group (accessed August 30, 2018)
44. *U.S. Foreign Aid by Country.* Source: https://explorer.usaid.gov
45. *U.S. Relations With Egypt.* Bureau of Near Eastern Affairs, Fact Sheet, July 18, 2018. Source: https://www.state.gov/r/pa/ei/bgn/5309.htm (accessed October 17, 2018).
46. Zanotti, Jim. *U.S. Foreign Aid to the Palestinians.* Federation of American Scientists, December 12, 2018. Source: https://fas.org/sgp/crs/mideast/ RS22967.pdf
47. George, Susannah. *US ends funding for UN agency for Palestinian refugees.* The Washington Post, August 31, 2018. Source: https://www.washingtonpost.com/world/national-security/us-ends-funding-of-un-agency-for-palestinian-refugees/2018/08/31/
48. Lopez, Clare. *History of Muslim Brotherhood Penetration of the U.S. Government.* Gatestone Institute, April 15, 2013. Source: https://counterjihadreport.com/history-of-muslim-brotherhood-penetration-of-the-u-s-government/ (accessed Sept. 24, 2018)
49. Samuels, Brett. *Muslims running for office in record numbers: report.* The Hill, July 16, 2018. Source: http://thehill.com/homenews/campaign/397158-muslims-running-for-office-in-record-numbers-report
50. *Muslim congressman envisions Muslim house speaker.* WorldNetDaily, January 11, 2019. Source: http://www.wnd.com/2019/01/muslim-congressman-envisions-muslim-house-speaker/
51. Stracqualursi, Veronica. *New House Democrat Rashida Tlaib: "We're gonna impeach the mother****r."* CNN, January 4, 2019. Source: https://www.cnn.com/ 2019/01/04/politics/rashida-tlaib-trump-impeachment-comments/index.html
52. Weiss, Bari. *Ilhan Omar and the Myth of Jewish Hypnosis.* The New York Times, January 21, 2019. Source: https://www.nytimes.com/2019/01/21/opinion/ilhan-omar-israel-jews.html
53. *The ACW Letter: A Common Word between Us and You.* October 13, 2007. Source: http://www.acommonword.com/the-acw-document/
54. *"A Common Word" Christian Response.* Yale Center for Faith & Culture, November 18, 2007. Source: https://faith.yale.edu/common-word/common-word-christian-response
55. Arnsdorf, Isaac. *Interfaith service at Washington National Cathedral promotes religious tolerance.* Washington Post, June 26, 2011. Source: https://www.washingtonpost.com/local/dc-politics/interfaith-service-at-washington-national-cathedral-promotes-religious%20tolerance/2011/06/26/ (accessed March 24, 2019).
56. Feoktistov, Ilya. *How Foreign Terrorist Funders Get U.S. Public Schools to Teach Anti-Jew Propaganda.* The Federalist, October 3,

2018. Source: https://thefederalist.com/ 2018/10/03/foreign-terrorist-funders-get-u-s-public-schools-teach-anti-jew-propaganda/

57. Murphy-bates, Sebastian.

58. Source: https://www.thirteen.org/edonline/accessislam/ lesson.html (accessed December 27, 2018).

59. Bennetta, William J. *Arab World Studies Notebook lobs Muslim propaganda at teachers.* The Textbook League (e-mail letter to Stuart Elliott), October 8, 2003

60. Texas State Board of Education, Summary of Action Items, Sept. 24, 2010.

61. Sewall, Gilbert T. *ISLAM IN THE CLASSROOM: WHAT THE TEXTBOOKS TELL US,* American Textbook Council, June, 2008. Source: www.historytextbooks.org

62. Spencer, Robert. *The Islamization of Public Schools.* Gellar Report, May 19, 2018. Source: https://gellerreport.com/2018/05/islamization-public-schools.html/

63. Pullmann, Joy. *What do American Schools teach about Islam?* The Federalist, August 16, 2016. Source: http://thefederalist.com/2016 /08/16/what-do-american-schools-teach-about-islam-pc-or-nothing/ (accessed October 28, 2018).

64. Binkley, Collin and Chad Day. *US colleges face scrutiny for financial links to Saudi Arabia.* Christian Science Monitor/Associated Press, October 30, 2018. Source: https://www.csmonitor.com/USA/Education/2018/ 1030/US-colleges-face-scrutiny-for-financial-links-to-Saudi-Arabia (accessed December 22, 2018).

65. Rosiak, Luke. *Saudi Arabia Funds Politically Influential University That Promotes Pro-Muslim Agenda.* The Daily Caller, October 31, 2018. Source: https://www.dailycaller.com/2018/10/31/saudi-arabia-georgetown/

66. *Muslim Student Assn of the U.S. & Canada.* Discover the Networks. Source: http://archive.discoverthenetworks.org/groupProfile.asp? grpid=6175 (accessed August 30, 2018)

67. Bodine Al-Sharif, Mary Ann and Penny A. Pasque. *Addressing Islamophobia on College Campuses.* Higher Education Today, May 4, 2016. Source: https://www.higheredtoday.org/2016/05/04/ addressing-islamophobia-on-college-campuses/ (accessed October 27, 2018).

68. Rosiak, Luke.

69. *Islamophobia is Racism: Resource for Teaching & Learning about anti-Muslim Racism in the United States.* Georgetown University. Source: https://islamophobiaisracism.wordpress.com/ (accessed December 1, 2018).

70. Starnes, Todd. *College Warns Saying "God Bless You" is Islamophobic.* Fox News, March 7, 2018. Source: https://www. toddstarnes.com/values/college-warns-that-god-bless-you-is-islamophobic/

Chapter 15

A Clarion Call to Action

*... men of Issachar, who understood the times
and knew what Israel should do. . .*

1 Chronicles 12:32

W here do we go from here? In spite of all the horrors presented in the foregoing chapters committed by certain devout followers of Islam, it is not the intention of this author to provide a license or excuse for the reader to verbally or otherwise attack Muslims.

Muslims are among the lost, just like anyone else who does not know Jesus Christ as Lord and Savior. They need to hear the Gospel or receive revelation knowledge of Jesus as much as anyone who is spiritually separated from God.

Many Christian denominations have missionaries serving in Muslim countries with a desire and hope of sharing the Gospel of Jesus Christ. However, in many Muslim countries, preaching the Gospel or even sharing one's Christian faith is forbidden. Even carrying a Bible in public or having a home Bible study or prayer meeting can bring severe consequences. Sometimes it takes years to develop trusting relationships with a Muslim in order to have the opportunity to share a little about Jesus.

On the flip side, very few churches in the United States have ministry outreaches that share the Gospel with Muslims living in their towns or neighborhoods. In America, the Church should see the growing Muslim population in the U.S.—as hard as it may be—as a blessing and not a curse. For now—and the window is narrowing quickly—it is not illegal to share one's faith, pray with or for someone, invite someone to a Bible study, or share the Gospel. Yet, far too many Christians and church leaders are afraid of doing just that. If the Church and Christians are not vigilant and stand up for the truth of the Gospel, as well as the protections for religion provided in the U,S, Constitution, those that are anti-Christ will be quick to close all doors to religious freedom in America, and the lost will remain lost and the Church will die.

Some Christians believe that God has raised up Islam at this time to punish the Church for its multitude of sins of disobedience and apostasy. That remains to be seen. For now, the Church needs to repent of its unfaithfulness to the Gospel and move on with the work of the Gospel of Jesus Christ, with all power and majesty.

If you have diligently and attentively read through this entire *Compendium,* I congratulate you. You now know more about Islam than

99.99% of non-Muslims. You also understand that Islam represents an ideology unlike any other the West and the Free World has ever encountered. If you have been born in or raised in a Western culture where freedom of thought, decision-making and choice are paramount to a free society, you now comprehend the oppression under which the Muslim believers live. Also, to evangelize a Muslim for the sake of Christ and their personal salvation is not like sharing Christ with your next door neighbor who, while he or she may be an agnostic or atheist, likely grew up in a free Western society. Witnessing to a Muslim is first and foremost a spiritual battle. To testify to your faith in Jesus to a Muslim is entering into Satan's camp and you better first lay the spiritual foundation of prayer and intercession for yourself and the one with whom you seek to share the love of Christ.

In addition, with your newfound knowledge or enhanced understanding, I highly encourage you to spread the word by offering to lead a class on the subject at your church, community education center or elsewhere. You could also try to write polite, factual letters to the editor at your local newspaper. Or you could establish your own online blog to share your new insights, express concern and give testimony of any Muslim outreach you might prayerfully consider. Most of all, I challenge you to seek the Lord on whether or not He might desire for you to be a part of the vanguard of Christian spiritual warriors to reach out to Muslims in your community with the unadulterated and uncompromising Word of God—the truth of the Gospel of Jesus Christ.

But everything exposed by the light becomes visible—and everything that is illuminated becomes a light. This is why it is said: "Wake up, sleeper, rise from the dead, and Christ will shine on you."
Be very careful, then, how you live—not as unwise but as wise, making the most of every opportunity, because the days are evil.
Ephesians 5:13-16

Because you are concerned about the rise of Islam in America or elsewhere does not make you an Islamophobe or a Muslim hater, although some may choose to label you such. Look upon yourself as one of God's watchman, sounding the alarm for your community and future generations. More importantly, should God call you to do so, see yourself as a voice crying in the wilderness to bring the Good News of the Gospel to the lost Muslims in your community. First and foremost, you can choose to be a prayer warrior, breaking down spiritual strongholds for those who are seeking to reach Muslims in the West. You can also help financially support ministry outreaches to Muslims in the West or elsewhere.

The 21ˢᵗ Century Challenge for the Church. Around 65 A.D., Jude, Jesus' brother and disciple, wrote a warning letter to the fledgling church. In his one chapter letter, he wrote, "save others by snatching them from the fire; to others show mercy, mixed with fear—hating even the clothing stained by corrupted flesh" (**Jude 23**).

In Psalm 145, David provides the church and all Christians with this reminder: "All your works praise you, LORD; your faithful people extol you. They tell of the glory of your kingdom and speak of your might, so that all people may know of your mighty acts and the glorious splendor of your kingdom" (**Psalm 145:10-12**). The time is now. The only way to stem the tide of the Islamic advance is to reach out with the Good News. God is looking for more watchmen; more communicators of the word of God to share His redemptive salvation message with the lost and those held in spiritual bondage.

Jesus said, "No one comes to the Father [God] except through Me (**John 14:6**). If, as Christians—true followers of Christ—we believe that proclamation by Christ, then why are we not more demonstrative and vociferous about our faith; more concerned about non-believers going to hell?—Especially those who are in bondage to a satanic ideology. If we do not believe Christ's admonition as being germane to our day and age, then why are we Christians?

"And even if our gospel is veiled," the Apostle Paul wrote, "it is veiled to those who are perishing. The god of this age has blinded the minds of unbelievers, so that they cannot see the light of the gospel that displays the glory of Christ, who is the image of God. For what we preach is not ourselves, but Jesus Christ as Lord, and ourselves as your servants for Jesus' sake" (**2 Corinthians 4:3-5**).

Jesus, in His Sermon on the Mount, testified to His followers, **"You are the salt of the earth.** But if the salt loses its saltiness, how can it be made salty again? It is no longer good for anything, except to be thrown out and trampled underfoot. **You are the light of the world.** A town built on a hill cannot be hidden. Neither do people light a lamp and put it under a bowl. Instead they put it on its stand, and it gives light to everyone in the house. In the same way, **let your light shine before others**, that they may see your good deeds and glorify your Father in heaven" (**Matthew 5:13-16**; author's emphasis).

Satan is using people of Islamic faith to persecute those of the blood covenant, whether they are Christians or Jews, because Satan, in the name of Allah, despises the only true God and Jesus whom he could not corrupt. He has blinded Muslims to the truth with his hatred of Christ. Is it any wonder that those who follow the Islamic faith do so only because they were born into a Muslim family; were persecuted into doing so or are ignorant of its tenets of the faith? The fulfillment of Ishmael's legacy as the seed of a woman of bondage, and whose descendants would be *against everyone*, has been fulfilled and capitalized on by Satan's continued bondage-inducing hold on the people of Islam. Until they are set free in Christ, they will forever persecute and be adversaries of those of the only true blood covenant—Jews by heritage and Christians through Jesus' sacrifice on the cross.

"Because the church has failed to understand Islam, the Islamic people have not been stirred or touched by the Gospel of Jesus Christ. They remain in darkness of a fanatical religion which forces them to have faith in a god who is unreachable, untouchable and unknowable," wrote Pastor Reza Safa in 1996 (*Inside Islam: Exposing and Reaching the World of Islam*, p. 10).

A Spiritual Battle Requiring Spiritual Warfare. Muslims are in spiritual bondage—bondage so oppressive that we in the free world and as Christians cannot fully comprehend. Any effort to set the captives free starts with prayer and intercession, not only for God's guidance, but to break the spiritual strongholds that hold the Muslim captive to the darkness. Jesus told His disciples, ". . . how can anyone enter a strong man's house and carry off his possessions unless he first ties up the strong man? Then he can rob his house" (**Matthew 12:29**).

Jesus was not teaching His disciples how to be thieves. He was instructing them in spiritual warfare against the spirits of darkness. It is through prayer, fasting and intercession that spiritual bondages are broken. "I have given you authority," Jesus reminded those who follow Him, "to trample on snakes and scorpions and to overcome all the power of the enemy; nothing will harm you" (Luke 10:19).

"When a strong man, fully armed, guards his own house, his possessions are safe," Jesus said. "But when someone stronger attacks and overpowers him, he takes away the armor in which the man trusted and divides up the spoils" (**Luke 11:21-22**). Again, the analogy is that the strong man is Satan, but Jesus' disciples have one even stronger—Almighty God and the power of the Holy Spirit—who disarms Satan and releases his spoils (those held captive).

Where to start. Where should the Judeo-Christian faithful start to prepare for this spiritual battle? The prophet Joel provides a not so subtle clue. "Blow the trumpet in Zion, declare a holy fast, call a sacred assembly" (**Joel 2:15**). Prayer and fasting is the best place to start. All the wisdom of God must come to bare in this challenge. "Oh, my anguish, my anguish! I writhe in pain," cried the prophet Jeremiah. "Oh, the agony of my heart! My heart pounds within me, I cannot keep silent. For I have heard the sound of the trumpet; I have heard the battle cry" (**Jeremiah 4:19**). Have you and your church heard the battle cry? Perhaps it happened on September 11, 2001. Perhaps much sooner, but the church was not listening and was not vigilant.

The prophet Ezekiel was called of God to be a watchman for the house of Israel (**Ezekiel 3:17; 33:7**). The watchmen of the people of the only true God are called of God to warn His people of pending danger—whether it is from their sin from within or from their enemy without.

> *Son of man, I have made you a watchman for the house of Israel; so hear the word I speak and give them warning from me. When I say to a wicked man, 'You will surely die,' and you do not warn him or speak out to dissuade him from his evil ways in order to save his life, that wicked man will die for his sin, and I will hold you accountable for his blood. But if you do warn the wicked man and he does not turn from his wickedness or from his evil ways, he will die for his sin; but you will have saved yourself.*
>
> *Again, when a righteous man turns from his righteousness and does evil, and I put a stumbling block before him, he will die. Since you did not warn him, he will die for his sin. The righteous things he did will not be remembered, and I will hold you accountable for his blood. But if you do warn the righteous man not to sin and he does not sin, he will surely live because he took warning, and you will have saved yourself"*
> (**Ezekiel 3:17-21**).

God has given clear instructions. The people of Jehovah God—the pastors and rabbis in particular—are to call sin, *sin*, no matter in whose camp it resides. As the imams of Islam rail from their mosques and rooftops about the "evils" of Christianity and Judaism, the Judeo-Christian community of watchmen remains mostly silent. They are afraid to call the wickedness within Islam sin and an abomination to God Almighty. They are hesitant to call the sinner out of the darkness and bondage of Muhammadism into the light of Jesus Christ.

God loves all people and He loves the Muslims too, and wants them to experience the light of His salvation. As the Apostle Paul expressed to the Christians who were under oppression in Rome: "How, then, can they call on the one they have not believed in? And how can they believe in the one of whom they have not heard? And how can they hear without someone preaching to them? And how can they preach unless they are sent? As it is written, 'How beautiful are the feet of those who bring good news!'" (**Romans 10:14-15**).

The watchmen of God have a great and grave responsibility. He or she is called to warn God's people of impending doom or attack. If the watchman knows the attack is coming but fails to warn the people, the blood of the people will be on his or her hands. In like fashion, if the watchman sees a man in sin but does not warn him to repent and turn from his sin, then his eternal damnation shall be the responsibility of the watchman.

> *Son of man, speak to your countrymen and say to them: 'When I bring the sword against a land, and the people of the land choose one of their men and make him their watchman, and he sees the sword coming against the land and blows the trumpet to warn the people, then if anyone hears the trumpet but does not take warning and the sword comes and takes his life, his blood will be on his own head. Since he heard the sound of the trumpet but did not take warning, his blood will be on his own head. If he had taken warning, he would have saved himself. But if the watchman sees the sword coming and does not blow the trumpet to warn the people and the sword comes and takes the life of one of them, that man will be taken away because of his sin, but I will hold the watchman accountable for his blood'"* (**Ezekiel 33:2-6**).

Once again, the Spirit of the Lord needs to come upon His watchmen like it did for Gideon; to blow the trumpet of warning for His people (**Judges 6:34**). "Shout it aloud, do not hold back," Isaiah proclaimed. "Raise your voice like a trumpet. Declare to my people their rebellion and to the house of Jacob their sins" (**Isaiah 58:1**).

As the venerable Apostle Paul said, "if the trumpet does not sound a clear call, who will get ready for battle?" (**1 Corinthians 14:8**). Where are the blasts of the trumpets and who will sound the alarm?

"To whom can I speak and give warning? Who will listen to me?" exclaimed Jeremiah the prophet. "Their ears are closed so they cannot hear. The word of the LORD is offensive to them; they find no pleasure in it" (**Jeremiah 6:10**). When the watchmen do speak up, the people better listen or the consequences could be devastating.

> *I appointed watchmen over you and said, "Listen to the sound of the trumpet!" But you said, "We will not listen." Therefore hear, O nations; observe, O witnesses, what will happen to them. Hear, O earth: I am bringing disaster on this people, the fruit of their schemes, because they have not listened to my words and have rejected my law* (**Jeremiah 6:17-19**).

How did we get to this Juncture in American History? An often quoted (and sometimes misquoted) scripture is **2 Chronicles 7:14**, which says: "if my people, who are called by my name, will humble themselves and pray and seek my face and turn from their wicked ways, then I will hear from heaven, and I will forgive their sin and will heal their land." This is clearly a call to God's people, but the part that is often left out or glossed over is, "and turn from their wicked ways." One might ask, *What does the church have to repent for today?*

Over the last several decades—and likely much longer—America has become a culture of death and decadence. Why has America—once the center of Judeo-Christian principles and experience—degenerated into a wanton, hedonistic society? The reasons, from this author's perspective are many, but a few glaring ones will be listed.

- **Separation of Church and State.** Americans readily accepted this lie in 1947 and the Church was silent. Barring the Church from the public and political arena of everyday life gave way to debauchery and godless living.
- **Prayer and Bible were taken out of education in 1962-63.** Many of America's Founding Fathers took a strong position on the Bible and prayer. Dr. Benjamin Rush, a prominent physician, educator and signer of the Declaration of Independence said: "Religion is necessary to correct the effects of learning. Without religion I believe learning does real mischief to the morals and principles of mankind. . ." (letter to John Armstrong, March 19, 1783). By removing prayer and the Bible from our schools, the moral fiber and foundation for youthful guidance was obliterated. Once again, the Church stood silent.
- **Rejecting God and the Gospel of Christ.** Jesus said, "Whoever listens to you listens to me; whoever rejects you rejects me; but whoever rejects me rejects him who sent me" (**Luke 10:16**).
- **Roe vs. Wade, abortion and the culture of death.** See the discussion to follow.
- **Sexual perversion among youth and adults.** The esteemed George Washington, in his presidential Farewell Address, September 17, 1796, wrote: "Of all the dispositions and habits which lead to political prosperity, religion and morality are indispensable supports. In vain would that man claim the tribute of patriotism, who should labor to subvert these great pillars of human happiness, these firmest props of the duties of men and citizens. The mere politician, equally with the pious man, ought to respect and to cherish them." Gouverneur Morris, one of the signers of the U.S. Constitution, wrote: "Religion is the only solid basis of good morals: therefore education should teach the precepts of religion, and the duties of man towards God."
- **Pornography.** America is by far the leading source of the world's pornography. In 2012, it was reported that America, that by gone Christian nation, provided 89 percent of the world's pornographic production.
- **Educational dumb down—rewriting true American history.** All

the despotic leaders of the past—Hitler, Mussolini, Marx, and others—and those of the present, know, that to control the minds of a nation's youth, resulted in controlling the future. If one controls the narrative, one can dictate the destiny of a people. The great Winston Churchill is credited with saying, "A nation that forgets its past has no future." History—American history—once the backbone of American primary education, has given way to political correctness and social engineering substitutes. Real American history no longer exists.

- **Destruction of the family unit.** In the post-World War II era and before, the man/husband was the consummate breadwinner and the woman/wife stayed home as the family "nest builder" and nurturer. Such a concept is alien to today's families. If there are two parents, in most cases they are both working, leaving others to raise their children, or in the worst case, leaving the children to raise themselves. In addition, the family is being pressured and assaulted emotionally and psychologically from many directions from the growing complexities and challenges of daily living.
- **The perverted church.** In far too many churches, sin has crept in, ever so deceptively at first, but now as a flood, as more and more churches bow at the altar of perversion and a false gospel.

And, who is responsible for the ever-growing decadence of America and Americans? It is the Church—the Church of Jesus Christ—that was to set the standard; to uphold it and defend it at all costs, and it has failed miserably.

For it is time for judgment to begin with God's household; and if it begins with us, what will the outcome be for those who do not obey the gospel of God? (1 Peter 4:17). Judgment starts with the church. Oh, Christians can easily point the finger of responsibility in al, different directions, but God will hold His Church responsible for the many lost souls who have fallen prey to the wicked one.

An Ex-Muslim's Perspective. In November, 2014 (updated in November, 2017), an unnamed Muslim who converted to Christianity and was working as an evangelist in a Muslim dominated country agreed to have his wisdom on how to witness to Muslims posted on the website for the Christian Reformed Church of North America. It is quite lengthy but very informative. Due to its length, only a small portion is presented here. However, for the serious seeker of wisdom, it is advised that you visit the website posting at this location: https://network.crcna.org/muslim-ministry/ex-muslims-suggestion-how-evangelize-muslim-reformed-echoes.

Here is his guidance, in part:

- *The testimony of the Gospels provides the most reliable witness to Christ. Preach the Gospel as it is! Do not soft-pedal around biblical terminology to please Muslim hearers. Be clear about what you believe and why you believe it.*
- *. . . Our apologetic discussion with Muslims should be to defend the Scriptures and prove that the Scriptures aren't corrupt as Muslims claim. . . .*
- *Always ask them the classic evangelistic questions. 'What about your salvation?' 'Can you be certain of this?' 'If you were to die, can you be certain you'd enter heaven at some point?' Their response is always, "No, I couldn't be certain, nor do I care."*
- *. . . The essence of Muslim evangelism is accurate communication about sin and grace: simply and clearly. Talk about the law and the gospel . . . Don't compare the Bible with the Quran.*
- *. . . Avoid the use of Christian jargon. Speak about real sin, real guilt, real shed blood! Do not be ashamed to use Jesus' direct and indirect titles . . .*
- *Be sensitive to their past - if they've had a bad experience with Christians, missionaries or churches, struggled with a particular sin etc., be understanding and compassionate! Muslims hate self-righteousness . . .*
- *Muslims will ask you many questions about your faith. Don't feel like you have to answer all of their questions in one day.*
- *Muslims will ask you to comment on their faith. Don't go there; they will not benefit from your criticism (or feigned approval) of other religions. Your job isn't to debunk Islam but to give a clear witness to the truth of the Gospel. . . .*
- *The message of the Gospel offends Muslims. It is okay! Don't worry! God will take care of the hearer. It is His message. Muslims will not convert to Christ if they are not offended by the message of the Gospel. Offend them by being very clear about the teachings of Christ!*

While the Gospel is meant to "offend" and challenge the hearer, we are not called to be offensive. There is much more wisdom to be gleaned from this believer, so visit the site.

The Sinner's Path to Salvation

Jesus answered, "I am the way and the truth and the life. No one comes to the Father except through me" (John 14:6).

NOBODY ELSE; NO OTHER DIETY CAN HELP YOU.

"For there is one God and one mediator between God and

mankind, the man Christ Jesus" (1 Timothy 2:5).

"For it is by grace you have been saved, through faith—and this is not from yourselves, it is the gift of God— not by works, so that no one can boast" (Ephesians 2:8-9).

WHAT YOU MUST DO:

1. **ADMIT** you are a sinner, and that only the Lord Jesus can save you.

    ". . . for all have sinned and fall short of the glory of God" (Romans 3:23).

2. **REPENT:** be willing to turn away from sin and submit to God (see Luke 13:5).

    Jesus said: "I tell you, no! But unless you repent, you too will all perish" (Luke 13:5).

    [The Apostle] "Peter replied, 'Repent and be baptized, every one of you, in the name of Jesus Christ for the forgiveness of your sins. And you will receive the gift of the Holy Spirit'" (Acts 2:38).

3. **BELIEVE** that the Lord Jesus Christ died on the cross and shed his blood to pay the price for your sins, and that he rose again.

    "If you declare with your mouth, "Jesus is Lord," and believe in your heart that God raised him from the dead, you will be saved" (Romans 10:9).

4. **ASK** God to save you (see Romans 10:13).

    ". . . for, 'Everyone who calls on the name of the Lord will be saved'" (Romans 10:13).

5. **ASK** Jesus Christ to be the Lord (take control) of your life (see Romans 12:1-2).

"Therefore, I urge you, brothers and sisters, in view of God's mercy, to offer your bodies as a living sacrifice, holy and pleasing to God—this is your true and proper worship. Do not conform to the pattern of this world, but be transformed by the renewing of your mind. Then you will be able to test and approve what God's will is—his good, pleasing and perfect will" (Romans 12:1-2).

IF YOU REALLY MADE JESUS YOUR LORD, THEN ACT LIKE IT!

1. Read your Bible every day to get to know Christ better. *Jesus answered, "It is written: 'Man shall not live on bread alone, but on every word that comes from the mouth of God"* (Matthew 4:4).
2. Talk to God in prayer every day. *Pray without ceasing* (1 Thessalonians 5:17).
3. Find a church where the Bible is taught as the complete word of God and is the final authority. *They devoted themselves to the apostles' teaching and to fellowship, to the breaking of bread and to prayer* (Acts 2:42).
4. Obey Christ's command to be baptized. See Acts 2:38 preceding.
5. Celebrate the Lord's Supper (communion) often. *For whenever you eat this bread and drink this cup, you proclaim the Lord's death until he comes* (1 Corinthians 11:26).
6. Seek forgiveness (where possible) of those you hurt and make restitution where required. Jesus said: *This is my blood of the covenant, which is poured out for many for the forgiveness of sins* (Matthew 26:28).
7. Forgive unconditionally others who have hurt you. *But if you do not forgive others their sins, your Father will not forgive your sins* (Matthew 6:15).
8. Be charitable. *Each of you should give what you have decided in your heart to give, not reluctantly or under compulsion, for God loves a cheerful giver* (2 Corinthians 9:7).
9. Share your new faith with others, both fellow believers and non-believers. *Therefore go and make disciples of all nations, baptizing them in the name of the Father and of the Son and of the Holy Spirit,* (Matthew 28:19).

More Books by the Author

Be Pruned, To Bear Fruit That Will Last, 2010, 2019, 2022.
Bond Slaves: Confessions of Hard Core Bikers, 2010.
Bond Slaves: Confessions of Hard Core Bikers (Memorial Edition), 2022
Deceptions and Lies of Islam and the Preaching of a False Gospel, 2019.
Embracing the Anti-Christ: The Heresy of Interfaith Dialogue, 2020, 2022
Hop-A-Long: Abandoned but not Forgotten, 2010.
I Remember When . . . Growing Up In Post-World War II America, 2011.
Islam & Christianity, A Revealing Contrast, 2009.
La Iglesia Católica: Las razones porqué la dejé, 2014.
Overcoming the Storms of Life, 2010.
Revelation 18 and the Fate of America, 2013.
Revelation 18 and the Fate of America (2021 Edition), 2013, 2021, 2022.
The Catholic Church: Why I Left It, 2012.
Understanding Islam in the Light of Christianity (Student Edition), 2019, 2022.
Understanding Islam in the Light of Christianity (Compendium), 2019.
Understanding Islam in the Light of Christianity (Compendium), 2019.
Wall of Separation: Jefferson's Intention or Judicial Fabrication?, 2010, 2022.
We the People: Laying *the Foundation*, 2003.
We the People: Birth of a Nation (Second Edition), 2014.

Author website: https://booksbygauss.com

Author Blog: ampatriot.wordpress.com

Author e-mail: gaussbooks@gmail.com

About the Author.

Dr. Gauss has been writing for publication since 1962. He is the author of hundreds of newspaper articles and columns; numerous magazine and trade publication articles and various university extension publications.

A thorough and precise researcher, his first book was published in 1998. Since then he has written and published over 20 books, the vast majority on Christian themes and spiritual insights.

He has been a featured guest on many regional radio and television programs, including satellite TV.

Understanding Islam in the Light of Christianity is the result of years of dedicated research and personal experience. The end product reveals insightful comparisons of Islam and Christianity not found in similar works.

Made in the USA
Middletown, DE
20 July 2023

35301439R00235